Advance Praise for POWER GAMES

"*Power Games* is a collection of provocative and very courageous reflections on psychoanalytic training past, present, and future. The authors share their own experiences of humor and humiliation, transformation and terror, pleasure and pain as they lead us through the dark shadows and illuminating potential of training and supervision. As gifted analysts, they then structure experience with sophisticated theory, helping us to intellectually appreciate what they have given us to feel. This much needed volume should be required reading and discussion for psychoanalytic trainees, teachers, supervisors, and analysts."

—Mary Gail Frawley-O'Dea, Ph.D., author of *Perversion of Power: Sexual Abuse in the Catholic Church*

"This courageous book fills an unwritten chapter in psychoanalytic history—of power and influence in training institutes. Outstanding are the revealing accounts of personal experiences of vulnerability, trauma, and recovery during training which surely can be repeated manifold across the spectrum. Eloquent pleas are made for education to replace doctrinaire training. By encouraging critical thought and diversity, this important book itself is a reflective space in which authors vividly describe experiences and thoughts about improving education. It fosters hope that institutional impasses can be resolved so that our artful science can find forms appropriate for the 21st Century."

—Malcolm Pines, M.B., F.R.C.P., Psych, D.P.M., founder, Institute for Group Analysis, London

"I am a passionate believer in the 'talking cure,' but have seen that organizations and training can easily lead to abuse. We need to guard against this and insure the vitality of our field through ongoing self-examination. Dr. Raubolt and his contributors have made a very important contribution to this ongoing self-examination both on a scholarly and gripping real-life storytelling level."

—Stuart Perlman, Ph.D., training and supervising analyst, Institute of Contemporary Psychoanalysis; author of *The Therapist's Emotional Survival*

"It is a sign of the maturing of psychoanalysis and psychotherapy as social sciences (what used to be called, accurately, the *moral* sciences) that they are increasingly examining their moral credentials, their capacity for good and ill. *Power Games* brings needed attention to the dangers of indoctrination, discipleship, and clinical harm, inherent in authoritarian institutions and training models, and proposes alternatives well worth thinking about. This compelling collection of essays and clinical papers is a valuable addition to the literature of psychotherapeutic control and manipulation about which much needs to be written."

—Jonathan Cohen, M.D., author of *Apart From Freud: Notes f*

Power Games

Influence, Persuasion, and Indoctrination in Psychotherapy Training

Edited by
Richard Raubolt

OTHER

Other Press
New York

Permission is gratefully acknowledged for the right to reprint "Covert Methods of Interpersonal Control" from Gaslighting, The Double Whammy, Interrogation and Other Methods of Covert Control in Psychotherapy and Analysis by Theodore Dorpat, published by Jason Aronson.

Production Editor: Mira S. Park

This book was set in 11 pt. Goudy by Alpha Graphics of Pittsfield, New Hampshire.

10 9 8 7 6 5 4 3 2 1

Library of Congress Cataloging-in-Publication Data

Power games : influence, persuasion, and indoctrination in psychotherapy training / Richard Raubolt, ed.
    p. ; cm.
Includes bibliographical references and index.
ISBN-13: 978-1-59051-173-2
ISBN-10: 1-59051-173-5
1. Psychotherapy—Study and teaching.   2. Psychoanalysis—Study and teaching.   3. Psychotherapists—Training of.   4. Psychoanalysts—Training of.
5. Control (Psychology)   I. Raubolt, Richard R. (Richard Raleigh)
[DNLM: 1. Psychoanalysis—education.   2. Interpersonal Relations.   3.
Power (Psychology) WM 18 P887 2006]
RC459.P69 2006
616.89'14—dc22
                                        2006007110

Contents

.

Acknowledgments

This edited book is the result of the collaborative efforts of a great many people. There are two people, though, who deserve special recognition and credit for their unwavering belief in this project.

Mary Krzeminski, project assistant, tireless supporter, and always a dearest friend, gave herself over to this book without reserve. She could always be counted on, never complained, and treated each chapter and author with loving care. This book would never have gotten from the dream in my mind to the printed page without Mary's kind and wise guidance. By way of saying thank you I dedicate this book to "my Mary."

My wife, Linda, also deserves special credit even if it embarrasses her. She bravely and lovingly lived through the abuse from my professional training that prompted the writing of this book. She believed in this publication so much and knew when I didn't that "a wise editor will see the importance of these ideas and experiences." She even predicted it would be a woman and it was, Judith Feher-Gurewich of Other Press, but that as they say is another story. Thank you, dear Linda.

Contributors' Biographies

Doris Brothers, Ph.D. Cofounder, training and supervising analyst, the Training and Research Institute for Self Psychology (TRISP); author, *Falling Backwards: An Exploration of Trust and Self Experience* and *The Regulation of Uncertainty: Psychoanalysis, Trauma and Relational Systems.*

Theodore Dorpat, M.D. Training and supervising analyst, Seattle Institute for Psychoanalysis; author of many book chapters and articles; coauthor, *Clinical Interaction and the Analysis of Meaning: A New Psychoanalytic Theory*; author, *Wounded Monster: Hitler's Path from Trauma to Malevolence.*

Paula B. Fuqua, M.D. Faculty, Chicago Institute for Psychoanalysis; council member, International Association for Psychoanalytic Self Psychology; associate editor, *International Journal of Psychoanalytic Self Psychology* (formerly *Progress in Self Psychology*).

Arthur Gray, Ph.D. Private practice, New York City; instructor and supervisor, Postgraduate Center for Mental Health and Jewish Board of Family and Children's Services.

Irene Harwood, M.S.W., Ph.D., Psy.D. Assistant clinical professor, UCLA School of Medicine, Department of Psychiatry, where she is also director, Prevention of Insecure Disorganized Attachment Project; psychoanalyst and faculty, Southern California Psychoanalytic Institute and Society; cofounder of the Society for the Study of the Self; coeditor with Malcolm Pines, *Self Experiences in Group: Intersubjective and Self Psychological Pathways to Human Understanding*; president-elect, Group Psychotherapy Association of Southern California; has supervised at Wright Institute, Los Angeles and California Institute for Clinical Social Work; conducts individual and group consultation in her private practice.

Patrick B. Kavanaugh, Ph.D. Former president, International Federation for Psychoanalytic Education; founding president, Academy for the Study of the Psychoanalytic Arts; visiting artist in psychoanalysis, Cranbrook Academy of Art, Bloomfield Hills, MI; former member of the teaching and supervisory faculty, Program for Advanced Psychoanalytic Studies, Wyandotte, MI; former director of training, University of Detroit; private practice, Farmington Hills, MI.

Michael Larivière, Ph.D. Private practice, Strasbourg, France; former associate professor of psychiatry, Faculty of Medicine, University of Strasbourg, France; former associate editor, *Etudes Freudiennes* (*Journal of Psychoanalysis*), Paris; published numerous articles in France, Italy, Canada, and United States, and has led seminars in psychoanalysis in Turin and Padua, Italy.

Conrad Lecomte, Ph.D. Full professor, clinical psychology, University of Montreal; trainer and supervisor; coauthor, *Rapprochement et Integration en Psychotherapie: Psychanalyse, Humanisme et Behaviorisme*, Gaetan Morin, Montreal; author of numerous articles and book chapters on supervision and psychotherapy.

Molyn Leszcz, M.D., F.R.C.P.C. Associate professor and head, Group Therapy, University of Toronto, Department of Psychiatry; coauthor with

Irvin Yalom, M.D., *The Theory and Practice of Group Psychotherapy*, 5th ed.

Marty Livingston, Ph.D., C.G.P. Editor, *Group*; director, Group Therapy Training Department, Postgraduate Center for Mental Health, New York, NY; author, *Near and Far: Closeness and Distance in Psychotherapy* and *Vulnerable Moments: Deepening the Therapeutic Process*.

Gershon J. Molad, M.D. Clinical psychologist, private practice, Tel Aviv, Israel; faculty of medicine, Program of Psychotherapy, Tel Aviv University; faculty of Social Welfare and Health Studies Program of Advanced Studies in Psychotherapy, University of Haifa; teaching and writing focus mainly on the discourse about the personal and professional life-span development of analysts and therapists, and on the autobiographical dialogue between analysts in conference space.

Linda Raubolt. Founder and director, Learning Disabilities Consultants; author and workshop leader on women's issues.

Richard Raubolt, Ph.D. Clinical psychologist, independent practice in individual and group psychotherapy for adults and adolescents, Grand Rapids, MI; supervising psychologist, Aquinas College Counseling Center; chair, Trauma Committee, International Federation for Psychoanalytic Education; editor, *Power Games: Influence, Persuasion, and Indoctrination in Psychotherapy Training*; special editor, *Group, The Journal of the Eastern Group Psychotherapy Society*, vol. 27, no. 2/3.

Annette Richard, M.Ps. Clinical psychologist, private practice; member of the Quebec Order of Psychologists; former lecturer at the Université de Montréal Department of Psychology; author of several articles, book chapters, and papers.

Joan E. Sarnat, Ph.D., A.B.P.P. Clinical and supervisory practice, Berkeley, CA; member and faculty, Psychoanalytic Institute of Northern California; adjunct faculty, Wright Institute, Berkeley, CA; co-author with Mary Gail Frawley-O'Dea, *The Supervisory Relationship: A Contemporary Psychodynamic Approach*.

Daniel Shaw, L.C.S.W. Private practice, New York City and Nyack, NY; clinical supervisor and faculty, National Institute for the Psychotherapies (NIP), New York, NY; faculty, Object Relations Institute, New York, NY; cochair, Continuing Education Committee, International Association for Relational Psychoanalysis and Psychotherapy (IARPP).

Charles B. Strozier, Ph.D. Professor of history, John Jay College and Graduate Center CUNY; training and supervising analyst, Training and Research Institute for Self Psychology, New York, NY; author, *Heinz Kohut: Making of a Psychoanalyst* and *Apocalypse: On the Psychology of Fundamentalism in America*.

Judith E. Vida, M.D. Founder, faculty member, Institute of Contemporary Psychoanalysis, Los Angeles; associate clinical professor of psychiatry, University of Southern California; has taught the demonstration of psychodynamic psychotherapy to psychiatric residents; past president, Southern California Psychiatric Society; fellow, American Psychiatric Association; member, International Psychoanalytic Association, and Sándor Ferenczi Society of Budapest; president, International Federation for Psychoanalytic Education; private practice, Pasadena, CA. The mutual and intensive collaboration of Vida and Molad since 1999 has led to papers and lectures reflecting on and exploring the possibilities of a less defensive dialogue among analysts, and to examining its clinical and theoretical relevance in their current seminars on the autobiographical dialogue.

Ernest Wolf, M.D. Faculty, training and supervising analyst, Chicago Institute of Psychoanalysis, Chicago, IL; author, *Treating the Self*.

Foreword

Ernest S. Wolf

After having been deeply involved in psychoanalysis as an analysand, student, analyst, training analyst and supervisor, psychotherapist, administrative assistant and faculty member at an institute, researcher, and writer on psychoanalytic and psychiatric topics—from the 1950s to today—I have long felt the need for a serious discussion in our literature on two main topics that are usually slighted or even passed over: first, the relation in psychoanalytic education between student and supervisor, and, second, the collaboration and/or conflict between two very different psychoanalytic approaches to psychoanalytic work, namely deriving one's primary guidance from a commitment to a theoretical position versus deriving one's guidance from one's attunement to the clinical experiences of both analyst and analysand. It is therefore with a great deal of anticipation and also of satisfaction that I welcome Dr. Raubolt's book as a most valuable contribution to the literature and development of psychoanalysis.

There can be no doubt that the chosen topics of education and supervision are among the most basic activities in which psychoanalysts and psychotherapists are engaged. Dr. Raubolt has chosen leading writers in assembling this outstanding collection of essays discussing these educational tasks and their associated problems. By presenting us with such a wealth of ideas and experiences Dr. Raubolt is helping shape our field to meet the demands of the twenty-first century.

Introduction

Charles B. Strozier

Psychoanalysis occupies a unique position in the history of healing. It burst on the scene in the 1890s as a quirky method for the treatment of hysterics developed by a talented young medical doctor eager to make a name for himself. In time this new mode of cure through talk became a movement that pushed traditional psychiatry into the backwaters and transformed many aspects of popular culture in the twentieth century. In our era of Prozac, however, psychiatry has returned to the clinical, psychotherapeutic fray with a vengeance. Psychoanalysis is no longer hegemonic, and probably never will be again. But it has clung tenaciously to the intrinsic value of conversation in the Platonic sense and free association as a meaningful form of treatment. Psychoanalysis in the contemporary era, somewhat ironically, has become at last true to itself. Many fundamental changes in the field have occurred. It has significantly loosened its links with psychiatry, and at least in the United States has been largely feminized as it recruits from beyond medicine, especially social work. The couch is no longer iconic and the interaction of patient and therapist is empathic, relational, open, and engaged.

In this new context, psychoanalysis may be finally able to turn with some modesty to ask some honest questions about the inner dynamics of its training. This book, *Power Games*, is at the forefront of this new spirit of inquiry. What one learns from the book's analysis is not altogether reassuring. The world of psychoanalysis is full of false saints and mighty sinners. Some astonishing things have been done in its name, and destructive cults by any name have grown at the edges of the movement. But the tale this book tells is also the beginning of wisdom for a tradition certainly worth clinging to and embracing.

Power Games includes moving personal stories of pain and suffering at the hands of cultic groups masquerading as psychoanalytic training institutes, commentary on many aspects of training by insiders, and astute analysis from several different theoretical points of view. The emphasis in this material is relational and much is specifically self psychological, but the authors avoid pushing a line and seek in their own terms to understand their experience. The authors are able to draw on their extensive psychological understanding to probe their own subjugation to the tyranny of training gone mad. Some write intensely personal asides to illustrate theoretical points. And all seek to understand the perversions of a grand project at the hands of some practitioners.

In the spirit of this book I want to center my introduction around two stories. The first is vicarious. Robert Jay Lifton, one of the first to think about psychoanalytic training in cultic terms, had as well an extraordinary personal experience with his own training. In the late 1950s he was a candidate at the Boston Psychoanalytic Institute. He was then undergoing a personal analysis with Beata (Tola) Rank, whom Sigmund Freud at first recklessly misjudged in a letter to Karl Abraham in December 1918 (Gay 1988, pp. 471–72) as "a little Polish-Jewish wife whom no one finds congenial and who betrays no high interest" but whom Freud soon came to appreciate as an attractive and thoughtful young woman whom he got to know personally. In addition to his analysis, Lifton (personal communication, August 21, 2005) completed two years of courses at the institute. In 1960, however, Lifton got permission from the training committee at the institute to take advantage of a two-year grant to work in Japan, a research stint that in the end became two-and-a-half years and included his interviews with survivors of the atomic bomb in Hiroshima and led to his study, *Death in Life* (1969), which won the National Book Award. After he returned from Japan in 1963, Lifton assumed the Foundations Fund for Research in Psychiatry Professorship at Yale and quietly withdrew from the institute.

But in fact his relationship with his training was not at all that quiet. During the period of his intense involvement in psychoanalytic training between 1958 and 1960, Lifton was writing his classic study, *Thought Reform and the Psychology of Totalism: A Study of "Brainwashing" in China* (1961), based on interviews conducted several years earlier. This book, familiar to all scholars who have had any interest at all in cultic behaviors and motivations, explores in great detail how those dissenters from Communist totalism had been systematically "reeducated" by the Chinese after the revolution of 1949. The Chinese perfected a method of indoctrination that drew on the experience of the Russians and others before them. Lifton showed the many sides of this process of what he called "thought reform," especially its larger ideological context, in decidedly human terms that lend his study continuing relevance. Many people leaving cults still carry around on their person a copy of Lifton's chapter 22 on the general nature of "ideological totalism" as a talisman against further psychological infection.[1]

For those who read on into the next chapter of the book, "Approaches to Re-Education,"—and those readers included Lifton's analyst, Beata Rank, and the senior figures at the Boston Psychoanalytic Institute—one finds a remarkably clear and insightful analysis of what I would call the cultic undertow of psychoanalytic training. The ethos of the psychoanalytic enterprise, Lifton notes (1961, pp. 446–447), "is in direct opposition to that of totalism." Its emphasis on the inquiry into the human psyche that Freud lent to the project is in the best Western tradition of humanism, individualism, and the openness of the scientific tradition. But organizationally, just like other movements that become dogmas, psychoanalysis has struggled to hold onto its liberating spirit. There have been schisms more like religious battles than intellectual disagreements. Freud himself was both charismatic and

---

1. I actually saw a student once, who had gotten out of a cult, walking around with a copy of chapter 22 in her purse. I later spoke with Amy Siskind about this issue, and she confirmed that it was common to distribute copies of chapter 22.

grandiose in ways familiar to anyone with knowledge of cultic movements. And most of all the training procedures in institutes too often
cross a line into indoctrination.

The structural problem is that institutes require the trainee to be
a patient, a student, and a candidate all at once in the same setting and
with senior figures who overlap roles as analyst, teacher, and supervisor. Lifton asks a series of pointed questions about this deep and abid-
ing confusion:

> From the standpoint of the criteria for ideological totalism, we may raise
> the following additional questions: Does this combination of personal
> therapy, professional instruction, and organizational influence—all me-
> diated by a single training institute—create a tendency toward milieu
> control? Does it cause the institute itself to become surrounded with a
> near-mystical aura? Do these circumstances—especially the candidate's
> learning a scientific doctrine in connection with its therapeutic applica-
> tion to his own psychological distress—create an implicit demand for
> ideological purity? And do they raise the possibility that his analyst and
> his institute, by bringing about his "cure," will become (even if inadvert-
> ently) the arbiters of his neurotic and existential guilt? Could the con-
> fession process of therapy in this way take on an extratherapeutic function
> of binding the candidate to the psychoanalytic movement, thereby mak-
> ing him hesitant to criticize its teaching? Is there sometimes a tendency,
> in the descriptive and reductive overemployment of a particular school's
> or institute's favorite technical terms, to load the language or to suggest
> a sacred science? Is there thus a danger of establishing (perhaps uncon-
> sciously on everyone's part) a pattern of intellectual conformity as a
> prerequisite for a successful training experience or in other words, estab-
> lishing a primacy of doctrine over person? And when questions of ideo-
> logical difference influence decisions about who is to be recognized as a
> legitimate psychoanalyst, is there a tendency toward the dispensing of
> existence? [Lifton 1961, pp. 447–48]

As Lifton sees it now (personal communication, August 21, 2005),
he was only able personally to appreciate the depth and grandeur of the
work of Sigmund Freud after he withdrew from the confining atmosphere of the institute. Lifton needed to be free of the institute to take
in the Freudian tradition, its radical message, and appreciate its real
contribution to human knowledge. Until then, Lifton had to separate
himself from what Erik Erikson at the time characterized as the monk-

hood, the monkishness, and the monkery of psychoanalytic institute training (Erikson 1958). Lifton's freedom from all that after the early 1960s, furthermore, became a source of his lifelong creative inquiry into the deeper meanings of the psychoanalytic tradition, including his underappreciated work of genius, *The Broken Connection* (1979), which he characterizes as an extended conversation with Freud.

The second story is my own. I have no doubt that psychoanalytic training often tends to foster in candidates a turn from their original idealism to a kind of quiet fanaticism. I have always been appalled at the religious nature of much of the discourse in the field. The authority to control all aspects of the lives, indeed the souls, of others can all too easily create monsters of senior analysts, teachers, and supervisors. The extreme examples in this book must serve our field as cautionary tales.

And yet that was not my personal experience. I found graduate school at the University of Chicago, where I received my Ph.D. in history in 1971, oppressive beyond my worst expectations. I hated with a passion all the hierarchy at the university, the exalted and remote and vain and pampered and obnoxious professors. I felt constantly insecure, inadequate, and bad. I struggled with all the languages I was studying and the fussy way we had to learn everything from this or that period in history. I got an ulcer. It was only when I graduated and left the university that I found myself finally able to breathe.

Five years later, in 1976, as a young professor and after my own analysis, I enrolled as a research candidate at the Chicago Institute for Psychoanalysis. The institute was equally divided then between those committed to classical psychoanalysis and the work of Sigmund Freud and the young Turks who gravitated to Heinz Kohut and his new ideas about what he was calling self psychology. I quickly moved into the Kohut camp, where I skirted at the edges of what was called "the group." I was not Kohut's patient, or his supervisee, or even his student. But the aura that surrounded him had all the dangers of a cult and Kohut himself was, of course, incredibly charismatic. As Ina Wolf put it (Strozier 2001) Kohut was not entirely clear where his arm ended and that of his followers began. The group was definitely cultic in many ways, an aspect of the Chicago psychoanalytic world in the 1970s that I describe in some detail in my biography of Kohut (2001).

But Kohut, for all his faults, set limits. In 1978, for example, he headed off a movement by some of his followers to break from the

Chicago Institute and establish a separate self psychology institute. Kohut was easily as grandiose as Freud, but he was also level-headed and professional. I discovered to my surprise and delight that he was quite taken with my early work on Abraham Lincoln, which resulted in my first book, *Lincoln's Quest for Union*, in 1982. I felt understood and appreciated. Kohut made me feel worthwhile. In the institute training itself, I found the courses and general conversation wonderful and much more interesting than my seminars in history had been at the university. My friend, Robert Jay Lifton, has commented to me many times that I could resist the oppressive pull of the ideological totalism at the institute because my career did not hinge on my relationships with my teachers at that point in my life, as it was only later that I began my own clinical practice of psychoanalysis. I am sure he is right, though the observation fails to puncture my idealization of what I experienced as a candidate at the institute.

There are no simple conclusions. Psychoanalysis is an enterprise fraught with dangers and yet capable of exalted purpose. Its training is ridiculously insular and always subject to abuse. Its reach continues as well after training, for a young analyst depends for his or her livelihood on referrals from exactly those senior figures who control all aspects of institute life. Shunning in psychoanalysis can have profound economic consequences.

And yet the tight world of psychoanalysis can generate creativity and hope. I am not at all sure the potential for good outweighs that for pure evil. But I am struck with the complexity of the story, and I have to admit, for all my grousing, that I am hugely satisfied to be myself a practicing psychoanalyst, a teacher in an institute, and a supervisor of young analysts-in-training. I have to wonder why, in light of all my criticisms. I am sure it is partly idiosyncratic and personal. My training in psychoanalysis was not the first time in my life that I have survived and grown in potentially difficult situations. But perhaps I benefited more than I even recognized at the time from my immersion in the earliest moments of the new and empathic form of psychoanalytic practice that now prevails in the field. In the 1970s, Kohut's radical ideas about the self were new and a great intellectual discovery for me. They also change the way one understands human beings. The theory requires an ethical adjustment. It assumes mutuality and a deep respect for the experience of the other in the consulting room, in class, in supervision, and in life. It is often said, correctly, that self psychology is basically a theory of empathy. And in privileging empathy, Kohut's work in turn opened up a floodgate of humane research and thinking in areas as seemingly diverse as intersubjectivity, postmodern analysis, constructivism, and the conversational model that appear to be coalescing under the general umbrella of relational psychoanalysis.

So ideas matter, though at the same time we all need the critique of this book to remain alert.

REFERENCES

Erikson, E. H. (1958). *Young Man Luther: A Study in Psychoanalysis and History*. New York: Norton.

Gay, P. (1988). *Freud: A Life for Our Time*. New York: Norton.

Lifton, R. J. (1961). *Thought Reform and the Psychology of Totalism: A Study of "Brainwashing" in China*. New York: Norton.

——— (1969). *Death in Life: Survivors of Hiroshima*. New York: Vintage.

——— (1979). *The Broken Connection*. New York: Simon and Schuster.

Strozier, C. B. (1982). *Lincoln's Quest for Union: Public and Private Meanings*. New York: Basic Books.

——— (2001). *Heinz Kohut: The Making of a Psychoanalyst*. New York: Farrar, Straus & Giroux.

SUPERVISORY EXPERIENCES: PERSONAL REFLECTIONS

A Therapist's Initiatory Journey Through Submission in a Coercive Training Program

Annette Richard

> *The need to make meaning . . . can serve the need for leaps of creativity and growth and yet, given a slight perturbation, ever so subtly glide into a need to cling to a defensive and constrictive belief system.*
>
> [Ghent 2002, p. 804]

> *The paradox in the dogmatic process . . . is that it reveals fundamental questions within our culture . . . , deep uncertainties which torment us outside of our awareness.*
>
> [Roy 1998, p. 96]

This is a book about the emotional ecology of the groups in which we learn to become psychotherapists. Living in a world in transition from an epistemology of modern objectivism to a postmodern relativism seems to have thrown that process into a crisis to which each of us has responded differently. In a context of rich pluralism, an exciting plethora of new metaphors, new insights, and new ways of thinking is being created and offered to newcomers in the profession as well as to experienced practitioners. But the understanding of individual experience as wholly cocreated leaves us in a dizzying state of "Cartesian anxiety." This is the cultural context in which a newcomer to the profession, or even an experienced therapist in quest of new meanings, is looking for safe and reliable teachers and community with whom to explore vulnerable states of uncertainty. Our attempt to create stability in this situation is in a constant balanced flux with uncertainty, creating one of the existential dilemmas of life. This is the story of my own journey.

I have decided to tell my own story not because it is unique but because I hope to make my small contribution in order to help understand such derailments of ideals that lead to indoctrination, fanaticism, and abuse of power in psychotherapy practice and training. My narrative is probably very similar to that of many others who, in the 1960s and 1970s, attempted to liberate themselves from a confining cultural environment. The human-potential movement was then bringing thousands of young adults in North America to "growth centers," searching for new psychological moorings in the midst of profound cultural changes. I think this crisis has left its mark on our current political and social situation as well as in today's cults. As a therapist, I was involved in this countercultural movement personally and professionally.

In a 1981 story about the disintegration of the Center for Feeling Therapy (CFT) in Los Angeles, the *Los Angeles Times* reported that many former patients had filed a $95 million lawsuit against their therapists in which they charged that they had been "defrauded of their money, brainwashed, and abused physically and emotionally" (Timnick 1981). Investigators in a CBS broadcast about the group labeled it the "Cult of Cruelty" (1981). A book was also written describing the rise and fall of the CFT was titled *Therapy Gone Mad* (Mithers 1994). I was there. I was a patient and a therapist-trainee in this psychotherapy cult. I was both the abused and an abuser in my idealized search for a cure.

Understanding my involvement in the CFT is a painful but, I hope, curative process. My suffering is tied both to the shame of having myself been abused psychologically and to the guilt I feel for having abused my patients. My hope for cure lies in the sobering and humbling acceptance that my personal world of experience is continually shaped by and shapes the personal worlds of others. This is the realization of what Stolorow and Atwood (1992) have called the "intolerable embed-dedness of being" (p. 22). As I attempt to reveal my participation in CFT, as a patient and as a therapist, I feel painfully torn between my longing to make my experiences known and my need to hide them in order to protect my autonomy and integrity.

The intersubjectivists believe that all psychological theories reflect the personal struggles of their authors, their existential tensions and quests (Atwood and Stolorow 1993). As human beings, we all have an evolving private implicit belief system about the good life, about the ideal quality of experiencing and awareness, theories about suffering and its cure that draws us to choose among the different models of the mind. I believe that every practitioner in psychotherapy from any theoreti-cal allegiance is liable to fanaticize his own theories of suffering and cure since the latter were constructed in his innermost experiential history. With Orange and colleagues (1997), I think that one of the ways we can avoid going down this slippery slope is a continuing process of re-cognition of these personal theories, conscious and unconscious, and their recontextualization. The observer must become the observed (Atwood and Stolorow 1984).

I will differentiate three periods in my journey. During the first, my Rogerian period, I fervently adhered to the therapeutic humanistic ideals of Carl Rogers. Professional disillusionment and personal life crisis brought me to the "feeling-therapy" period. Following the brutal break-down of the feeling-therapy group, I went through a long recovery pe-riod from which emerged a new personal and professional perspective. I will now tell my tale.

MY SEARCH FOR "UNEMBEDDED BEING"

Upon entering my undergraduate and graduate studies at the Université de Montréal in 1963, the naive idealism of my early twen-ties was both impressed and hurt by the strong oppositional polarities between the mainstream schools of thought in psychology. The differ-ent theories of mind and of human existence excluded each other. The study program, largely dominated then by experimental psychology based on a Cartesian scientific philosophy favoring objectivism, the quantifiable observations of behavior at the expense of internal factors and intrapsychic events, left me confused and disappointed. Having grown up as a girl and as a member of an Acadian minority in a French-Canadian ghetto, would I have to survive again by submitting to the dominant culture? There was a second option for clinicians: psychoanalysis, considered in the academic circles as the "bastard child" of scientific psychology.

But the traditional Freudian therapeutics based on the analyst's authoritative knowledge of the patient's unconscious and on a pessimistic vision of human existence did not fit with my romantic ideals either. When I was introduced to the "third force" (Tageson 1982) in psychology, the existential-humanistic psychology, I was convinced I had found a home at last. I fervently embraced the countercultural ideals of the human-potential movement with its optimistic beliefs in self-determination, freedom, and the responsibility of the individual in relation to his social environment.

During my graduate studies, I trained as a Rogerian client-centered therapist (Rogers and Dymond 1954) outside of the official curriculum. I joined a marginal group of students who adhered to convictions that were revolutionary in that academic setting, an ideology fitting the so-called social and political Quiet Revolution in Quebec of the 1960s. I was convinced that authentic empathic understanding and unconditional acceptance allow patients to relinquish their self-protective defenses and restore their self-actualizing motivation. Not only did I believe that by adhering to Rogers's teachings I could avoid the dogmatism that seemed to pervade psychoanalysis, I thought I could provide patients with precisely what had been lacking in my own development and social/familial environment. By applying these ideals at home, I imagined I would be a better parent to my son than my parents had been to me. Another source of my enthusiastic adherence to the Rogerian ideal was my hope of breaking free of a life-long conflict; my longing to feel attached to others seemed incompatible with my wish to experience myself as assertive and fully differentiated.

I now see that while the Rogerian approach exalted the subjective, personal, and singular reality of the patient and glorified an empathic perspective, it failed to recognize that therapists cannot observe without theory or without organizing what is observed. I pushed the ideals of the existential-humanistic approach to very painful extremes before I understood the necessity of scrutinizing my own self organization in interaction with others, especially in therapeutic relationships—the "fallibilistic" attitude described by Orange (1995).

FIRST MAJOR DISILLUSIONMENT

In 1974, when I was in my early thirties—a recently divorced single parent, and a practicing psychotherapist for eight years—I was overwhelmed by a number of painful personal and professional crises that all occurred simultaneously. Personally, my dream of creating a family, through which I hoped to rescript (Brothers 1995) the affective isolation that marked my childhood and adolescence, was shattered when I became aware that I was involved in a deep relational impasse. Professionally, I was confronted with frequent failures. My exclusive focus on immediate here-and-now subjective experience had led me to deny the persistent influence of past formative experiences on the present. Having neglected the complexity of the change process, I was unable to understand or cope with difficult and tenacious clinical problems. At the same time, my attempts to rectify my own past by helping patients rectify theirs had locked me into a "should-be" stance of empathic responsiveness that was every bit as confining as the "should-be" neutrality of psychoanalysis. Once again I felt caught in the submissive position. I felt totally inadequate as a Rogerian client-centered therapist since my efforts failed to relieve the suffering of patients who were most in need. As I tried ever harder, but without success, to live up to my ideals I experienced prolonged periods of anxiety and depression. These led me to a frantic search for alternative therapeutic approaches.

Looking back, I realize that my therapeutic stance had become more and more difficult to maintain because it was based on a negation of my own vulnerability and selfobject needs. My attempts to smother my own experience alternated, at times, with bouts of confrontative and explosive assertions of my perspective that I rationalized as providing "authentic relating." Such authenticity was recommended by Rogers himself, mostly at the end of his own life and career. Maybe he was also struggling with his idealization of what he called "the necessary and sufficient" therapeutic conditions (Rogers 1957).

I clearly remember feeling so overwhelmed with concerns about my most disturbed patients that I was unable to enjoy myself. How could

I have a good life if those who depended on me couldn't have one? I longed for vacations, but was unable to profit from them. I recall how powerless I felt in the face of what I saw as destructive behavior on the part of my patients. The very behaviors that made them seek my help would, of course, derail the treatment, but I had no way to deal with them. There were moments when I hated my patients and I wished they would leave. But mostly I felt shame and intense dread. To make matters worse, I had become aware that I was going nowhere in my personal treatment. Painful disillusionment of my ideals on all fronts!

Yet, I was still very young and full of hope for repair. I believed there must be a way to work more effectively. It was the early 1970s, a time of throwing away all constraints. Many marginal groups promising radical recipes for self-improvement and transformation had sprung up, tempting those who searched for alternatives. This is the context in which Feeling Therapy appeared to me as the antidote to my intolerable pain and helplessness. As Dorpat (1996) observes, people tend to join cults when they are emotionally disturbed or in transitional periods.

THE CENTER FOR FEELING THERAPY

The CFT was founded in 1971 by a group of nine dissidents of Arthur Janov's Primal Institute, which also had developed in the margins of the traditional therapy community. In June 1974, I left Montreal for Los Angeles with eight other colleagues to participate as a patient in an intensive psychotherapy program at the CFT, and eventually as a therapist-trainee. During the winter prior to this trip, I had met Richard Corriere and Jerry Binder, two of the CFT founders. My colleagues and I had been fascinated to hear CFT founders speak about having discovered a theory of personality, psychopathology, and therapy that had taken them far beyond the "miserable failures" of other approaches developed in the human-potential movement. In the hope of recruiting us for their therapeutic community of "transformed persons," they claimed it was our only chance to confront "reasonable insanity," a universal psychopathology maintained by an "insane society." This community, they promised, would provide continuing support for a process they called "going sane" (Hart et al. 1975) through which we would transcend "the alienation of emotional authenticity."

Talking directly to my despair, they offered a solution to my failed search for a differentiated identity that would not sacrifice my longing for intimacy with others. All I had to do, they insisted, was join a community of individuals who shared my search. Although initially as suspicious as I was fascinated, I was finally seduced by the closeness they seemed to share with one another, and the certainty with which they presented their arguments. The limitations of other approaches, they claimed, were attributable to the failure by those involved to contact their own insanity. In contrast, their community of equal therapists offered protection against having the neurotic projections of any one person determine a system. They argued that they submitted their patients only to those therapeutic practices that had proven effective on themselves.

That, it seemed to me at the time, was it: I had not gone "all the way" to change my own life, so I could not guide my patients to change theirs. The CFT therapists proposed a specially designed program for us: as patients, we would have two intensive psychotherapy sessions lasting two months each in the course of one year. This would enable us to be feeling therapists for our own patients when we got back to Montreal.

Like primal therapy, feeling therapy initially emphasized very early relationships. The founders celebrated Janov's rediscovery of abreactive, cathartic reexperiencing of childhood traumas previously denied consciousness, the method Freud developed with Breuer and then discarded (Hart et al. 1975). Insisting that emotion is more important than understanding and insight, their basic general principle held that human beings have a bodily need for "completing" feelings.

The founders of CFT believed that pathology, or "craziness" as they called it, originates during the course of socialization when we develop defenses such as withholding, repressing, or substituting "true feelings" in order to cope with a "reasonably insane world." This defensive disordering of feelings was considered the one and only explanation for patients' unhappiness and dissatisfaction. As Hart and colleagues (1975) expressed it, "Without being in an integral state, a person is insane. There are two states of being: balanced or unbalanced. There is no in-between. There is balanced feeling or disordered feeling" (p. 13). In my search for wholeness, freedom, and pristine authenticity, this fully dichotomized notion of self, sane or insane, true or false, was quite appealing to me.

The feeling-therapy view of "insanity" required a radical and revolutionary therapeutic approach that aimed not only at change or cure, but a total transformation of the personality. The CFT attempted to go beyond the abreaction of Janov's primal scream by tearing down defenses that supposedly interfered with the full expression of feelings and, therefore, a "sane" way of life. Of course this required highly aggressive and confrontative techniques. As Hart and colleagues (1975) explain:

> In Feeling Therapy we use a person's craziness to transform his life. By evoking and provoking crises we bring craziness to the surface. The person must then undergo a disintegration of his defenses and an unbalancing of his familiar integration. [p. 63]

They retained the primal-scream format of a three-week intensive program, which mostly involved individual therapy followed by group sessions several times weekly in the context of communal living arrangements. The intensive program was designed to break down the insane personality structure and to create a bond with the therapist. After being broken down in isolation with a therapist, the patient was thought to access a "true feeling state." Whether or not this occurred was solely determined by the "feelingful" therapist, who, very much like a lie detector (Ayella 1998), was able to determine the true from the false, the real from the unreal in his patient's experience:

> A person is either responding from his feeling or he's going away from his feeling. If he's going away, he's defending and you can feel it, if you are clearly in the present yourself. You can feel whether the other person is there responding with you. So you just respond over and over again to his going away and you can do that in millions of ways. [Hart et al. 1973]

Although the true feeling state was supposed to become an internal reference for a new way of life, it had to be continually nurtured by a community of "feelingful people." Only other CFT patients and therapists, "the first true friends," could be trusted to be "response-able" and therefore to create a sane life. Eventually the patient-trainee was allowed to participate in co-therapy training and practice with peer patients in group settings supervised by senior therapists.

These dichotomous absolute conceptions of health and pathology can only lead to a dogmatic and even sectarian therapeutic practice. It represents the ultimate attempt to redeem the Cartesian project of freeing the individual from the influence of his environment by the absolutization of subjective emotional reality: "I feel, therefore I am." Rogers and Dymond (1954), Winnicott (1960), and others have also proposed these romantic narratives of a true self forced to hide from environmental impingements behind a false self. Representing our hopes for a fully autonomous individuality (or unembedded being), it can create the illusion that an entity, a fully formed true self, deeply buried inside us, is waiting to be liberated (Mitchell 1993, Strenger 1998). The CFT therapists were carrying this conviction to its extreme. Nevertheless, I believed it. Eigen (1999) describes my experience in his definition of the "area of faith" in the "quest for 'ideal' experiencing": "A way of experiencing which is undertaken with one's whole being, all out, with one's heart, with one's soul, and with all one's might" (p. 3). It was meant to be my own attempt for a new begining, a ready-to-wear antidote to my depressive disillusionment as a young adult and therapist.

THE "THERAPY GONE MAD"

From June 1974, when I started my first intensive CFT therapy program, until November 1980, when the CFT disintegrated over a period of three days, I lived intensely in an adventure that was at times extremely uplifting but, more often, nightmarish. The nightmare started in my second individual therapy session, on the second day of my intensive program, when my therapist, Konni, who was charismatic leader Richard Corriere's girlfriend, "busted" what she called my "defensive mousie, ass-kisser" behaviors and attitudes. Having prepared herself by reading an extensive autobiography I had sent in advance of joining the CFT, along with the nonrefundable $2,500 fee for my three-week program (a fortune for me at the time), Konni presented herself as if she had omnipotent knowledge of my truths and my lies. This "busting" went on for hours during which I was told to exaggerate my so-called defensive behaviors. For example, I would talk "mousily," lie under a rug, and so on. I was told that not until I could fully feel my defenses would I have the choice to feel and express who I really was.

Konni was tough. She trapped me from every angle until I crumbled in tears of exhaustion and pain. I felt devastated, torn open. Then she would become sweet, tender, and loving as she acknowledged my pain as the denied feelings of an affectively deprived child who had been forced into being nice and undemanding. Konni would then insist that I shout out my anger at my parents for having stopped my impulses as a child and that I hit a racket against a padded wall until I was exhausted. Eventually she told me that I had reached a new level of feeling, from which I could choose to have a full life or to retrogress and feel badly and lonely again. I believed that by being loud, loquacious, and shocking I had opened a door to an aliveness I had never known.

I was also instructed to demand what I needed and wanted from her and from others in my "special group," my "feeling community." People in my therapy group were there, I was told, to support my "going sane" transformation, and I was there to support theirs. We were to bust old defensive ways of being, especially pretenses at change, to which we would all resort at times in our attempts to avoid humiliating and terrifying attacks. We were kept off-guard by the unpredictability of our therapists' humiliating attacks, which alternated with loving validation. These were what CFT called "transforming cycles of complete feelings" (Hart et al. 1975, p. 39). Looking back, I can now recognize a coercive facsimile of an ongoing noncoercive intimacy: the never-ending cycles of breakdown and repair, separation and reunion.

Cut off from all former ties, I underwent a radical destructuring of my sense of self. I regard this as very similar to the process of identity change through thought reform and coercive persuasion that has been observed in prison settings and hostage situations (Ayella 1998, Dorpat 1996, Roy 1998). An essential difference was that I was there voluntarily. We were reminded of this whenever we objected to a therapist's cruel behavior. Any resistance to what was taking place in the process was deemed "defensive," "resistive," being "back in our crap," or "acting out" our craziness. Although I was often terrified and despairing, the alternations of abuse and loving tenderness I experienced in this coercive environment sometimes produced in me the intensely exhilarating conviction that I was part of an elite group in a revolutionary process of change. Moreover, I came to feel that there was nowhere else to go.

Upon returning home to Montreal with my group of colleagues after my first two months of therapy and training, I found that my personal and professional way of being had indeed been effectively transformed. I was in such a deep state of confusion and vulnerability that I clung to CFT's teachings and kept in touch with members of the L.A. community. Adding to my sense of childlike desperate dependency was the strong taboo in our group against keeping anything private. If I had failed to comply with the CFT directive that all secrets must be made public, I risked having them shamefully exposed. Not only did I share my innermost experiences, but also my life space, work, and even my personal therapy (we did therapy for one another). Although we strongly believed that we were on the road to individual freedom, we depended more and more on one another to know what that was!

Our fervently held beliefs, combined with the heady sense of elitism we shared, contributed to wild swings of powerful emotions that contrasted dramatically with the depression, emptiness, and isolation of our past lives. Indeed, the intensity of my feelings led me to believe that I was living a heroic and meaningful life. Some good moments kept my hopes alive, especially in the first years: childhood wounds were acknowledged, opening me up to loving feelings and to the joy of a community. However, my exhilaration was usually short-lived, and intensely dysphoric periods invariably followed. Whatever I felt, however, was rigidly interpreted as moving toward or away from my genuine feelingful self. "If you don't feel good, it's because you don't choose to," I heard over and over. In retrospect, I can recognize the slippage of my convictions and those of the CFT community in general toward ever greater dogmaticism and fanaticism. Our preoccupations, the themes that shaped our lives, grew narrower and narrower to the point of rigid stereotypy.

Increasingly, I demanded the same commitment that I felt toward the CFT from my peers and my patients. It is this part of my experience that is the most painful and difficult to admit. That I was unable to protect myself is mortifying, but knowing that I hurt people who were seeking my help through the imposition of my beliefs makes me feel even more ashamed and guilty. I was not training as a therapist as much as I was involved in a total lifestyle transformation, trying to "convert" my patients to the same. Although I never managed to become the omnipotent and arrogant healer I was required to be (and thought I should be), I would sometimes "bust" a patient's so-called defenses when I was told to do so. I felt terrible doing it. But if I failed to comply, I knew I would be dropped from the group of the elite and I dreaded feeling destitute, isolated, and despairing once again. Behind closed doors with my patients, I often allowed myself to care about them. I connected with them on a human-to-human basis rather than with the rote responses I was trained to provide. However, we were closely monitored. If a patient dropped out of therapy with me, I would be blamed for manifesting "defensive negativity" about our "new philosophy," the only valid and true one.

I recall having had glimpses of the disavowed but massive accommodations I made in order to survive in my totalistic environment, and the similar demands I made on others who appeared to share my new convictions. I began to feel so inadequate as a therapist, I even fantasized about being a restaurant waitress. Then I condemned myself for not having the guts to leave and become one. But how could I go against the group and my therapists? How could I leave when all of life's meaning was tied to these relationships?

THE COLLAPSE

It would take too long to describe in detail all the circumstances that led to the disintegration of the CFT in November 1980 (Ayella 1998, Mithers 1994). Briefly, Richard Corriere, one of the founders, had become an extremely autocratic leader and had exercised increasingly abusive control. His colleagues, senior CFT therapists, confronted him in an attempt to even out the power imbalance. They decided to allow patients to express their dissatisfaction, a move that was like holding a match to a powder keg. In the explosion that occurred over the next 72 hours, we became brutally aware of our own abuse and how abusive we had been to our patients and to each other. There was a surge of combined relief, pain, and horror in all of us. The relief came from being suddenly free from the coercive system that had so totally controlled our lives, as well as from having our long suppressed doubts validated. We were then compelled to face the painful and terrifying collapse of our belief system and way of life. It would take me and my colleagues years to fully feel and make sense of what had happened to us. We were face to face with our fallibility on all levels! Even more haunting was our concern that, had the CFT not ended, we would not have had the strength to leave.

After the collapse of the CFT, I experienced a long period of social and professional withdrawal. I hid myself partly in shame and partly to find some space in which to reconstruct my shattered world. To combat the sense of meaninglessness and anomie that replaced the intensity of my former life, I desperately needed to make sense of what had happened to me. I read frenetically, although I was extremely wary of being influenced by any theory again. Miserable as I felt, I was too apprehensive about losing myself again to seek therapy. Who could I trust? Not even myself!

I finally managed to seek therapeutic help five years after the collapse. Through this process, I did gradually regain my lost confidence in the change process. However, my understanding of how change occurs is now profoundly different from what it was. Almost twenty-five years have passed since the collapse of the CFT. The community of colleagues I have found among self psychologists and intersubjectivity theorists has allowed me to acknowledge and deal more creatively with what I now recognize as a continuous process of mutual influence. It is fraught with uncertainties, tensions, and pain, and sometimes unbearably so in the therapeutic endeavor. Yet, having known the alternative, I more often embrace these with an open heart.

AN INITIATORY JOURNEY

Many authors have studied and written about what Doris Brothers (Brothers 2001, Brothers and Richard 2003) calls the "intersubjective regulation of uncertainty" and about the phenomena of fanaticism and indoctrination in groups forming around authoritarian leaders (Ayella 1998, Roy 1998). Starting with Freud, some therapists have been suspicious of religious faith and its possible alienating power. Paradoxically, many have also been blinded to their own abuse in fostering dependency in vulnerable patients. The contemporary intersubjective or relational model of the therapeutic relationship allows us to acknowledge and reflect on issues of influence and autonomy in analytic or therapeutic dyads (Mitchell 1997). Nevertheless, while paying exquisite attention to the details of therapeutic relationships, supervisory dyads have long neglected to recognize the complexities of their own relationship. This failure to develop a congruent model for supervision and training has created the context for the emergence of an authoritarian and elitist transmission of knowledge. The CFT therapists claimed they were remedying this incongruence by having all therapists submit to their own treatment before and while being trained; indeed, the therapy was the training, since we believed that by having access to a level of "true" feelings we would be totally "response-able." Cut off from outside influence and failing to reflect on relational experience, this therapeutic practice and training, among other aspects, led to indoctrination and abuse of power. I am reminded here of similar situations in certain training institutes. Lately, a few authors in psychoanalysis have been questioning the use and abuse of power in psychotherapy as well as in training programs [Dorpat 1996; also see *Psychoanalytic Inquiry*, 2004, vol. 24(1), on problems of power in psychoanalytic institutions]. Some have proposed new models of supervision (Frawley-O'Dea 2003, Frawley-O'Dea and Sarnat 2001, Lecomte and Richard 1999).

The literature mentioned above will be amply reviewed by other contributors to this book, and I will not add to it here. In my attempt to contribute to an understanding of coercive training programs, I turn now to my own participation in order to tease out some of the meanings it held for me. Why seek out such experience? What is the nature of this quest? Why stay in and hold on to such an abusive environment?

In my search for meanings after the collapse, I came across the writings of Heinz Kohut (1971, 1977), in which he described different transferential experiences in the analytic patient. These were manifestations of healthy yearnings for developmental selfobject experiences and the pathological results of past failures in such experiences. I recognized my search for an idealizing selfobject experience in the midst of my painful states of confusion and hopelessness, personally and professionally. It had led me to this unimaginable leap of faith in trusting the CFT therapists-trainers. They appeared to me to know what I needed to learn, as being what I wanted to be; I hoped that by totally surrendering to their guidance I would be transformed. My hopes, which are probably present in all therapy patients, and I would add in every person (therapist) seeking a teacher, were "not purely regressive nor purely progressive" as Mitchell (1993, p. 221) wrote. What a relief it has been for me to see the "tendrils of healthy self-strivings" (Tolpin 2002, p. 168) intertwined with the repetitive and pathological dimensions of my motivations. Seeing leaders and followers of cults as only pathological, fails to recognize how vulnerable to indoctrination is any person who, in the throes of a growth crisis, is striving for wholeness and restoration.[1]

But something went terribly wrong! In my hope to break through my emotional numbness, my stultifying defensiveness, I had gone all out. Eigen (1999) captures this very well: "A way of experiencing which is undertaken with one's whole being, all out, with one's heart, with one's soul, and with all one's might" (p. 3). I subscribed totally to being stripped of my defensive self-protective stances. Looking back, I remember how I started a denial process by pushing aside my first wary perceptions of inequality and submissiveness in the women involved in CFT: power was distributed unequally among the gender dividing line, hinting at the inequality also present between patients and therapists, trainees and trainers. Being desperate to avoid the familiar and to erase the impact of my past experiences, I denied my continual suspicions and doubts. I trusted my therapists-trainers in an undifferentiated manner (Brothers 1995), opening myself up to reliving a past traumatic betrayal.

The repetition compulsion has been studied and theorized extensively since Freud coined the term in his 1919 paper, "The Uncanny." Brothers (1995) views these phenomena as "sadomasochistic enactments undertaken in the hope of rescripting trauma scenarios" (p. 85). I believe both the leaders and followers of CFT were involved in such a pursuit, which is bound to fail. Wanting desperately to believe that this time around would be different we all fell blindly into this powerful collective enactment of betrayer and betrayed retraumatization.

We easily recognize the need for self-preservation, one that is deemed as the supraordinate motivational striving in human life (Atwood and Stolorow 1984, Kohut 1984). This survival thrust is often quite explicit

---

1. Studies of former followers in cults by Latkin (1993) and by Richardson (1995) (both cited by Roy 1998) identify two groups: the new followers in their early twenties who are described as idealists, meaning seekers in countercultural explorations, and others in their thirties and forties identified as the "disillusioned travelers" in the universe of convictions. None of them showed significant pathological traits.

and visible in its outward expression. When manifested in the therapeutic arena, clinicians have tended to call them resistances or defenses. Self psychologists have given us a more empathic view of those phenomena by illuminating their self-protective aspect. Neverthelesss, they sometimes blind us in perceiving the inherent growth thrust present in the same manifestations (Tolpin 2002), a motivational striving that is, I believe, equally as fundamental as the need for self-preservation. Searching for a new beginning (Balint 1968), the hope of "rescripting [a] trauma scenario" (Brothers 1995, p. 85), and the "forward edge transferences" (Tolpin 2002, p. 171) are different ways of describing the attempts to heal and resume growth in the person. But these notions fall short in fully accounting for the deliberate search to destabilize myself to the point of disorganization.

The word *surrender*, as described by Emmanuel Ghent (1999), conveys to me more fully the sense of my longing in submitting to the CFT therapy and training. Ghent's paper, titled "Masochism, Submission, Surrender: Masochism as a Perversion of Surrender,"[2] fascinated me, particularly his description of the longing to surrender as the motivational force operating toward growth, the obverse of resistance or of the motivation to maintain the status quo. Ghent's position is similar to that of the humanistic-existential movement to which I had adhered earlier in my life and which had led me to the CFT. He sees psychoanalysis as based on "a belief in the fundamental need of people for the expansion and liberation of the self, the letting down of defensive barriers and the dismantling of the false self" (editors' introduction, p. 211; I would say: the experience of a false self). This need, he believes, is rooted in the more general longing to be known and recognized, and the corresponding wish to know and recognize the other. He remarks: "Surrender might be reflective of some force towards growth for which, interestingly, no satisfactory English word exists" (p. 215). He describes "the vagaries of the force that is on the side of psychic healing, the impulse to grow, to surrender, to let-go" (p. 235), which may be manifested in the blackwashing or perversion of surrender into submission as seen in sadomasochistic relationships. The sadism in such instances of domination of the other

---

2. The Surrender paper was first presented at New York University in 1983 and was published in *Contemporary Psychoanalysis* in January 1990. It was reedited in 1999 by Mitchell and Aron as part of the seminal papers of relational psychoanalysis.

could be seen as the reversal of submission, or the perversion of the active, penetrative version of the yearning to surrender (to know the other). I felt that he was describing the CFT enterprise. My experience in therapy and in training comes out alive in the following:

> Submission . . . the ever available look-alike to surrender . . . holds out the promise, seduces, excites, enslaves and in the end, cheats the seeker-turned-victim out of his cherished goal, offering in its place only the security of bondage and an ever amplified sense of futility. By substituting the appearance and trappings of surrender for the authentic experience, an agonizing, though at times temporarily exciting, masquerade of surrender occurs: a self-negating submissive experience in which the person is enthralled by the other. [Ghent 1999, p. 220]

In his Afterword, Ghent (1999) insists that even though surrender and submission are distinct and even opposite phenomena, they are paradoxically tied to each other. He distinguishes them although he acknowledges that nothing lives in a state of such dichotomized reality and that we often find them together. Holding in mind that at any given therapeutic moment, both surrender and submission are part of any relational process, is what he calls later a capacity for entertaining paradox (Ghent 1992). Submission and its active counterpart, the impulse to impose oneself, are often, in many practices (especially in the Eastern philosophies and spiritual disciplines), a necessary prelude to surrender and growth. In much the same way regression, which may "function as a special case of surrender" (Ghent 2001, p. 36), is often seen in psychoanalysis as preliminary to healing. Wishing change involves seeking while at the same time fearing a dissolution of the familiar self organization. In his later work, Ghent (2001) uses the language of nonlinear dynamic systems theory to suggest that this state of surrender (also sought in other experiences like falling in love) is "a system poised on the edge of chaos, a state optimal for change" (p. 38). But Ghent (1999) also signals "the ever-present peril of this impulse being exploited" (p. 242). There is a fork in the road that opens up in the micro-moment when an experience could become surrender or submission, a kind of strange attractor, an "edge of chaos" moment. The extreme sadomasochistic patterns found in coercive training programs could well be instances of the derailment of such moments. The emotional ecology of dogmatic and coercive training groups seems to load the dice toward submission.

DISCUSSION

What leads to such derailments in psychotherapy training? Can we avoid them? In the words of Adam Phillips (2001), is it "possible to conceive of a psychoanalytic training (or treatment) that is not . . . a Procrustean bed?" As Doris Brothers wrote, "The regulation of uncertainty cannot be accomplished by the operation of an isolated mind" (Brothers and Richard 2003). To learn, to grow, and to change our belief system or world of personal meanings requires a trustworthy relationship in which we are able to open ourselves up to outside influences. This applies also to the patient in the therapeutic relationship and to the trainee therapist in his relationship with teachers-supervisors or within a community of teachers and colleagues. Faith and surrender are part of this process, which can also be understood as idealizing selfobject experiences. After my training experience in the CFT, I became extremely wary of Procrusteanism—defined by Phillips (2001) as "cutting people down to size and making them fit" (p. 10). Therefore, in opening myself up to being influenced again, I was drawn to idealize (to surrender/submit to) the teachers and theoreticians who were also wary of any Procrustean tendencies. This helped me open up to being with my patients (also with my supervisors and my supervisees) in such a different way that I could learn from and grow with them in unpredictable directions. In this brief discussion, I would like to point out some of the personally meaningful learning experiences I had that I believe helped me to differentiate emotional ecologies in training environments that load the dice in favor of surrender and may avoid getting locked into the extremes of submission.

First, I think we need to consider carefully experiences of authority, of power and the nature of responsibility in therapeutic and training practices. My experience through submission to dogmatic authoritarian knowledge has led me to adhere to this major epistemologic shift in our professional culture: any understanding of a person's world of experience (including one's own) emerges and is co-constructed from mutual emotional participation in unique relational fields, and as such, it can only be partial and perspectival. Such a contemporary acknowledgment of the intersubjective nature of any therapeutic enterprise and a renewed continuous commitment to this view is to me the most prized anchor of self-discipline and responsible participation in the therapist and in his trainer. This epistemic stance is conducive to more humility and fallibility (Orange 1995) in all participants. It contributes to a decentering in the experience of authority in the expert: we hold our theories lightly, and we are no longer sure of the correctness of our interpretations of the lived experiences in relating with patients and trainees. As experts, we rely instead on our abilities for intimate dialogue and self-reflexivity, or "relational process skills" (Preston and Shumsky 2004, p. 197). Developing such skills based on an intersubjective clinical sensibility in the therapist is a lifelong process, and should be one of the main foci of any training environment. It can optimally take place in an environment where a dialogue about the relationship between trainers and trainees is central to the task, making the training model congruent with the therapy model by anchoring it in an intersubjective clinical sensibility (Lecomte and Richard 1999; see also Lecomte, Chapter 12, this book).

Having experienced both extremes of submissiveness to and imposition of arbitrary therapeutic authority, I have come to value as a safeguard the continuous recognition of the ongoing mutuality in experiences of surrender/submission in the therapeutic as well as in the training arenas. My own experience confirms the emerging opinion of many authors who believe we are in this profession partly because we are seeking our own personal healing and growth (Brothers and Lewinberg 1999, Ghent 1999) often through surrendering, and sometimes masochistically submitting to our patient's use of us. Through the lens of a relational selfhood, we now recognize what philosophers have already noted (Loomer 1976 as cited by Riveschl and Cowan 2003): "The capacity to be influenced is as truly a sign of power as the capacity to influence" (p. 109). In defining an intersubjective clinical sensibility, Stolorow and colleagues (2002) write that it "requires the empathic connection of which Gadamer so eloquently speaks as 'undergoing the situation' with the other" (p. 118). Lichtenberg and colleagues (1996) beautifully describe a nonlinear view of such dyadic affective communication within a mutual-influence system by a powerful metaphor: the therapist has to walk on an "affective-cognitive tightrope" (p. 122). Under the impact of powerfully evocative affect states of the patient, or when the patient frustrates the therapist's needs for certain kinds of selfobject responsiveness from him that the therapist had come to expect or take for granted (Bacal 1995), the latter will sway either in the direction of restricting his emotional involvement or being overwhelmed while enacting complementary or concordant reaction to the patient's enactments. I believe self-reflexivity in the therapist means being able to contain those reactions and to understand them as expressive of his own historically shaped subjectivity and at the same time, as a resulting impact of the patient's communication (Lecomte and Richard 1999). This awareness may enable the therapist not only to regain his affective-cognitive equilibrium or his subjective centeredness, but also to respond optimally to the patient's conscious and unconscious communications, that is, to be resonantly attuned to the patient's experience and at the same time, able to contribute a response from his unique subjectivity. These understanding and responsive abilities constitute the "self-supervisory" competence that I think we should aim to develop in the therapist-trainee through an integrative educative-therapeutic-experiential process (Lecomte and Richard 1999; see also Lecomte, Chapter 12, this book). Self-supervision in both therapist and supervisor-trainer could then be defined as the awareness (although partial and limited) and ongoing regulation of one's own organizing activity in interacting with similarly and differently organized perspectives in patients and trainees. This constitutes a profoundly embedded emotional participation and response-ability fraught with uncertainties, suffering, and limitations. Moments of surrendering to this embedded process can create unexpected emergent new patterning of experiences for patients and therapists, trainees and trainers.

Again, to augment the safeguards against extremes of submissiveness, I want to emphasize the importance of attending to the necessary and useful asymmetry present in the above egalitarian view of the therapeutic and training relationships. Given my understanding of what led me to these extremes with the CFT training program, I am inclined to both value and carefully reflect upon the facilitation of regression ["as a special case of surrender" (Ghent 2001 p. 36)] in therapy and training. Any asymmetry in relationships, as the one between therapist and patient, or between trainer and trainee, might be evocative of the universal asymmetry between adult and infant, in which the child's experience is extremely permeable and receptive to his caregivers' organized unconscious world of experiences. Learning with a teacher, and growing and changing with a therapist, involve seeking while at the same time dreading a similar state of surrender, which permits a "controlled" dissolution of familiar self organization in the individual so that he can learn and grow. Ghent (1999) describes the state of surrender as "an experience of being 'in the moment,' totally in the present, where past and future, the two tenses that require 'mind' in the sense of secondary processes, have receded from consciousness" (p. 216). Others might call this an encounter with what is the primary quality of experiencing (Eigen 1999), or activating the subsymbolic processing in the treatment situation to bring about a resymbolization of experiences (Bucci 1997), or accessing the affect states of global experiencing at the core and intersubjective relatedness levels (Stern 1985). Scharff (2004) offers this description of Ghent's process of surrender: "Dipping into less organized parts of self and being able to 'use objects' for our own emergent self organization." Therefore, surrendering is not a voluntary activity but more a state of mind, a yielding, a letting-go, which is the expression of an open system, a letting disorganization/change happen. This is made potentially possible only if and when we can tolerate and permit our patients to disorganize/use us in many ways while they are struggling with their own pursuit of surrender through submissiveness and sadistic protest. But the extreme vulnerability involved in this pursuit makes us want to control it by sometimes either making ourselves or our theories into God or uniting with another (a trainer-supervisor) as God so as to avoid retraumatizations.

Another safeguard against being controlling when we are trying to be liberating, as therapist and as trainer, is to respect the meanings embedded in states of resistance and self-perpetuation. Uncovering the unthinkable destructiveness of a significant other is a profound act of destabilizing one's own mind, often a quasi-death experience. Ever so gradually surrendering to (fully accepting) that "apperception of disorganizing meaning" (Ghent 1999, p. 229) is only possible after long periods of avoidance or protest. Any attempt to induce a state of surrender in such a context leads at best to submissiveness or constrained resignation, or at worst to a retraumatizing self-burial and self-annihilation. Any subtle or implicit requirements to relinquish a sense of self-agency in a therapy or training setting can be destructive when it has to be disavowed by the participants. Finally, I believe we do not facilitate surrender or transformation but we can (or fail to) allow it to potentially occur.

There are many oversimplifications in my formulations. I have used concepts in powerful dichotomies: it is very easy to slip into valuing one over the other, potentially leading to developmental moralism and dogmatism in the clinical and training setting. As Phillips (2001) wrote:

"Procrusteanism is, as it is, a well-known analytic approach" (p. 10). We can always say that there are powerful dialectical tensions between such polarities that we need to deal with in our lived experiences and awareness. I think we also need new models, new ideas to be able to transcend those dichotomies so as to more fully apprehend (at the same time knowing it is never totally possible) and surrender to the embeddedness of human existence, a major paradigmatic shift. The dynamic systems theory, a postmodern complexity theory, seems to be offering us many promises toward this goal. Like many others in my profession, I am struggling to live on that razor's edge, in between too much structure and too much randomness in knowing, a state known as the "edge of chaos."

CONCLUSION

My tale describes what people seeking richer lives can do to one's self and to others when they want to change and learn. My own hopes for such personal and professional change, "not purely regressive nor purely progressive" (Mitchell 1993, p. 221), have led me to explore the extremes of the central paradox of my being: the need "to be with" and the need "to be distinct from" an Other (Sander 1995) in an attempt to avoid what was for me the intolerable tension of my embeddedness. My experience of extreme submission to abusive treatment was initiatory in the sense that it carried to its destructive extreme a longing for an absolute autonomous self, the foundation of desired truthful and authentic free living. Paradoxically, it created the emergence of a new paradigm, personally and professionally, that allowed me not only to recognize the anguish of my deeply embedded being-in-the-world but also ever so gradually to surrender to it and deal with it more creatively.

I believe we need to acknowledge the authenticity of the question that led people like me into this dogmatic extreme and sectarian withdrawal from the larger culture. Changes bring out a mute, unthought suffering and the need to integrate it into a symbolic system culturally embedded in therapeutic rituals (Levi-Strauss 1949, cited by Strenger 2002). The desire for an absolute autonomous self seems to be still central to contemporary Western culture of which our psychotherapeutic practice is a part. The emphasis placed on individuality, on accepting responsibility for one's life and actions, on acquiring a sense of agency or mastery, on making the unconscious conscious, seems to have led us all through a crisis and to a search for what was missing: the vital relatedness of Being. Faith and surrender, so central in the Eastern culture, seem to be part of this quest. Failing to recognize and meet the need for it and for safe dependency in learning and changing does not produce autonomy but leads to abuse and perversion of those involved.

REFERENCES

Atwood, G. E., and Stolorow, R. D. (1984). *Structures of Subjectivity: Explorations in Psychoanalytic Phenomenology*. Hillsdale, NJ: Analytic Press.

———— (1993). *Faces in a Cloud: Intersubjectivity in Personality Theory*, 2nd ed. Northvale, NJ: Jason Aronson.

Ayella, M. F. (1998). *Insane Therapy: Portrait of a Psychotherapy Cult*. Philadelphia: Temple University Press.

Bacal, H. A. (1995). Discussion of "Countertransference: What the Self Psychological Lens Obscures," by Suzan Sands. Paper presented at the 18th Annual International Conference of the Psychology of the Self, San Francisco, CA. September.

Balint, M. (1968). *The Basic Fault*. London: Tavistock.

Brothers, D., (1995). *Falling Backwards: An Exploration of Trust and Self Experience*. New York: W.W. Norton.

———— (2001). Ghosts of the silver screen and other self-psychological reflections on the acceptance of death. Paper presented at the 24th Annual International Conference on the Psychology of the Self, San Francisco, CA. October.

Brothers, D., and Lewinberg, E. (1999). The therapeutic partnership: a developmental view of self-psychological treatment as bilateral healing. In *Progress in Self Psychology*, vol. 15, ed. A. Goldberg, pp. 259–284. Hillsdale, NJ: Analytic Press.

Brothers, D., and Richard, A. (2003). The cult of certainty: a self-psychological view of the quest for "unembedded being" in a coercive training program. Paper presented at the 26th Annual International Conference on the Psychology of the Self, Chicago, IL. November.

Bucci, W. (1997). *Psychoanalysis and Cognitive Science: A Multiple Code Theory*. New York: Guilford Press.

CBS affiliate. (1981). Cult of Cruelty. Five part television series, Los Angeles, May.

Dorpat, T. L. (1996). *Gaslighting, the Double Whammy, Interrogation, and Other Methods of Covert Control in Psychotherapy and Analysis*. Northvale, NJ: Jason Aronson.

Eigen, M. (1999). The area of faith in Winnicott, Lacan and Bion. In *Relational Psychoanalysis: The Emergence of a Tradition*, ed. S. A. Mitchell and L. Aron, pp. 1–37. Hillsdale, NJ: Analytic Press.

Frawley-O'Dea, M. G. (2003). Supervision is a relationship too: a contemporary approach to psychoanaltyic supervision. *Psychoanalytic Dialogues*, 13(3):355–366.

Frawley-O'Dea, M. G., and Sarnat, J. E. (2001). *The Supervisory Relationship: A Contemporary Psychodynamic Approach*. New York: Guilford Press.

Ghent, E. (1992). Paradox and process. *Psychoanalytic Dialogues* 2:135–159.

——— (1999). Masochism, submission, surrender: masochism as a perversion of surrender. In *Relational Psychoanalysis: The Emergence of a Tradition*, ed. S. A. Mitchell and L. Aron, pp. 211–242. Hillsdale, NJ: Analytic Press.

——— (2001). Need, paradox and surrender: commentary on paper by Adam Phillips. *Psychoanalytic Dialogues* 11(1):23–41.

——— (2002). Wish, need, drive: motive in the light of dynamic systems theory and Edelman's selectionist theory. *Psychoanalytic Dialogues* 12(5): 763–808.

Hart, J., Corriere, R., and Binder, J. (1975). *Going Sane: An Introduction to Feeling Therapy*. New York: Jason Aronson.

Hart, J., Gold, S., and Cirincione, D. (1973). Feeling therapy and primal therapy: the Topanga seminar. Presented at Topanga, CA. March.

Kohut, H. (1971). *The Analysis of the Self*. New York: International Universities Press.

——— (1977). *The Restoration of the Self*. Madison, CT: International Universities Press.

——— (1984). *How Does Analysis Cure?* Chicago: University of Chicago Press.

Lecomte, C., and Richard A. (1999). The supervision process: a self-supervision developmental model for psychotherapists. Paper presented at the 22nd Annual Conference on the Psychology of the Self, Toronto.

Lichtenberg, J. D., Lachmann, F. M., and Fosshage, J. L. (1996). *The Clinical Exchange: Techniques Derived from Self and Motivational Systems*. Hillsdale, NJ: Analytic Press.

Mitchell, S. A. (1993). *Hope and Dread in Psychoanalysis*. New York: Basic Books.

——— (1997). *Influence and Autonomy in Psychoanalysis*. Hillsdale, NJ: Analytic Press.

Mithers, C. L. (1994). *Therapy Gone Mad*. New York: Addison-Wesley.

Orange, D. M. (1995). *Emotional Understanding: Studies in Psychoanalytic Epistemology*. Hillsdale, NJ: Analytic Press.

Orange, D. M., Atwood, G. E., and Stolorow, R. D. (1997). *Working Intersubjectively: Contextualism in Psychoanalytic Practice*. Hillsdale, NJ: Analytic Press.

Phillips, A. (2001). A celebration of the work of Emmanuel Ghent. *Psychoanalytic Dialogues* 11(1):1–21.

Preston, L., and Shumsky, E. (2004). Who tore the web? Thoughts on psychoanalytic authority and response-ability. In *Progress in Self Psychology*, vol. 20, ed. W. J. Coburn, pp. 189–206. Hillsdale, NJ: Analytic Press.

Riveschl, J. L., and Cowan, M. A. (2003). Selfhood and the dance of empathy. In *Progress in Self Psychology*, vol. 19, ed. M. J. Gehrie, pp. 107–132. Hillsdale, NJ: Analytic Press.

Rogers, C. R. (1957). The necessary and sufficient conditions of therapeutic personality change. *Journal of Consulting Psychology* 21:95–103.

Rogers, C. R., and Dymond, R. F., eds. (1954). *Psychotherapy and Personality Change*. Chicago: University of Chicago Press.

Roy, J.-Y. (1998). *Le Syndrome du Berger: Essai sur les Dogmatismes Contemporains*. Paris: Boréal.

Sander, L. (1995). Identity and the experience of specificity in a process of recognition. *Psychoanalytic Dialogues* 5(4):579–593.

Scharff, D. E. (2004) Commentaries on "Masochism, Submission, Surrender—Masochism as a Perversion of Surrender," by E. Ghent. IARPP Online Colloquium Series, Ghent Colloquium, November 1–23.

Stern, D. N. (1985). *The Interpersonal World of the Infant: A View from Psychoanalysis and Developmental Psychology*. New York: Basic Books.

Stolorow, R. D., and Atwood, G. E. (1992). *Contexts of Being: The Intersubjective Foundations of Psychological Life*. Hillsdale, NJ: Analytic Press.

Stolorow, R. D., Atwood, G. E., and Orange, D. M. (2002). *Worlds of Experience: Interweaving Philosophical Dimensions in Psychoanalysis*. New York: Basic Books.

Strenger, C. (1998). *Individuality, the Impossible Project: Psychoanalysis and Self-Creation*. Madison, CT: International Universities Press.

——— (2002). From Yeshiva to critical pluralism: reflections on the impossible project of individuality. *Psychoanalytic Inquiry* 22(4):534–558.

Tageson, C. W. (1982). *Humanistic Psychology: A Synthesis*. Homewood, IL: Dorsey Press.

Timnick, L. (1981). Nineteen File Suit Against their Ex-Therapists. *Los Angeles Times*, June 30.

Tolpin, M. (2002). Doing psychoanalysis of normal development: forward edge transferences. In *Progress in Self Psychology*, vol. 18, ed. A. Goldberg, pp. 165–190. Hillsdale, NJ: Analytic Press.

Winnicott, D. (1960). Ego distortion in terms of true and false self. In: *The Maturational Process and the Facilitating Environment*. New York: International Universities Press.

2

One Wife's Story:
A Relational Systems Perspective

Linda Raubolt and Doris Brothers

When Richard Raubolt asked me (D.B.) to respond to his brave and moving account of his involvement in the Bar Levav Education Association (BLEA) and his membership in a cult-like supervision group (Raubolt 2003), I felt honored. I welcomed the opportunity to offer my thoughts on the intense connection that so often seems to develop between charismatic leaders and their followers (Brothers 2003a). In the course of our work together (Richard became the special editor of the issue of *Group* in which our articles appeared), I met his wife, Linda. I wondered what it was like for this beautiful, vivacious, intelligent woman while her husband was caught in BLEA's relentless grip. Then Richard called me again. This time he asked if I would help Linda write about her experiences for this book and comment on them. Again, I felt honored to be part of a very courageous enterprise. I asked Linda to develop a timeline chronicling the BLEA years. We then met to discuss the extraordinary document she sent me, much of which was derived from the journals she kept during her painful ordeal. Sitting together for hours one September afternoon, we discussed her heart-wrenching and inspiring journey. What follows is Linda's story:

American romanticist and author Elizabeth Peabody wrote in 1834 that one should learn from life "the simple creed that everything that can happen to a human being is either for enjoyment in the present or instruction for the future." I begin my story here.

1971

The marriage of our spirits took place on May 7, 1971, at St. John the Baptist Byzantine Church in Detroit, Michigan. Young and alone together, Richard and I set off on a journey in search of our future. The pathway led to New York City, where Richard began his studies in psychology. As his companion and fellow explorer, we attended numerous training sessions, which included psychosynthesis, Gestalt Therapy, psychodrama, and even Dan Cassriel's "Scream Therapy." Richard came to settle in on an analytic training program and I went into analytic therapy.

I thought I knew him well, knew him as a man, a husband, and a "becoming" analyst. We developed a common language about life and what we held to be important. I don't mean to imply that we always saw eye to eye (actually that would be impossible given our height differential, 4'11" and 6'), but we clearly had differences. However, through our common language we always managed to find our way to each other.

And life went on.

Richard's training continued, our first son was born, and an internship took us back to Michigan. Broadening his scope, Richard continued to seek out training and professional groups. And boy did he find one! Little did I know that the language Richard and I shared could be stolen. It would be replaced by words and ideas so very foreign to me. Richard, however, would come to embrace this new language with what appeared to be great ease, ultimately becoming fluent not only in the words but in the structure. Without a textbook available, I was unable to grasp this new alien language.

The man I thought I knew, I knew not at all. And life went on.

1982

I met Reuven Bar Levav, M.D., for the first time when my sons and I accompanied my husband to the spring meeting of the Michigan Group Psychotherapy Society (MGPS), an organization he had joined the previous year. Our older son was 7 and our younger son was 9 months old at the time. When Richard introduced me to Reuven, rather than saying hello, Reuven asked, "How long did you nurse your baby?" Taken aback by his audacious question, I waited a moment and then responded, "Long enough." My suspicions and distrust were born at that moment. I would come to detest this man and the Bar Levav Education Association (BLEA), the psychotherapy training institute he founded, for the devastating effects they had on me, my marriage, and my family.

Richard's association with MGPS afforded him the opportunity to develop relationships with not only Reuven but also the rest of the faculty of BLEA. Little did we realize that MGPS was and continues to be controlled by BLEA. For me, MGPS and BLEA have always been one and the same. I could never tell where one ended and the other began. In the early months of his involvement with MGPS, Richard would often comment, "Aren't they nice people? They treat you so nicely." While there was nothing yet about which to be suspicious, other than Reuven's abrasive tone, I remained wary. Who were these people who seemed so appreciative and kind to Richard, I wondered. Like me, they seemed to believe in Richard, to recognize the qualities that made him such an excellent therapist. I gradually learned that while they truly did understand how brilliant and creative he was, they did not have his best interests at heart. They were only interested in using him to achieve their own goals. It now seems obvious that they hoped he would enable them to expand their program into west Michigan.

1986 TO 1990

Richard was elected treasurer of MGPS in the spring, but it was I who actually did all the work and kept the books. As the society's pseudo–financial officer, I was able to learn a great deal about BLEA and MGPS and the individuals who made up these groups. To me, they all seemed to be cut from the same cloth; their individuality blurred together. Their conversations seemed to center around the organization, not about themselves. Yet they wanted to know everything about us.

During this period, as Richard's relationships with Reuven and the BLEA faculty deepened, I would accompany him to meetings, dinners, and other MGPS-sponsored events. Once, we were invited to a brunch at the home of Natan HarPaz, M.S.W., dean of training for BLEA (an opportunity for Richard to meet more people). Natan was aware that we had just purchased a new home and in front of everyone there, asked Richard, "How much did you pay for it?" Much to my surprise, Richard told him! I was livid. How could this man dare to ask such a personal question? And what had made Richard so quick to disclose information that I regarded as confidential between us? Richard had not asked my permission to reveal these facts. Suddenly I realized that our private life was fair game. It was then that I first felt that I was in danger of losing Richard. And I became aware that I must always be on guard around Natan.

Around this time, Richard began to attend weekly seminars offered by BLEA. (He was personally invited to attend by Reuven, free of charge.) Richard would make the 2½-hour drive from East Grand Rapids, where we lived, to Detroit for the seminars. It was during these drives that his sporadic "anxiety attacks" began. As he continued to attend these seminars, the frequency and severity of his attacks increased. For Richard and me life was changing rapidly and dramatically. We purchased a building, brought in a number of other therapists, and created a large mental health clinic, the Center for Professional Psychology. The center offered individual and group psychotherapy, and psychological evaluations for various county agencies. I became the business/building manager for this major undertaking. Aware that life had become extremely stressful for me, I wondered if Richard's anxiety was also stress-related.

To rule out the possibility that his anxiety attacks were physical in nature, Richard underwent intensive medical testing. Nothing was found. Because the attacks showed no sign of letting up, he felt that a session with Reuven might be helpful. I agreed to accompany him to Detroit for this meeting and at the end of the session, Reuven asked me to come into his office (said the spider to the fly). His question to me was, "What frightens you about Richard's attacks?" I answered that my greatest fear was that since Richard experienced these attacks while driving, he might have an accident and be killed. I would not only lose Richard, I would be left with the entire responsibility of the clinic as well as caring for our family.

Reuven sternly accused me of thinking only of myself, not about Richard. Despite the responsibilities I had assumed in order to help Richard professionally and at home, Reuven told me that Richard alone shouldered all the responsibilities in our marriage. To the extent that Richard had to worry about me, Reuven said, he could not take care of himself. What was I going to do, he asked, to relieve the pressure Richard was under? I made no response. I left Reuven's office believing I was responsible for Richard's anxiety. My downward spiral began.

Reuven's pronouncements made me question all that I had come to believe about myself. I had always thought of myself as tremendously responsible—even when I was a very young child. When I was 7, my father was hospitalized for what was described as "severe depression." I can still remember the marks that electrodes left on his head, remnants of the shock treatments that he received even though he was only 27 years old at the time. Recovering at home, he told me how smart I was and that it was up to me to help my mom get through this ordeal. His words changed our relationship, crumpling the world in which I had been "Daddy's girl." He had been the strong man I could lean on. Believing there was nothing really wrong with him, I wanted to be able to say, "Get up, you can do it yourself." Now, I believe that my father gave me a gift. I learned how to take care of myself and others with only the barest level of support. Now years later, I see that, at least in part, it was this lonely strength that enabled me to survive BLEA.

As his anxiety attacks grew more frequent and severe, Richard's dependence on MGPS/BLEA increased. Because Reuven had identified me as the problem, Richard leaned heavily on Reuven and Natan for the support and understanding they so willingly offered. Once again, I felt that I had been emotionally abandoned by the significant man in my life.

This journal entry is dated January 26, 1990:

> Dick told me this morning he hasn't felt very close to me lately. He feels a distance between us. I too have felt the distance. But unlike him I have enjoyed it. He drains me. We have had low points in our marriage but

never like this. Could this possibly be the beginning of the end? I am afraid perhaps it is. If I were to take a deep look at myself, I would find an angry volcano ready to erupt. Although I love the boys more than anything in the world, and I do truly love Dick, I find my life to be a continuous responsibility. I am so tired of being responsible for everything and everyone. I could scream. If I try to tell Dick, I am met with "Well, you're not the only one who is feeling bad." . . . Dick always says, "Get a life." But I don't know where to find one. I don't even know if I want to. . . . Just remember, be positive. The only one that can help you is you. Pull yourself together and get on with this life. It does no good to cry over spilt milk. I will make the best of it, get through it, and sustain—at least until the next crisis.

To my dismay, Richard's relationship with Natan grew closer and closer. When Natan decided to pursue a doctoral degree in psychology, Richard introduced him to the Fielding Institute in Santa Barbara, California. As an alumnus Richard enthusiastically recommended Natan as a candidate for the program. When Natan was accepted, Richard developed the required doctoral internship for him at our office. As part of this internship, Natan did therapy with patients who Richard referred to him. Although we furnished the office and secretarial services without compensation, Natan kept *all* of the money he was paid by patients. However, when Richard saw supervisees at Natan's office in Detroit, they paid Natan's office for the services Richard rendered and Natan kept 40 percent of the fee for himself. Richard saw nothing wrong with this unbalanced picture; I was enraged.

Richard also recruited colleagues to participate in a group supervision program that was to be led by Natan. Because of Richard's solid reputation, his colleagues eagerly joined. Soon after the program started in Grand Rapids, in May 1990, Richard and I had a major falling out. Natan would stay at our home, holding the groups either at our home or at the office. Having Natan as a houseguest was infuriating. Once again we provided everything, including my menial work, and Natan made all the money. Even more upsetting was the fact that Richard thought we should be grateful to Natan for gracing our lives. My objections to this arrangement met with harsh contempt from Richard. As his words to me became increasingly brutal and degrading, I began to see myself as a burden to him. I worried that perhaps Reuven was right, perhaps I was the problem. But then again, since Richard had never been abusive before, I could only assume that he learned these new harsh words and attitudes in supervision.

Marathon therapy weekends (28-hour intensive group therapy sessions) are a crucial part of the BLEA model, so of course Richard was invited to be a participant. While he was not yet in therapy with anyone in Detroit, he and Natan both thought this would be most beneficial for him. Although Richard felt I was not supportive, my journals state otherwise.

In my journal dated November 17, 1990. I wrote:

> Dick is at a marathon therapy weekend with Natan. Hopefully it will be a very meaningful experience for him. His fears and anxieties are eating him alive. I believe they have been for a very long time. Maybe this weekend will help ease some of those pressures. The one fear that has become constant is the fear of losing Dick. For me, the most difficult part is that I am not first in Dick's life, I can't blame him. . . . I feel like an emotional cripple searching for crutches to hold up this worthless mass for just a little longer. It is hard to admit that I don't have any dreams for the future. I have begun to live only for tomorrow. I firmly believe that forever *is* tomorrow.

1991

Convinced that I greatly needed therapy, Richard recommended that I see someone from the BLEA organization. This of course provoked a major outburst from me. I responded that there was no way on God's earth that I would share any of my intimate thoughts with "those people." But I worried that Richard might be right, that I was losing my mind. I had always been told that I was my father's daughter. Were the demons that pursued my father now coming after me? I began looking over my shoulder, constantly waiting for the shadows to overpower me. If Richard was right, no one could save me.

In my journal dated March 17, 1991, I wrote:

> I believe I am becoming the "Madwoman" of East Grand Rapids. . . . I'm the crazy one around here. He shares nothing with me. I share only with myself now.

At this very weak moment for me, a woman we had known for years, who was now also a member of Natan's supervision group, suddenly began to pursue a closer relationship with me. Since she and Richard co-led a therapy group, they spent a great deal of time together. Pressured by Richard, I accepted her overtures. My meetings with her proved devastating insofar as she repeatedly conveyed to me that she knew Richard better than I. Whatever remaining trust in Richard I had managed to salvage over these months now dissolved. I realized that while growing more and more estranged from me, he had grown closer and closer to "them."

Here is what I wrote on May 17, 1991:

> Although I have a husband, I could never feel safe in expressing my feelings with him. . . . I know he can share . . . feelings with others (in group supervision) but not with me. I am glad he has some way of ridding himself of his phantoms. I am jealous. As always I deal with my demons alone. The sadness which overcomes me when I look back on my childhood keeps me from moving forward. I try to transform the sadness into anger vowing to achieve and accomplish in adult life what childhood lacked. However, the reality is, my childhood continues to haunt me. My personal possessions are vast, more than anyone deserves, but emotionally I am a "bag lady."

By the end of this period my journal contains references to my "feeling nothing," and of my marriage as a "black hole" from which I cannot escape. I was overcome with depression, and what felt like breakdowns were occurring over and over. I felt as though bits and pieces of me were crumbling, falling deep within.

Once again my inner voice saved me. From my journal dated June 14, I wrote:

> Crying over spilt milk again, Linda? Grow up. What do you have to be sad about? Yes, it's me again, pick yourself up and get on with it. Who told you life would be a paradise? Who told you everything would be perfect? You seem to have fared a hell of a lot better than most. Be grateful, stop whining, and kick ass. So you don't have a friend but me? So what? I haven't steered you wrong or let you down yet, have I? No! So stop your yapping and get on with life.

At this point, I began to understand that there were many sides to me, all of them different, but yet not fully separate. Although I managed to push the old "me," the strong, vital voice in my journal, deep into hiding, she emerged every now and then. My problem was when "she" was not around I felt nothing, including love for others.

1992

When Richard began therapy with a BLEA associate in Detroit, I questioned his choice of therapist. "What do you know?" Richard said. To myself, I answered, "Nothing." What I thought or felt no longer mattered. Richard seemed to have all the answers. For me, the only benefit of Richard's therapy was that he was away in Detroit every Friday and I found some peace alone. The animosity between us escalated, resulting in many heated arguments. Clearly Richard resented my anger. He became more belligerent as he experienced Crisis Mobilization Therapy techniques (BLEA's model of aggressive therapy), while I learned to strengthen my resolve by expressing my anger. Richard's involvement with BLEA, including the supervision group, and his own therapy, now controlled every aspect of his life.

At one point Richard attended an intensive therapy workshop led by Reuven in Portland, Oregon. Everyone from the supervision group attended. Prior to this workshop, everyone called Richard "Dick." When he returned, he insisted that we must call him "Richard." He said it was a major turning point for him. I, very obstinately, told him that he was Dick when I met him, Dick when I married him, and for me he would remain Dick. Richard is the name BLEA gave him, the name of the man who had become a stranger to me. Today when I speak about him with others, I refer to him as Richard. But at home together, I still call him Dick and so do family members.

Gradually at first, and then more and more forcefully, my determination to sustain my own life took hold, even as the chasm separating Richard and me deepened. Matters came to a head on my birthday, following a shopping trip with the woman Richard had urged me to befriend. After this outing I clearly saw how she had continually attempted to discredit me. Since Richard believed her and not me, there was no way for me to defend myself. I determined at this point I had to take a stand, so I told Richard I would not attend an upcoming MGPS black-tie dinner-dance with him. In fact, I decided I would no longer attend any MGPS or BLEA functions. It was the "birthday" of my independence! That following weekend when Richard went to the MGPS dinner-dance alone, I stayed home and took pictures of our older son as he went off to his last homecoming dance (he would graduate in June 1993). I was where I wanted to be! As it turned out, this was a major milestone in my life. I had finally said no to Richard and to MGPS/BLEA.

1993

While I was saying no to Richard and to MGPS/BLEA, Richard was saying yes. He was elected president of MGPS, a six-year commitment that consisted of two years as program director, followed by two years as president, and finally two years as consultant to the president. Richard eagerly accepted the presidency and the commitment it entailed, even though it meant that he would have to spend a great deal of time in Detroit, away from home. I objected angrily. My question was, "Where does this leave the family?" Richard accused me of being jealous of his friends in MGPS/BLEA. Of course I was jealous, for I had no one.

Here is my journal entry for March 1993:

> I think the problem lies in the fact that at one time all we had was one another. Now he shares with these newfound friends and his therapist. I share with me. All alone once again. I feel as if I'm the loser in the deal. But how can I be the loser? I'm not, for I have my sons and their love. They are truly my whole world now.

Richard's acceptance of the presidency of MGPS was the final straw. After this last confrontation, I stopped writing in my journal. While I did not record any details, I can recall every situation and many of the horrible moments of this time as they related to MGPS/BLEA. During this period there were also many cherished moments that I spent with my sons. They *were* the main reason I survived the MGPS/ BLEA years.

1995

In August, while presenting a paper at the Ferenczi conference in Sao Paolo, Brazil, Richard suffered a major panic attack. I was amazed that during this crisis he never once thought of calling his BLEA therapist for help. Instead he called me at home, and I once again became his lifeline. I spoke soothingly to him and helped him secure an early flight back to the United States. While questions had always lurked for Richard regarding BLEA tactics and style, he had not sought answers. Once safely home, the pieces of the BLEA puzzle began fitting together for him. This marked the beginning of the end of his association with MGPS/BLEA. Although he stayed in his BLEA therapy, Richard realized he needed something else. This model no longer worked.

Sao Paolo was a turning point in another major way for me. This event threatened our sons with exactly the calamity against which I had been trying to protect them. I felt determined to fend off an intergenerational repetition of my own trauma. Knowing all too well the emotional burden involved, I wanted to spare my boys any responsibility for the care of their father.

Up to this point, Richard and I had kept our sons out of the conflict between us. Since Richard was so frequently away both physically and emotionally, I had created a little family of three in which we weathered life's ups and downs without him. With our older son away and busy with college and our younger son immersed in high school and sports, it had been easy to shield them. However, when Richard called from Brazil, both boys were home and the crisis could not be hidden. I decided to sit them down and tell them about Richard's plight. I explained that he was in trouble emotionally, that he suffered from panic attacks. I mentioned that Richard would return the next day after a lengthy flight involving a prolonged layover in New York. Our oldest son immediately suggested that he fly to New York to meet his father. "We can't leave him there alone," he said adamantly. While I was deeply touched by his loving, generous offer to help his father, I answered firmly, "No, he is a man. He got himself there and he'll get himself back." Nevertheless, he insisted on accompanying me to the airport in Grand Rapids to pick him up.

I realized that I needed to prepare both of my boys to encounter a father who no longer resembled the impeccably dressed, supremely confident man they thought they knew. Yet I decided that it was important that my sons see their father with all of his human frailties. I wanted them to see his struggle, not out of heartless revenge, but because I felt confident that they would witness his recovery. I knew he would find the strength to pull himself together.

1996

After speaking to a number of colleagues throughout the United States, Richard decided to seek treatment with a noted self psychologist. For me, this doctor was our savior. We owe him a great deal. Although at first Richard believed his BLEA therapist supported the change, it was not long before the therapist told Richard that he had made a grave mistake. The therapist hinted that leaving would cause Richard to feel intense anger. Challenging his loyalty, Richard's female colleague accused him of "leaving the family." Richard then steeled himself to leave the supervision group in the face of what he knew would be fierce opposition. Natan proved to be no match for Richard; his resolve to take back control of his life was now unshakable. His strength had returned.

The "crisis in Brazil," as we came to call it, created the opportunity for me to develop a different relationship with Richard. Humbled by his experience, he felt uncertain and confused. This created an opening, a crack in which I again was able to insert myself. Since I now had his attention, I was able to explain to him how I felt, tentatively at first and then with greater force and honesty. Through my words, I was able to show him how he appeared to me. To my surprise and to his credit he did not retaliate. Instead he listened as I poured out my soul to him— my hurt, anger, hatred, and, yes, love. There were still doubts about whether we could make it back together, and if not, could we create something new, something with vitality and respect. Could we love each other again? We talked for what seemed like days on end to make up for lost time. We needed to create a space just for us, a space where we could drain the illness that had overtaken our relationship. To do so we stepped back and away from others. This was private work.

We made it, sometimes I think, miraculously. Our scars are tender and have threatened to reopen at various moments. However, recovering from the MGPS/BLEA years has also made us stronger, more supportive and more loving with each other. We did, after all, go to hell and back.

On May 7, 1996, we celebrated our 25th wedding anniversary with a black-tie dinner. We were only at the beginning of our journey, becoming stronger and closer with each day. And, yes, we invited Natan HarPaz and his wife, the female associate and her husband, and a few other "BLEAbots" (they are robots of a sort) to our celebration of perseverance, strength, and love. All the power was mine that evening and I relished every moment.

Also that spring, in an article that Richard wrote for the MGPS Newsletter he dared to question the BLEA model of therapeutic practice. Predictably he became the target of their rage. Reuven used every means at his disposal to humiliate and demean Richard, questioning not only his leadership but his integrity as well. Richard weathered this "storm of discontent" in fine style. As president of MGPS he attended monthly meetings until November 1996. With six months left in his term, he refused to attend meetings. If he was needed, he said, they could contact him by phone. They never did.

1998

Despite Richard's limited contact with other BLEA members, word apparently reached Reuven through the grapevine that Richard was writing a paper, describing BLEA as a psychotherapy cult. He sent Richard a letter asking if all was well, to which Richard did not respond. The day Richard finished his paper was the day Reuven was shot and killed by a patient.

With the news of Reuven's death, waves of feeling washed over me. First I felt angry at the damage his charisma and authority had caused. I recalled how strenuously I had tried to avoid him when he pursued me at parties, always wanting to dance with me or to talk. Then I felt sad, especially for the young man who killed himself and another patient at the time he murdered Reuven. Oh the desperation, despair, and anger that drove him to carry out such a violent act! By far my strongest feeling was relief. Reuven could no longer intrude on my family. His ominous shadow would no longer darken our lives. I could now speak freely. My fearful silence of these many long years was finally broken.

LIFE GOES ON . . .

I am able to tell my story today because of the love, strength, and patience Richard and I share. I am also grateful for the wisdom I acquired through this devastating ordeal. Peace, tranquility, happiness, and love now give my life balance, for I can now be "both intellectual comrade and light of my home" (Elizabeth Peabody, September 1835).

And life goes on at "Moonsbreath Manor," our wonderful home where we reside with our two Irish Wolfhounds (Belle and Brina). After thirty-five years of marriage, Richard and I continue to explore all that the future may hold in store for us, speaking the same language once again.

UNCERTAINTY, TRAUMA, AND RELATIONAL SYSTEMS

Linda Raubolt tells us that, from the very beginning, she felt wary and mistrustful of BLEA. Unlike her husband, she never fell under its treacherous spell. Yet as her story so poignantly demonstrates, the traumas she experienced during the BLEA years were no less devastating than Richard's own. How are we to understand her suffering? What enabled her to survive her ordeal? And where did she find the strength to restore her life and her marriage? Being neither Linda's therapist nor her confidante, I cannot presume to offer definitive answers to these questions. I am not even sure that definitive answers are possible. Nevertheless, several aspects of Linda's story lend themselves to examination from the relational systems approach to trauma I have been developing, an approach that centers around experiences of uncertainty and its intersubjective regulation (Brothers 2000, 2001, 2003a,b, Brothers and Richard 2003). I will first briefly summarize this approach and then attempt to show how it relates to Linda's situation.

What I am calling a relational systems approach has its roots in what has variously been termed nonlinear dynamic systems theory, chaos theory, or complexity theory. This theoretical perspective is now being applied to the clinical situation by a number of prominent psychoanalysts (e.g., Beebe and Lachmann 2002, Coburn 2002, Stolorow 1997, Sucharov 1998, 2002). According to Esther Thelen and Linda Smith (1994), psychologists who have applied the principles of dynamic systems to early human development, these principles "concern the problems of emergent order and complexity: how structure and patterns arise from the cooperation of many individual parts" (p. xiii).

Until quite recently, I attempted to understand trauma at what nonlinear dynamic systems theorists refer to as "the local level of the individual." At this level, trauma seemed to me to involve betrayals of trust in oneself and others to provide experiences needed for the development, maintenance, and restoration of self-experience—self psychologists call these selfobject experiences (Brothers 1995). I now believe that this understanding is far too limited. From a relational systems perspective, I see that trauma also involves profound disruptions of the processes by means of which experiences of uncertainty over psychological survival are intersubjectively regulated (Brothers 2003a,b).

Regulation, as I have come to use the concept, pertains to variations in the orderliness that emerges out of the reciprocal engagement or mutual influence of people in a living system (Beebe and Lachmann 2002, Stolorow and Atwood 1992). Since experiencing any sort of shared regulatory activity heightens expectations (enhances trust) that needed relational experiences will be consistently, predictably, dependably available, I have suggested that an aspect of all regulation is the regulation of uncertainty. This means that, to some extent, feeling, knowing, forming categories, communicating, sensing time, remembering, forgetting, and fantasizing—all of which involve intersubjective regulatory processes—may contribute to the intersubjective regulation of uncertainty (Brothers, forthcoming).

As I see it, we tend to experience disorder—or "chaos" in the language of dynamic systems theory—when systemwide efforts at uncertainty regulation fail or are disrupted. Now, some disorganizing experiences are not only inevitable but they seem to be necessary for psychological existence. Mahoney and Moes (1997), for example, conceptualize development in terms of "cascades of disorganization" (p. 187). The very idea of unruffled order seems alien to the tumultuous complexity most of us associate with being alive. Trauma, on the other hand, is a starkly different experience. In contrast to the disorganization that results when our efforts at uncertainty regulation are temporarily thwarted, the profound disorder that characterizes trauma threatens a living system with annihilation. I propose that disorder of this magnitude is likely to result when the systemically emergent certitudes that continually arise out of, and bring order to, our relational worlds are destroyed.

I use the term *systemically emergent certitudes* (SECs) in much the same way that Stolorow and Atwood (1992) use *structures of experience* or *organizing principles* and Orange (1995) uses *emotional convictions.* Insofar as SECs refer to the conditions that people come to believe are necessary for the fulfillment of their relational needs, their destruction signals the end of certainty about psychological survival. With the sudden loss of what had once lent stability, order, and meaning to life, people within traumatized systems seem to experience the dread of psychological extinction, or what Kohut (1971) so aptly termed "disintegration anxiety." Moreover, with the destruction of SECs and the failure of what had previously regulated uncertainty within a system, desperate and extreme modes of uncertainty regulation tend to emerge. These extreme modes often involve efforts to simplify experience—to "decomplexify" it as Orange (2000) puts it—by such means as the use of dichotomous thinking, and by the formation of extremely rigid, brittle certitudes that may be fiercely defended.

It seems to me that Linda experienced Richard's abandonment not only as a traumatizing betrayal but also as retraumatizing. According to Coburn (2002), the meanings of psychological phenomena emerge out of the complex interactions that have occurred in a system's history together with its current state and environment. Linda tells us that this was not the first time she felt abandoned by a man she had trusted. Her father had done as much in her childhood. After his hospitalization for severe depression, he informed her that she had to care for the emotional needs of her mother. No longer convinced that she would always be "Daddy's girl" with a strong man to lean on, Linda seems to have taken her father's directive to heart. In other words, a compelling certitude seems to have taken form for Linda involving her conviction that she could maintain needed connections to others by assuming responsibility for their emotional well-being. (Similar certitudes are to be found among those patients who were overburdened and parentified in childhood such as those described by Alice Miller [1979].)

Linda's certitude appears to have been all but demolished during the BLEA years. We have seen that despite assuming responsibility for the care of her home and children, administering MGPS, accompanying Richard to BLEA events and functions, and many other supportive activities, she still experienced the emotional loss of the man she loved. And, adding insult to injury, Bar Levav thoroughly assaulted her sense of herself as a trustworthy and responsible caregiver by accusing her of adding to her husband's burdens.

An important aspect of the traumatic loss of certainty about psychological survival involves the destruction of what Coburn (2001) has described as one's "sense of the real." There can be little doubt that Linda's sense of what was real, her very sanity, was attacked when her experience of herself as a loving and responsible wife was thrown into question. How devastating it must have been for her to learn that her husband confided in others more than in herself! This attack appears to have thrust Linda back onto what the poet Adrienne Rich (1979) calls the "bleak, jutting ledge" of a world without trusted others. A theme of despairing loneliness among indifferent and/or hostile people pervades Linda's story. "As always," she wrote in her journal, "I deal with my demons alone." Little wonder that she worried about becoming the "Madwoman of East Grand Rapids."

I believe that Linda has hinted at what kept her from madness. She tells us that after Bar Levav's death she felt she could "speak freely" at last. "My fearful silence of these many long years was finally broken," she says. But as far as I can tell, Linda had never been completely silenced during her ordeal; she had recorded her voice, her truth, in her journals. As I see it, Linda's journal writing constituted a wonderfully healing form of uncertainty regulation. It involves what Orange (2000) has identified as "bearing witness." Again and again, as Linda painstakingly described the devastation she was enduring, and her emotional response to that devastation, she reminded herself, and, perhaps some imagined readers, that through her own strength, and the strength of her devotion to others, she would survive.

A relational systems perspective, I believe, allows for the hopeful possibility that in recovering from the effects of a devastating trauma our self-experience may actually grow stronger and more vital. Mahoney and Marquis (2002) observe that "when the system manages to wrestle out of the disorder into which it was thrown, the emerging system tends to be both more complex and more capable" (p. 798). I suspect this occurs for an individual as extreme modes of uncertainty regulation are relinquished and the capacity to tolerate the unpredictability and ambiguity of relational life is increased. When Richard once again turned to Linda in his hour of great need, I believe she had already discovered that her worth transcended her caregiving role in relation to him. Having proved to herself that she could survive without him, that her survival was not contingent on caregiving, she was ready to open herself to the enormously difficult but profoundly satisfying work of rebuilding a marriage.

Linda has told a story that may help to relieve the silent suffering of those, who, simply by virtue of being part of the relational system of a cult survivor, have also been traumatized. If, as I tend to believe, all living systems are interrelated on some level, perhaps we are all survivors.

REFERENCES

Beebe, B., and Lachmann, F. (2002). *Infant Research and Adult Treatment: Co-Constructing Interactions*. Hillsdale, NJ: Analytic Press.

Brothers, D. (1995). *Falling Backwards: An Exploration of Trust and Self Experience*. New York: Norton.

———— (2000). Faith and passion in self psychology, or, swimming against the postmodern tide of uncertainty. Paper presented at the 23rd International Conference on the Psychology of the Self, Chicago, November.

———— (2001). Ghosts of the silver screen and other self-psychological reflections on the acceptance of death. Paper presented at the 24th Annual International Conference on the Psychology of the Self, San Francisco, November.

———— (2003a). Clutching at certainty: thoughts on the coercive grip of cult-like groups. *Group* 27(2/3):79–88.

———— (2003b). After the towers fell: terror, uncertainty, and intersubjective regulation. *Journal for the Psychoanalysis of Culture and Society* 8(1):68–76.

———— (forthcoming). *The Regulation of Uncertainty: Psychoanalysis, Trauma, and Relational Systems*. New York: Routledge.

Brothers, D., and Richard, A. (2003). The cult of certainty: a self-psychological view of the quest for "unembedded being" in a coercive training program. Paper presented at the 26th International Conference on the Psychology of the Self, Chicago, IL. November.

Coburn, W. J. (2001). Subjectivity, emotional resonance, and the sense of the real. *Psychoanalytic Psychology* 18:303–319.

———— (2002). A world of systems: the role of systemic patterns of experience in the therapeutic process. *Psychoanalytic Inquiry* 22(5):654–677.

Kohut, H. (1971). *The Anaysis of the Self*. New York: International Universities Press.

Mahoney, M. J., and Marquis, A. (2002). Integral constructivism and dynamic systems in psychotherapy processes. *Psychoanalytic Inquiry* 22(5):794–813.

Mahoney, M. J., and Moes, A. J. (1997). Complexity and psychotherapy: promising dialogues and practical issues. In *The Psychological Meaning of Chaos: Translating Theory into Practice*, ed. F. Masterpasqua and P. A. Perna, pp. 177–198. Washington, DC: American Psychological Association.

Miller, A. (1979). *Prisoners of Childhood* (R. Ward, Trans.). New York: Basic Books, 1981. (Original work published in 1979.)

Orange, D. (1995). *Emotional Understanding: Studies in Psychoanalytic Epistemology*. New York: Guilford.

——— (2000). Discussion of Doris Brothers' "Faith and Passion in Self Psychology, Or, Swimming Against the Postmodern Tide of Uncertainty." Paper presented at the 23rd Annual International Conference on the Psychology of the Self, Chicago, November.

Raubolt, R. (2003). Attack on the self: charismatic leadership and authoritarian group supervision. *Group* 27(2/3):65–77.

Stolorow, R. (1997). Dynamic, dyadic, intersubjective systems: an evolving paradigm for psychoanalysis. *Psychoanalytic Psychology* 14:337–364.

Stolorow, R. D., and Atwood, C. E. (1992). *Contexts of Being: The Intersubjective Foundations of Psychological Life*. Hillsdale, NJ: Analytic Press.

Sucharov, M. (1998). Optimal responsiveness and a systems view of the empathic process. In *Optimal Responsiveness: How Therapists Heal Their Patients*, ed. H. Bacal. Northvale, NJ: Jason Aronson.

——— (2002). Representation and the intrapsychic: Cartesian barriers to empathic conflict. *Psychoanalytic Inquiry* 22(5):686–707.

Thelen, E., and Smith, L. B. (1994). *A Dynamic Systems Approach to the Development of Cognition and Action*. Cambridge, MA: MIT Press.

3

Trauma Sketches, Translations, and a Dialogue of Love: A Personal Response to L. Raubolt and Brothers

Richard Raubolt

EDITOR'S NOTE

Despite the potential accusation of conspicuous self-disclosure or criticism for sentimentality unwarranted in a professional text, I am exercising the editor's prerogative to respond to the previous chapter. This is a serious book about the training of psychotherapists and psychoanalysts. It's also a book about people deeply affected when such training turns from its rightful purpose and crosses over to create traumatic abuse.

Trauma is about aloneness. Even though professional trauma is interpersonal, it too, is still about aloneness. Maybe even more so. The ravages of professional trauma are brought home, distorting all who are present. There are no bystanders. A spouse is neither set apart nor spared the damage. Such trauma consumes, as each treats, interacts with, and creates an other, separate from the humanity of either. Commonality is broken, fear reigns, and deep wounds are inflicted. Helpless against the onslaught of pain, which both closes down and cuts off the spirit. Cracked shells are left exposed as the kernels of self go ever deeper inside—alone, wordless and detached. Waiting against hope, desperate longing still prevailed. Sleeping beauty was suspended in time and space. Separate, bereft of meaning and purpose, adrift from love: can they join the world, the land of the living? How to learn to love again? What is the language of love that begins to heal? How does it look, feel, sound? How does one wake up to find a love life made more vibrant by the trauma that caused such deep sleep?

TRAUMA SKETCHES: MY OWN STORY

My mother wasn't there at my birth. She was lost along the way. A child was not her desire; my father was her sole love. I was the cost of being with him, but she wouldn't make the emotional payments. I was her gift to him. A gift my father took down from the shelf for sporting events, work in the yard, and of course to carry the name. Not my name, the name of his firm. Connections were fleeting, but without the brooding unhappiness of the mother burdened with the unwanted. We moved further away from each other, my mother and I. Silence was our communication; neither of us knew the other. We were wary and afraid. Still she entered me, secretly as a psychic phantom (Abraham and Torok 1994), creating a wound filled with shadows, absence, and the unknown. I could only feel the symptoms of her presence: nightmares, isolation, and bouts of crippling anxiety accompanied by terrible stomach pains. All too frequent for chance but beyond reason, or at least beyond my ability to reason or understand. I was possessed.

A new teacher came on the scene. He was cunning, seductive, and welcoming. He knew my feelings before I spoke them. There was magic in his message that filled my emptiness with certainty and aggressiveness. His pursuit was power and replication, creating clones to carry out his conquests. He was one type of Steiner's (2003) masters: "The vampire in the domain of the soul" (p. 3). This war-hardened Israeli psychiatrist was to save me by making me a soldier in his personal army. Toughness was the way to life; submission was the vehicle of love. Crises were created, empty gestures, techniques devoid of the real were his battle plans. Such excitement induced sleep. I resigned my commission but not before I lost even more of myself. I had taken on a voice that was not mine.

Alone on the battlefield surrounded by strangers, Sao Paulo, Brazil, scared me back into life. In a foreign country and again alone, I was there to present a paper in conflict with life as I was living it. A paper on the trauma I was about to drown in. Helpless souls around; my first analyst was there but more scared than I, offered words covered with ash—bitter and light. All that was within shattered; the terror of being alone consumed me, drenching me in sweat and tears. The Israeli warriors were in retreat. I had no desire to summon their forces. They could not save me. Self-hatred was in full supply and I needed no reinforcements. My heart beat out of my chest, a man still possessed, seeking a kind word and a piece of safety.

R.R. phone home. A surprised voice once tinged with fear but still coated with love. "What do you wish of me?"

"Save me, dear. Stay on the line, don't let me go."

"I'm here. I always was. We'll get you out. We'll get you home." The voice of love crackled through the phone and settled in my heart. I was heard. I was not alone. And so the healing began with words that awoke the dead and brought union once again.

On my journey my second analyst emerged from Germany. In escaping Hitler he had learned about aloneness; Einstein hair, the impish Balint smile I had seen in so many photos, and a name revered in analytic circles. He was formal in his manner, kind in his words and heart; more Kohut than Kohut. My consultation was fueled with grief. I told him my life stories, and spoke of images, fears, and terror. Calmly he sat, unmoving. He offered a referral.

"No, I want to see you."

"Then I will see you," delivered with the full German accent.

"But I come from a distance. I must work. I can't come for analysis."

This classically trained, elderly training analyst replied, "Then we will try a nontraditional analysis, if you are willing. And we will see."

My first session sitting in a chair a universe apart, five feet or so, I said, "You are so very far away."

Hearing my longing and with a gentleness that brought me in, he said, "You know the couch is much closer to me." And so we began my analysis, fractured by distance and interrupted by time, but a life line tied deep into my soul. Foreignness was bringing me home.

SOME THOUGHTS ON THEORY: PERSONAL AND OTHERWISE

Trauma is about aloneness, about silence. Healing, coming together is about talking, repeatedly. Repeating the same story, with the same language, is necessary to make the experience real. In talking, finding words, any words, one's own words begin to form the experience outside of oneself. The terror does have words that break open the disavowal, the silence, the withdrawal of dissociation. Language forms a structure, at first, for and of the head only. An intellectualized language, detached, elusive, and barren, becomes the first attempt at recognizing and bringing into consciousness details of the horror hiding in the shadows. Unconscious, previously denied associations, images, and sketches may then begin to form with feeling tones emerging and merging with intellectualized descriptions. This is an uneven, jumpy process. New life is given birth.

Talking and talking to, in a loving, patient dialogue creates movement. Moving in and moving out: "Is *it* real?"; Did *it* really happen?"; "How did *it* happen?"; "How did I cause *it* to happen?" Shame runs like a wide winding ribbon of pain and despair. Speaking about *it* with someone alters and changes *it*.

Memories of pain recede to a midway station: present but off to the side, if only slightly. New memories can now move forward; more historical (life before or beyond), broader and deeper, true of self, these memories are the representation of a fuller narrative of one's life. Trauma folds into the life story; more pieces to be known as "me." This is who I am, as J. Vida (personal communication, 2004) has noted "there is no unnecessary pain."

These traumatic experiences are integrated through surrender and introjection. Surrender is a difficult word to use with trauma but I am using it as Ghent (1990) has suggested: "a quality of liberation and expansion of self as a corollary to letting down of defensive barriers" (p. 108) and as "deeply buried or frozen, a longing for something . . . to make possible the surrender, in the sense yielding, of false self" (p. 109). To my way of thinking it is a giving into, accepting deeply and profoundly the damage within, and then to let go again to become whole with oneself and the world. The isolation leading one to feel mad and apart can begin to heal.

Surrender is not always possible. The wounds can cut so deep that no more vulnerability can be tolerated. Bleeding from the heart, the traumatized, especially perhaps the professionally traumatized, are imprisoned, their will is taken and they remain lost. Submission has supplanted surrender. Back to Ghent (1990): submission is "loving oneself in the process of the other, becoming enslaved in one way or other way to the master" (p. 115). Submission is about exploitation and entrapment. Losing one's way, a false self is reinforced through identification with the traumatic aggressor. We are now in Ferenczian territory. So bereft of self, so utterly dependent, fearful, and terrorized, the traumatized seek entry into the mind of the aggressor. Dissociated and lost they seek connection, a longing attachment, and a sense of safety by becoming like their master aggressors. To be alike is to be different from self, mastering the art of attack; enslavement is felt to be broken: "I am free to violate you so I am no longer violated. Such power shall set me free."

An illusion of course, a desperate plea for safety but hell on those who love as aggression is unleashed. I was living Buddha's untamed heart. Kornfield and Frondsdal (1993) translate the Buddha's description in the following fashion: "Friends, I know nothing which brings suffering as does an untamed, uncontrolled, unattended, and unrestrained heart. Such a heart brings suffering" (p. 85). Any scent of vulnerability brings the full measure of abusive power: "I am not weak, you are. I shall save myself by destroying you." Unconscious, disavowed aggression disguised, however, as help, "for your own good," was the banner I marched under in my relentless marital attacks. Not able to face my helplessness, pumped up by rage and misguided by "loving confrontation," I sought to remake my wife. I sought to destroy her differences from me, crush her independence, and steal her language. Thank God I failed.

She fought back but I did not notice; she would come around. Righteousness was on my side. I owned the language in an absolute and fundamental way. I would define and redefine what was proper and good. There were no exceptions, there were no interpretations. Translation was rendered mute. Sao Paulo split this identification like an atom. "Now where was I, where was she?"

RETURN TO THE LANGUAGE OF LOVE

She was there. She never left. It was not she who abandoned the union; clearly I did and had been absent for years. There was a gulf of emptiness. I was missing something. My life had become too familiar, drowning in routine I cast about for something to open the crypt, to feel myself as real, active, and alive. Angry and feeling alone, I had sought refuge in the shockingly different and found myself in the grotesque and traumatic. I was lost and empty. Could we now make it back together? Could we translate these experiences of violence as love gone seriously awry? Could we again surrender to love?

"You didn't hear me. You don't love me. You want me to be different, like them. You wanted my soul. You lost your kindness. You are not the man I married. I don't recognize you. They are in control of you. You are impatient. You put others before me. I am glad you are broken now. I prayed for this day. I bided my time. I love you. Come back to me."

I listened. I cried. I apologized. I saw myself. I did not like what I saw, the hurt I caused, or the me I had become. I had taken in much: the coldness of my mother, the arrogance of my first analyst, and the cruelty of the underground Israeli psychiatrist. I abhorred what I had become. Through my wife's loving translation I could come to see and accept this transformation. No longer disavowed I could hear her call to be different, to be more. I had to remember our forgotten language of long ago. Like a stroke victim, I had to learn again our words of love. I had to learn to discard the false language of submission for the true language of intimacy. An intimacy not forced by words of domination or rendered shallow by guilt. A new coming together finding vows long misplaced, taken for granted, and almost lost.

Yes, these traumatic sketches changed me. They did in some way expose more of who I was and would be. They exposed dangerous, violent, aggressive aspects of me. These could not be simply cast aside as aberrations. They were new parts of me to be accepted, owned, and integrated. This was for me a difficult, painful process of introjection closer to Abraham and Torok (1994) than Ferenczi. I had come to believe and accept introjection as a pathological process of "internalizing the bad object." In an earlier paper, I had written that when compared to identification with the aggressor: "Introjection is on the other hand, a more profound, consuming, damaged and fixed internal state" (Raubolt 2004, p. 39). Another traumatic agent was now in me, I had ingested the toxic threat. I had brought yet another transgressor more fully into me, forming another crypt for this phantom and he, she, they could no longer be seen and fought with as outside of me. I feared I had become what I feared.

Abraham and Torok and more specifically Molad and Vida (2004) provided a different perspective and understanding of introjection. Abraham and Torok defined introjection as "a constant process of acquisition and assimilation, the active potential to accommodate our own expanding desires and feelings as well as events and influences of the external world" (p. 9).[1] I found new ideas such as acquisition and assimilation, adjustment and change. My task was to "create forms of coherence in the face of emotions, panic, and chaos" (p. 14).

Or as another way of putting it, I had to develop what Loewald (1978) refers to as "moral responsibility." ("Had to" implies force, which I don't really mean, but it did feel like a moral imperative.) For Loewald this involves "appropriating" one's own history: a reworking, reorganizing, and transforming of history to create a present life. Living outside the cult's shadow of feelings gave me space to be neither too detached nor too entangled in my past.

I began to accept more of that which I had, heretofore, tried to disown. By talking and loving again, I had the room and the recognition that there were times where aggressiveness on my part was necessary, even required. The round edges of earlier years needed sharp elbows to defend, initiate, defy, and achieve; love and aggression were mingling together, building the foundation of life. In owning my aggressiveness I was challenging some of my early emptiness. With the aggressiveness came a strength to find and fill in mute psychic zones or enclaves that were decades old (Abraham and Torok 1994). I found my missing mother so I could then say good-bye. And my second analyst said simply, "The boy is becoming the man." His impish smile remained intact.

I do not mean to suggest the wounds have fully healed. I continue to write about these experiences to fill in some of the space, to grasp

---

1. "If viewed as a complete process, introjection encompasses three successive stages: (1) Something new or foreign (whether good or bad) occurs in or to me. (2) I turn myself into that which this new "thing" has done to me; I familiarize myself with it through play, fantasy, projection (or any number of other activities); in sum, I appropriate it for myself. (3) I become aware of what has occurred and of my own gradual encounter with it. As a result I am now able to give the whole process a place within my emotional existence; I also understand why and how the scope of 'myself' has been modified and expanded" (p. 14).

more fully the unmet desires at play that caused such pain and to learn to "work with" all that I have and continue to go through. Now "work with" is an interesting and upending notion, at least for me. Vida in a personal communication (2004) first suggested to me that "working through" is a tragic misconception. Trauma never goes away; trauma will never be what never happened. To quote her, "Over time and with much 'working with' it can be re-woven to some extent, or transformed, but it is always inexorably there." Melanie Klein (1960) some 45 years ago wrote of the irreducibly fluid nature of mental life, that is, multiple alternating states of being. To navigate the turbulence of life without drowning is mental health. The ideas of a conflict-free existence and overcoming emotional difficulties completely are illusions best cast aside. And so life goes on: messy, unpredictable, and, yes, vibrant as well.

REFERENCES

Abraham, N., and Torok, M. (1994). *The Shell and the Kernel*. Chicago: University of Chicago Press.

Ghent, E. (1990). Masochism, submission, surrender: masochism as a perversion of surrender. *Journal of Contemporary Psychoanalysis* 26:108–136.

Klein, M. (1960). On mental health. In *Envy and Gratitude and Other Works (1946–1963)*. New York: Dell, 1975.

Kornfield, J., and Frondsdal, G. (1993). *Teachings of the Buddha*. Boston and London: Shambhala.

Loewald, H. (1978). *Psychoanalysis and the History of the Individual*. New Haven, CT: Yale University Press.

Molad, G., and Vida, J. (2004). From identification-relations (of power) to introjection-relations (of love): a note on identification with the aggressor. Workshop presentation for psychoanalysis, history, dream, and poetry organized by the European Association for Nicolas Abraham and Maria Torok, Paris, France, October.

Raubolt, R. (2004). Charismatic leadership as a confusion of tongues: trauma and retraumatization. *Journal of Trauma Practice* 3(1):35–48.

Steiner, G. (2003). *Lessons of the Masters*. Cambridge, MA: Harvard University Press.

4

Narcissistic Authoritarianism in Psychoanalysis

Daniel Shaw

Some time ago I played, for a psychoanalytic study group of which I am a member, a comedy sketch, recorded ages ago, in which Elaine May and Mike Nichols portray a psychoanalyst and her patient. Having had a good laugh each of the numerous times I have listened to this sketch over the years, I gleefully, and as I now know naively, imagined my typically serious and scholarly group uncharacteristically doubled over, wiping tears of laughter from their eyes, enjoying a good joke on us all. In the sketch, the patient (Nichols) informs his analyst (May) that in the following week he will have to miss the last of his five sessions per week, since it is Christmas Eve and he plans to be with his family that day. Instantly shattered by the news of her patient's plan to desert her, May attempts to maintain her analytic stance and mask her spiraling self-fragmentation by demanding that her patient explore, be curious about, reflect on, and associate to his need to miss his session. In the face of his insistence that he just wants to be with his family on Christmas Eve, the analyst begins to weep quietly, then to sob in despair, then to scream with rage. Unable to help her recompensate, the patient quietly retreats, wishing her a Merry Christmas, as the analyst continues to unravel. When I turned off the recording, I faced a silent group, with some members finally confessing to a sense of excruciating anxiety while listening. There was little further discussion. We moved on quickly to the material we had planned to discuss. In showbiz parlance, I had bombed. Though unable to articulate at the time why the sketch repeatedly cracks me up, I can now say that for me, it helps to laugh about the ever-present, always not fully analyzed narcissism of the psychoanalyst—that is, to laugh at it, but not to laugh it off.

Narcissism is a problem for our patients, but it is just as much a problem for the profession of psychoanalysis and for every psychoanalyst. It is a problem that has shadowed our profession from the beginning, and it is a problem that our profession still struggles to address adequately. As analysts, we have long been concerned with our patients' narcissism, and as teachers and supervisors, with narcissism in psychoanalytic candidates (e.g., Brightman 1984–85). But it is increasingly the case (Cooper 2004, Hoffman 1998) that *our* narcissism as analysts, teachers, and supervisors occupies the field of our observation.

In this chapter I explore aspects of the analyst's narcissism and discuss the connection between narcissism and authoritarianism, especially as it pertains to psychoanalytic training. I discuss authoritarianism in the context of individual supervision, and I discuss how narcissistic authoritarianism can become malignant and infect therapeutic communities.

PROFESSIONAL NARCISSISM

Freud formulated his conceptualization of narcissism in 1914 and proceeded to enact some of its more problematic aspects by deeming himself the only analyst not in need of an analysis by another analyst by setting up a book of rules for the analytic process that he exempted himself from following and by marginalizing innovative followers and favoring those whom he could more easily control. Authoritarian control and suppression of dissent may have seemed, at the time, like a necessary means to the crucial end of establishing psychoanalysis as a profession, but in the long run these methods have proven ineffective. To the contrary, Balint's (1968) portrayal of the banishment of Ferenczi from the analytic community as a trauma to the profession still remains relevant. Although it is increasingly more likely in our professional publications and conferences to see rival psychoanalytic schools seeking common ground, years of rampant factionalism and internecine power struggles, along with authoritarian, incestuous training systems (Levine and Reed 2004), have substantially contributed, I believe, to the embarrassing fact that the majority of the public in the United States no longer has a clue as to what we mean when we say "psychoanalysis."

The worst potential of narcissism, for which we reserve the word *malignant*, was fortunately not realized by Freud, whose work, in spite of his imperial tendencies and some serious mistakes, has nevertheless been profoundly generative. But because the psychotherapist is a potent transference figure—not a parent, not an oracle, not God Almighty, but, for many patients, something like all three—it is within our power, in a worst-case scenario, to gain almost total control over our patients and supervisees, and, in the name of psychotherapy and with the power invested in us, control and exploit them for the sheer narcissistic gratification of it.

The abuses of power therapists are capable of, in training and clinical situations, and the damage done to students and patients, should not be underestimated. We pay a steep price as a profession, both in terms of the vitality and integrity of our training institutions and in terms of maintaining the public trust, when we do not attend to these problems adequately. Even more importantly, we have a moral imperative to protect students and patients from abuse, to "do no harm," and this means that we must address these problems where they begin, in the training of our candidates, and in the training of our teachers and supervisors. I link the presence of these abuses to the lingering presence of narcissistic authoritarianism in our profession. Before presenting examples of such abuses, I will offer my view of narcissism and of the connection between narcissism and authoritarianism.

PATHOLOGICAL AND MALIGNANT NARCISSISM

The pathological narcissist,[1] in my view, is a person obsessed with matters of superiority and inferiority, in both the moral and the material spheres. Of course everyone is concerned with these matters to an extent—no one is without some vanity, shame, pride, envy, and desire for control. The degree of obsession with these matters, its pervasiveness, and the behaviors employed to maintain the sense of superiority are the chief factors that determine when these concerns become pathological.

The pathological narcissist maintains a tight grip on a brittle, delusional sense of omnipotent superiority as a defense against deeply repressed shame, and feelings of inferiority and envy, which have typically been traumatically instilled and reinforced in the family of origin. The pathological narcissist has been the child of a pathological narcissist and has developed a profound unconscious identification with the aggressor parent. Unconsciously, the pathological narcissist seeks repeatedly both to expel and to induce in those around him the sense of shame and inferiority that has been instilled in him in an effort to externalize and disavow the toxic shame within, a process that Benjamin (2004) and Davies (2005) have referred to as "passing the hot potato." This compulsive disavowal and externalization of shame can reach the level of what I would call a narcissistic psychosis, in which the pathological narcissist comes to believe in his unquestionable righteousness, viewing those who disagree or challenge him as hostile, cruel, crazy, ignorant, and morally repulsive. Because the pathological narcissist believes he is always right, never wrong, those who have any conflict or grievance with him are kept on the defensive because, according to the pathological narcissist, they are always wrong, never right.

The obsession with unassailable, unimpeachable perfection represents the narcissist's desperate need for control and is the link between

---

1. I have elaborated these ideas in a previous work entitled "Traumatic Abuse in Cults: A Psychoanalytic Perspective" (2003). The following authors have influenced my formulation of pathological narcissism: Rosenfeld (1964) and the modern Kleinians of London profiled by Schafer (1997), and also Fromm (1964), Kernberg (1985), Kohut (1966, 1971, 1972, 1976), and Josephs (1992).

narcissism and authoritarianism. The authoritarian's oppressive demands for submission are based on the pathologically narcissistic need to maintain omnipotent control and superiority. Authoritarianism, like pathological narcissism, is based on defining others as inferiors and, through whatever control methods are possible, maintaining them as such. Pathological narcissists use a kind of reverse Fairbairnian moral defense (Fairbairn 1952): they give someone else all the burden of the badness and always claim the moral high ground for themselves.[2]

The naked, raw dependency displayed by the analyst in the Nichols and May sketch is precisely what the pathological narcissist is desperately defending against. The pathological narcissist, having suffered early, severe trauma in connection with dependency issues, is terrified of his dependence. Dependence has come to mean to him that, to his great shame, he is despicably weak, not perfect, and not omnipotent. To solve the problem of his mortifying dependence, he induces dependence in others—his partner (or children), subordinates, students, supervisees, or patients. He achieves this by using his position of authority to set himself up as the ultimate judge, proclaiming those he seeks to control to be either pitiable (and thus redeemable by the pathological narcissist) or contemptible (and thus dispensable). With others who might be less readily influenced, he gains control and induces dependence through seduction or displays of grandiose magnanimity, switching only later, when his omnipotence is questioned in any way, to belittling and shaming. He assumes infallible righteousness and dispenses favor or disfavor, leading others to base their self-esteem on his judgment of them. By provoking and cultivating in others the sense of moral failure and inferiority, the pathological narcissist, manically denying his own shameful dependence, bolsters his delusion of omnipotent self-reliance by projecting his contemptible dependence onto others.

While not all narcissists function as authoritarian figures, I believe narcissism always underlies authoritarianism, in which an authority figure views himself as always deserving of devotional attention and submission from those around him. Authoritarian figures, in accord with

---

2. I am developing this formulation more fully in a future paper entitled "The Family Tragedy: The Intersubjective Web of Pathological Narcissism and the Moral Defense."

their pathological narcissism, justify interpersonal acts of deception, intimidation, coercion, suppression, and exploitation because they believe in their omnipotent righteousness. For them, the end (maintaining delusional omnipotence as a defense against unbearable shame and dependence) justifies any means.

I distinguish the pathological narcissist from the malignant by the tendency in the latter toward sociopathy, the ability to commit and justify criminal acts such as sexual violations, robbery, blackmail, assault, and murder. Like the malignant narcissist, the pathological narcissist is often cruel, but will stop short of being criminal.

EVERYDAY NARCISSISTIC AUTHORITARIANISM

While there have been numerous examples of pathological and malignant narcissism in psychotherapy communities, far more common are minor intrusions of the analyst's narcissism in his role as teacher and supervisor. I focus on these everyday examples of minor narcissism in supervision because I believe they are ubiquitous and not adequately examined. The examples I will give are meant to show how vestiges of narcissistic authoritarianism in psychoanalytic training continue to haunt our training situations in spite of theoretical and cultural shifts away from authoritarianism. While the supervisors in the following examples were trained in the 1960s and 1970s, by the late 1990s they were known for their connections to contemporary self psychology, intersubjectivity, and relational theory, which is to say that their theoretical schools are not associated with the more orthodox schools in which authoritarianism might be expected. The incidents I will recount exemplify small lapses in otherwise constructive supervisory experiences, and they occurred against the background of the supervisors' considerable generosity, intelligence, and dedication. Yet when disruptions like these occurred for me and for my fellow candidates in training, and they often did, we felt confused, disconnected, intimidated, and ashamed. This tradition in psychoanalysis, of bullying, shaming, and intimidating (whether mild or severe), and refusing to take responsibility and apologize for errors, has roots that go back as least as far as Freud and the case of Dora, a treatment now widely perceived as misattuned and insensitive, and to the disagreements between Freud and

Ferenczi (see Berman 2004, Chapter 1). I believe my supervisors had taken far more of this sort of thing from their analysts and supervisors than they were dishing out. But now and then the occasional flashback would surface, and I would then be treated to a narcissistic lapse, a taste of what it was like in the "olden days."

In addition to issues of transgenerational transmission of narcissistic behaviors, analysts of course bring their own history of narcissistic vulnerability to the situation. Analysts are often fulfilling deeply cherished, idealistic aspirations in choosing their profession, aspirations that transcend narcissistic concerns regarding power and prestige. The desire to help, to be loving, caring, understanding, and healing are expressions of altruism that many analysts value highly. Many of us are continually moved and grateful to be able to witness the growth and change process in those we help. Yet along with these kinds of motivations can be found more selfish ones, which I believe are quite common. Among these would be the use of our professional status as a means of establishing ourselves as "the sane, healthy one," usually in defense against a parent's or sibling's projections of craziness. We may have needed to distinguish and differentiate ourselves from a crazy parent, or we may be driven to rescue people successfully because rescuing a family member was impossible. We may be seeking to gain the higher moral ground in a power struggle happening in real time with significant others or with archaic internal objects. We may be seeking to acquire virtue as helpers in an effort to extinguish a sense of worthlessness. Certainly the motives for our choice of profession are complex and overdetermined, and always include to some degree the fulfilling of our narcissistic needs. The acquisition of prestige, power, and control is usually somewhere in the mix, even in the face of highly effective assaults on our power, control, and prestige from the insurers and their beloved behavioralists.

The various kinds of personal historical factors, such as those mentioned above, that influence our choice of profession play a crucial role in determining what our narcissistic vulnerabilities are, which in turn determine where we fall on the authoritarian continuum in terms of our work. We cannot be professionals without assuming authority. Professional narcissism becomes problematic when it drives us to seek power and control by becoming authoritarian, that is, infallibly righteous and controlling by means of belittling, condescending, intimidating, blaming, and shaming. The more narcissistically vulnerable one is, the more potential there is for authoritarian control to be employed defensively.

As analysts, teachers, and supervisors, we all struggle with (at least) the following four areas of narcissistic vulnerability, any one of which could lead to authoritarian control behaviors as we attempt to establish our authority as teachers and supervisors: (1) the temptation to exhibit our superior expertise and power so as to invite idealization and defend against our own anxieties about inadequacy; (2) envy, competitiveness, and the fear of being surpassed; (3) the need to be admired and to feel indispensable, along with the fear that we will be rejected (excruciatingly expressed by Elaine May in the comedy sketch); and (4) concerns about our reputation, especially in institutional situations. Regardless of the supervisor's theoretical orientation, the potential always exists for these vulnerabilities to emerge in the supervisory process. Such vulnerabilities can engender in the supervisor narcissistically defensive behaviors, such as exhibitionism, intimidation, and shaming, which are behaviors that assert the supervisor's superiority and promote the supervisee's sense of inferiority and dependence.

Whether the supervisor sees her role as that of an objective, didactic expert, as in the classical tradition, or as an embedded participant, as in the contemporary relational school (Frawley-O'Dea and Sarnat 2001), the above general narcissistic vulnerabilities, and many that might be more individually idiosyncratic, will inevitably emerge in supervisory work even if only to the mildest degree.

EVERYDAY NARCISSISM
IN PSYCHOANALYTIC SUPERVISION

Let me offer two examples of what I think of as typical, everyday kinds of authoritarian supervisory moments. I completed my M.S.W. in 1996, and my analytic training in New York City in 2000. My supervisors were well-seasoned, highly intelligent, sincerely dedicated psychoanalysts with the same narcissistic vulnerability as most humans. By no means would I consider either of these supervisors to be pathologically narcissistic. Nevertheless, I examine here moments in my work with them when the line between authority and authoritarianism was crossed, suggesting the presence of narcissistic issues in the supervisor.

Supervisor 1

In my second year of analytic training, I spent most of a weekly supervision session bristling but accommodating to a supervisor I found condescending and didactic. "Speak in short, precise phrases," she told me one day, and she demonstrated how she thought analysts should speak. I have never much cared for the stereotypical ways that analysts sometimes speak (sounding too much like Elaine May in the comedy sketch), and I wasn't planning to emulate such stereotypes. Additionally, I was reasonably certain that my supervisor didn't always practice what she preached, and that she probably prattled on and on, too, at times. Saying nothing of any of this, I nodded my head. I didn't want to be a resistant, narcissistic candidate—as candidates who are not sufficiently submissive are often labeled. We finally had a real argument in a later supervisory session where, in response to my disclosure of some countertransference difficulties I was having, she took out a book and read a whole page about analytic technique to me. Discouraged and angry that my countertransference struggles seemed of no interest to her other than as technical errors to be intellectually disposed of, I expressed my frustration. She was astonished and admonished me for not taking in the bountiful good things she was giving me. A week later, I tried to patch things up by mentioning that I sometimes found it difficult to relate to authority figures. She responded with a nod, at most, and proceeded as though nothing had happened. We never discussed it further.

My chief impression of our work together over the course of a year was an internalized admonition about being long-winded, and I've kept it in mind all these years. But I question myself at times as to how much I control my speech for my patients' benefit, and how much control stems from a "thought police" mind-set that I reject but that nevertheless creeps in, shaming me in spite of myself.

The need to be admired, feared, and imitated is, in my view, an expression of the supervisor's narcissism. A supervisor who presents herself as the model for how the supervisee should speak and think is assuming that the supervisee is looking for the supervisor to be an idol to imitate. On the contrary, I believe most supervisees are looking for support and encouragement to develop and grow as persons and analysts in their own right. If we offer supervisees technical and theoretical models based on our own biases and preferences, and of course we always do, I think we at least owe it to them to acknowledge our biases and preferences, explain to some extent the basis for our preferences, and encourage them to form their own. The value of keeping this information mystified eludes me.

Many institutes now elicit evaluations of supervisors from supervisees, no doubt sincerely hoping to promote collegiality rather than indenture. Yet I believe it is rare for supervisees to disclose their critique of a supervisor fully. Supervisees in this situation often feel themselves to be, and possibly actually are, at risk of being diagnosed as narcissistic (note the projection) and judged by their institute as difficult, in need of further analysis, and so on. Compliance is the safer route for many. Defiance risks punishment by tarnishing the supervisee's reputation within the institute, which could mean losing opportunities for referrals and for playing significant roles in the institute after graduation, such as becoming a training analyst there, teaching, supervising, and serving on the board of directors.

Supervisor 2

I was presenting a patient in my final year of training, whom I liked a great deal. I was speaking of a struggle I had been having with listening to her, connected to my sense that she was defending against a great deal of shame. As a result, she seemed to use at times a very contrived, theatrical persona when she communicated with me, a persona that stood in sharp contrast to what seemed like another aspect of her that emerged in some sessions—a more related, reflective, alive version of her. My patient and I had begun to be able to talk about this, and I was relating this to my supervisor. I repeated a remark I made to the patient, to the effect that I found myself more engaged and connected to the real person than to the theatrical persona. Without waiting to learn how my patient reacted, my supervisor colored, stiffened, and said quite sharply, in a tone of rebuke I don't think I had heard since about seventh grade: "And who do you think you are to have said that to her?"

I was a fourth-year candidate, and tired of being afraid of my supervisors, no matter how much I was depending on their support, so I raised an eyebrow or two and looked quizzically into my supervisor's eyes as if to say, "you aren't really taking that tone with me, are you?" After a tense momentary standoff, he softened. The supervisor went on to be less reproachful and more facilitative. We did not return to or try to work through what happened until the following week, when while reporting on the same patient, I let my supervisor know that I was aware, during my session with the patient subsequent to my supervision, of imagining my supervisor negatively judging all of my interventions, including "uh-huh" and "mmm-hmmm." Without hesitation, my supervisor said that he had been having a stressful day the week before and that I should go ahead and work without imagining him disapproving of me. Although I was the one initiating all the processing of what had happened, I appreciated his concession, and we got on well from there. And yet, I would have to say that my trust was somewhat shaken from that point on.

This supervisor was willing to be accountable for his shaming, intimidating behavior, but only after I brought it up, and only nonchalantly, and with no apology. It is of course entirely expectable that one might slip up and err as a supervisor by being too didactic, or reacting hastily in a shaming way. This can and does happen with most supervisors, sooner or later. But as I see it, the supervisor then has the responsibility to process with the supervisee what has happened and to repair the disruption. In the absence of such willingness to process, the supervisee, who is likely to be vulnerable to a shaming and intimidating supervisor, may develop more anxiety about disapproval than would already be normally present. His work as he presents it could then become organized around receiving the supervisor's approval, around meeting supervisory requirements that are subjectively biased toward the supervisor's particular theoretical and technical preferences, and that are shaped by the supervisor's narcissistic concerns. The supervisee learns to develop a "false supervisee self" based on compliance. In my view, this also greatly increases the chances that the supervisee will go on to elicit similar results with his patients.

In considering the examples I have presented, I have avoided attempting to identify the specific narcissistic vulnerabilities these supervisors might have been influenced by because I have no idea what they might be, and even if I did, it would be inappropriate to reveal that information, even speculatively. What is relevant to this discussion is that the presence of authoritarian behaviors in these supervisors, such as their use of shaming and intimidation to promote compliance, indicates a link between narcissism and authoritarianism. In both of these examples, we see a supervisor taking a strong position against the supervisee, who is perceived as violating a theoretical or technical principle the supervisor particularly values. There are elements of shaming and intimidation in both examples, and in the first we see the supervisor expecting the supervisee to adopt the supervisor's preferences and speak as she does. In the second case, the supervisor was willing to acknowledge his role in the disruption, but in the first case, in spite of the disruption, the supervisor proceeded without further exploration of what had happened between us. In both cases, the behaviors I describe could be means by which these supervisors unconsciously sought to raise the candidate's anxiety about the supervisor's approval, a situation that might give the supervisor a feeling of greater power and control. Because candidates are typically investing so much in becoming analysts, it is easy for them to base their self-esteem as people on their performance as rated by their supervisors. This is especially true given the amount of power, both personal and professional, candidates typically perceive supervisors as having. The fiction that our supervisors and training analysts can be assumed to be free of narcissism potentially sets up a no-win situation for the candidate, who then always has to "hold the hot potato" in a conflict because the supervisor is always "right," and the candidate is always being "narcissistic." Here is where supervisors and supervisees must learn to draw the line between authority and authoritarianism or risk turning training into indoctrination. Suppressing individuality and creativity in candidates in favor of compliance and accommodation strikes me as the Orwellian version of psychoanalysis, of which we should all be very afraid.

As supervisors, we have the opportunity, by being comfortable with and acknowledging our fallibility, to model to our supervisees and students our ability to negotiate and regulate our narcissistic vulnerabilities thus potentiating in turn the supervisee's release from undue shame and fear of imperfection and aiding the development of a sense of unique professional identity. By so doing, we protect ourselves, and our supervisees and patients, from the danger of authoritarian domination, indoctrination, and theoretical dogmatism, which are hallmarks of the narcissistic need for omnipotence in the psychoanalytic training context.

MALIGNANT NARCISSISTIC AUTHORITARIANISM

Having looked at the ways everyday narcissistic authoritarian behaviors occur in psychoanalytic supervision, it behooves us to be familiar with just how destructive severely pathological narcissistic authoritarianism can become in psychotherapy communities or among therapists influenced by authoritarian teachers. In such cases, a psychotherapy community can become a cult—isolated, paranoid, and with the potential for devastation. Chapter 9, by Richard Raubolt, in this book offers a shocking example of this situation. What follows is an example of how psychotherapists have been influenced by a pathologically narcissistic, authoritarian religious leader. In this example, only one of many I might include if space permitted, we see the tendency toward sociopathy in malignant narcissism.

Siddha Yoga is a religious organization that teaches that meditation and worship of the Siddha Yoga guru (currently, an Indian woman in her early fifties known as Gurumayi) constitute the path to spiritual enlightenment, in which one may purify and cleanse one's bad karma and come to experience God within oneself while recognizing and welcoming God in others. Siddha Yoga is a group that attracts a wealthy clientele, including celebrities, socialites, performers, and academics, in spite of the fact that the extensive history of sexual and other abuses perpetrated by the leaders of this group is well documented in a *New Yorker* article by author Lis Harris (1994) and in various online groups where former members give testimony about the group (also see Rodarmor 1983).

Less well known is the influence of Siddha Yoga on mental health practitioners. The Siddha Yoga organization began holding annual conferences for mental health professionals in the mid-1980s and were still doing so, to my knowledge, as late as 1997. Though not yet a mental health professional, I attended the first two of these conferences during a period of time when I was a participant in the Siddha

Yoga community. I recall the presence of several hundred practitioners, gathered in a retreat facility in upstate New York for a full-day seminar, conducted by staff members of the organization. These seminars, as I know from personal contact with their organizers and as an eyewitness, primarily served to encourage mental health practitioners already practicing Siddha Yoga to invite their patients to get involved. Therapists were taught to display altars with pictures of Gurumayi in their offices, and were advised on how to talk about the benefits of their own use of Siddha Yoga meditation when their patients noticed the altars and made inquiries. Also in these programs, therapists who were Siddha Yoga devotees discussed their experiences, in coached presentations, of how Siddha Yoga transformed their therapy practices, how they shared Siddha Yoga with their patients, and how it transformed those patients' lives. These therapists had brought groups of their patients to the retreat facility to meet Gurumayi, and received special attention from Gurumayi for their recruitment efforts. Therapists not already involved in Siddha Yoga were actively recruited at these conferences, in which they were led through various meditation exercises, and finally given a special audience with Gurumayi, who made a regal impression in her bright red silk robes, seated on a throne before which the attendees were invited to prostrate themselves at her feet.

In addition to encouraging devotee therapists to recruit their patients into Siddha Yoga, Gurumayi referred many of her devotees, whether they asked for referrals or not, to other devotees who were mental health professionals. According to several of these professionals I spoke with, who eventually severed their ties to Siddha Yoga, Gurumayi then solicited reports from these devotee therapists about those she had referred, and discussed details of their treatment with these therapists in the presence of other members of her entourage, often in mocking tones.[3]

---

3. In 1995, I and others who knew of these practices contributed information about the conferences to an online discussion group about abuses in Siddha Yoga. I have been told by a participant that in the last conference, held in 1997, therapists were specifically warned against recruiting patients. Nevertheless, I continued to receive inquiries as recently as 2004 from psychotherapy patients who have observed a picture of Gurumayi in their therapist's office.

Gurumayi was engaged in a long vendetta against her brother, a rival Swami named Nityananda, throughout the 1980s and beyond (Harris 1994). During this time, staff members of Gurumayi's organization were ordered by her to organize local Siddha Yoga followers to develop ways to harass her brother. The most notorious of these incidents, in which skunk oil was thrown at audience members listening to a lecture by Nityananda, was executed by a licensed psychologist, one of those to whom Gurumayi had often referred members for psychotherapy.

Gurumayi and her closest advisors perpetrated, justified, and condoned many other illegal and unethical behaviors, and persuaded followers, including mental health professionals, as in the above example, to do the same. The malignant narcissist acts in conformance with the underlying belief that she (in this case, the Siddha Yoga guru) is perfect, superior, and ultimately entitled, and therefore any means will always justify the end—the end being the fulfillment of the delusion of omnipotent perfection. In authoritarian communities, this goal becomes the shared goal of the followers, even though this invariably entails the betrayal of their own moral values, as in the case of therapists who dissociatively overlooked the flagrant ethical violation of recruiting their patients into Siddha Yoga. Followers of a pathological narcissist assume a masochistic position, becoming pathological narcissists by proxy. Through dedicating themselves to the leader in total submission, and by taking on the leader's goals (typically grandiose plans to transform the world that would simultaneously enrich and empower the leader).[4]

In the last 10 years, I have often worked with former members of cults, and have learned of many other authoritarian psychotherapy groups. The problem is all too common, and while some former members have succeeded in actions against practitioners leading to the revocation of their licenses, many of the leaders of such groups have no professional credentials to begin with. To address this problem, we must first develop a greater understanding of the problem of narcissistic authoritarianism, from its mildest to its most pathological forms, and

---

4. This dynamic was well elaborated by Erich Fromm (1941) in *Escape from Freedom*, in which he describes the concept of the Magic Helper.

recognize it and study it as an ongoing professional phenomenon that will always require our attention. This chapter, and this book as a whole, are steps toward that goal.[5]

CONCLUSION

Psychoanalysts have struggled since the beginning of the profession to understand their power and to use their power responsibly and therapeutically. Power is never a simple matter for humans to negotiate. Power is always potentially corrupting. On the one hand, we set ourselves the goal of expanding the freedom of our patients, and on the other hand, we establish training methods that all too often lead to accommodation, compliance, and conformity in our trainees. As I have attempted to show, it is unconscious, disavowed narcissism in psychoanalysts that engenders authoritarianism, which is a corruption of power characterized by the employment of interpersonal strategies for domination and control as a means of defending against narcissistic vulnerability.

It is in no small measure the postmodern trend toward the interrogation of authority that has begun to resuscitate and reinvigorate the psychoanalytic profession. It is this willingness to level with ourselves, to confront our own professional narcissism, and to question all our assumptions about our authority and the use of our power that may yet rescue psychoanalysis from the brink of obsolescence—the perilous position our own professional narcissism has, to a great extent, helped to put us in.

ACKNOWLEDGMENTS

The author wishes to thank Lew Aron, Linda Jacobs, and Jill Salberg for their helpful critique and encouragement. Thanks also to *Contemporary Psychoanalysis* for permitting the use here of parts of a previously

---

5. Efforts toward this end are represented as well by recent publications such as Levine and Reed (2003), and Berman (2004).

published book review entitled "Madness and Evil: An Insider's View of the Sullivanian Institute." (*Contemporary Psychoanalysis*, Volume 41, #4, October 2005, pages 765–773.)

REFERENCES

Balint, M. (1968). *The Basic Fault. Therapeutic Aspects of Regression*. London: Tavistock Publications.

Benjamin, J. (2004). Beyond doer and done-to: an intersubjective view of thirdness. *Psychoanalytic Quarterly* 63:5–46.

Berman, E. (2004). *Impossible Training: A Relational View of Psychoanalytic Education*. Hillsdale, NJ: Analytic Press.

Brightman, B. (1984–85). Narcissistic issues in the training experience of the psychotherapist. *International Journal of Psychoanalytic Psychotherapy* 10: 293–317.

Cooper, S. (2004). State of the hope: the new bad object in the therapeutic action of psychoanalysis. *Psychoanalytic Dialogues* 14(5):527–551.

Davies, J. M. (2005). Whose bad objects are we anyway? Repetition and our elusive love affair with evil. *Psychoanalytic Dialogues* 14(6):711–732.

Fairbairn, W. R. D. (1952). *Psychoanalytic Studies of the Personality*. London: Routledge & Kegan Paul.

Frawley-O'Dea, M., and Sarnat, J. (2001). *The Supervisory Relationship*. New York: Guildford Press.

Fromm, E. (1941). *Escape from Freedom*. New York: Farrar and Rinehart.

——— (1964). *The Heart of Man: Its Genius for Good and Evil*. New York: Harper & Row.

Harris, L. (1994). O Guru, Guru, Guru. *The New Yorker*, November 14, pp. 92–109.

Hoffman, I. (1998). *Ritual and Spontaneity in the Psychoanalytic Process*. Hillsdale, NJ: Analytic Press.

Josephs, L. (1992). *Character Structure and the Organization of the Self*. New York: Columbia University Press.

Kernberg, O. (1985). *Borderline Conditions and Pathological Narcissism*. Northvale, NJ: Jason Aronson.

Kohut, H. (1966). Forms and transformations of narcissism. *Journal of the American Psychoanalytic Association* 8:567–586.

——— (1971). *The Analysis of the Self: A Systematic Approach to the Psychoanalytic Treatment of Narcissistic Disorders*. New York: International Universities Press.

——— (1972). Thoughts on narcissism and narcissistic rage. *Psychoanalytic Study of the Child*, 27:360–400. New Haven, CT: Yale University Press.

——— (1976). Creativeness, charisma and group psychology: reflections on the self-analysis of Freud. In *Freud: The Fusion of Science and Humanism: The Intellectual History of Psychoanalysis*, ed. J. E. Gedo and G. H. Pollock. New York: International Universities Press.

Levine, H., and Reed, G., eds. (2004). Problems of power in psychoanalytic institutions. *Psychoanalytic Inquiry* 24(1):1–139.

Rodarmor, W. (1983). The secret life of Swami Muktananda. *CoEvolution Quarterly* (Reprinted by permission of CoEv Q in two issues of *CAN/FOCUS News*, April–May 1984:5–6, and Summer 1984:5–6).

Rosenfeld, H. (1964). On the psychopathology and psycho-analytic treatment of schizophrenia. In *Psychotic States: A Psychoanalytical Approach*, ed. H. Rosenfeld. London: Hogarth Press, 1965.

Schafer, R. (1997). *The Contemporary Kleinians of London*. Madison, WI: International Universities Press.

Shaw, D. (2003). Traumatic abuse in cults: a psychoanalytic perspective. *Cultic Studies Review* 2(2):101–129.

Siskind, A. (2003). *The Sullivan Institute/Fourth Wall Community: The Relationship of Radical Individualism and Authoritarianism*. Westport, CT: Praeger.

5

Discussion: Vulnerability, Charisma, and Trauma in the Training Experience: Four Personal Odysseys

Marty Livingston

Psychoanalytic theory always reflects personal experience. A writer writes and a theorist theorizes partly as a personal attempt to bring order and meaning to the subjective impact of disturbing experiences. Trauma, by definition, refers to events that overwhelm and disorganize. Without sufficient environmental support, a child, or at times an adult, is unable to regulate his affective experience. To avoid the subjective experience of total annihilation, painful and intolerable affect is often walled off and dissociated. Seeking to understand and to be understood, to find validation once again for one's sense of identity and self, is a central mechanism of a striving to heal the wounds of these traumas.

This quest for healing draws patients into treatment and professionals into training. The training institute and its leaders, like the therapist for a beginning patient, represent a hope for a new beginning. The more charismatic the leaders of training programs, or the therapist, the more intensely these yearnings for nurturance and meaningfulness are stirred. In its most fruitful form, charisma invites vulnerability and surrender to a process within a safe surround. Vulnerability allows old organizing principles to soften and be reflected upon. It is in what I have referred to as "vulnerable moments" that old self-limiting defenses are relinquished and new structure becomes a possibility (Livingston 2001). Vulnerable moments are windows for change.

The *Encarta World English Dictionary* (1999) defines charisma as "the ability to inspire enthusiasm, interest, or affection in others by means of personal charm or influence." In its positive form, charisma is the use of one's own subjectivity and affect to deepen connection and process. It is related to a sense of faith and a set of values. In the case of a group leader or teacher, these values, and the leader's passionate belief in them, can contribute to a sense of safety and the space to explore and grow. However, when a charismatic training institute, or a therapist, is driven by needs for personal aggrandizement and power, the seeker of meaning and healing is betrayed. The chapters in this first section of the book are reporting on and conceptualizing the traumatic effects of pathological narcissism, authoritarian domination and control, and masochism and submission. These are the results of leaders' unbridled narcissistic needs unchecked by a disciplined self-reflection and a commitment to analytic exploration and the welfare of students and patients. To provide a balance, I would like to share some of my own experiences with charisma as a positive force with some pitfalls.

One aspect of charisma that sets off a sense of danger is that the leader's sense of passion can at times lead to a forcefulness. The use of the force of the leader's personality and conviction can be potentially damaging. However, the sense of the leader as a person with values rather than a blank or neutral screen is actually a key to providing safety and promoting depth. When group members approach an abusiveness toward each other, are attacking and derogating, it is important that the leader compellingly establish that such behavior is "not all right." Forcefulness and dedication to analytic exploration, with a sensitive understanding of each group member's needs and abilities to tolerate stress, allow a charismatic leader to encourage patient's to stay a little longer in an uncomfortable space. It provides a sense of containment for previously disavowed painful affect.

Charisma invites vulnerability and trust. Vulnerability is pivotal in therapeutic change, but it also is a vulnerability to shame, disorganization, and unhealthy influence. These are the stories told in the chapters in this section. They are stories of betrayal of vulnerability. They are stories of retraumatization and confusion. They are also tales of courage and persistence. Our writers in this section continue to strive for healing and meaning. They write to work through the shattering of their trust. With the help and support of loved ones and therapeutic responsiveness, they have been largely able to reestablish the organization of their self-experience. They write to continue their healing process, to make sense of disturbance and disorder, and to seek validation and understanding. They also write to warn us.

They warn us of the danger of falling prey to the narcissism of charismatic leaders and also of the pitfalls of our own narcissism and charisma. The warning is poignant and well taken. These writers are both courageous and clear in their sharing. One cannot be untouched by their journey. I believe that all of us who seek the holy grail of analytic understanding have, unfortunately, suffered similar betrayals both in our childhood and in some of our training experiences. It is easy for me to identify with the traumatic experiences described and to care about and resonate with the pain. Perhaps some readers may not be able to identify with these experiences, or perhaps need to disown identification with the sense of having been subjected to abuse by a caregiver. In any case, I found it easy to take in this warning and to be on guard against the dangers it cautions us about. Yet I am also alarmed at the warning itself. Perhaps that is because I also identify with the object of these warnings. No, I do not see myself in the category of malignant and destructive leaders like the ones portrayed in these pages. However, in my youth, my zeal for the group leader's use of his own vulnerability, humanness, and affective involvement made many of my colleagues uncomfortable and critical. Our professional world has changed drastically since the rigid dehumanizing expectations of the 1960s. Much of what I tried to develop and talk about then is now considered within the scope of concepts like Bacal's (1985) "optimal responsiveness." Back then any personal expression was considered as a "boundary violation" and viewed as "acting out" on the leader's part. It made people uncomfortable, and as a young, relatively new, group leader, I became defensive. Hurt and believing that my teachers had betrayed me, I withdrew from the academic scene for two decades.

Because of my own experience with being misunderstood and treated as dangerous, I am much more cautious about deciding that a leader is dangerous or about discouraging my students from developing their own unique charisma. Despite the dangers so well illustrated in these chapters, I am speaking for the value of charisma. I believe that there is a danger of throwing out the baby with the bath water, a danger of discarding one's own unique, affective, creative, forceful, and passionate qualities in order to avoid being labeled as charismatic and dangerous. As you have already no doubt noticed, I am not "discussing" these chapters in the way most discussions are written. Personal odysseys and the sharing of such vulnerability don't call for analysis. Instead, I prefer to react personally and to share some of my own flirtations with charisma. At this point in my life, I think that I have traveled through a number of healing paths. I, too, write to be understood and to heal. However, at the moment at least, my associations don't run to retraumatization. Instead, I feel fortunate that I have had some experiences with both sides of the charismatic leadership and for the most part no longer experience myself as betrayer or betrayed.

My father was as charismatic as they come (at least as my whole extended family portrays him). Everyone I have ever talked to about him remembers him as warm, forceful, and wonderful. He changed the lives of not only my mother, but also of my grandparents and uncles and aunts as well. His death when I was only 3 left an unfulfillable hole in my life and my sense of self. It left me with a hunger for charisma and for leaders who stirred this promise. I also felt an impossible need to be such a man—a very tough task for a little boy. His early death left a myth without a chance to deidealize him gradually. As a youngster, I remember presenting the "George Sandelman Medal," given in his name each year to the student in the school where he taught, who most exemplified his qualities of selfless dedication and strength. To me, he sounded like a world-famous football coach and molder of men. He was a good junior high physical education teacher. His death was itself a traumatic betrayal. It was only as an adult in analysis that I began to feel that he did not "choose" to abandon me.

Clearly, this history left me vulnerable to passionate causes and leaders. My analyst was, like my image of my father, a powerful and highly respected, perhaps even revered, figure. He was also the dean of training and a very influential figure in both the individual analytic and group therapy departments at my training institute. At any institute party, or meeting, his booming voice was present as soon as one entered the room. He was my individual and group analyst, my teacher, and a key administrator. Boundaries were quite blurred. He was a passionate advocate of classical Freudian theory with a dogmatic stress on the centrality of the oedipal conflict. He was very upset with me when I began to write and chose to focus on early conflicts with the mother as a central factor. He read my first paper and angrily chastised my neglect of oedipal dynamics in my patient. I can still feel the scathing sense of his displeasure and remember his words quite vividly. He told me that the paper was okay up to a point, but that "most people had fathers."

At one point when I was disagreeing with him, probably quite contemptuously and provocatively, he threatened to throw me out of treatment. When I asked what that would mean for my training, he snapped at me: "You would never be a Freudian, you would be a Livingstonian." When I think of that now, it is not such a bad thing to develop your own ideas. However, as a young man desperately wanting to belong to both the Freudian institute and to him, this was a traumatic moment that I have never forgotten. I cried for hours afterward. I felt condemned to a path of aloneness and distance. I heard him saying that my contempt and distance was "unanalyzable." Later that night I realized that my crying and fear of loss was a breakthrough. I was human after all. I was able to go back the next day and share this with my analyst. It was a real turning point for me. I realized years later that not only had I established in my mind that I was human, but also that I could have an impact on the powerful man. He, too, was human. His theory would never have allowed him to work this out as an intersubjective interaction. Still, it became "good enough" once he understood my process in working with it.

So, why am I relating these incidents? I think I am sharing this to give you an idea of the dangers of my analyst's charisma and unworked-out narcissism. I later heard that he had thrown a colleague out of treatment. It was not an idle threat. The point that I am slowly getting to is that I was in danger and in some ways I was hurt, but my overall feeling about my analysis was, and still is, that this man helped me grow. He pushed me to find the man in me and modeled a kind of warm and forceful leadership that is a valued part of me.

My positive memory of him and his charisma is so much a wordless sense impression that it is hard to convey. I felt his presence, his compassion, and his zest most, paradoxically, when he said nothing. I recall the experience of Mannie sitting in group and laughing with his whole body as he enjoyed a patient's excitement about newfound strength. I can feel the way he would turn attentively to me when I was struggling to express what I felt toward him. It made little difference whether I felt rage or deep affection. His expression, his posture, and his mannerisms all said, "Come on, I'm ready to engage with you. I can take it." One mannerism I particularly visualize, and often find myself expressing, is a simple, quiet, beckoning gesture he often made. It left the responsibility with me, but he clearly welcomed direct emotional contact. This emotional availability was closely linked to a charismatic style.

One incident stands out in my mind as a part of his charisma that I have come to appreciate in myself. Occasionally, one of us would come to the group room early and take Mannie's chair. He responded differently with the meaning he felt from each of us who sat in his place, but it was always an exciting and meaningful experience. In fact, it usually electrified the group. One day, a class of group therapists-in-training that he was teaching talked about their discomfort when a patient "displaced" them. Many leaders voiced uneasiness about whether to respond to the challenge or to allow the patient to "get away with it." Eventually, they wondered how Mannie handled such occurrences. I told them about my experience in taking his chair. He came in and sat in another chair without comment. As the group progressed I started to experience the chair as growing more and more huge. Eventually, I expressed this. That led to a very meaningful experience. The class was puzzled and asked Mannie how he was able to contain his response to the challenge. His reply was, "If the only seat left was on the chandelier, I'd still be the leader." I laughed heartily because I knew so well what he meant.

What I remember most about Mannie is a sense of his vigorous, passionate presence. For me, his charisma was an important part of him. It was connected at the core to his sense of the true spirit of analysis as a love of freedom and individuality. My experience of his presence as a man involved in my struggle to actualize my own uniqueness enabled me to be me. That "me" includes an ability to be passionate and forceful, and at times charismatic. I think that with the benefit of a self-psychological grounding and a stress on returning to what Louisa Livingston and I (Livingston and Livingston 2006) refer to as a "sustained empathic focus" on each patient's subjective/affective experience, I can harness the forces of charisma and respond sensitively, at times forcefully and at times tenderly, to the underlying vulnerability individuals bring to me in their yearnings. An understanding of these underlying vulnerabilities and narcissistic needs, both in our patients and ourselves, must accompany forcefulness, passion, and charisma if we are not to betray the delicate trust that patients and therapists-in-training bring to us. Like my father, Mannie passed away, too soon and without warning, shortly after I left treatment. I often wonder whether he would have come to the wisdom and balance I am suggesting if he had been alive through the changes in our field since the late 1960s. I would love to have had a chance to talk with him as the seasoned clinician and theorist I have become. I know that he would have delighted in my growth and in the conversation.

The warning of the chapters in this section is, as I have said, well taken. However, let us not, in protecting our trainees and patients from what Daniel Shaw, in Chapter 4, refers to as "pathological narcissism," betray them and a part of our own identities by withholding forcefulness, passion, and tenderness.

REFERENCES

Bacal, H. (1985). Optimal responsiveness and the therapeutic process. In *Progress in Self Psychology*, vol. 1, ed. A. Goldberg, pp. 202–227. New York: Guilford.

Encarta World English Dictionary. (1999). Microsoft Corporation.

Livingston, M. (2001). *Vulnerable Moments: Deepening the Therapeutic Process.* Northvale, NJ: Jason Aronson.

Livingston, M., and Livingston, L. (2006). Sustained empathic focus and the clinical application of self-psychological theory in group psychotherapy. *International Journal of Group Psychotherapy* 56(1):67–85.

II

THEORETICAL AND TECHNICAL CONSIDERATIONS

6

Covert Methods
of Interpersonal Control
Theodore Dorpat

It has been said that fish don't know they swim in water until they are out of the water. Similarly, most people do not know about the subtle and covert types of interpersonal control, domination, and abuse they are exposed to all of their lives in their families, at their schools, or in their workplace. Not until they have experienced relationships that are more caring, respectful, and nonmanipulative are they able to recognize how much they have been covertly manipulated, controlled, and abused by others. In this chapter I describe and discuss the widespread use and significance of different methods of covert interpersonal control in everyday life and in psychoanalytic treatment.

The covert methods of interpersonal control include "gaslighting" and a variety of other types of projective identifications wherein individuals, through different kinds of manipulation, exert control over other persons. Two defining characteristics of covert methods of interpersonal control are (1) the action, manipulation, or practice is one in which an individual attempts to exert control over the feelings,

thoughts, or activities of another individual; and (2) the action or practice is carried out covertly. By covertly I mean that these actions are
not carried out in an overt or direct way. My definition of covert methods of interpersonal control specifically excludes *overt* methods of control and verbal abuse such as threats of violence, explicit expressions
of rage and anger, as well as tantrums, denunciations, hostile name-
calling, or other openly hostile actions that may be taken by individuals to dominate, control, or abuse other persons.

This chapter focuses on covert methods of interpersonal control
and other indoctrination methods, their effects on interpersonal relations including the analytic interactions, and the reasons why so many
individuals are unaware of their existence or their importance both in
everyday life and in psychoanalytic treatment.

Any kind of intervention, including interpretations, questions,
confrontations, clarifications, and the like, can be used for purposes of
interpersonal control and domination. Though I claim that some methods such as questioning and confrontation are often used by clinicians
as covert methods of interpersonal control, I recognize that sometimes
they are not. Only by a study of the context in which some intervention
occurs can an investigator make reasonable inferences and judgments
about whether a particular intervention was intended to be controlling,
directive, or intimidating.

An appreciation of interactional dynamics requires us to recognize
the surprising extent to which presumably therapeutic interventions can
be used for controlling, harassing, manipulating, demeaning, patroniz-
ing, humiliating, intimidating, and gaslighting patients.

In what follows, I shall list, explain, and illustrate with vignettes
various ways in which practitioners use covert methods of interpersonal
control (usually unconsciously) and discuss the implications of these
practices for their effects on their patients and the treatment process.

PROJECTIVE IDENTIFICATION AND COVERT
METHODS OF INTERPERSONAL CONTROL

Nearly all of the tactics and methods of interpersonal control I
shall discuss may be considered to be different species of projective identification. The widespread ignorance about or denial of the employment

of indoctrination methods in psychoanalytic treatment also pertains to the prevailing conceptions about projective identification. One group of psychoanalytic writers would limit it to include a mode of primitive defense found only in psychotic or other seriously disturbed patients. I believe the use of projective identification is far more widespread among both the general population and among mental health professionals than is generally recognized. Far from being rare, projective identification is one of the most common modes of communicating and relating in groups of two or more. (For similar views, see Bion 1959 and Langs 1978.)

The most effective communications containing projective identifications are ones in which the victims do not know that they have been manipulated. One of the most destructive effects of projective identification occurs when victims identify with what has been projected onto themselves. The harmful effects of projective identification are nullified when victims are capable of disbelieving the negative and pathologic ideas attributed to them and when they can disidentify with whatever negative introjects result from the projective identification (Dorpat 1985).

Ogden's (1982) view of projective identification as having three aspects [i.e., (1) a type of defense, (2) a mode of communication, and (3) a primitive symbiotic kind of object relation] has gained wide acceptance.

The therapist's use of covert methods of interpersonal control tends to create a pathological symbiotic mode of interacting characterized by mutual projective identification; in the therapeutic context this mode of interaction has been called a type B field by Langs (1978). In the type B field, both the therapist and the patient extensively employ projective identification and use the other member of the dyad as a container for disruptive projective identifications. My clinical and supervisory experiences with psychotherapy trainees in various mental health professions and with psychoanalytic candidates indicate that a type B field is a common one in both psychiatric and psychoanalytic practice and that psychotherapists and analysts often unconsciously either initiate or maintain this pathological mode of relatedness. Langs's (1976, 1978, 1979, 1980, 1981) psychotherapy seminars for psychiatric residents suggest the alarming prevalence of the type B field in the practice of psychoanalytic psychotherapy.

The basic interactional mechanism in projective identification and in many of the different methods of covert interpersonal control is one in which one individual manipulates another individual in such a way as to evoke disturbing ideas and affects (such as shame, guilt, and anxiety) in the other person. Through the manipulation and its effects on the victim's thoughts and feelings, the perpetrator gains some control over the victim. In projective identification, the subject's first unconsciously project unwanted aspects of themselves onto another person and pressure the object to contain, as it were, the subject's disavowed affects and other contents.

The induction of emotions such as fear, shame, and guilt are powerful methods used in families as well as larger groups and institutions (government, schools, churches, the military, and the like) for controlling and regulating the cognitions and behaviors of individuals.

COVERT METHODS OF INTERPERSONAL CONTROL IN THE THERAPEUTIC SITUATION

Gaslighting

Gaslighting is a type of projective identification in which an individual (or group of individuals) attempts to influence the mental functioning of a second individual by causing the latter to doubt the validity of his or her judgments, perceptions, or reality testing in order that the victim will more readily submit his or her will and person to the victimizer. (See Chapter 2 in *Gaslighting, The Double Whammy, Interrogation, and Other Methods of Covert Control in Psychotherapy and Analysis* for a more comprehensive discussion of gaslighting.)

Gaslighting is a common and powerful interpersonal dynamic in a variety of different tactics and techniques both individuals and groups have used for attaining interpersonal and social control over the psychic functioning of other individuals and groups. Gaslighting is an important aspect in many of the brainwashing and indoctrination techniques employed by cults and by totalitarian fascist and communist regimes in their coercive management and oppression of political prisoners and prisoners of war.

The various types of gaslighting have in common two defining features. The first is an attempt to impair or destroy an individual's confidence in his or her psychic abilities. After this first aim has been achieved, the second aim is to attain control over the feelings, thoughts, and behaviors of the victims.

By making another person feel fearful, guilty, or ashamed, the manipulator is in a position to gain control over the other individual's affects, thoughts, and behaviors by substituting his own beliefs. This is the basic mechanism of gaslighting whether used in everyday life, in psychotherapy situations, or in the thought-reform and mind-control manipulations of cult leaders. Some advertising and many social interactions in which one person attempts to gain control over another are based on this principle.

Questioning

Questioning, especially if it is repetitive and directive, is a method by which clinicians can and often do gain control over their patients' mental functions and communications. (See Chapter 3 in *Gaslighting, The Double Whammy, Interrogation, and Other Methods of Covert Control in Psychotherapy and Analysis* for a more comprehensive study on the use of questioning as a method of interpersonal control.) As I indicated in previous publications, questioning tends to promote in the patient a mode of thinking and communication opposed to the methods and goals of psychoanalysis (Dorpat 1984, 1991). Frequently, questioning shifts the patient's communication away from the type A mode[1] of communication (also called derivative or symbolic communication) toward the type C mode (communication that is literal, superficial, impersonal, and affectless).

---

1. Langs (1978) describes three communicative modes: types A, B, and C. The type A mode is characterized by symbolic imagery and authentic affects, and it is the optimal mode for both therapist and patient. Projective identification is the defining feature of the type B mode. The defining property of the type C mode is the absence of primary process derivatives. In a previous publication, I labeled as the type D mode of communication a specific type of interactional defense consisting of inauthentic communication, and I described it as a defining property of what Winnicott (1960) called the False Self (Dorpat 1994). The significance of shifts in the patient's modes of communication is also discussed in chapter 10 of *Gaslighting*.

In inexperienced or anxious psychotherapists, one can note a common interactional pattern connected with the use of questions. Sometimes, when such therapists are unable or unwilling to tolerate frustrations such as silence, they attempt to control the situation by questioning the patient. Patients typically respond to such questions by defensively adopting a type C mode of communicating.

Defense Interpretation

Lomas (1987) presents a convincing argument that many classical analysts have given too much weight to the masculine qualities of disciplined reticence, toughness, and control—qualities that are often considered valuable in the interpretation of defenses. In preserving their sexual identity, such tough analysts not only seek to distinguish their mode of being from that of women but also attempt to define the latter's realm as inferior.

Lomas correctly, in my view, believes there is an excessive need on the part of some psychotherapists to make defense interpretations. Such zealous assaults by the therapists on their patients' defenses often constitute the enactment of hidden agendas for the control and domination of the patient. In my supervisory experience I have found that the excessive and inappropriate use of interpretations of unconscious defense is often done for purposes of controlling the patient. Compliant or type C responses are the most common ways patients react to these forceful attacks and confrontations on their defenses, and such responses are illustrated in the following vignette.

A repetitive but unconscious sadomasochistic interaction between therapist and patient occurred in which the therapist repetitively and unempathically confronted the patient with his defenses of intellectualization and isolation of affect.

> The patient was a socially isolated middle-aged scientist with severe narcissistic problems who suffered from deep feelings of inferiority and shame. On the manifest level, the patient responded to these defense interpretations by compliance, withdrawal, and type C communications. The therapist aggressively made interventions such as the following: "What's happened to your feelings today?" "Your voice sounds flat and

devoid of all emotion," "Your talk is very intellectualized. Can't you bring out more feelings?" At a conscious level, the patient responded compliantly and without protest to the therapist's impatient and repetitive confrontations and interpretations about his affectless and intellectualized mode of communication.

An examination of his primary process derivatives (e.g., affects, imagery, metaphors, narratives, and nonverbal communications) following the therapist's interventions about his defenses revealed that he unconsciously had evaluated the therapist's interventions as attacking and humiliating. My efforts as a supervisor consisted of using the patient's primary process derivatives to show the therapist how the patient had experienced her defense interventions as harsh and humiliating.

One day, for example, the patient began a session by telling in a somewhat halting and reserved manner some insights he had attained after his last session with the therapist. In his characteristically distant and cautious way, he told about his new understanding into why he had become "addicted" to watching Clint Eastwood movies. He described how he came to understand his fascination for identifying with Clint Eastwood as a compensation for his feelings of shame and inferiority.

At this point, the therapist interjected, "You sound like a boy whistling in the dark." At first, the patient was startled by the therapist's inopportune and tactless remark so lacking in attunement with his state of mind and with the suppressed pride he felt for his new insights. Then, he became depressed and in the following session he spoke of quitting the therapy. Fortunately, the therapist, with the supervisor's assistance, was able to understand how her poorly timed defense interpretation about "whistling in the dark" had disrupted the mirror transference and precipitated a depressive response. When the therapist was then able to acknowledge to the patient her own contribution to the patient's depressive response, the selfobject transference and the therapeutic alliance were restored.

Confrontations

The technique of confrontation is made to order for serving purposes of controlling, directing, humiliating, or dominating. Though some of the older texts on psychoanalytic technique describe confrontations as an acceptable and useful technique, my own experience in doing, teaching, and supervising psychoanalytic treatment has witnessed few occasions in which confrontations have facilitated the therapeutic process. Often confrontations are antitherapeutic projective identifications in which therapists consciously, or more often unconsciously, attempt to intimidate or at least influence and control patients by engendering painful emotions such as fear, guilt, shame, or anxiety. (For similar views on confrontation see Langs 1982.)

Interrupting or Overlapping?

Interrupting another person who is talking, especially if it is done in a loud and commanding tone of voice, is another way individuals may assert their dominance and need to control others in interpersonal situations.

However, the fact that one speaker begins talking to another person while the other person is already talking should not always be interpreted as controlling or abusive. The person who begins speaking while another person is talking and who does so in a way that is affectively and thematically attuned to the first speaker may be doing what professor of linguistics Tannen (1990) calls "overlapping." In her view, overlapping speech is not destructive and not intended to exercise dominance and violate others' rights. Instead, it is cooperative, a means of showing involvement, participation, and connection. In short, simultaneous talk can be supportive. Tannen (1990) describes regional differences in speech patterns. Individuals from the West Coast may often (as I did until 20 years ago) mistakenly consider the custom of some individuals on the East Coast to participate in overlapping speech as evidence of Easterners' need to rudely dominate the conversation.

Abrupt Change of Topic

A therapist's abrupt change of topic in psychotherapy situations can be emotionally disruptive, fragmenting, and disorganizing to the patient. Such unexpected and disturbing kinds of interventions most often stem from the therapist's unresolved countertransference problems. Though the need to intimidate and control the other person is often an unconscious aspect of this technique, I do not think it is always present. Sudden changes in the topic derail the psychoanalytic dialogue, and they are disturbing because they are unempathic and not attuned to the patient's state of mind. Frequently this kind of intervention leads to the patient's becoming emotionally disturbed or disorganized. In response to such disruptive interventions, many patients may withdraw and shift to a type C mode of communication and defense.

FRAGMENTING THE PATIENT'S EXPERIENCE

Interventions such as questions or interpretations that focus on details that are not relevant to the patient's concerns and current state of mind tend to derail the patient, to fragment the patient's experience, and to disrupt the selfobject transference. They may bring about at least temporary affective turmoil and disorganization. The fragmenting influence of this type of intervention is illustrated in the story of the centipede who became disorganized and unable to walk after he was asked, "What's wrong with your 34th left foot?"

In the following vignette, a patient became disturbed and withdrew into a compliant type C communication when the analyst fragmented her experience by directing her attention to a detail in a reported dream.[2]

A 32-year-old married woman in analysis for anxiety attacks and disturbed relations with men dreamt about being in a bedroom. She described the bedroom as a sunny room with a beautiful view of nearby snowcapped mountains. Sunlight was streaming through the window near the bed. A revolver was lying on a dresser. After a few minutes of the patient's anxiously discussing her associations to the dream and a recent quarrel with her husband, the analyst interrupted her with a question, "What comes to your mind about the gun?"

The patient replied in a matter-of-fact way, "A penis comes to my mind. I believe a gun is a symbol of a penis—oh—I guess that the gun in the dream has to do with my penis envy." The patient proceeded in a monotonous tone of voice in which her associations were impersonal and vague. All emotion drained from her speech and for the remainder of the hour her mode of communication was predominantly a type C mode.

The analyst's unempathic question was disruptive to the patient's psychic equilibrium, and it did not reflect adequate attunement with the patient's anxiety. Furthermore, his intervention was premature and

---

2. I am indebted to Dr. Joseph Lichtenberg for this vignette.

intrusive because she had not associated to this detail of the manifest dream.

In response to the analyst's disruptive intervention, the patient experienced a momentary threat of self-fragmentation. To allay this fragmentation and to prevent further cognitive and affective dyscontrol, she switched to using a type C communication as a mode of defending herself and distancing herself from the analyst. Her affectless response about the gun being a symbol for the penis was a compliant response in which she unconsciously told the analyst what she thought he expected her to think.

In her discussion of the different modes of overt and covert verbal abuse, Evans (1992) lists the following types of covert verbal abuse: "withholding," "countering," "discounting," "verbal abuse disguised as jokes," "blocking and diverting," "trivializing," and "undermining."

COVERT METHODS OF INTERPERSONAL CONTROL IN EVERYDAY LIFE

Gaslighting and other covert methods of interpersonal control are common modes of relating in our culture, and most people, including mental health professionals, are unaware of their existence or they consider them normal (Carter 1989, Elgin 1980, Evans 1992, Tannen 1990). Covert methods of control are *some of the time* embedded in the ways nearly all individuals in Western societies talk and relate to each other. In some people, these methods are used *most of the time* in communicating with others.

For the purposes of this chapter, I use the terms *covert methods of interpersonal control* and *covert verbal abuse* as synonyms because in my view the various covert types of interpersonal control, with few if any exceptions, are abusive.

The findings and conclusions I have reached from clinical studies on the use of covert methods of interpersonal control and other methods of indoctrination are similar in two ways to the findings and conclusions of investigators in cognate fields such as studies of verbal abuse and investigations on the mind-control methods employed by cult leaders (Langone 1993a, Singer 1995). First, my repeated clinical observations while doing individual and group supervision and the examination of process notes of hundreds of hours of psychotherapy and psychoanalysis have revealed the widespread use of these methods of indoctrination. Though there are important differences in the frequency, style, and tactics used for covert interpersonal control by clinicians, their use is alarmingly prevalent and widespread. Second, I found that most often both clinicians and their patients were not consciously aware of the abusive and controlling quality of covert methods of interpersonal control.

Another finding in my informal clinical studies and the investigations of others in cognate fields is the presence of a universal property in both overt and covert verbal abuse: the aim of controlling, dominating, and exercising power over others. Anger, contempt, hatred, envy, and a host of other affects and aims may or may not be expressed in both covert and overtly abusive communications, but the wish to control the other is always present.

My major findings and conclusions are supported by investigations carried out in three different disciplines: feminist studies, linguistics, and Marxist studies (Chodorow 1989, Flax 1990). Many studies in the above three disciplines support the conclusion that there is a widespread pattern of relationships in Western societies in which certain individuals and groups exert control and dominance over other individuals. Feminist studies emphasize, document, and attempt to explain male domination of women, and studies by Tannen (1990) and Elgin (1980) demonstrate that men tend to commit more verbal abuse than women. Marxist scholars emphasize the domination in capitalist countries of the have-nots by those who have money, power, and status.

The conclusions I have reached both about the extensiveness of methods of covert interpersonal control and about the unawareness of it are supported, as I mentioned, by extensive investigations of speech patterns of individuals in the United States. Tannen (1990) investigated gender differences in communication and she concludes that men live in a hierarchical social order in which they are either one-up or one-down. She states, "In this world conversations are negotiations in which people try to achieve and maintain the upper hand if they can, and protect themselves from others' attempts to put them down and push them around. Life then is a contest, a struggle to preserve independence and avoid failure" (p. 25).

In her book *The Verbally Abusive Relationship*, Evans (1992) notes that "verbal abuse is an issue of control, a means of holding power over another" (p. 13). Later she writes, "all verbal abuse is dominating and controlling" (p. 40). Carter (1989), in his volume about verbal abuse, emphasizes that the major dynamic in verbal abuse is the need to control the victim, and he writes about Hitler as a prime example of someone who was exceedingly abusive and who did so out of a persistent, deep need for dominating and controlling other persons.

THE CONTRIBUTIONS OF ELGIN

Professor of linguistics Suzette Elgin (1980) has described a common type of covert verbal abuse that, to the best of my knowledge, has not been noted in the psychiatric or psychoanalytic literature. Though many persons in our American culture are both perpetrators as well as victims of this kind of projective identification, few are aware of its existence or its significance in everyday life or in psychotherapy. This kind of mental abuse is more common, according to Elgin (1980), in men than it is in women.

In this type of projective identification, emotionally disturbing messages are hidden away or concealed, as it were, as a *presupposition* of the subject's communication. Using psychoanalytic terms, one could say that the benign manifest content of the message covers a latent content consisting of an abusive message.

In the following examples, all but the final one are taken from Elgin's (1980) book. The explicit communication in these examples is given first, followed by the unspoken presupposition. I have added the last item (i.e., "affects evoked") because in my opinion the affective responses of the victim are important interactional effects of this type of covert verbal abuse. The evoked affects and the cognitions linked with the painful affects are what make these communications abusive and disturbing.

Example 1
   "If you *really* loved me, you wouldn't go bowling."
Presupposition
   "You don't really love me."
Affects Evoked
   Guilt, shame.

Example 2
"Don't you *care* about your children?"
Presuppositions
"You don't care about your children."
"You should care about your children; it's wrong of you not to."
Affects Evoked
Guilt, shame, depressive affect.

Example 3
"Even an *elderly* person should be able to understand this rule."
Presuppositions
"There's something wrong with being an elderly person."
"It doesn't take much intelligence or ability to understand this rule."
Affects Evoked
Guilt, shame, depressive affect.

Example 4
"*Some* husbands would object to having their wives going back to school when the kids are still just babies."
Presuppositions
"It's wrong for you to go back to school."
"I'm not like other husbands—I am unique and superior to them because I'm not objecting to your going back to school."
Affects Evoked
Anxiety, fear, guilt, shame.

Example 5
To a patient who had been in psychotherapy for many years, his therapist asked, "Are you still worried about whether people like you or not?"
Presuppositions
"You are childish to still worry about whether people like you."
"There is something wrong with you for continuing to worry about whether people like you."
Affects Evoked
Shame, anxiety, anger.

As Elgin explains, victims of covert verbal abuse may be unaware of the abusiveness of such communications because they have not been taught to watch out for presuppositions, or to pay attention to them instead of the words that form the surface (i.e., manifest) sequence. Consequently, they feel hurt or insulted in response to something that sounds on the surface level like a benign and reasonable thing to say. Victimizers, as well as victims of this kind of verbal abuse, according to Elgin, are most often unaware of the abusive character of their communications. As a protection against this type of verbal abuse, Elgin (1980) recommends watching out for and identifying the hurtful presuppositions contained in the victimizer's communication.

As a second line of protection, she recommends that the victim or potential victim adopt what she calls the "computer mode" of communication, which consists of speaking in generalities and abstractions and reducing to a minimum any body movement or emotional expression. The mode of communication she recommends is identical with what Langs (1978) calls type C communication. (See Dorpat 1993 for more on the "computer mode" and type C communication.)

THE IDEALIZATION OF "POWER AND MASTERY OVER PEOPLE"

Controlling, abusive, and coercive modes of communicating and relating are embedded in many speech patterns of Western societies because power over people is idealized and sought for in the Western world (Gruen 1988). A disturbing and vulgar illustration of this passion for power over people is the popularity of books by Van Fleet and others of his ilk. Van Fleet (1983) makes his living conducting seminars and writing books on techniques for gaining power and control over individuals.

In his popular book, *25 Steps to Power and Mastery Over People*, Van Fleet claims that by reading his books and following his recommendations the reader "can gain power, influence, and control over others and *attain complete mastery over people*" (p. 7, italics added).

Van Fleet understands, as few people do, the interpersonal power accruing to individuals who know how to evoke strong emotions of fear and desire in others. He explains in detail effective methods for covertly gaining control and how these methods require some knowledge of human emotions and motivation. He recommends motivating a person to do something like buying a car he does not need by arousing his desire. If you can't control a person by arousing his desire, then he suggests trying to make him feel fearful. Van Fleet said, "If you can't move a person to action by arousing his desire, then turn the coin over and move him to action by arousing his fear" (p. 131).

Another of his recommended strategies for obtaining interpersonal control is attacking a person's weak and vulnerable points. With no trace of conscious guilt, he suggests, "Always go for a weak one where she cannot protect herself" (p. 141). Van Fleet accurately describes his coercive and abusive methods as "verbal brainwashing."

Unconsciously, Van Fleet, I surmise, at some level has some questions about the unethical and grossly immoral quality of his recommendations. I infer the above from his extravagant and defensive claims about his techniques being legitimate and morally correct:

> It is *certainly not illegal or immoral* for you to use brainwashing as a powerful but fully *legitimate* technique for persuasion to convert a person to your way of thinking so he will do what you want him to do [p. 217, italics added].

Van Fleet cites John Wesley's extraordinary charismatic abilities in the seventeenth century to convert thousands to Christianity as an example of how to use brainwashing to "change behavior patterns." Van Fleet is unusually perceptive in understanding the similarity between the methods evangelists such as Wesley use for bringing about conversion with the methods totalitarian political regimes use for brainwashing. In political, psychotherapy, and religious cults, the authorities in charge are able to gain control over their hapless victims after they have first managed to convince them of their actual or imagined failings and inadequacies, be they moral, cognitive, or psychiatric. (See Chapter 9 in *Gaslighting* for more about the use of brainwashing methods in political, religious, and psychotherapy cults.)

Van Fleet's recommendation ("constant repetition is the key to success in brainwashing") explains the efficacy of repetitive defense interpretations in attaining control over patients. (For a case example of this, see my commentary on the repeated interpretations of defense made by the analyst Silverman in the case report in Chapter 4 of *Gaslighting.*)

My initial reaction to reading Van Fleet's book was one of moral outrage over his recommended techniques and disbelief about his claims for how the reader could attain financial success and power over people by following his strategies and techniques. Further reflection and study led me reluctantly to conclude that Van Fleet was correct in concluding that brainwashing methods could win "power and mastery over people" as well as achieve professional and financial success.

The use of both overt as well as covert methods of interpersonal control is a common and popular pathway to success in business and some professions, such as law. Attorneys who command the highest hourly fees and who have a reputation for success are too often the ones who are the meanest, most unscrupulous, and harshly dominating individuals one could imagine living outside the walls of penal institutions. They are the "hired guns" of America in the twenty-first century.

My experience in doing forensic psychiatry supports the appraisal of the attorney Benson (1991) about the legal system in the United States. Today's adversarial system creates a warlike atmosphere for attorneys in which they are pressured by their clients to win at any cost and by any means available. Lawyers who act ethically often put themselves at a competitive disadvantage. Benson concludes, "We have created a profession in this country that by its very nature encourages being disagreeable, pushy and sometimes even dishonest to be successful" (p. 10).

INDOCTRINATION TECHNIQUES
USED BY INSTITUTIONS

The covert methods of interpersonal control used mainly unconsciously by some mental health professionals are similar in some ways to the indoctrination, brainwashing, and social control methods used by various institutions (e.g., governmental, educational, religious, etc.). A major difference is that these institutions for the most part consciously and deliberately use overt as well as covert methods for interpersonal and social control, whereas clinicians use only covert methods and these are carried out for the most part unconsciously. (See Chapter 9 in *Gaslighting* for a discussion of the use of overt and covert methods of interpersonal control and brainwashing methods in cults.)

Many types of psychiatric treatment and psychotherapy are deliberately organized to systematically carry out methods for shaping, controlling, or directing the behaviors of patients. The widespread support of directive techniques is illustrated in the recent writings and seminars of psychotherapist Jay Haley. About thirty years ago, he wrote a satirical polemic against psychoanalysts for using controlling and directive methods (Haley 1969). In his attack on psychoanalysts, he accused them of practicing "one-upmanship" with their patients, and he criticized them for being masters of the art of putting their patients "one-down." He appears to have changed his attitude toward "directive" methods because he now conducts summer conferences on Cape Cod for instructing therapists on how to conduct "directive" therapy.

Some of the damaging effects of using covert or overt methods of interpersonal control in psychoanalytic treatment stem from the fact that their use is contradictory to the avowed purposes, methods, and traditions of psychoanalysis. In situations where patients receive contradictory messages about the nature and purpose of the therapist's communications, the patients may be placed in what Bateson (1972) and others call a double-bind. The therapist's implicit or explicit message, "What I say is not directive or prescriptive. My purpose is to enlighten you, not to control you," is contradicted by messages and communications of the therapist which are directive, controlling, or manipulative.

BEHAVIOR MODIFICATION THERAPY

The explicit aim of behavior modification therapy is the control of patients' behavior through the use of rewards and punishments. Though Skinner claims his findings and theories about operant conditioning are science, he has not discovered anything *new*, nor has he enlightened us about anything *old*. Humans and certain other mammals (for example, mother bears) have used reward and punishment as effective means of training and attaining social control over others, especially their offspring, for millions of years. Though Skinner did not, in my opinion, make an important contribution to knowledge or science, he did develop an efficient technology and an effective methodology for shaping and controlling the behaviors of animals (including humans) through the systematic application of rewards and punishments.

PSYCHOLOGICAL EFFECTS OF BEHAVIOR MODIFICATION THERAPY

The following vignette illustrates how behavior modification can support the formation and consolidation of a false self personality organization and inauthentic communication.[3] (See Chapter 4 in *Gaslighting* for a clinical case study of a patient with false self psychopathology.)

A 32-year-old single man was admitted to the psychiatric service of a hospital for treatment of depression and an attempted suicide. The hospital staff treated him with behavior modification treatment, which consisted of attempts to control and modify his behavior through rewarding behaviors the staff deemed acceptable and ignoring or punishing behaviors they considered "sick" or in other ways unacceptable. He became deeply disappointed when the psychiatric staff did not want to listen to him or to understand him. In fact, at most times they ignored him, except on occasions when they would unaccountably praise him for "behaviors" he did not care about.

He came to the realistic judgment that the staff members were not interested in what he felt or what he thought. They were, however, sometimes very much concerned about "behaviors" he considered to be among the more unimportant and superficial things about himself. They praised and "rewarded" him for his good manners, for "socializing" with other patients, for keeping his room tidy, and for dressing in ways pleasing to the staff.

To protect himself from being disappointed over not being understood in an empathic way and not having his experience validated in any way, he became more vigilant about what the staff wanted from him and he gradually learned what would win staff approval and eventual discharge from the psychiatric ward. Above all, he should at all times *act* normal. Moreover, he should not express his genuine feelings or bother staff members by talking to them about his problems.

---

3. I am indebted to Dr. Robert Bergman for this vignette.

What I have just described is, of course, a formula or recipe for the reinforcement and maintenance of inauthentic ways of relating. The psychiatric ward's behavior modification program succeeded all too well in getting the patient to suppress his symptoms, to conceal his spontaneous feelings and thoughts, and, most importantly, to shape and support his inauthentic ways of relating to others. In short, behavior modification therapy suppressed his true self and supported and partly shaped his false self. Partly because of such dehumanizing and affectively damaging experiences on the psychiatric service, many months of psychotherapy were necessary before he could trust his therapist not to attempt to stifle his individuality or to control his "behavior."

GROUP DENIAL

Other investigators who have noted the fact that both victimizers as well as victims are often unaware of the existence or of the significance of covert methods of interpersonal control and abuse include Carter (1989), Elgin (1980), Evans (1992), Lakoff and Coyne (1993), and Tannen (1990).

Carter (1989) notes that only 1 percent of persons are intentionally verbally abusive. In his view, "Twenty percent do it semiconsciously as a defense mechanism. The rest of us do it only occasionally, usually unconsciously and unintentionally" (p. 9).

Elgin (1980) discusses the widespread unawareness, especially among men, of the controlling and abusive aspects of their verbal communication. She concludes, "Take as a given that men are brought up to be verbally abusive, *usually without conscious awareness* of that fact" (p. 286, italics added).

Individuals who have been systematically subjected to covert methods of interpersonal control and who have been followers of religious, political, or psychotherapy cults most often do not understand the traumatizing ways they have been manipulated and exploited by their oppressors (Singer 1995). Patients I have treated or examined who have been subjected to these covert kinds of interpersonal control and abuse by their families, by cults, or by their previous therapists have, for the most part, denied either the fact or the meaning of these oppressive practices until they, like the victims of childhood sexual and physical abuse, are able to work through the denial defending against the awareness of their cumulative trauma and then begin to understand the significance of their traumatic experiences.

How do we account for the prevailing and widespread unawareness of the various methods of covert interpersonal control and abuse not only among mental health professionals but also in the general population? Though there are, of course, individual differences in both the degree and quality of unawareness, I believe there is a collective denial among many persons in Western societies of various aspects of these practices. I suspect but cannot prove that this collective denial accounts for a substantial part of the prevailing unawareness of the existence as well as effects of covert verbal abuse.

The covertness of covert methods of interpersonal control partly serves to conceal the abusive and controlling nature of the communication. In my professional experience, many therapists who use covert methods of interpersonal control rationalize the use of such methods and deny the controlling oppressive aspect of their communication. Dewald (1972), for example, rationalizes what others, including myself, consider his oppressive and controlling use of questions by stating that questions are required to get the patient to follow the basic rule and to prevent silences.

The highly prevalent unawareness of victims of verbal abuse that they are being controlled and abused has also been demonstrated by investigators who have studied this in cults. Cult experts Langone (1993b) and Singer (1995) report that cult members are rarely aware of the subtle techniques and mind-control methods used for shaping their behavior, thoughts, and feelings. Cults are able to operate successfully because at any given time most followers are either not yet aware that they are being controlled, abused, and exploited, or, less commonly, they cannot express such awareness because of uncertainty, shame, or fear of doing so.

Here is a brief, familiar example of a group denial involving medical and surgical residents. In a previous publication I reported that residents in training and graduates of residency training programs tended to deny certain emotionally disturbing aspects of their physically and psychologically abusive and harmful training programs (Dorpat 1989). I refer here particularly to the excessively long hours—often exceeding 100 hours a week—of work required of residents, as well as the con-comitant fatigue and sleep loss. Their denial of the traumas and stress they had sustained for many months was organized and shaped by their relationships to their peers and to their teachers. The unconscious message they received from others at their training institutions was to minimize and discount their work stress and its harmful effects on their physical and mental health. In fact, many residents rationalized their situation by patently false assertions about how much their arduous work schedule added to their personal and professional development.

In a group as with the self, schemata[4] shape the flow of informa-tion. In any group, the relevant schemata are those that are shared by members, the subset of schemata that are the "we." Groups, whether large or small, are as vulnerable as individuals to denial and self-deception. In the groups of residents the group schema used to deny the stress and its effects could be put into words in this way: "Don't com-plain! The long hours of work, the loss of sleep, and the fatigue are good for you." According to Bion (1959), a most crucial aspect of a group mentality are those basic assumptions about how to handle anxiety-evoking information. This includes an unconscious collusion by the group members about what to deny.

Persons in groups come to share a large number of schemata, most of which are communicated without being spoken of directly (Reiss 1981). Foremost among those shared, yet unspoken, schemata are what group members are tacitly enjoined to deny. When the persons in a group have made the tacit or unconscious choice about what they will deny, they have established a shared defense. (See also Dorpat and Miller 1992 for more discussion about shared defenses.)

GROUP DENIAL AMONG PSYCHOANALYSTS

I believe the group denial (or ignorance) in the general popula-tion concerning covert methods of interpersonal control also applies

---

4. Schemata are memory structures that organize the mind and serve as its con-tents. A schema functions as a template for organizing and interpreting lived experi-ence. A schema is not a carbon copy of the event it represents; rather, a schema is an abstraction representing the regularities in a particular type of person–event interaction.

to American psychoanalysts and psychoanalytic psychotherapists. As evidence of this I cite the responses of a group of analysts to the presentation of a case in which there was flagrant and repeated use of different covert methods of interpersonal control.

The treating analyst, Dr. Martin Silverman (1987), provided uncensored process notes of four successive analytic hours. Thirteen eminent analysts provided discussion papers on Silverman's process notes. Only one, Merton Gill, noted and discussed what I, along with Gill, consider to be the central interactional dynamic of the four analytic sessions—namely, the analyst and the analysand are engaged in a continuing sadomasochistic interaction. Neither the patient nor the analyst explicitly addresses this ongoing pathological interaction. Their sadomasochistic interaction and the analyst's repeated employment of gaslighting tactics, as well as other methods of covert interpersonal control, provide a unifying frame of reference for understanding what is occurring in the analysis and for explaining the prolonged stalemate in the analysis. One discussant, Dr. Charles Brenner, who explicitly shares the same classical theoretical orientation as the treating analyst, Silverman, found nothing to criticize in Silverman's conduct of the analysis.

DENIAL LEADS TO IGNORANCE AND DYSCONTROL OVER WHAT IS DENIED

When I discuss the unawareness of persons who use covert methods of interpersonal control, I ascribe it to two possible factors: denial and ignorance. Although I have no hard evidence, my clinical experience and self-analysis lead me to believe that the most common cause of the wide prevalence of covert abuse and covert methods of interpersonal control is the defense of denial, and that the lack of knowledge (i.e., ignorance) about the existence and various meanings (such as its harmfulness) of covert abuse and covert methods of interpersonal control is secondary to the denial.

The ignorance or defect in knowledge secondary to denial responses I explained in previous publications in this way (Dorpat 1985, 1987): In denial reactions, a subject shifts his focal attention from whatever is disturbing or experienced as potentially disturbing to something, and this shift away from the disturbing object I call *cognitive arrest*. This cognitive arrest in clinical reactions prevents subjects from fully and accurately symbolizing in words whatever it is that they have defensively disavowed. Denial thus prevents the formation of secondary process products (i.e., verbal representatives) about whatever is disavowed.

I believe we should exercise some restraint in criticizing mental health professionals and other persons who use these directive methods. Most often they do not consciously intend to injure others, and most often because of the group denial they are unaware of what they are doing and of the psychic effects of what they are doing.

An important consequence of denial is the avoidance of responsibility and the rejection of authority or "ownership" over what is denied. The one who denies is not irresponsible; he or she is *aresponsible* (the prefix "a" has the same meaning as in words like *amoral*). Denial, then, is marked by an unconscious rejection of personal responsibility for some action, rather than a conscious shirking of responsibility. The denier does not intend to act in an immoral or irresponsible way but, rather, cuts short self-reflection regarding his actions before even knowing what he is doing.

Another consequence of denial is dyscontrol, the subject's loss of control over whatever he has denied. The denier's failure to avow and to assume responsibility over what he denies (disavows) leads to a loss of direct, conscious control over what is denied. The widespread, excessive, and damaging effects of covert methods of interpersonal control among mental health professionals is then a type of dyscontrol.

In sum, denial leads to ignorance about and dyscontrol over what is denied.

CONCLUSION

I have little doubt that the various covert methods of interpersonal control are used more extensively by nonpsychoanalytic therapists than by psychoanalysts and psychoanalytically oriented psychotherapists. In psychoanalysis, however, the use of such methods of indoctrination are opposed to both the values and traditions of psychoanalysis from Freud on. Respect for the patient's autonomy, the rule of neutrality, and the value placed on being nondirective are just three traditional psychoanalytic principles standing in opposition to using methods of indoctrination.

It is not my aim to have therapists eliminate any type of unconscious influence or suggestion because it would not be either possible or desirable to do so. However, the influence exerted by the covert methods of interpersonal control is harmful to human well-being and normal development. One of the major ways such methods work is through the evocation of human misery in the myriad forms of shame, guilt, and anxiety.

My hope is that this chapter will help persons doing psychoanalytic therapy to work through and identify their unawareness or denial of covert methods of interpersonal control. In this way, psychoanalytic therapy can bring about truly permanent changes produced by constructive forces within the patient rather than by the temporary changes made in compliance to the therapist's use of methods of indoctrination.

In psychoanalytic treatment there exists a prevalent error of putting an excessive faith in the certainty of doctrine at the expense of an open-ended exploration between patient and psychotherapist. When psychoanalytic practitioners overvalue their theory and method and assume the right to control the conditions and content of the dialogue, they are making the same kind of destructive error as the unethical politician or the shady used-car salesman.

The ideas and methods of Freud and his heirs can be and have been used for dominating rather than healing by far too many psychotherapists. They do this by undermining people's respect for their conscious perceptions and judgments (as for example in gaslighting) and by degrading ordinary caring in favor of techniques that fly in the face of common sense.

The abuse of power in psychotherapy is linked with an idealization of technique in human relations (Lomas 1987). A mode of behavior is advocated or required on the basis of a theory that either claims or implies a right to supersede the ordinary caring and respect that people have a right to expect from others.

REFERENCES

Bateson, G. (1972). *Steps to an Ecology of Mind.* New York: Ballantine.

Benson, S. (1991). Why I quit practicing law. *Newsweek.* November 4, p. 10.

Bion, W. R. (1959a). *Experiences in Groups*. New York: Basic Books.

Carter, J. (1989). *Nasty People*. New York: Dorset.

Chodorow, N. J. (1989). *Feminism and Psychoanalytic Theory*. New Haven: Yale University Press.

Dewald, P. A. (1972). *The Psychoanalytic Process*. New York: Basic Books.

Dorpat, T. L. (1984). The technique of questioning. In *Listening and Interpreting: The Challenge of the Work of Robert Langs*, ed. J. Raney, pp. 55–74. New York: Jason Aronson.

——— (1985). *Denial and Defense in the Therapeutic Situation*. New York: Jason Aronson.

——— (1987). A new look at denial and defense. *The Annual of Psychotherapy* 15:23–47.

——— (1989). Abusive practices in medical training. *King County Medical Society Bulletin* 68:20, 26.

——— (1991). On the use of questioning as a psychoanalytic technique. *Psychoanalysis and Psychotherapy* 9:106–113.

——— (1993). The type C mode of communication—an interactional perspective. *The International Journal of Communicative Psychoanalysis and Psychotherapy* 8:47–54.

——— (1994). On inauthentic communication and interactional modes of defense. *Psychoanalytic Psychotherapy Review* 5:25–35.

——— (1996). *Gaslighting, The Double Whammy, Interrogation, and Other Methods of Covert Control in Psychotherapy and Analysis*. New Jersey: Jason Aronson.

Dorpat, T. L., and Miller, M. L. (1992). *Clinical Interaction and the Analysis of Meaning: A New Psychoanalytic Theory*. Hillsdale, NJ: Analytic Press.

Elgin, S. H. (1980). *The Gentle Art of Verbal Self Defense*. New York: Dorset.

Evans, P. (1992). *The Verbally Abusive Relationship*. Holbrook, MA: Bob Adams, Inc.

Flax, J. (1990). *Thinking Fragments—Psychoanalysis, Feminism, and Postmodernism in the Contemporary West*. Berkeley: University of California Press.

Gruen, A. (1988). *The Betrayal of the Self: The Fear of Autonomy in Men and Women*. New York: Grove.

Haley, J. (1969). *The Power Tactics of Jesus Christ and Other Essays*. New York: Avon Books.

Lakoff, R. T., and Coyne, J. C. (1993). *Father Knows Best: The Use and Abuse of Power in Freud's Case of Dora*. New York: Teachers College Press.

Langone, M. D. (1993a). *Recovery From Cults*. New York: Norton.

——— (1993b). Helping cult victims: historical backgrounds. In *Recovery From Cults*, pp. 22–47. New York: Norton.

Langs. R. (1976). *The Bipersonal Field.* New York: Jason Aronson.

———— (1978). *The Listening Process.* New York: Jason Aronson.

———— (1979). *The Therapeutic Environment.* New York: Jason Aronson.

———— (1980). *Interactions: The Realm of Transference and Countertransference.* New York: Jason Aronson.

———— (1981). *Resistances and Interventions.* New York: Jason Aronson.

———— (1982). *Psychotherapy: A Basic Text.* New York: Jason Aronson.

Lomas, P. (1987). *The Limits of Interpretation.* Northvale, NJ: Jason Aronson.

Ogden, T. (1982). *Projective Identification and Psychotherapeutic Technique.* New York: Jason Aronson.

Reiss, D. (1981). *The Family's Construction of Reality.* Cambridge: Harvard University Press.

Silverman, M. (1987). Clinical material. *Psychoanalytic Inquiry* 7:147–165.

Singer, M. T. (1995). *Cults in Our Midst—The Hidden Meaning in Our Everyday Lives.* San Francisco: Jossey-Bass.

Tannen, D. (1990). *You Just Don't Understand.* New York: William Morrow.

Van Fleet, J. K. (1983). *Twenty-five Steps to Power and Mastery Over People.* West Nyack, NY: Parker Publishing.

Winnicott, D. W. (1960). Ego distortion in terms of true and false self. In *The Maturational Processes and the Facilitating Environment*, pp. 140–152. New York: International Universities Press, 1965.

7

On Cutting the Grass, Psychoanalytic Education, and the Interweave of Ideology, Power, and Knowledge: An Historical and Philosophical Perspective

Patrick B. Kavanaugh

We see men haying far in the meadow, their heads waving like the grass they cut. In the distance, the wind seemed to bend all alike.

Thoreau

It was an early November morning some 35 to 40 years ago. I was on my way to the county psychiatric hospital located far out in the country, conveniently distanced from the city and the everyday life of most people. I could tell I was approaching the institutional grounds as I found myself riding alongside the black, iron-spiked fence that encircled the main buildings of this massive residential treatment facility. After about a mile or so, there was a break in the iron spikes and I slowed, turned in at the main entrance, and entered the grounds. With a sense of nervous excitement, I slowly began the long, winding drive up to the Victorian-styled admissions building where I was to report for the final processing of my paperwork and begin orientation for my first professional position.

I still remember seeing about fifteen to twenty men cutting the grass with push-mowers as I drove up the long, winding drive. They were lined up behind each other in staggered, overlapping rows so that as they walked in their stiff and lurching kind of unison, they cut a swath about 20 to 25 feet wide. It was one of those very late fall, early winter Michigan mornings when the sky is still a blackish-gray, streaked with deep purples and rich bluish-reds. A foggy mist was hanging heavily in a kind of suspended state just above the ground. I pulled over to the side of the road and watched. It was quite an eerie sight to see the men walking stiffly, pushing their mowers, and cutting the grass that no longer needed cutting. Completing their rows, they would then turn, once again line up, and begin walking in staggered precision down the next row until, one by one, each disappeared back into the thick, foggy mist. Several minutes later, they would reemerge from the thick fog, one by one, about 20 feet further over. After watching for awhile, I restarted the car and continued on my way to the steeple-tipped admissions building where I filled out the final paperwork authorizing my admission into the institutional community behind the iron-spiked fence.

Situated on about 900 acres, this institution had its own farm and the equipment necessary to raise animals and crops, a patient-run laundry and store, a printing press and newsletter, a police and fire station, a community center and hospital, living quarters for patients and many of the staff, and a cemetery where over 7,000 former patients were buried. In the place of the person's name, however, each tombstone was marked by a four-digit number corresponding to his or her medical chart records. Upon admission, a chart number such as 3296 was assigned to each person. This chart number constituted the person's identity in the community; it shepherded him or her through the complexities of the community's bureaucratic and social maze from the time of admission to, most often, their final resting place (Hunter 1998). In this massive edifice complex, many of the seventy-five buildings were alphabetized from A through Z; A-Building was, of course, the admissions building; B-Building was the staff residence; C-Building was the patient-run store; and D through G signified and housed the back-wards patients. And these were the ABC's of institutional life and the structures that held its people.

As I gradually came to learn during the years of my stay, these medical chart numbers and building letters were kinds of communal languages; they were the technocratic practices that functionally contributed to establishing the discursive rationality, constructing the social reality, and providing a sense of social coherence for residents and staff alike. Inside the perimeter of its black, iron-spiked fence, this community had its own distinct culture in which its institutional(ized) systems of thinking, sets of beliefs, and core values structured, signified, and legitimized certain ways of thinking about the world and each of the people who passed through A-Building. Its institutional rationality and discourse defined the natural order of things in the community: power and prestige flowed inherently from the hierarchically ordered relationships between the staff and patients; privilege and prerogative derived from the dichotomized distinctions between the *sane* and the *insane*. In so doing, the institutional discourse made the world(s) behind the iron-spiked fence more understandable, comprehensible, and coherent. And these were the ABCs of the social order that structured the lived experiences of everyday institutional life for the staff (the sane) and residents (the insane) alike.

These same systems of signification also provided a context in which was written something of the historical text of the community. I eventually came to learn, for example, that those who pushed the mowers in their predetermined rows were affectionately known in the community as the "Lobo Brigade," an abbreviated reference to the Brigade of the Lobotomized. Back in the 1940s and 1950s, the institution's treatment of choice had been to routinely perform prefrontal lobotomies on the mentally ill. In the evolution of psychiatric treatments, lobotomies at that time were in the forefront of the more sophisticated and scientific of psychiatric interventions to alter mood and behavior. Those people who had silently greeted me at the entrance to the grounds were living and breathing monuments to the ways of thinking of that earlier time, a time that had long since faded into the foggy mist of days past. The Lobo Brigade constituted an iconic chapter in the historical text of the community.

As times change, so do the sociocultural and philosophical assumptions regarding that which constitutes the mentally ill, effective treatment strategies, and institutional philosophies and practices in the delivery of therapeutic health-care services. And with the passage of time, this particular institution was downsized. More specifically, its chart-numbered patients were deinstitutionalized, its alphabetized buildings were demolished, and its black, iron-spiked fence was re-moved. The demolition of its alphabetized structures housing the pa-tients could be understood as a literalized form of deconstructing an institutional(ized) treatment philosophy, influenced in no small mea-sure by the sociopolitical economics of increasing property values as the suburbs gradually enveloped the countryside. Those few buildings that remained were updated, renamed, and continued to provide psychiat-ric services to the surrounding communities as a regional psychiatric hospital. Where there was once the patient-run store, there now sits a MacDonald's fast-food restaurant serving the local community under its golden arches.

Since leaving the grounds of this institution, I have had occasion to be at several other residential treatment facilities and various edu-cational institutions: universities, pre- and postdoctoral training pro-grams, and teaching hospitals. Over the years, I gradually came to notice some rather striking similarities between the residential community surrounded by its iron-spiked fence and the educratic institutions. As a member of various teaching and supervisory faculties, I came to more fully know and appreciate the inseparable and largely unexamined in-terweave of ideology, power, and knowledge in psychoanalytic edu-cation and training. And more and more frequently, I found myself thinking of the Lobo Brigade as they appeared and disappeared into the thick foggy mist, cutting grass that no longer needed cutting and, in so doing, monumentalizing an historical time and ways of thinking that had long since passed. It seems to me that in many respects our psy-choanalytic institutions, theoretical beliefs, and empirical researches have remained insulated—and isolated—behind their own conceptu-ally constructed iron-spiked fence forged from a nineteenth-century positivist philosophic premise, a positivist-medical ideology that houses people in the alphabetized structures of diagnostic and statistical manu-als, and an empirical discourse that speaks scientifically produced bodies of knowledges about human beings at the .05 level of truth.

As a fourfold contribution to the study of authoritarian practices and the exercise of power in psychoanalytic education and training, this chapter examines the interweave of ideology, power, and knowledge by considering first the theoretical and philosophical assumptions under-lying the vertically arranged, hierarchically organized structure of our educratic institutions, their technocratic rationality, and their institutional discourse (in this context, consideration is given to the authoritarian exercise of power both within the walls of the institute and, more recently, within the parameters of the larger psychoanalytic community); second, the theoretical and philosophical assumptions underlying our psychoanalytic bodies of knowledge; the medical-positivist ideology that dominates the process of our knowledge production and its acquisition, and the defining influence of this interweave of ideology, knowledge, and power in the identity formation of the psychoanalyst; third, the question of authoritarianism and power, on the one hand, and the sociopolitical and socioeconomic context of the training analysis, the heart of psychoanalytic education, on the other; and fourth, several alternatives to the institute model of education and training. There seems to be a pressing urgency to discussing these issues, particularly when one considers the results of the Strategic Marketing Initiative, a recent survey commissioned by the American Psychoanalytic Association (Zacharias 2002).

The Strategic Marketing Initiative surveyed psychoanalysts, mental health professionals, and patients in the hopes of discovering better means of making psychoanalysis more successful in getting more patients (Zacharias 2000). The perception and attitudes among the groups surveyed were as disturbing as they were revealing: psychoanalysts were percieved as authoritarian, arrogant, and aloof. The perceptions, attitudes, and issues highlighted by the survey appear to run much deeper than those that might be remedied by psychoanalysts' simply making efforts to be more engaged, involved, and relevant through, for example, developing outreach programs in the community. Indeed, this chapter raises these questions: Are the seeds of these perceptions and attitudes unwittingly planted, nurtured, and cultivated by the theoretical and philosophical assumptions underlying our educational institutions, their bodies of knowledges, and the image of the analyst around which psychoanalytic education and training are organized? Do these theoretical and philosophical assumptions lend substance to the perception and attitudes of the analyst as authoritarian, arrogant, and aloof?

This chapter is written from the perspective of a skeptical phenomenalist and is intended as a contribution to the study of the psychoanalytic arts.

INSTITUTIONAL STRUCTURE, RATIONALITY, AND DISCOURSE: THEORETICAL AND PHILOSOPHICAL ASSUMPTIONS

At the end of the end of the twentieth century, our seventeenth-century organizations are crumbling. . . . It is interesting to note just how Newtonian most organizations are. The machine imagery of the spheres were captured by organizations in an emphasis on structure and parts.
Margaret Wheatley, *Newtonian Organizations in a Quantum Age*
Institutional Structure, Rationality, and Discourse

Birthed in a culture of positivism, psychoanalysis was a child of the Westernized cultures; psychoanalytic education was a product of its times. Freud was profoundly influenced by the assumptions, ways of thinking, and the historical approach of Darwinian biology. Indeed, Freud was known as the "Darwin of the Mind" (Jones 1953). Darwin's historical approach provided a scientific solution to the problem of species. His researches in biology extended the validity of the historical approach as a scientific method of inquiry from the inorganic world of geology to the organic world of biology (Ritvo 1990). With the publication of the *Studies on Hysteria* (1895), Breuer and Freud adopted the historical approach as the scientific method of inquiry and applied it to the human mind and mental phenomena. As a model, evolutionary biology provided a way of thinking by which psychoanalytic theory could understand the development of people and mental life as sequential, orderly, natural, and law-governed; evolutionary doctrine and methodology rooted psychoanalysis in biological and scientific foundations. And as one of the natural sciences, classical psychoanalysis had the tendency to order the human universe in a developmental hierarchy, mirroring the seemingly natural hierarchies of evolutionary biology (Strenger 1998). The conceptual foundations of its theories, techniques of practice, and educational institutions were grounded in these presumed natural hierarchies of the real world. In a culture of positivism, positivist thought is committed to only one form of social formation: those institutional structures that support principles of hierarchy and control (Giroux 1997).

Founded in 1920 by Max Eitingon, the Berlin Psychoanalytic Institute embodied these principles of control in its vertically arranged, hierarchically organized structure. Consistent with a nineteenth-century worldview, its institutional structure provided clear lines of authority and chains of command; its sharp boundaries and demarcations provided a clear delineation of the specific function and purpose of each element, component, and part in its tripartite system of education (Wheatley 1992). In its hierarchically organized structure, those higher up in the hierarchy possess power and authority over those who are situated lower down; power is expressed through the institutional discourse consisting of the hierarchically organized structure (training analyst, analyst, candidate); a positivist-medical ideology (symptomatology-etiology-psychopathology); an espoused theoretical orientation (ego psychology); and the image of the analyst around which psychoanalytic education was organized (social scientist-artist). The institutional discourse expressed its power through the technocratic language of those standards, rules, and regulations that defined its pedagogical philosophy and principles and governed its educational practices.

The Exercise of Authoritarianism and Power
Within the Walls of the Institute

At its inception, the Berlin Psychoanalytic Institute adopted the tripartite system for psychoanalytic education, an educational model consisting of an institutional or didactic analysis (the training analysis), theoretical or didactic instruction, and the supervised analysis of control cases. In the winter of 1923–24, the training committee of the Berlin Psychoanalytic Society imposed standards and regulations on each of these learning activities and experiences of the candidates. In so doing, an institutional wisdom and oversight replaced everything in the realm of the candidate's individual and personal choice; a technocratic rationality guided the decisions about each phase of the candidate's education. And psychoanalysis became institutionalized (Safouan 2000). Standards and regulations now applied to the selection of candidates; the requirement of a personal analysis of 6 months duration; the designation of the training analyst; in collaboration with the training analyst, deciding when the candidate was ready to participate in further stages of training; and deciding when the candidate's personal analysis was completed. Decisions regarding education and training were removed from the control of the individual psychoanalyst-educator and the respective candidate and were placed under the control of the institute. With this authoritarian exercise of power by the training committee, psychoanalytic education became institute-centered as opposed to student-centered.

Standards standardize, regulations regulate, and institutions institutionalize. With these standards and regulations, the other-as-third became an integral aspect of institute training; a triumph of triangulation prevailed among the institute, the analyst, and the candidate. In the evolutionary narrative of psychoanalytic education, the candidate's educational development and progression through the institute's hierarchical system eventuates, theoretically, in the attainment of the power, prestige, privileges, and prerogatives of the training analyst. Movement within the institute from the lowest position of *candidate* to *analyst* to the highest level of *training analyst* took place under the institute's oversight and decision-making control. The philosophy underlying such hierarchically organized institutions can be simply and succinctly stated: without the developmentally advanced ultimate knower imposing his structure and direction through standards, regulations, and curriculum, candidates would be totally incapable of creating a meaningful educational setting and experience (Safouan 2000). This nineteenth-century theory of institutions is one of the cornerstones of the Berlin Institute and model of education. Its institutional structure, educational philosophy and model, and scientific view of history and psychoanalysis has remained virtually unchanged since 1920, longstanding whispers of discontent in the analytic community notwithstanding. For the past 80 years, the quantitative logic of its technocratic rationality has defined the framework for debating differences in thinking about psychoanalytic education with the major focus of the debate centering on the frequency standard of the training analysis: Is the *real* training analysis defined by meeting two, three, or four times per week? And which frequency of meetings produces the *real* psychoanalyst?

**The Exercise of Authoritarianism and Power
Beyond the Walls of the Institute**

The exercise of authoritarianism and power has more recently extended beyond the walls of the institute. In the summer of 2001, the consortium, a coalition representing the pedagogical and political interests of the four major psychoanalytic associations in the United States, adopted national standards and regulations for psychoanalytic education and training. National health-care accreditation standards now define and regulate the selection and eligibility of candidates (mental health professionals); the extensive didactic course work (3 years minimum); the frequency and duration of the training analysis (three times/week for 3 years minimum); and the supervised control cases (two adult cases, three times/week minimum). Also, the training institute formally assumes the responsibility for evaluating the candidate's educational experiences through the Candidate Progression Committee. In adopting these standards, psychoanalytic education becomes more entrenched in its own technocracy, further infantilizes the candidates-in-training, and more narrowly restricts the diversity of thinking in our educational institutions. *And more and more frequently I found myself thinking of the Lobo Brigade as they appeared and disappeared into the thick foggy mist.*

Standards standardize, regulations regulate, and institutions institutionalize—and infantilize. Indeed, the former president of the International Psychoanalytic Association, Otto Kernberg's, critique of psychoanalytic education speaks not only to this infantilization of candidates-in-training but also to the cocoon-like isolation of our educational institutions from the intellectual advances of other disciplines during the twentieth century (Kernberg 2000), and, it could be added, the intellectual advances within our own discipline of psychoanalysis (Kavanaugh 1999a). Through its institutionalized power relations in the larger community, organized psychoanalysis now represents the identity, purpose, and ethics of a psychoanalyst as exclusively those of a mental health professional who has graduated from an accredited institute. With the adoption of national health-care accreditation standards, the consortium's educratic rationality answers some rather perplexing and confounding questions left over from the past century: *What is psychoanalysis?* Psychoanalysis is a health-care profession, or a specialty thereof. *What is psychoanalytic education?* Psychoanalytic education is the demonstrated competence of those educational experiences taking place in an institute meeting health-care and accreditation standards. *Who is a psychoanalyst?* A psychoanalyst is a mental health professional who graduates from an accredited institute. Through this rather circular reasoning, the consortium achieves certain political objectives in its advancement of psychoanalysis as a medical specialty; endorses philosophical assumptions supportive of a positivist's view of history, knowledge, and science; and continues psychoanalytic education into the twenty-first century in the science and pathology tradition of the Berlin Institute, the tradition providing the organizing conceptualization, purpose, content, and format for psychoanalytic education and training since 1920 (Kavanaugh 2001). The authoritarian exercise of political power by organized psychoanalysis now extends beyond the walls of the Institute to trump the innovative advances in educational theory, psychoanalytic thinking, and conceptual developments in other related disciplines during the past century.

The triangulation among analyst, institute, and candidate legitimized in the winter of 1923–24 now interweaves with an equally complex triangulation of analyst, institute, and government legitimized in the summer of 2001. The institutional discourse of organized psychoanalysis now joins with various governmental agencies to standardize, regulate, and further institutionalize psychoanalytic education and training. The analyst as a health-care professional constructs our identities as practitioners and educators; implicitly and explicitly prescribes the nature and purpose of psychoanalytic education; and standardizes, homogenizes, and qualitizes the pedagogical strategies of the analytic culture. Moving ever forward, the consortium now seeks to establish an independent and autonomous National Accrediting Board in Psychoanalysis. Given the history of licensing in the health-care professions, a government-issued license to practice psychoanalysis looms on the horizon for all psychoanalysts. The political, philosophical, and economic question of the right to train seems to have been answered: only accredited institutes will be able to train and certify candidates to receive a government-issued license to practice psychoanalysis. Another question, however, awaits its answer: Do the authoritarian practices of our educational institutions, guided by an aloof technocratic rationality, combine with rather arrogant claims to being the only legitimate sources of education and truth lend substance to the perception of their graduate-analysts as authoritarian, aloof, and arrogant?

If psychoanalysis is what our educational and political institutions profess it to be, then psychoanalysis in the U.S. is a medical way of thinking with conceptions of people signified and housed in the numbered and alphabetized structures of diseases, disorders, and deficiencies. The *Diagnostic and Statistical Manual of Mental Disorders*, 4th edi-tion (DSM-IV) stands as a monument to this shared communal pre-occupation with psychopathology, treatment, and curative factors. The interweave of ideology, power, and knowledge that characterizes the pedagogical philosophy and practices within the institute now extend beyond its walls in the form of national health-care accreditation stan-dards for education and training. As our institutes qualify practitioners for a government-issued license to practice psychoanalysis, however, it becomes all the more important to speak to these questions: What are the intellectual and conceptual bases underlying these qualifications to practice psychoanalysis? What are the theoretical and philosophical assumptions underlying the truth claims of their therapeutic bodies of knowledges?

PSYCHOANALYTIC BODIES OF KNOWLEDGES: PHILOSOPHICAL AND THEORETICAL ASSUMPTIONS

It is indeed precisely philosophical discourse that we have to challenge and disrupt, inasmuch as this discourse sets forth the law for all others, inas-much as it constitutes the discourse on discourses. . . . This domination of the philosophic logos stems in large part from its power to reduce all others to the economy of the Same [emphasis added].
Luce Irigaray, *This Sex Which Is Not One*

It has been greatly underappreciated, if not generally unrecognized, that the medical model of psychoanalysis is grounded in philosophy, the philosophic tradition of logical positivism. Its philosophical assump-tions of naturalism, linear time, determinism, atomistic thinking, no-mothetic principles, and an amorality in science are those that underlie the modernistic systems of thinking of a nineteenth-century worldview or model (Kavanuagh 1999a, Slife 1997). Infused with a medical ide-ology, these largely unquestioned philosophical assumptions unite to structure the epistemological and intellectual foundations of the medi-cal model of psychoanalysis. The shadow of a nineteenth-century meta-physics continues to be cast over the truth claims of our psychoanalytic bodies of knowledges . . . *The Lobo Brigade was a living and breathing monument to the ways of thinking of that earlier time.*

A Culture of Positivism and the Rational Narrative: Naturalism

The *Studies on Hysteria* (Breuer and Freud 1895) was birthed in the larger cultural context of latter nineteenth-century Germany, a culture of positivism in which there was little, if any, tolerance for departures from reason, logic, and rational explanations in the understanding of the world and physical phenomena. The assumptions held and the modes of inquiry pursued by Breuer and Freud in the *Studies on Hysteria* (1895) were based on a nineteenth-century worldview in which the epistemological methods of knowing interwove in the cultural fabric with the philosophy of naturalism, which provided the philosophical context for scientific inquiry and advances in knowledge. Naturalism assumes that the world is mind-independent and knowable, and that it functions by rational and natural laws according to the intricate, predetermined, and preordained designs of nature (Ronca and Curr 1997). A grand and unifying rationality underlies these intricate and complex designs. Nature was understood as a rational and intelligent workman, with its creations possessing just those powers and attributes permitting generation, growth, and evolutionary progression (Robinson 1989). Further, naturalism assumes a unified theory of nature, life, and science in which all natural phenomena are governed by predictive, rational, and natural laws. People and society are assumed to be part of this natural order and design; the world and people function according to common principles and rational laws, as do all other natural phenomena in the physical world. In a culture of positivism, the principles of rationality in the natural sciences are seen as vastly superior to the hermeneutic principles underlying the more speculative social sciences (Giroux 1997, 1991). Freud was embedded in this historical context, construction, and contingency. His psychological insights and theories were produced within the contingency of this militant rationalism and positivism.

With the publication of the *Studies on Hysteria* (1895), psychoanalysis was founded as an historical discipline. For Freud (1914), Breuer's cathartic treatment of Anna O. revealed "the fundamental fact that the symptoms of hysterical patients are founded upon scenes in their past lives" (p. 8). With its publication, a revolutionary way of understanding the cause-effect relationships of mental life was introduced: hysterics suffer from reminiscences. Far from being arbitrary and capricious, symptoms had rhyme and reason and meaning and purpose;

the past events of Anna O.'s life were of causal significance in the formation of her current symptoms. In Freud's new conception of mind, the historical approach was the primary mode of scientific inquiry; a most rational method for understanding a most irrational content matter had been discovered. Anna O.'s reminiscences were filtered through an historical mode of thinking and comprehending. And her reminiscences were understood from the prevailing perspective of the times, an historical positivism situated in the rationalist's narrative.

The rationalist's epistemology prevailed in psychoanalysis as it did in the science, philosophy, and art of the times. In commenting on the literature of those times, Walter Kendrick (1996), professor of English at Fordham University, notes that the rationalist's perspective contextualizing the *Studies on Hysteria* (1895) was quite consistent with the narrative in English fiction written during the middle to latter part of the nineteenth century. One of the core assumptions of being contained in the stories of people in the *Studies on Hysteria*, for example, was the idea that there is a fixed essentialist foundation in a pre-given and rational nature:

> No matter how much villainy or foolishness came into the story, both storyteller and audience stood aloof, rationally observing them, sustained by a logical, linear style of writing that asserted the triumph of reason even when it narrated irrationality. [Kendrick 1996, p. 106]

Freud's sane, intelligent, and judicious voice that speaks to the reader of the *Studies on Hysteria*, Kendrick asserts, never failed to assume that Anna O.—and the reader—inherently possessed those same qualities of rationality. The rationalist's assumptions, values, and beliefs organized a psychodynamic way of thinking; the rationalist's grammar and syntax structured the set of rules accounting for the formation of symptoms; and the rationalist's voice narrated the irrational content matter of Anna O.'s symptoms from the truth of historical positivism. The rationalist's epistemology rests on certain theoretical and philosophical assumptions:

Historical and Causal Realities: Nomothetic Principles

As a scientist-historian in the positivist tradition, the analyst inquires into a real, knowable, and singular past through the historical approach, discovering historical events as found objects in the hallways of time past, and then bearing witness to their having occurred. In the positivist's view of history, "The objects of the historian's inquiry are precisely that, objects, out there in a real and single past. Historical controversy in no way compromises their ontological integrity" (Gay 1974, p. 210).

The analyst functions as an historian of the individual's history, deciphering her or his personal record of past events and then speaking as if from outside the story being told. In this positivist view of history, the language of the analyst simply refers to the found historical objects and their causal influences in the current symptom picture. The assumptions of historical and causal realities in the positivist tradition make it possible for the analyst to trace back to earlier or more primitive stages of development the origins of symptoms as Darwin had traced back the origins of organisms functionally resembling each other to the same primitive structures (Ritvo 1990). These assumptions of historical and causal realities made it possible to develop as a nomothetic discipline. As a derivation from the Greek *nomos*, meaning *lawful*, and *thetikos*, meaning *knowledge*, the term *nomothetic* translates as "lawful knowledge," "lawful thesis," or "dogma" (Lemiell 1987). As a branch of the biological sciences, psychoanalysis continued to model itself on the empirical methods and assumptions of the natural sciences for the greater part of the past century.

Linear Time and Determinism

Linearized assumptions of time and place and logic and causality laid a deterministic foundation in psychoanalytic thinking in which past trauma psychically determines, of necessity, present symptoms or deficits. In the positivist's tradition, temporal succession and spatial proximity are axiomatic in determining the causal explanations of mental phenomena. Linearized notions of time, place, logic, and causality provide the foundational assumptions for the medical model's organizing conceptual framework of symptomatology, etiology, and psychopathology in which behaviors considered abnormal are understood as symptoms (symptomatology) caused by the repression of archaic traumatizing events (etiology) that interfere with current adaptations to the objective and knowable world (psychopathology). In the *Studies on Hysteria* (1895), for example, past traumatizing events in Anna O.'s life are located at specific points along a continuum of linear time and space. These past events, in turn, determine her later symptoms; that which precedes in time is related to that which follows in a causal, deterministic, and evolutionary manner. All scientific processes, including the view of history as a veridical science, must occur along this invisible line of linear time (Slife 1997). Anna O.'s symptoms were understood as disguised representations of past traumatizing events, correspondent to the actual people and events of her past life. Her symptoms were contingent on—and produced by—these archaic events; her current symptoms had meaning and purpose that derived from an earlier time and place. This spatiotemporal framework also makes it possible to infer past events, retrospectively, from present symptoms, thereby enabling accurate and precise genetic reconstructions of what must have happened to have resulted in the current configuration of symptoms.

The medical model of psychoanalysis continues to rather naively assume that the individual's history is empirical in which what happens and what will happen result largely from what has happened in the person's earlier surround of childhood. Such dogmatic unities as the past preceding the present as cause precedes effect have been foundational in our conceptions of mind, causality, and science since the publication of the *Studies on Hysteria* in 1895, presuppositions that have remained largely unquestioned and unexamined in the analytic community. Linearized assumptions of time, place, logic, and causality are premised on Newtonian conceptions of space and time and are understood as separate and physically independent, autonomous entities. Our modernistic theories of mind and causation developed within this spatial and temporal context. Rooted in a Newtonian framework, such causal theories commit psychoanalytic thinking to a Cartesian view of mind in which actions are understood as the consequence of interactions between the outer objective states of the physical (reality) and the inner subjective states of the mental (fantasies) (Child 1996). The theoretical and philosophical assumptions underlying this Newtonian-Cartesian worldview continues to premise much of the thinking in the modernistic psychologies of psychoanalysis, e.g. Drive, Ego, Object, and Self.

Amorality and a Logical Atomism

For the greater part of the past century, the psychoanalytic community held science as its epistemic ideal. Consistent with the empiricist's thesis and doctrine, analytic theory, process, and interpretation must transcend the analyst's subjectivity. They should attain an objective scientific standard as if science and its methodology are unmediated by values, presumptions, and ideological context, indeed as if scientific knowledge itself is mind-independent and value neutral, that is, amoral. Put another way, nomothetic principles and laws governing mental life are believed to simply exist "out there" in an objective and knowable world, awaiting their discovery as do the laws of nature and society. In this way, the modernistic myth is perpetuated that research, science, and the empirical knowledge generated in the social sciences exist outside of historical, cultural, and socioeconomic influences; empirical validation of psychoanalytic constructs is essential to validate the discipline as a science of mind.

In the prevailing medical ideology, empirical research rests on the assumption that everything the person experiences can be reductively analyzed into component elements and the interrelationships between those elements, with the result that mental processes are reduced in complexity and simplified into predictable, measurable, and lawlike behaviors (Russell 1985). Logical atomism walks hand in hand with logical positivism; both assume that people are the sum total of their atomistic experiences. Premised on these philosophical assumptions, science can hold everything in its objectivizing gaze as it discovers linearized knowledge and explanations. Indeed for the hard-core reductionist, the soul can be empiricized; in the neurosciences, the soul is reduced to the whirring activity of the brain. The psychology implicit in such causal theories, however, is thoroughly Cartesian, as is their epistemology (Hyman 1992).

THE INSTITUTE AS THE KEEPER OF TRUTH: THE INTERWEAVING OF IDEOLOGY, POWER, AND KNOWLEDGE

Institutional training is probably antithetical to analysis.
Adam Limentani, *Journal of the American Psychoanalytic Association* (1974)

A Cartesian Construction of the Subject

In the Cartesian world, the subject is constructed as fully conscious, autonomous, coherent, and self-knowable, and as speaking without being spoken (Sarup 1993). Identity and being are found in thought and the rational mind; thinking is the essence of human nature: *I think, therefore I am*. In the Cartesian world, a self-evident and dichotomous metaphysics is foundational in thinking and speaking about the world and people; dichotomous distinctions between the sacred and profane, the mind and body, and the outer objective and inner subjective are developed in a binary system of logic, beliefs, and values. Descartes distinguished the outer physical world from the inner world of the mental and claimed to prove that the physical has a separate existence from the mental (Clarke 1997). In so doing, the subject of modernity was constituted as a rational subject with the body subordinated to rational thought, a dualistic solution that privileges mind over body. Subsequent scientific preoccupations have been with the interactions that take place between the mind and body. Thus, from this perspective, the conceptual has primacy over the physical; cognition, thinking, and objectivity take primacy over passion, intuition, and subjectivity. In the Cartesian tradition, psychoanalytic education is an education of the mind, as the body is not considered to be a source of knowing, thinking, or knowledge (Capra 1982, Hooks 1994, Maher and Tetreault 1994).

Language, Knowledge, and Truth

In a culture of positivism, bodies of knowledges are produced and organized around the assumptions of a metaphysics of presence in which "something Real could be represented in thought, the Real was understood to be an external or universal subject existing 'out there,' and 'truth' was understood to be correspondence to it" (Flax 1990, p. 34). In the positivist's worldview, there is only one world, which functions by the same natural, universal, and rational laws as do society and people. This scientific vision of reality and people constitutes the only legitimate, neutral, and objective way of seeing, knowing, and thinking about the world and people; science and its methodology is the only paradigm of knowledge production. A positivist rationality speaks to the technical mastery of people through the scientific production of knowledge and its acquisition: the assumptions underlying a metaphysics of presence structure a linearized relationship to language, knowledge, theory, and truth. In the fixed, static, and linearized Newtonian world, language is object-based and knowledge is understood as objective, mirror-like reflections of reality discovered-as-it-is. The word corresponds to the object it represents and simply reflects the object or the causal relationship as it exists out there in reality. Truth, understood as discovered rational knowledge, transforms knowledge into a scientific thing-like object that corresponds to the real world. In this way, knowledge takes on the appearance of being objective, bounded, and context free, far removed from the individual, political, and cultural traditions that structure its meaning. A positivist's relationship to the world and reality and to the word and knowledge makes psychoanalytic knowledge knowable, teachable, and learnable. The positivist's relationship to language, knowledge, theory, and truth defined the ABCs of knowledge production and its acquisition in the institute.

As knowledge is cumulative, psychoanalytic theory can be continuously developed, refined, and advanced as new discoveries are made. Eventually, theory comes to stand for the scientifically discovered (nomothetic) laws, concepts, and principles about psychopathological conditions, their causes, and symptoms. A theoretical reality corresponding to objective clinical observations can be constructed and handed from one person to another. Bodies of knowledges consisting of prethought thoughts, prepackaged theoretical formularies, and predetermined ways by which others "ought to be" can be objectively recorded in the sacred text of truth discovered, inscribed in the institute's standardized curriculum, and taught as discovered rational knowledge about the historical and causal realities producing the various symptom pictures (Kavanaugh 1998). Derived from an empirical analytic discourse, these bodies of knowledges are taught as factual, axiomatic givens, inherently devoid of ethical values, and existing outside of a cultural or historical context. In the United States, particularly, the bodies of knowledges of the analyst have become more certain, predictive, and explanatory; theory has become linked to a search for the truth at the .01 level of confidence. The positivist's relationship to language, knowledge, and truth encourages the learning of received wisdoms; unfortunately, it also discourages reflective thinking.

In the analytic culture, science is the paradigm of knowledge production; the institute is the site of knowledge acquisition. In the positivist's tradition, a privileged relationship to knowing the truth of self (the training analysis) and other (didactics and supervision) are integral aspects of psychoanalytic education and training. As the only legitimate center for psychoanalytic education, the institute became the keeper of theoretical truth, teaching this truth through the science of teaching—or pedagogy. As a derivation from the Greek *paidos* meaning *boy* and *agogos* meaning *guide*, pedagogy literally translates as *to guide the boy*. The institutional wisdom and oversight imposed by the training committee of the Berlin Society in the winter of 1923–24 continues to guide the candidate through these scientifically discovered bodies of knowledge of self and other, irrespective of the particular theoretical reality. The candidate passively receives and learns knowledge; the teacher actively imparts and teaches this knowledge. The institute is the keeper of the theoretical truth, its institutional discourse speaks the voice of this truth, and wrapped within the cloak of the truth of its theoretical reality is found the moral piety of those who know—and those who are in the process of coming to know—the reality (theoretical), the good (ethics), and the truth (knowledge) for others through the predesigned, preapproved, and presanctioned program of study that speaks the analyst in its preordained image as a social scientist-artist.

Bodies of Knowledges and the Identity Formation of the Analyst

Does the institute's educational philosophy, milieu, and bodies of scientific knowledge unwittingly nurture and cultivate the image of the analyst as arrogant, authoritarian, and aloof? Pedagogical strategies are organized around the image of the analyst as a social scientist-artist. In so doing, they fulfill Freud's legacy that every psychoanalytic proposition be the consequence of a dialectic that blends scientifically based knowledge with the creative artistry of humanistic compassion (Bornstein 1985). In the learning and practice of psychoanalysis as a science, the analytic setting is implicitly, if not explicitly, understood as one might conceive of a scientific laboratory in which the analyst seeks to understand the psychic laws by which the raw data of the patient's associations, moods, or states of mind are organized. A scientific methodology modeled on rational intuitionism, in the Greek and medieval philosophic tradition, provides the framework for listening, understanding, and responding: the analyst listens to or observes the raw data from the patient, formulates a hypothesis based on sequenced observations made during the session, interpretively intervenes as one might manipulate an independent variable, and rules out or confirms the accuracy of the intervention(s) as determined by the subsequent data of the patient's thoughts, associations, or states of mind. In the positivist tradition, the scientific method is the model of data collection in psychoanalysis; an empirical-medical system of thinking developed that validates itself through its own linearized theory and methodology.

Those committed to the positivist-scientist tradition of psychoanalysis continue to press for a "canon of inference" that would provide a more scientific basis for the psychoanalyst's interpretations. This canon of inference would

> represent an evolving refinement of the correspondence criteria underlying clinical interventions. If some day we developed such a methodology, we could substantially improve the present dismal state of our evidential support for our theoretic and clinical claims because we *could state explicitly what the patient said or did that was the basis for a specific intervention.* [Boesky 2004, p. 8, emphasis added]

According to Boesky, the purpose of such a canon of inference is to develop a better methodology for single-hour process research and to then successfully teach the correspondence criteria for specific interpretations in our institutes. In this way, lawful knowledge is discovered, fostering the illusion that the nomothetic principle(s) and law(s) hold for each of many individuals. A positivist rationality speaks to the technical mastery of psychoanalytic theories of human development in our educational institutions and of human beings in the analytic discourse.

In certain key respects, there is very little difference between the twenty-first-century empiricist and the nineteenth-century rationalist: both share the same assumption of a general correspondence between language and reality. They differ only in the way to establish what the nature of the world might be. The empiricist concludes by actual logical analysis via science and its methodology rather than concluding by rationally asserting the self-evident truth by a priori reasoning. For the twenty-first-century empiricist, a Cartesian rational objectivism, resting on a Newtonian-based science, method, and explanation, displaces the nineteenth-century Aristotelian rational intuitionism, resting on intellectual insight. Both, however, are scientists in the positivists' tradition: both are committed to rigorous techniques, mathematical expression, and law-like regularities that support only one form of scientific inquiry. In both the empiricist and rationalist traditions, the task remains the same for the analyst as a social scientist-artist: (s)he searches for the repeatable structures and lawful relationships existing between internal mental events and the external social realities that determined or caused those events. Valid knowledge of and about these historical and causal realities is possible only if the knowledge discovered is objective and scientific. Thus, in the quest for knowledge, historical truth must be separated from narrative truth—fact separated from fiction—as the analyst is obligated to scientifically validate the causal connections between current symptoms or developmental deficits and the earlier events of childhood. Consistent with the dualistic Cartesian construction of mind and body, the analyst ultimately must validate the links between the mental functions of the person and the neural substrate of the organism (Gedo 1999, Rubenstein 1997).

Questioning the Interweave of Ideology, Power, and Knowledge

Is there a relationship between the interweave of ideology, power, and knowledge in the institute model of psychoanalytic education, on the one hand, and the image of the analyst as authoritarian, arrogant, and aloof, on the other? Positivist principles, standards, and correspondence criterion have stood like an iron-spiked fence around the perimeter of the analytic community producing bodies of knowledges that speak of the analyst as the knower of the master discourse of personality development, the causal factors underlying various pathological conditions, and treatment and its curative factors. Such an authoritative relationship to knowledge places the analyst in a privileged relationship to the theoretical truth of and for the other. Through psychoanalytic education, the analyst, for example, can know the meaning of a symptom, the causes of the symptom, and the degree of pathology in the childhood surround that resulted in the symptom—without even meeting with the person—and in so doing lend considerable substance, it would seem, to the perception of the analyst as arrogant, aloof, and authoritarian. The social scientist-artist continues as the image around which psychoanalytic education and training is organized. This conception of scientist, however, is rooted in a late–nineteenth-century social science and the conception of artist is rooted in a mid–nineteenth-century view of art and fiction. As noted by Donald Spence (1987), the analyst occupies an epistemologically neutral middle ground that supposedly exists somewhere in between this science and art, claiming the privileges of both scientist and artist yet refusing to be held to the critical standards that obtain in either.

In the hallways of the institute, knowledge is power, as understood by Nietzsche (1901) in his concept of the will to power and as elaborated by Foucault (1972) in his discourse on the relationship between power and knowledge. Succinctly stated, "All thought that pretends to discover 'truth' is but an expression of the will to power, even to domination, of those making the truth-claim over those who are being addressed by them" (Snyder 1988, p. xii).

Unfortunately, the idea that knowledge is power seems embedded in the image of the analyst around which psychoanalytic education is organized. Discovering the secrets of unconscious motivations and the role they play in personality development seems to have seductively contributed to the image of the psychoanalyst who, as a scientist-artist, has the ability to predict and control human behavior. Is there not a certain degree of arrogance and aloofness embedded in this image and understanding of the analyst as a social scientist? Is the illusion of having such omniscient abilities and powers something that might be better off being understood as opposed to being a foundational and integral aspect of the identity formation of the analyst?

Bodies of psychoanalytic knowledges intersect with power when, in the mind of the analyst, normative standards move from how things are to representing truth claims as to how things ought to be for the other, irrespective of one's theoretical truth, that is, Drive, Ego, Object, and Self Psychologies. Further, knowledge intersects with power when the analyst claims the moral justification, obligation, and power to evaluate the other; to signify her or his meaning, purpose, motive, and intent; and then to directly or indirectly influence, if not abridge, an individual's political, social, and personal freedoms and responsibilities (Kavanaugh 1999b). Universalizing and totalizing conceptions of people contain core ethical issues for the analytic practitioner and educator when psychoanalytic theory and practice are based on normative conceptions of people. Indeed, more than simply an epistemological doctrine, positivism "is a potent form of ideology that smothers the tug of conscience and blinds its adherents to the ideological nature of its own frame of reference" (Giroux 1999, p. 20).

Premised on the theoretical and philosophical assumptions of positivism, the institutional discourse of our educratic institutes reflects and embodies the ways of knowing, thinking, and perceiving emblematic of classical epistemology; it reproduces the ways of thinking, perceiving, and knowing about people and life premised on a nineteenth-century view of history, science, and causality (Bevan 1991).

In the United States, psychoanalytic education, theory, and practice are organized around an implicit, if not explicit, expectation of a conformance and compliance to certain theoretically anticipated outcomes. As suggested by Kincheloe, the consequences for psychoanalytic education have been quite stultifying:

> In the culture of positivism, education becomes a form of social regulation that guides humans toward destinies that preserve the status quo. Reflection on the formation of "what is" vis-à-vis "what should be" is dismissed from the positivistic culture. In other words, *consciousness of historical forces and their relationship to everyday life has no place in the technocratic rationality of the culture of positivism.* [Kincheloe et al., cited in Giroux 1997, p. x, emphasis added]

The interweave of ideology, power, and knowledge in psychoanalytic education appears to have molded the historical discipline of psychoanalysis into an unreflective and uncritical discipline that has failed to question its most cherished assumptions, theoretical beliefs, and ways of thinking. Our educational institutions appear to have unwittingly encouraged in its candidates a distinctly antihistorical attitude and relationship to individual historical consciousness. How could this be? If psychological laws, explanations, and meanings about a person can be discovered independently of that person's cultural context, then much of the current thinking and theorizing in the analytic community is historically neutral and unwittingly encourages an uncritical reflection upon oneself. Empirically based psychologies, formularies, and wisdoms have become ahistorical, universalizing, and impersonal knowledges about people as if such knowledge exists independently of human beings and the historical context in which it was produced. A positivist mode of rationality and history operates, paradoxically, to undercut the value of history and undermine the importance of individual historical consciousness and insight . . . *And more and more frequently I found myself thinking of the Lobo Brigade as they appeared and disappeared into the thick foggy mist.*

In many respects, our educational institutions have become echo chambers of received wisdoms, recycling analytic orthodoxies that rest on Cartesian-Newtonian assumptions about people and life, and housing people in our alphabetized diagnostic and statistical manuals. Critical thinking atrophies in such a technocratic system as individual judgment and decision-making are co-opted by the institutional discourse. A lack of critical thinking is fostered and encouraged as ethical decision-making and historical consciousness are separated from the everyday lives of the psychoanalytic educator, practitioner, and candidate, except, of course, when it might further the interests of those vested in the institutional discourse. The need and concern for individual theories of ideology, ethics, and political action are far removed from ourselves in our increasingly standardized and qualitized analytic culture. Does the consciousness of historical forces and their relationship to everyday life no longer have a place in our educratic institutions? Contextualized by a positivist-medical ideology, our educational institutions have remained frozen in time resting on the conceptual foundations of a nineteenth-century worldview. And frozen in time, they are being left behind.

WHISPERS OF DISCONTENT WITHIN THE WALLS OF THE PSYCHOANALYTIC INSTITUTE: THE TRAINING ANALYSIS

The training analyst is regarded as possessing the psychoanalytic equivalent of omniscience. . . . Consciously or unconsciously, the mythology of the institutes infiltrates the training program. . . . Mythologies, moreover, do not remain suspended in mid-air. They are translated into institutional practices.
Jacob Arlow, *Journal of the American Psychoanalytic Association* (1969)

Shortly after the institutionalization of psychoanalysis in the winter of 1923–24, whispers of discontent with our pedagogical philosophy and practices began echoing through the hallways of our training institutions, a discontent that centered on their inability to match their institutional forms of training with psychoanalytic theory (Safouan 2000). For the most part, this discontent centered on the training analysis, the educational experience that provides the candidate with the opportunity to come to intimately know something about the unconscious process and dynamic of self, the heart of psychoanalytic education. With the consortium's adoption of health-care accreditation standards, the institute secures the right to train. Within the institute, the training analyst is the only one with the right to train the candidate through the mandatory training analysis.

Jacqueline Rose (2000) has deftly gathered succinct comments and critiques of psychoanalytic training that stretch back through the hallways of time to the very beginning of psychoanalytic education and training at the Berlin Institute. She cites, for example, from Max Eitingon's almost apologetic report to the international training committee that "nobody learns pure psychoanalysis as such," and further that "the point in which institutional or didactic analysis differs from therapeutic analysis . . . is not in having a special technique but, as we say in Berlin, in having an additional aim, which supersedes or goes in hand with the therapeutic aim" (Eitingon 1927, cited in Rose 2000, p. 4). An additional aim? Can psychoanalysis be taught through the training analysis? Is there not an inherent contradiction between having a didactic aim and a therapeutic aim in the training analysis? In the early beginnings of the Berlin Institute, Hans Sachs, the first training analyst, legitimized two goals for the institutional or didactic analysis: "One was to transmit the understanding of the unconscious which had been so laboriously accumulated by Freud and his co-workers, and the other was *to enforce absolute obedience to the theoretical position of the school*" (Fine 1987, p. 93, emphasis added).

Is the training analysis little more than an institutionalized form of indoctrination into the theoretical truth of the training analyst or the institute? Controversies about the training analysis have been at the heart of all dissensions and splits within the psychoanalytic movement since the founding of the Berlin Institute in 1920. And the discontent with the training analysis is long-standing, reflected, for example, in Anna Freud's explicit critique of "the deviations from the classical technique when analyzing candidates" (1938), and Theresa Benedek's observation that "the problem of teaching through psychoanalysis" is something no one wrote about, "as if it were a tabooed subject" (1969) (cited in Rose 2000, pp. 2–3). These and other more recent whispers of discontent gather into a strong historical voice of dissatisfaction with the institute model of education and training and, in particular, with the cross-purposes and objectives of the training analysis.

Lewin and Ross (1960) speak to the long-standing history of institutional ambiguity and confusion surrounding the training analysis. They describe the candidate and the analyst as situated in two conceptual frameworks and systems that at different times oppose, complement, and alternate with each other. At once, the candidate is situated in the untenable position of being the object of analytic inquiry for the purpose of change or cure and the object of didactic instruction for the purpose of learning theory and technique. In the course of the training analysis, when is the candidate a candidate, a patient, or an analysand? All too often, it appears that the additional aim of the institutional or didactic analysis takes precedence over the therapeutic aim, with the training analysis becoming little more than the institutional conduit for transmitting the particular worldview of the analyst or the institute, unfortunately at the expense of listening and translating the candidate's associative material. The candidate's acquisition of the prescribed theoretical truth via the training analysis often leads to the development of a "false expertise," as discussed by Kirsner (2001):

> Institutional "false expertise" invokes the aura of anointment where training analysts passed down received truth through an esoteric pipeline depending on genealogy instead of function. Quasireligious thinking and politics rush in to fill the gap between the level of claimed knowledge that affords qualification and the far lower level of real knowledge. [p. 195]

Does this aura of an anointment lend substance to the perception and attitudes of the analyst as authoritarian, arrogant, and aloof? That is, is this "false expertise" of graduate-analysts related to their receiving the theoretical truth-to-be-learned at the expense of their continuing ignorance of a more intimate knowledge of self? Does this false expertise develop into a compensatory arrogance conveyed, at once, through an authoritarian attitude and an aloof posturing of self as the omniscient knower of the master discourse of other? And, in the radiant aura of becoming an anointed one, does the arrogance of omnipotence serve as a mask to disguise the ominous-impotence of ignorance?

As suggested by Safouan (2000), the candidate's free associations become enveloped in an institutional(ized) code of silence in which unconscious process and dynamic are not permitted a voice in the training analysis. Kirsner (2000, 2001) states his belief that the position of the training analyst maintains power based on hierarchical patronage and anointment. Unfortunately and all too often, muting the voice of unconscious process and dynamic unwittingly becomes the unspoken educational experience of the candidate. Is it possible to engage in an analytic discourse within the walls of the institute? How free are the candidate's associations when they might clash with the theoretical beliefs or institutional duties and ethical responsibilities of the training analyst? Perhaps an unconscious collusion among the analyst, analysand, and institute to neither acknowledge nor state certain unconscious experiences in the training analysis underlies the frequent phenomenon of the candidate's getting a training analysis for the institute and, later, a personal analysis for him- or herself. In such instances, the training analysis becomes little more than a course requirement to be completed for graduation. And in such instances, it would seem that the iron-spiked fence surrounding the institute refuses entry to and acknowledgment of the candidate's unconscious process and dynamic in the training analysis.

Training analysts are situated in an equally untenable position between their responsibilities to the institute, on the one hand, and to the candidate, on the other. As agents of the institute, they have certain institutional and ethical responsibilities, not the least of which is the responsibility to evaluate the candidate's suitability and progress as a psychoanalyst-in-the-process-of-becoming. As agents of the candidate, however, they have the inherently contradictory responsibility of listening with evenly suspended attention to the candidate's free associations with neither therapeutic agenda nor ambition. With the adoption of the consortium's education and training standards, training analysts are now in an even more untenable position as they now take on additional legal and ethical responsibilities for the candidate's education. In so doing, they become triple agents of the institute, the candidate, and the government. Do the consortium's standards not lead to tacit expectations, if not explicit pressures, for the candidate's free associations to conform with the particular sociopolitical ideology of the training analyst, the institute, or the governmental licensing entity? The added legal, ethical, and political realities of an ever-broadening institutional discourse place even more emphasis on training analysts for quality assurance and to ensure an outcome-based analysis rather than simply listening and translating the candidate's associative material. This is not to suggest that the training analyst cannot be part of an institute model of education. It is to suggest, however, that the institute model of education cannot be a part of the training analyst's identity as an analyst. The training analyst's allegiance must be always and only to the analytic discourse and the associative-interpretive process, an increasingly difficult, if not impossible, task given the adoption of the consortium's standards for psychoanalytic education.

Power, Authoritarianism, and the Training Analysis

Those in hierarchical structures have a tendency to seek legitimacy from those situated higher up in the hierarchy. The institute, for example, seeks power and authority from the government to validate its scientific vision of reality and people, its empirically derived bodies of theoretical knowledge, and the analyst as a health-care professional via a government-issued license. In so doing, the institute's version and vision of psychoanalysis is legitimized. Within the institute, the same tendency to seek legitimacy from those higher up in the hierarchy holds for the training analyst in relation to the institute and the candidate in relation to the training analyst; achieving legitimacy in this hierarchical arrangement translates into the illusion of accumulating power and status, privilege and prerogative, and economic security and well-being as one ascends the hierarchical ladder.

The question of training analysts' power and their role in granting legitimacy to the candidate cannot be separated from the question of the candidate's future career; economics contextualize the training analysis and its outcome. For example, will the candidate receive the necessary endorsement(s) to graduate, receive a government-issued license to practice, teach at the institute, receive referrals, publish in the first-tiered journals, and eventually become a training analyst? In the culture of our educational institutions, an outcome-based education and training analysis are good career moves (Kavanaugh 1998, 1999c). "Power, patronage, referrals, and income are intertwined with the question of succession, of being anointed with legitimacy and money through referrals. Anointment to the status of training analyst provides candidates, which brings greater legitimacy and allows more practice with four- or five-times-per-week patients" (Kirsner 2001, p. 206). But at what cost to the profession when the technocratic rationality and discourse has a vested interest in sustaining hierarchical principles and in denying the significance of an individualized historical consciousness? There is a certain ironic symmetry to the notion that those who study a psychoanalysis of conformity and compliance are expected to conform and comply to the prethought and preapproved ways of thinking, being, and knowing advanced in the educational institutions in which they study. But at what cost to the candidate when institutionalized codes of silence collude to ensure a "not knowing" of unconscious process and dynamic in the training analysis? . . . *And more and more frequently I found myself thinking of the Lobo Brigade as they appeared and disappeared into the thick foggy mist.*

If power corrupts and absolute power corrupts absolutely, then the question arises: Has the institute's absolute power over the candidates' education, beginning in Berlin in the winter of 1923–24, corrupted our educational institutions and pedagogical practices in an absolute sense? Admonitions to be more sensitive to the exercise of power and its abuses in training programs—or to change or exchange the various parts in the institutional structure or philosophy—overlook the complex interweave of ideology, power, and knowledge in the positivist's tradition. Irrespective of how benevolent, benign, or empathic a particular administrator, training analyst, or supervisor might be, the institutional structure, educational philosophy, and image of the analyst remain rooted in a nineteenth-century worldview. A positivist ideology continues to dominate each aspect of our educational institutions, theories, and researches. In perhaps the most thoroughgoing and revealing account of the political histories and inner workings of arguably the leading psychoanalytic institutes in the United States affiliated with the American Psychoanaltic Association, Kirsner (2000) concludes that one of the major aspects underlying the problems of such institutions is that "a basically humanistic discipline has conceived and touted itself as a positivist science while organising itself institutionally as a religion. . . . Ultimately, this fundamental misunderstanding in the analytic culture has retarded the development of the field with psychoanalytic education becoming akin to the process of anointment" (p. 233).

ALTERNATIVE MODELS OF EDUCATION

We are difference . . . our reason is the difference of discourses, our history the difference of times, our selves the difference of masks. That difference, far from being the forgotten and recoverable origin, is this dispersion that we are and make.

Michel Foucault

Culture and psychoanalysis are inseparable. As times change, so do the sociocultural and philosophical assumptions underlying that which constitutes psychoanalysis in each of its aspects: theory, practice, education, and ethics. Indeed, the culture produces the psychoanalysis most needed by the culture. Prior to the 1970s, for example, there was a general consensus in this country as to the description and definition of psychoanalysis as theory and practice. Positivist notions of history, science, and causality provided the largely unquestioned assumptions for the development of psychoanalytic theory; correspondence theory, rules, and evidence constructed an objective framework for the collection of data that matched with the theoretical truth from a positivist perspective. For the past quarter of a century, however, the mythology of psychoanalysis as a positivist-medical science has been unraveling as the conceptual foundations of its theories, ethics, and education have been questioned, challenged, and rethought outside the positivist's iron-spiked fence. During this same period of time, science has been moving away from our normative conceptions of people and our existing power structures, grounded in the presumed natural hierarchies of nature (Strenger 1998). Our more contemporary conceptions of people are moving toward more global and interactive models of complex dynamical systems rather than the hierarchical models of yesteryear (Kavanaugh 2000). In adopting national health-care accreditation standards, organized psychoanalysis appears to have overlooked that the very concept and meaning(s) of psychoanalysis have been changing during the past quarter of a century. The consortium's adoption of national health-care standards prematurely forecloses on the questions raised for psychoanalytic education by the current theoretical pluralism in the analytic community.

Contemporary psychoanalysis is characterized by a rich and creative pluralism in conceptualization and theory. A world of differences currently exists between the various theoretical and methodological positions that derive from the more contemporary orientations of existential-humanistic, relational, transpersonal, philosophical, integrationist, and hermeneutic psychologies, to name just a few. These various psychologies rest on different philosophical assumptions, premise different understandings as to the basic nature of people, posit different methods of knowing about people, and assume very different purposes, objectives, and understandings for the analytic discourse. Psychoanalysis has been irreversibly altered by these different ways of seeing, knowing, and representing life, people, and reality. Clearly, the days of a monolithic psychoanalysis are far behind us, if indeed there ever truly was a monolithic psychoanalysis. The current project of rethinking psychoanalysis includes rethinking the intellectual and conceptual foundations of its bodies of knowledge and also the conditions of the acquisition of those bodies of knowledge. We must bring into question our traditional educational institutions and organizational structures, the underlying assumptions of our educational philosophy and model, and the image of the analyst around which education is organized (Kavanaugh 1995, 1999b,c).

The creative rethinking of psychoanalysis during the past quarter of a century has yet to take up the question of education and training in ways that match our institutional structures and forms of education with the particular concept and meaning of psychoanalysis for which one seeks training (Kavanaugh 1998). As a causal empirical science, for example, psychoanalysis derives from a radically different conceptual framework than does psychoanalysis as an hermeneutic discipline. Causal empirical theories commit us to a Cartesian worldview; an hermeneutic focus is a fundamentally anti-Cartesian perspective. It is virtually impossible to coherently combine both points of view in the same educational philosophy, model, and set of practices. The various answers to the question *What is psychoanalysis?* shape the different answers to the question *What constitutes psychoanalytic education?* What are the educational processes and experiences that contribute to the identity formation of a psychoanalyst as, for example, an existential-humanist, a skeptical phenomenalist-hermeneuticist, or a poet-philosopher and artist? What are the institutional structures and forms of education that match with these distinctly different ways of thinking about psychoanalysis?

A philosophy of differences founded by Nietzsche and Heidegger recognizes that the world is a world of interpretations of the world. The world of differences that characterize our more contemporary understandings of psychoanalysis speaks to the many possible and equally meaningful interpretations of human behavior. Those who aspire to know, translate, and speak the uniqueness and complexity of the analytic discourse must have the opportunity to learn in ways that match their respective theory with its appropriate forms of education. As suggested by the consortium's national health-care accreditation standards for education and training, a positivist-medical ideology trumps the pluralism of contemporary psychoanalysis; one size continues to fit all, unless, of course, it doesn't. Pedagogical, philosophical, and political differences in the United States place the question of psychoanalytic education back into question, the authoritarian exercise of power by organized psychoanalysis notwithstanding. As psychoanalysis is rethought, rewritten, and reinterpreted in the cultural context of the twenty-first century, its theoretical pluralism must have the analytic community's respect and encouragement for a plurality of educational philosophies, models, and strategies (Kavanaugh 1999c, 2001).

In the European community, the diversity of training programs more fully preserves the diverse and interdisciplinary quality of psychoanalysis (Meisels and Shapiro 1990). The faculty-centered model in the Berlin tradition and the student-centered model in the Vienna tradition are but two of the European training models available; coexistence with differences suggests a solution for the North American community: a continuum of training possibilities with the institute model at one end and those educational opportunities in which there is no organizational structure whatsoever at the other (Hyman 1990). This continuum of educational possibilities has the threefold advantage of recognizing the diversity of thinking in contemporary psychoanalysis, matching institutional forms of education with the particular theory under study, and acknowledging in a meaningful way the individualized nature of a student's educational experiences. Three different models of education situated at the less structured end of the continuum serve as illustrative examples: the Michigan model (Hyman 1990), the free-association model (Thompson 2000), and the formation of a society of psychoanalysts (Safouan 2000) that rests on certain minimalist principles. The educational philosophy and principles of each of these models reflect, in varying degrees, Siegfried Bernfeld's (1962) view that psychoanalytic education be student-centered.

Perhaps what is most radical in each of these educational philosophies and models is the underlying view of the candidate as self-directed, self-motivated, and self-selecting into a largely self-designed program for the study of psychoanalysis. Each of these narratives of training values and encourages individual responsibility and critical thinking as foundational and integral characteristics of the educational process; candidates are understood to be the responsible author of their own professional life. They make the decisions, for example, as to whom they might meet with for learning about different aspects of psychoanalytic thinking or theory, supervision of their analytic conversation with others, and engaging in the experiences of their personal analysis. Thus, people interested in psychoanalysis could, on their own initiative, seek psychoanalytic supervision, didactic experiences, and a personal analysis with someone who seems to know a bit more and is deserving of their trust. In the Vienna model, the candidate is the one who ultimately decides when the analysis is ended and when certification of self-as-analyst is warranted, the time-worn and threadbare arguments of protecting the public notwithstanding. The authority to authorize self-as-analyst is inextricably tied to the question of the end of analysis, which can only be answered, in the final analysis, by the candidates themselves. The authority to translate unconscious experience, process, and dynamic of other derives from one's own experiences in and of analysis. Much can be learned in the praxis of the analytic discourse; very little, however, can be taught, as human experience, analytic or otherwise, is not didactic.

Psychoanalytic education in the twenty-first century must be premised and organized around the freedom to question the structures of our traditional social institutions; the assumptions of our received knowledge, values, and moral pieties; and the constituted experience(s) of our culture and the individual. This includes the freedom to question the received wisdoms, values, and pieties of the institutional(ized) truth and ethic of psychoanalysis itself through the study of psychoanalysis in seminars, study groups, and tutorials; the supervised practice of psychoanalysis; and the experiences of one's own personal analysis, which includes the questioning of self as analyst and analysand in a continuing and mutual search for identity. In this conception of psychoanalytic education, identity as a health-care professional is not assumed, sought, or received. Indeed, one's identity as an analyst, itself, must be continuously questioned, the skeptical questioning of which, paradoxically, becomes a major aspect of one's identity as an analyst (Kavanaugh 1999b). The educational experiences contributing to this identity formation continue to revolve around the study, practice, and experiences of psychoanalysis. The underlying conceptual foundations of these experiences, however, are re-situated in philosophy, the humanities, and the arts as opposed to biology, medicine, and the natural sciences. As described elsewhere, psychoanalytic education might be organized around the psychoanalytic arts (e.g., the arts of critical thinking, the arts of continuity, and the arts of communication), which contribute to the identity formation of the analyst as a philosopher-semiotician, historiographer, and poet-artist (Kavanaugh 1998, 1999a).

As noted by Giroux (1991, 1997), critical thinking is a fundamentally political act when common sense assumptions are evaluated in terms of their genesis, development, and purpose. Unfortunately, a positivist-medical ideology forecloses on critical thinking about psychoanalytic education. It does not encourage the questioning of what is represented as fact; it encourages the acceptance of and adaptation to the fact. A psychoanalysis that questions its hidden assumptions and historical traditions, however, invites us to continuously engage in the difficult struggle of questioning our own history as a profession, which is, perhaps, the first step in escaping from our history and, in so doing, participating in reshaping the future of psychoanalytic education (Kavanaugh 2000). "To become aware of the processes of historical self-formation indicates an important beginning in breaking through the taken-for-granted *assumptions that legitimize existing institutional arrangements*. . . . Critical thinking demands a form of hermeneutic understanding that is historically grounded" (Giroux 1997, p. 27, emphasis added).

Historical awareness and consciousness makes possible the process of reflecting on our past; critical thinking is integrally linked with—and grounded in—the individual's historical sense.

Standards standardize, institutions institutionalize, and psychoanalysts psychoanalyze. And for the most part, disagreements with our pedagogical traditions have been dismissively interpreted as unresolved negative transferences with authority and authority figures. As a community of scholars, however, we must bring into question the underlying assumptions of our educational traditions, the consortium's political coalition and philosophical assumptions notwithstanding, lest we continue speaking of the analyst of the twenty-first century as written on the pages of a nineteenth-century historical text (Kavanaugh 1998). With the consortium's adoption of national health-care accreditation standards, our own communal version of the Lobo Brigade has been further institutionalized, continuing to cut grass that no longer needs cutting. In so doing, our educational institutions have become living and breathing monuments to an historical time and ways of thinking long since past. As to the future of psychoanalysis? Perhaps Christopher Bollas states it most succinctly: "Psychoanalysis just has to survive 'the psychoanalytic movement.' If it survives psychoanalysts and their schools, then it will grow and develop. But this remains to be seen" (cited in Kirsner 2000, p. 251).

REFERENCES

Arlow, J. (1969). Myth and Ritual and Psychoanalytic Training, in Three Institute Conference on Psychoanalytic Training. Pittsburg Psychoanalytic Institute, Pittsburgh.

Bernfeld, S. (1962). On psychoanalytic training. *Psychoanalytic Quarterly* 31: 453–482.

Bevan, W. (1991). Contemporary psychology: a tour inside the onion. *American Psychologist* 46(5):475–483.

Boesky, D. (2004). A neglected problem about clinical evidence. *Free Associations: Newsletter of the Michigan Psychoanalytic Institute and Society* 34(1):8–9.

Bornstein, M. (1985). Freud's legacy: science and humanism. *Psychoanalytic Inquiry* 5:87–98.

Breuer, J., and Freud, S. (1895). Studies on hysteria. *Standard Edition* 2:1–307.

Capra, F. (1982). *The Turning Point: Science, Society and the Rising Culture.* New York: Simon and Schuster.

Child, W. (1996). *Causality, Interpretation and the Mind.* Oxford Philosophical Monographs. Oxford: Clarendon Press.

Clarke, D. S. (1997). *Philosophy's Second Revolution: Early and Recent Analytic Philosophy.* Chicago: Open Court.

Cohen, A., and Dascal, M. (1989). *The Institution of Philosophy: A Discipline in Crisis?* New York: Open Court.

Fine, R. (1973). *The Development of Freud's Thought.* Northvale, NJ: Jason Aronson.

——— (1987). *The Development of Freud's Thought: from the Beginnings (1886–1990) through ID Psychology (1900–1914) to Ego Psychology (1914–1939).* Northvale, NJ: Jason Aronson.

Flax, J. (1990). *Thinking Fragments: Psychoanalysis, Feminism, and Postmodernism in the Contemporary West.* Los Angeles: University of California Press.

Foucault, M. (1972). *The Archeology of Knowledge and the Discourse on Language,* transl. A. M. Sheridan Smith. New York: Pantheon.

Freud, S. (1914). On the history of the psychoanalytic movement. The International Psycho-analytical Library (no. 7). E. Jones, ed. (vol. 1), New York: Basic Books, Inc.

Gay, P. (1974). *Style in History.* New York: Basic Books.

Gedo, J. (1999). *The Evolution of Psychoanalysis: Contemporary Theory and Practice.* New York: Other Press.

Giroux, H. A. (1991). *Modernism, Postmodernism, and Feminism: Rethinking the Boundaries of Educational Discourse.* Albany: State University of New York Press.

——— (1997). *Pedagogy and the Politics of Hope: Theory, Culture, and Schooling.* New York: Westview Press.

Hooks, B. (1994). *Teaching to Transgress: Education as the Practice of Freedom.* New York: Routledge.

Hunter, G. (1998). Forgotten cemetery blocks development. *The Detroit News,* November 1, pp. 1, 2.

Hyman, M. (1990). Institute training and its alternatives. In *Tradition and Innovation in Psychoanalytic Education,* ed. M. Meisels and E. R. Shapiro, pp. 77–85. Hillsdale, NJ: Lawrence Erlbaum.

——— (1992). The causal theory of perception. *Philosophical Quarterly* 42: 277–296.

Jones, E. (1953). *The Life and Work of Sigmund Freud.* New York: Basic Books.

Kavanaugh, P. B. (1995). Postmodernism, psychoanalysis, and philosophy: a world of difference for the future of psychoanalytic education. Paper presented at the International Federation for Psychoanalytic Education's VI annual conference, Toronto, Canada, November.

—— (1998). How will bodies of knowledges speak the psychoanalyst of the 21st century? Some thoughts on the arts of psychoanalytic education. President's address presented at the International Federation for Psychoanalytic Education's IX annual conference, Fordham University, Lincoln Center, New York, November.

—— (1999a). Thinking about psychoanalytic thinking: a question(ing) of identity, purpose, and ethics. President's address presented at the International Federation for Psychoanalytic Education's X annual conference, Sir Francis Drake Hotel, San Francisco, November.

—— (1999b). An ethic of free association: questioning a uniform and coercive code of ethics. *Psychoanalytic Review* [Special Issue, M. G. Thompson (ed) The Ethics of Psychoanalysis: Philosophical, Political, and Clinical Considerations] 86(4):643–662.

—— (1999c). Is psychoanalysis in crisis? It all depends on the premise of your analysis. In *The Death of Psychoanalysis: Murder? Suicide? Or Rumor Greatly Exaggerated?* ed. R. Prince, pp. 85–100. New York: Jason Aronson.

—— (2000). The decline of history as reminiscence, knowledge and tradition: reclaiming an historical sense in psychoanalytic thinking. Paper presented at the Michigan Society for Psychoanalytic Psychology's 20th Year Commemorative Program, Southfield, MI, November.

—— (2001). Codes of silence and whispers of discontent: pedagogical, philosophical, and political differences in the analytic culture. Paper presented at the XII annual interdisciplinary conference of the International Federation for Psychoanalytic Education, Ft. Lauderdale, FL, November.

Kendrick, W. (1996). Writing the unconscious. In *Psychoanalysis and the Humanities*, eds. L. Adams and J. Szaluta, pp. 97–118. Monographs of the Society for Psychoanalytic Training (6). New York: Brunner Mazel.

Kirsner, D. (2000). *Unfree Associations: Inside Psychoanalytic Institutes.* London: Process Press.

—— (2001). The future of psychoanalytic institutes. *Psychoanalytic Psychology* 18(2):195–212.

—— (2004). Psychoanalysis and its discontents. *Psychoanalytic Psychology* 21(3):339–352.

Lemiell, J. T. (1987). *The Psychology of Personality: An Epistemological Inquiry.* New York: Columbia University Press.

Lewin, B. D., and Ross, H. (1960). *Psychoanalytic Education in the United States.* New York: Norton.

Maher, F. A., and Tetreault, M. K. (1994). *The Feminist Classroom.* New York: Basic Books.

Meisels, M., and Shapiro, E. R., eds. (1990). Tradition and Innovation in Psychoanalytic Education: The Clark Conference on Psychoanalytic Training for Psychologists. Hillsdale, NJ: Lawrence Erlbaum.

Nietzsche, F. (1901). The Will to Power, transl. W. Kaufmann and R. J. Hollingsdale. New York: Random House, 1967.

Ritvo, L. R. (1990). Darwin's Influence on Freud: A Tale of Two Sciences. New Haven, CT: Yale University Press.

Robinson, D. N. (1989). Aristotle's Psychology. New York: Columbia University Press.

Ronca, I., and Curr, M. (1997). A Dialogue on Natural Philosophy (Dramaticon Philosophiae). Notre Dame, IN: University of Notre Dame Press.

Rose, J. (2000). Introduction. In Jacques Lacan and the Question of Psychoanalytic Training, ed. M. Safouan, pp. 1–49. New York: St. Martin's Press.

Rubinstein, B. (1997). Psychoanalysis and the philosophy of science. Psychological Issues, Monograph 62/63, ed. R. Holt. Madison, CT: International Universities Press.

Russell, B. (1985). The Philosophy of Logical Atomism, ed. D. Pears. Chicago: Open Court.

Safouan, M. (2000). Jacques Lacan and the Question of Psychoanalytic Training, transl. J. Rose. New York: St. Martin's Press.

Sarup, M. (1993). An Introductory Guide to Post-Structuralism and Postmodernism (2nd ed.). Athens, GA: University of Georgia Press.

Slife, B. (1997). Challenging our cherished theoretical and therapeutic assumptions. Paper presented at the Michigan Society for Psychoanalytic Psychology's Fall Workshop. Oakland University, Rochester Hills, MI, November.

Snyder, J. R., transl. (1988). Introduction. In The End of Modernity: Nihilism and Hermeneutics in Postmodern Culture, ed. G. Vatimo, pp. vi–lviii. Baltimore, MD: Johns Hopkins University Press.

Spence, D. (1987). The Freudian Metaphor: Toward Paradigm Change in Psychoanalysis. New York: W.W. Norton.

Strenger, C. (1998). Individuality, the Impossible Project: Psychoanalysis and Self-Creation. Madison, CT: International Universities Press.

Thompson, M. G. (2000). Free association: a technical principle or a model for psychoanalytic education? Psychologist-Psychoanalyst 20(2):8–11.

Wheatley, M. J. (1992). Leadership and the New Science: Learning about Organizations from an Orderly Universe. San Francisco: Berrett-Koehler.

Zacharias, B. L. (2002). Strategic Marketing Initiative. American Psychoanalytic Association: Marketing Research Report. Unpublished report. New Gloucester, ME: The Zacharias Group.

8

Institutional Cloning: Mimetism in Psychoanalytic Training

Michael Larivière

If, as Freud suggested in The Ego and the Id, *character is constituted by identification—the ego likening itself to what it once loved—then character is close to caricature, an imitation of an imitation. Like the artists Plato wanted to ban, we are making copies of copies, but unlike Plato's artists, we have no original, only an infinite succession of likenesses to someone who, to all intents and purposes, does not exist.*

Adam Phillips, *Terrors and Experts*

Mimesis is neither the theme nor the object of any given discourse. It is not immediately or simply translatable by imitation, reproduction, simulation, resemblance, identification, or analogy. It therefore should be remembered that if each of these concepts in some way implies, employs, or implicates mimesis, so do the concepts of originality, production, authenticity, and propriety. What mimesis says, what mimesis means, in other words, is that nothing is ever pure, unmixed, immune, innocent, and invulnerable. Mimesis reminds us that all thoroughbreds, paradoxically, are cross-bred; and so the analyst.

Mimetically speaking (i.e., taking into account the pervasive nature of mimesis), one could say that analysts are afflicted with authenticity problems—if by authenticity one understands at once the purity and the incontestability of provenance, birth, and authority. Hence the need for institutions: they are believed to deliver the seals of an otherwise always improbable, indeed more than doubtful, authenticity. This, of course, is a vast illusion. One needs only to briefly frequent the institutional milieu to realize what kind of intellectual conformism reigns therein: if certain members of the community indeed demonstrate admirable intellectual rigor, the vast majority is capable only of a dogmatic rigidity intolerant of any real questioning. In short, the analytic community (which, of course, is neither whole, nor undivided) is held together less by a common exposure to the unconscious than by a fascinated allegiance to great Analysts—Freud, Jung, Ferenczi, Klein, Lacan, etc.—who are seen as "leaders" or "guides": Führers. But it is only with Lacan and his followers that I am to occupy myself here, not with the more general issue of institutions.

Jacques Lacan founded his Ecole freudienne de Paris in June 1964, in the hope of countering the effects and aftereffects of what prevailed in all analytic institutions: identification with the analyst. Psychoanalysis needed, in his eyes, to be, as it were, readjusted to itself, it needed to relinquish the orthopaedic function it had come to fulfill after its exile in America. His theory was based on a reading, similar to that of Melanie Klein's, of Freud's second topic: the ego (*das Ich*) can in no way be seen as the result or the product of a progressive differentiation from the id (*das Es*), as a representative of reality whose function would be to contain, as well as to maintain, the individual's drives. Lacan thought, to the contrary, that there is no such thing as an autonomous ego. The ego is not the instrument of adaptation of the individual to external reality: it is an instance, progressively structured through the borrowing of different imagos. Lacan, in other words, by reexamining the notion of identification, defining it not in terms of the constitution of any definitive identity but, rather, in terms of a process that is seen as interminable, aimed at fundamentally deconstructing the fantasies of authority, mastery, and identity. What Lacan stressed is that identity is the product or the creation of language: that it is, literally (i.e., in the Latin sense of the word), a fiction. And in so doing, it is the analyst himself (or herself, as Adam Phillips would undoubtedly say) that Lacan dragged into a scene that he (or she) could not master; it is the analyst's authority that Lacan called into question. But asking analysts to acknowledge this as both the paradoxical condition of possibility and the self-subversive blind spot of their very being and thinking was asking too much. It was asking them to question their transferential relation to power and knowledge (as well as the uses thereof). How indeed could they have questioned a theory that guaranteed them so many advantages—"therapeutic" perhaps, but more to the point professional and financial? And how could they have reassessed their notion of transference when that particular transference had long been carefully set up, preserved, perpetuated in and by the institution itself? And indeed they didn't.

They joined his Ecole in an act of denegation, a denegation of almost everything he stood for—politically, ethically, theoretically and, even, clinically. Indeed, the vast majority of Lacan's followers simply could not read what he had nevertheless very clearly stated: that it was owing to the distortion of Freud's concepts by the International Psychoanalytic Association (IPA) that psychoanalysis had managed to survive. This, in my opinion, is an absolutely central issue that to my knowledge has never been raised by any of Lacan's disciples or readers. Not by chance. For if one is to follow Lacan's interpretation of Freud's decision to found the IPA, then one is forced to ask oneself why Lacan chose to repeat the operation. Why indeed did he choose to engage his troops on a path he himself had declared could only lead to failure? There is an unsolved paradox here: Why did Lacan, after having strongly and clearly stated in 1957 that it was owing to the IPA's failure to understand Freud's concepts that psychoanalysis was kept alive, decide eight years later to reengage his disciples on a track he could only know would inevitably lead to the same misunderstanding? Was he hoping against hope? Was he banking on his disciples' better judgment, or their capacity to relate differently to authority? Or his own capacity to rescue them from the kind of submission to ideals Freud's disciples had succumbed to? I doubt he was that naive. Lacan, who had read Kant, knew only too well that no institution had ever enabled psychoanalysis to delimit or delineate its own domain (*ditio*), field, territory (*territorium*), or domicile (*domicilium*). He knew only too well that psychoanalysis could not of itself establish its own legitimacy, produce its own concept (as well as the discourse on what it would produce), that it could not introduce itself on its own terms into the field that should contain it. And he knew only too well that no institution could ever preserve the essence of psychoanalysis. These problems are examined by Kant in the introduction of his *Critique of the Faculty of Judgement*. Derrida (1970) read this text and explained how what is without a clearly delineated "domain" (*Gebiet*) or field (*Feld*), without specific objects defining its domain, can still have a legitimate "territory" or "ground" (*Boden*).

It is this very issue of the legitimacy or legitimation of psychoanalysis that Lacan wanted analysts to come to terms with. His reasoning was the following: it was not by chance that the IPA was formed when it was formed, that is, in 1912. Indeed, psychoanalysis at that point in time had come to realize that it needed to expose itself, to open itself up to what largely exceeded the limits of its habitual field of inquiry. That is why Freud had asked Otto Rank and Hans Sachs, through the creation of Imago, to encourage, indeed to instigate, research in the field of what was to be known as applied psychoanalysis. This was not anecdotal. Freud, in acknowledging the necessity for psychoanalysis to be aware of what exceeded the limits of its would-be proper field of inquiry, was in fact acknowledging the necessity for psychoanalysis to ask itself where exactly its limits lay. In other words, Freud was telling his followers that the time had come for psychoanalysis to acknowledge the uncertainty of its own identity. This is something Lacan never ceased to remind us of: psychoanalysis never was and cannot ever hope to be assured of its legitimacy, it will never be safe and sound within the clear and solid limits of its "proper" field. This is not without very real, practical (political as well as clinical) consequences—and that is why the IPA was founded. Hence not only is the problem of the institutional grounding of psychoanalysis indissociable from that of its identification, it may even, with hindsight, be understood as the more or less conscious acknowledgement of the necessity, for psychoanalysis itself, of calling its very possibility into question. My point is that ever since Freud's acceptance of the necessity to entrench psychoanalysis in an institution whose function would be to provide it with international grounding and recognition, psychoanalysis knows and doesn't (want to) know that it must give up the hope of ever being sure of its own concept. In other words, Freud, through the institutional grounding of psychoanalysis, aimed at enabling it to, as it were, recover from the realization of the impossibility to inhere, to come together in the organic or logical unity of one concept. But things, of course, are not quite that simple.

For the question is not merely one of the possibility or impossibility, the legitimacy or illegitimacy, truth or falsehood (or fallacy), pertinence or impertinence of psychoanalysis, of its hypotheses, speculations, effects, efficacy, and practice. Hence Lacan's insistence on the necessity of remaining vigilant toward all discourses determined to establish, to institute the legitimacy of psychoanalysis and therefore to delineate the limits of its "field." And yet, as I have started explaining, Lacan felt he had to repeat—and not only once—Freud's operation. Indeed, not only did he first found his Ecole freudienne de Paris in 1964, he founded another institution, the Cause freudienne, immediately after having dismantled his Ecole in 1980. The Cause was in turn dismantled after Lacan's death the following year, only to be again immediately replaced, at the initiative of Jacques-Alain Miller, Lacan's son-in-law and legatee, by the Ecole de la Cause, which is still very much in existence, along with a myriad of other would-be Lacanian institutions founded by various people, some members of the old guard, others newcomers to the ever-widening circle of clerics devoted to the safeguard of the Lacanian gospel. I believe it is not unreasonable, given Lacan's own understanding of Freud's decision to institutionalize psychoanalysis, to read these successive acts of foundation, over and beyond Lacan's desperate determination to counter the effects and aftereffects of the initial internationalization of psychoanalysis, as its parodic ending, that is, as an operation through which psychoanalysis was once and for all forced to acknowledge the impossibility of being embodied, contained, preserved in any institution. This may very well be one of the major stakes of Lacan's work: to demonstrate, by making manifest how illusory all hopes of everlasting institutional entrenchment are, that Freud's effort at laying the institutional foundations of psychoanalysis was both inimitable and impossible to repeat, and further, that the very possibility, the very viability of psychoanalysis is predicated upon the acknowledgement of that double impossibility. In other words, Lacan's repeated acts of foundation could be read as the paradoxical recognition of the radical incompatibility between two logics: the psychoanalytic and the institutional. The reason I suggest we thus read Lacan's decision to repeat Freud's institutional operation is the following: in 1957, in a paper entitled "La Psychanalyse et son enseignement" (Psychoanalysis and Its Teachings), Lacan suggested that while Freud founded the IPA with the aim of preserving and transmitting his theory and method, he did so with the full knowledge of the facts: indeed, the IPA having mostly (if not only) given way, especially in America, to misinterpretations and even to distortions of his theory and method, one might be tempted to think that Freud had merely failed to reach his goal. Not at all, suggested Lacan; to the contrary. Freud obtained exactly what he wanted, namely a purely formal conservation of his message, something made obvious by the spirit of reverential authority in which the most manifest alterations of his message were made. Indeed, thought Lacan, not a single blunder was ever uttered in the insipid hodgepodge known as "analytic literature" that didn't take the precaution of leaning on Freud's authority. It was thanks to these distortions of his theory and method that Freud's most fundamental concepts were kept alive: they owe their survival to having been, for the greater part, misunderstood.

Lacan's starting point was the observation that no one had made before him, that Freud had founded the IPA 10 years before writing *Massenpsychologie*, that is, that he had engaged the analytic community on the institutional track without having beforehand clearly identified either the function or the role of the Führer, or the way in which the masses relate to him, a relationship Lacan understood, borrowing the concept from Hegel, as infatuation. And yet, Lacan chose to repeat it all. As if even he couldn't take responsibility for what he thought, for what he knew. This again is not simply anecdotal. What we need to ask ourselves, the only question that really matters concerning these problems, paradoxes, and contradictions, is this: to what inevitable denegation did Freud's decision to give institutional grounding to psychoanalysis lead? What denegation can the analytic movement only reiterate in order for the institution to keep on believing in its own necessity? The answer is obvious: what needs to be "forgotten" is that through his discovery of the unconscious Freud did away with the classical concept of conscience—and it is precisely that notion of conscience the institution clings to. For to want to train analysts, to want to manage or to administer a legacy, in this case Freud's legacy (but the problem is exactly the same today with Lacan's), whatever the modalities of the said training or management, is to want to restore that ancient conscience; it is to refuse to acknowledge the impossibility with which Freud confronts us—the impossibility of conceiving of the subject as whole. The *Ich* (ego) is *gespaltet* (divided), it is always in some way a stranger to itself—something that was best formulated, in my opinion, by Rimbaud: *Je est un autre* (I is an Other). Which explains, as I shall attempt to illustrate, the importance of mimetism in analytic "training."

Lacan wrote and spoke like no one else—or so it seemed. One might then ask: Who or what did he resemble? I am tempted to say: nothing and no one. Lacan resembled no one and that may explain why he would often declare himself to be totally alone. To which the horde, the rabble (as he would sometimes refer to them), his followers were quick to reply: "You may well be alone but we will not be without you." So they strove to write and speak (and dress and act) like him, as if these rallying symbols, these outward signs of belonging were more reliable than the institutional, clan-like protectionism they were otherwise offered. But they can't be made entirely responsible for this. Indeed, this rather pathetic form of mimetism was also their way of responding to Lacan's assertion that the only thing that is transmissible is a style. It is a complex issue, this. My understanding of it is that Lacan thought it necessary to constantly transgress the rule that founds the capitalization of knowledge upon the legibility of its terms or utterances. In other words, Lacan's position was similar to that which Freud had taken in 1895 in his and Breuer's *Studies on Hysteria*: psychoanalysis is predicated on the giving up of all scientific pretense and the acceptance of its literary essence. What Lacan asked analysts to consider, what he hoped they could try and come to terms with, is that the didactics of the unconscious are, essentially, an *ars mimetica*: as a contender to the position of "analyst" one is inevitably referred back to the first analytical "model," that is, to the autoanalyst himself. Which explains why the history of psychoanalysis reads like a perpetual "Imitation of Sigmund Freud," with all the appropriation and fratricidal rivalry consequences to which we are henceforth accustomed. In becoming an analyst, like it or not, one in some way inevitably claims to be representative of the Freudian "doctrine" or "truth"; one at least involves the memory of Freud, one uses Freud's name. But we must ask: What if Freud himself had claimed to be an analyst by identifying with "himself"? As long as we refuse to pursue our reflection on identification up to the point where the very model itself is seen for the fiction it is, we will not have effectively departed from the classical notion of conscience. As long as we refuse to acknowledge that Freud's descent—to use a dated word—real or mythical, is still more or less held together only thanks to this sustained mimetic endeavour, we will be resisting what psychoanalysis is about.[1]

One of the major difficulties of Lacan's endeavour is that he was forever confronted with an aporia: while aiming at doing away with the classical notion of subject(ivity), he unwittingly gave weight to the problems of identity. Indeed, he kept finding himself under the yoke of an ever more rigid logic (and syntax) that forbade his discourse from accomplishing what it had set out to do, distracting it from its anticipated course, collapsing it from within. In other words, the irresolvable paradox, the insurmountable contradiction of Lacan's endeavour was that it contributed to strengthen the very position it purported to render untenable, that of egotistical mastery. Lacan strove, through the use of deliberately arcane, sometimes seemingly almost amphigorical, indeed often baroque, magniloquent, euphuistic language, to incessantly dismantle the implied unity of meaning, because the truth of the unconscious was in his view incompatible with monolithic, indivisible, indiscerptible sense. Implicitly borrowing the notion from his friend Merleau-Ponty, Lacan aimed at maintaining dis-cursivity. But he knew he was fighting a losing battle. Disillusioned, shortly after having published his widely misread and misunderstood Écrits and in response to those who declared him illegible, he remarked rather cynically that it wouldn't be 10 years before everyone—not only all those who professed to share his interpretation of Freud's writings but quite a few of those who didn't as well—wrote like him. He was right.

In unison, Lacan's followers repeated what they heard and read, including their mentor's affirmations concerning the artificial and fictitious quality of any and all identity. Lacan told them their very iden-

---

1. This was expanded upon by Mikkel Borch-Jacobsen during a conversation we had in January 1986, published in the journal of which I was then co-editor, L'Artichaut (Strasbourg).

tity was unclaimable, they repeated this, but only to enjoy the feeling of plenitude, of completeness, of wholeness the knowledge of their *Ichlosigkeit*,[2] of the radical uncertainty of their identity paradoxically gave them.

But this may after all not be quite as paradoxical as it seems. Indeed, the Western history of subjectivity has long taken the form of a chronicle of an anticipated disappearance, of a disappearance forever taking place (at least from Montaigne to Blanchot, which doesn't mean it is an exclusively French chronicle. There are countless examples of various modalities of this disappearance in the works of such writers and philosophers as Nietzsche, Pessoa, Pynchon, Salinger, and Enrique Vila-Matas. Artists have also attempted to address these issues, such as Michelangelo Antonioni with his remarkable film *L'Avventura*, in which the characters are seen searching just as much for the God Nietzsche had pronounced dead as they are for their friend Anna on the Lisca Blanca reef—it is, in a way, with the enigma of the possibility of their own disappearance that they find themselves having to deal. I would venture that it was in the hope of escaping the inevitable, indeed the programmed disappearance of the subject, which Lacan's writings stressed, that his followers insisted on making themselves as visible as they possibly could. They did this mainly through publishing: analytic journals suddenly proliferated, both inside and outside their institution; major publishing houses gave editorial responsibilities to those analysts who were most influential in their community; works of analytical theory were published in numbers seldom before seen; seminars were taught, literally, by the hundreds; conferences were constantly being organized. In other words, Lacan's followers made themselves visible mainly through theorizing, and one should remember that theory and theater share the same etymology: *theorein*, that is, at once to look at and to make visible.

I can't here elaborate upon this terribly complex question of the relation between the theoretical and the mimetical. Suffice it to say that the question has always haunted Western culture: it is as old as Plato. Closer to us, several people devoted a great part of their work toward elucidating the problem—Nietzsche, Heidegger, and Derrida, among

---

2. The term is used, if memory serves me right, by Hugo von Hofmannsthal in his *Gespräch über Gedicht* (*Letter of Lord Chandos*); it translates literally as *egolessness*.

others. Each in his own way brought to the fore the well-known fact that there isn't a single utterance that isn't, at least, equivocal—*pater semper incertus est*—something "theory" is designed to remedy. And it never works. Indeed, the fundamental inaptitude of language for making itself (as, for example, the members of the Vienna Circle would have wanted) translucent to itself, is something we have no choice but to live with—and that Lacan never ceased to stress. It isn't, as George Steiner often suggests, that language has lost the capacity for truth, it is that language never could but operate, self-doubtingly, on the sharp edge of silence: Hofmannsthal, Kafka, Wittgenstein, Karl Krauss, Canetti, Heidegger, Celan, Mandelstam—authors Steiner constantly makes reference to—all speak to and of the impossibility of, as jurists say, telling the whole truth and nothing but the truth. This is something Lacan's followers have never ceased to repeat, often gleefully. But very few of them were (are) capable of the humility such a position entails. The loss could not, would not, be theirs. A quiet room and table (and couch and chair) to work in could never do. They need(ed) schools of psychoanalysis, where they could exercise their authority. They could never stay at the simplest and therefore most exacting level of intellectual integrity the Freudian eclipse of the ego calls for and that Lacan stressed. They offer(ed) instead what Steiner somewhere refers to as "loud vacancies of intellect." They could (can) at once celebrate Lacan's "return to Freud" as a reaffirmation of the dislocation and undermining of the old stabilities of the classical or Judeo-Christian "Self" and unwittingly consolidate the fiction of stable identity we label "I." Lacan's suggestion that no analyst can ever completely escape the feeling he is an impostor apparently went unheeded. And they in fact refuse to see how fatuous it is to hope for the restoration of the disseminated self, therefore of the personal *auctoritas* of the analyst. It is the radical solitude inherent in the position of analyst that they cannot accept, a position similar to that formulated by Nietzsche in the prologue of *Ecce Homo*: "I live off the sole credit I lend myself." Lacan's formulation was: "*L'analyste ne s'autorise que de lui-même—et de quelques autres.*" What it means is the analyst cannot defer to any authority outside himself; he alone, with the help of a few others, can know if and when he is ready to do the work: the "few others" will only have helped him prepare for the acid test for which he will be completely on his own.

This seems to be in contradiction with what I was saying before of the impossibility of restoring the analyst's disseminated personal auctoritas. It isn't: it is merely another way of saying that this auctoritas only exists as yet another fiction of stable identity. It says that no identity is stable. It is this narcissistic wound that analysts, regardless of their doctrinal choices, wish to remedy through institutional montages. In a letter to Richard Woodhouse, Keats wrote: "The poet has no identity." It may very well be that the analyst, that other rather fragile, uncertain figure, often resorts to writing in order to find himself, to claim his voice, a voice that will not be confused with those of the other people in the room. This anxiety is shared by all those who write, including the greatest. Freud hesitated reading Schopenhauer and Nietzsche; Thomas Mann hesitated reading Hermann Hesse's *Glasperlenspiel* and noted in his journal: "To be reminded that one is not alone in the world. Always unpleasant," thus unwittingly quoting Goethe, who asked: "Is a man alive when others are as well?" The paradox is that in order to claim a voice of their own, Lacan's followers most often would speak or write borrowing their master's voice. Lacan's disciples, like all disciples, were capable more of remembering than of thinking. They spoke with the master's voice, wrote with the master's words, wore the master's clothes, smoked the master's culebra cigars. Melancholy mimeticians, they might have wanted to use these lines from Borges's prologue to his *History of Infamy* as an epigraph to their own "writings": "These pages are the irresponsible game of a coward who didn't have the courage to write his own tales, and who enjoyed himself at falsifying and altering, sometimes without even an aesthetic excuse, the stories of others."[3]

Almost 25 years have passed since Lacan's death and the problem has worsened. The symptoms are many: peremptory dogmatism, militancy, recruiting, and proselytism on all fronts, astounding mimetism of style and expression, quarrels and vengeful passions similar to those seen in families around inheritances dividing the various groups or institutions founded since the dismantlement of the EfP. Jacques-Alain Miller has reawoken the project of a planetary expansion of psychoanalysis Freud had delineated in his *Selbstdarstellung*. For most Lacanians—and especially for Millerians—psychoanalysis is a cause to

---

3. My translation from the French. Paris, UGE, coll.10/18.

be defended. We would now need to assess what exactly Lacan's personal responsibility is in the present state of psychoanalytic affairs, for his responsibility is enormous—but this would far exceed the limits of this chapter. Indeed, in order to begin answering this question with the patience, the attentiveness, as well as the caution it requires, we would need to situate it in the wider context of a reflection on psychoanalysis understood as the institution of a name, Freud's, and ask how various other names, in this case Lacan's, had come to stand out, as well as what they had come to represent.

Lacan saw himself as Freud's legatee, and therefore needed to adopt as his own the question Freud had hoped to elucidate by founding the IPA: What exactly, psychoanalytically speaking, is a legacy? Lacan could not not know that founding a school in the name of a "return to Freud" and with the further aim of ensuring that Freud was given a "decent burial," could only mean creating for his own heirs circumstances identical to those Freud's followers had known. In other words, Lacan could not not know that he was abandoning his posterity to the impossible reckoning of the very same debt Freud's heirs had inherited. The unprecedented mimetism we have been witnessing for the past 40 years is only one of the many sorry consequences of Lacan's political shortsightedness.

I do realize, of course, how terribly unfair it is to end things so abruptly. There are so many issues begging to be examined here, which can't be, for lack of space. Suffice it to say that in spite of all the shortcomings of his institutional venture, we must acknowledge this simple fact: Jacques Lacan's contribution to psychoanalysis, whether considered from the theoretical, the clinical, or even the institutional point of view, compares with no other.

REFERENCES

Breuer, J., and Freud, S. (1895). Studies in hysteria. *Standard Edition* 2:1–307.
Derrida, J. (1910). *La vérité en peinture*. Paris: Champs Flammarion.

9

Coerced Discipleship: Indoctrination Masquerading as Training in Psychotherapy

Richard Raubolt

Do not force feelings of any kind, least of all the feeling of conviction.
Sandor Ferenczi

What we cannot speak about we must pass by in silence.
Ludwig Wittgenstein

"He talks like us" is equivalent to saying "He is one of us."
Edward Saper

As I have written previously (Raubolt 2003), I was a participant in what I describe as a psychotherapy cult. This training, in the form of group supervision, contained some of the extreme methods of control noted by others (Singer 1990, Temerlin and Temerlin 1982). However, by hovering more closely to the edge of respectability this group was more confusing and arguably more effective in using covert as well as direct methods of indoctrination.

My personal experiences and study of the literature on indoctrination, along with my supervision of others who have had similar abusive training, have contributed to my interest in the variations of power, control, and persuasion that threaten the integrity of training in psychotherapy and psychoanalysis. I am particularly interested in what I believe is the theft of personal language. Before exploring this area of inquiry, I will first present the framework that produces indoctrination instead of clinical supervision.

Indoctrination, for the purpose of this chapter, is defined as the process by which a proscribed and organized belief system is systematically imposed on others irrespective of their consent. With regard to psychotherapy, this process masquerading as a theoretical/psychological model seeks to restrict critical thinking and independent judgment. Rather than recognize the complexities, ambiguities, and subtleties inherent in clinical work, indoctrination forcefully presents a simplistic, stereotyped, and "sacred" dogma. "This sacredness," according to Lifton (1961), "is evident in the prohibition against the questioning of basic assumptions and in the reverence which is demanded for the originators of the word, the present bearers of the word and the word itself" (pp. 427–428).

Psychotherapy and psychoanalysis are restricted to what are defined as "scientific" methods by the leading exponents of a particular psychological model. Techniques are considered proper, acceptable, and most significantly correct only if they support the already-delineated theory. No significant advancement of clinical theory or method is possible in such a reified system that has claimed truth as its own.

Finally, compliant loyalty generated by charismatic and authoritarian leadership, the cycling of trauma and retraumatization, and the creation of multiple incestuous professional relationships provide the emotional glue required for successful indoctrination. In creating such loyalty the voices of dissent are silenced through manipulation, intimidation and the theft of personal language of the trainees. Through such a process trainees become disciples. They develop faith in the supervisor/ training analyst as the possessor of truth. Such disciples, Roustang (1982) writes, "must be ready to submit 'in advance' (*im voraus*) to his statements and judgments. This 'in advance' constitutes and maintains the transference and the faith: whatever happens, I shall serve him because he knows and he is right" (p. 20).

BY SEDUCTION OR FORCE: ESSENTIAL COMPONENTS OF INDOCTRINATION

My overview of the process of indoctrination identifies a number of connecting elements and strategies worthy of further attention:

1. Charismatic, authoritarian, and dominating leadership
2. Dichotomous and stereotypical thinking
3. Affiliation with an institution or group that fosters multiple conflicting professional relationships
4. Cycling of trauma and retraumatization
5. Theft of language

Charismatic, Authoritarian, and Dominating Leadership

Researchers of psychotherapy cults (Dorpat 1996, Langone 1993, Temerlin and Temerlin 1982) have described as central the critical and universal characteristic of charismatic, authoritarian, and dominating leadership. Harwood (2003), however, makes a useful distinction, which I will maintain in this chapter, between charismatic and self-serving charismatic leadership. A key difference is in intent. Charismatic leaders are often motivated by a crisis or a cause that requires purposeful strength and direction. Such leaders use the force of their personalities to encourage and inspire others. If it is done well, others will mobilize their ambitions and capacities to ward off feelings of discouragement or helplessness. Theirs is a call for action that seeks to enhance the best virtues in an otherwise unsure audience.

Self-serving charismatic leaders, by contrast, use their personalities to dominate and manipulate others. Such leaders are often charming, exciting, socially at ease, confident, and they present an attitude of absolute authority. Frequently forthright, they offer compelling answers to calm and quiet anxiety in their presence. They can listen with apparent tenderness and concern to mundane worries. On the surface, they allow no personal doubt of their own while they welcome and even incite the uncertainties of others. Usually male, this is the father imago of strength and influence dispensing words of inspiration and direction. Initially, they can be generous in their praise when they are pleased and only hints of sharpness appear when they feel threatened. As all-knowing fathers, they claim to develop resolve and success in their follower children. Disciples come to adopt the path of truth presented to them. Postmodern anxiety and questions are seemingly washed away as unnecessary, unworthy of them—as examples of their disciples' ignorance so simply resolved by the wisdom of charismatic leaders. Power, at this point, is implied but not exercised. Authority grows in strength as followers submit to the seductive message of "truth."

When trainees are faced with the confidence, grandiosity, and simplicity of the message offered by such leaders, they are particularly vulnerable at a point of transition (Dorpat 1996, Tobias and Lalich 1994), or due to traumatization feel empty, confused, or fragmented (Brothers 2003, Raubolt 2003). Trainees then become followers and self-serving charismatic leaders excite their devotion in a relationship of mutual dependency, or as Brothers (2000) describes "the intersubjective regulation of uncertainty."

For their part, self-serving charismatic leaders assert influence and control to avoid feelings of inferiority or depression. Such leaders need the idealization and dependence of followers as "a regulator to their self esteem" (Kohut 1976, p. 417). Often suffering from their own narcissistic injury, the dependency of others gives them resiliency. In a seemingly addictive process, they seek more control, adulation, and reverence. Self-serving charismatic leaders often grow paranoid, intolerant, and abusive. They come to demand exclusive fidelity in an attempt to solidify their parasitic vitality.

Followers, feeling increasingly dependent yet vulnerable and fearful, seek to meet the rising expectations of leaders through masochistic submission. Such submission, according to Ghent (1990) is "losing oneself in the power of the other, becoming enslaved in one way or another to the master" (p. 115), and offers "only the security of bondage and an ever amplified sense of futility" (p. 116).

Such leaders and followers only feel safe together. Each needs the other to feel valued, alive, and necessary. Each also provides the other with the requisite emotional supplies that are either unavailable or underdeveloped. Perhaps most succinctly, each makes the other feel more whole.

Dichotomous and Stereotypical Thinking

The establishment of dichotomies and stereotypical thinking seeks to eliminate the complexities and contradictions inherent in the practice of psychotherapy. Ambiguities lead to uncertainty that would undermine the process of indoctrination. Such a process relies on simplicity and absolutes. Lifton (1961), in describing such thinking, has written: "The most far reaching and complex of human problems are compressed into brief, highly reductive, definitive sounding phrases, easily memorized and easily expressed. These become the start and finish of any ideological analysis" (p. 429). Straightforward, direct certainties are required. Routine strategies reduce anxiety by clearly defining problems and interventions. No deviations are allowed, only answers defined by what the theory describes. Individuality, creativity, musing, exploration, since they are open and messy, are dismissed.

This latter "Negative Capability" is defined by Keats and cited by Phillips (2001) as "when a man is capable of being in uncertainties, mysteries, doubts without any irritable reaching after fact and reason" (p. 29). This is precisely the type of capability viewed as most threatening and, therefore, under greatest attack during indoctrination. Certainty and truth must be protected so as not to interfere with leader/follower dependence and as a result the entire training structure.

So how is the truth protected? One association that I am familiar with, the Bar Levav Education Association (BLEA), used repetition of therapeutic slogans to create an air of invincibility. In my meetings, with a group of former trainees, they cited examples from both supervision and their own therapy experiences. Supervision included the following "mantras," or to use Lifton's (1961) phrase, "thought-terminating cliché(s)" (p. 429), which were repeated session after session, week after week, month after month, until they became law and beyond question.

Examples included:

1. There is no "we" in psychotherapy.
2. Group therapy is the only way to treat shame.
3. Women therapists can't treat men patients.
4. The therapist should be the most important person in a patient's life, more important even than a spouse.
5. The therapist is the reality in the room.
6. Reality dictates that . . .

For psychotherapy the list changed little:

1. "Let me give you a hand (you can't change without me)."
2. "You are acting on your feelings" (if the therapist doesn't approve of certain behaviors).
3. "You are too much in your head (feel, don't think)."
4. "Say it five times, louder each time" (a phrase such as "I'm angry," said until the patient is screaming in rage after which the patient is expected to feel relieved and grateful).
5. "Put your feet on the floor, get your butt out, and breathe" (to help with expression of feeling).
6. "Say it straight."

I would like to note that after recalling some of these slogans or mantras, former supervisees/patients described experiences of nausea and disbelief, mixed with feelings of anger and shame, at how they were treated.

Affiliation with an Institution or Group that Fosters Multiple Relationships

Indoctrination is most effectively and persuasively completed through groups and in institutions. Training institutes run the risk of defining what is proper in treatment on the basis (and bias) of what senior therapists have deemed relevant and true. Explorations and questions are all too often received with suspicion. A sacred text or figure operates as a training superego.

Balint (1948) wrote of similar concerns in psychoanalytic training over a half century ago:

> The general aim . . . is to force the candidate to identify himself with his initiator, to introject the initiator and his ideals, and to build up from these identifications a strong super-ego which will influence him all his life. This is a surprising discovery indeed. What we consciously intend to achieve with our candidates, is that they should develop a strong critical ego, capable of bearing considerable strains, free from necessary identification, and from any automatic transference or thinking patterns. Contrary to the conscious aim, our own behavior as well as the working of the training system have several features leading necessarily to a weak-

ening of these ego functions and to the formulation and strengthening of a special kind of super-ego. [p. 167]

With a self-serving, charismatic leader/supervisor, his or her pre-dilections are passed off as knowledge. The status of master is then conferred and believers form groups to seek his or her instruction.

Phillips (2001), in writing about Lacan, offered some compelling advice about psychoanalytic training that also generalizes to other approaches:

> If there are to be usefully inspiring psychoanalysts in the future—rather than merely cult figures—they will have to stop trying to have new theories and aim instead just to write interesting sentences; and they should never teach their own work, only the work of others that they value (from a psychoanalytic point of view no writer can be the privileged authority on what he finds he has to say). What Lacan's life teaches us, unlike his fabulous writing, is that prestige should not be the name of the game. The lesson of the master is the one we should stop listening out for. "Experience," as Lacan wrote, "is not didactic." [pp. 111–112]

Of course, not all affiliations to institutes or training groups are destructive. Groups—here I am referring to therapy and supervisory groups—generally run along a continuum.

Harwood (1998) succinctly describes this process:

> Group dynamics enable connectedness, affiliation, attachment and security on one end of the spectrum ("a group object experience") with a contamination of affects, archaic identifications, and the acting out of destructive rage on the other, which becomes "a group traumatic experience" both for the participants and their targets. . . . destruction of the individual self in the group self of cults. [p. 163]

Training groups that create group traumatic experiences are under the direction of charismatic/master leaders who develop an emotionally intense experience where supervision is intentionally blurred with therapy. Trainees are treated as patients and all significant interactions occur between the supervisor and supervisee. These often sadistic interactions are usually challenging, crude, and demeaning confrontations. Supervisees are made to feel that they know nothing—nothing about the tenets of the program, but more dangerously nothing about themselves.

It is the self of the supervisee that is under attack, to eliminate traces of critical thinking and self initiative (Raubolt 2004). Singer (1990), in agreement, concludes that such programs "attack the core sense of being—the central self-image, the very sense of realness and existence of the self" (p. 103).

Such groups give the leader special status for the unique gifts he seems to display: power, authority, confidence and, most appealing of all, certainty. Groups then grow ever more silent and compliant. There is also the unconscious desire to sacrifice a member for the sake of co-hesion, and merger with the strength of the leader/master and unerring father. Livingston (1998) writes: "Any individual's need for self delineation threatens the group's need for basic alikeness. The demand for sameness is an attempt to maintain a precarious sense of safety and belonging" (p. 63).

Trainees are caught in what MacDonald (1988) calls a "loyalty/betrayal funnel" (p. 58). If trainees demonstrate any remaining loyalty to perceptions about what is right or true held prior to training, such independent thought is a betrayal of the group; if they remain loyal to the group or institution by silencing any doubts, misgivings, or critical questions, they betray any sense of individuality and ultimately them-selves. This "funnel" places members in a vortex of no choice. Blind submission based on dependency often is the only way out.

One supervisee in such a program kept a private journal of his thoughts and specifically his reservations about the training he was re-ceiving. With his permission I would like to quote one entry:

> My subjective sense of these things is that I am truly disturbed as I think about my own patients and how I could probably get most of them to go this route. Even if it is effective in many or even most instances (which I don't concede) it is anathema to me philosophically. What would be the reaction I would get in saying something like that? No one would try to elucidate what thoughts, feelings, ideas, experiences contribute to that sense that I have. It would simply be more evidence of deep character pathology. If I don't trust a person or a situation, does that mean there is something wrong with me? Always? It is intersubjective. How could it be otherwise? What is most dangerous about this that the therapist can consider himself to be righteous; the therapist has the right to act out in many ways. Even with all the supervision and therapy this is still pos-sible and likely. It is modeled.

Group supervisees are also bound to the leaders and senior thera-pists of the institution through multiple overlapping relationships that are both personal and professional. Such relationships, initiated by se-nior members, include social involvement with trainees (e.g., invita-tions to parties and special events such as birthdays, weddings, and anniversaries) as well as friendships while serving as a supervisor/thera-pist. Most disturbing is the myriad of conflicting professional roles adopted by the senior members: colleague, teacher, relative, supervi-sor, spouse, and parent. One author (Bar Levav 1990) even describes her participation as a patient in a marathon group therapy session led by her father. Significant relationships are then confined to the insti-tute's nucleus. All involved have vested interest in maintaining this "emotional incest" (Pepper 2002, p. 285) to keep the training center and each other together.

Such "emotional incest" is, however, not unique to this era. Falzeder (1994), in his creation of the "spaghetti junction" (p. 170), a highly detailed family tree of psychoanalytic affiliations, concluded that over-lapping intimate and professional relationships were "the rule and not the exception" (p. 171). On the basis of his research Falzeder concludes: "What we find in the factual history of psychoanalysis, are repeated patterns or series of affect-laden relationships, be they incestuous, hos-tile, erotic, or power relations, mixed with varying doses of analysis, leading to much confusion and suffering among those involved" (p. 187).

Cycling of Trauma and Retraumitization

Instillation (an exacerbation) of fear and shame is developed through the creation of crisis states that foster traumatic dependency. This particular element of indoctrination is the result of the first three components I have described. The charismatic authoritarian leader enlists the aid of the group and institution to sanction his use of highly provocative and demeaning language with the dissident supervisee. Repeatedly the supervisee's words are greeted with disbelief, ridicule, and contempt. Even agreement with the leader brings little relief as the intent of such supervision is to break open the personality of the trainee. At the Center for Feeling Therapy, for example, the process was referred to as "busting."

Feeling acute shame and fear, trainees turn to the leader as the only one with power to save them. Trainees temporarily lose their reflective capabilities and intelligence while feeling physically and morally help-less. The adult trainee becomes the abused and regressed child Ferenczi (1933) so effectively described. In delineating the profound effects of such fear he wrote: "The same anxiety, however, if it reaches a certain maximum, compels them to subordinate themselves like automata to the will of the aggressor, to divine each one of his desires and to gratify these; completely oblivious of themselves they identify themselves with the aggressor" (p. 162).

Supervisees involved in authoritarian training programs have often suffered from previous traumas (Brothers 2003, Raubolt 2004). These traumas may include physical or sexual abuse. More commonly they have known neglect or "traumatic aloneness" and as a result are prone to experience a "terrorism of suffering" (Ferenczi 1933, p. 166). As chil-dren, they often developed the compulsion to right all disorder in the family. They became particularly sensitive to the disappointment, fail-ings, worries, and fears of the maternal figure. As Ferenczi noted, "Of course this is not only out of pure altruism, but is in order to be able to enjoy again the lost rest and care and attention accompanying it. A mother complaining of her constant miseries can create a nurse for life out of her child" (p. 166). A nurse, yes, or more aptly for the present discussion, a therapist/analyst.

As the result of such histories, supervisees are exceedingly vulner-able to the seductive manipulations, prevarications, and retraumati-zations of doctrine supervision and training. Specifically, earlier traumas are reactivated through a "confusion of tongues" (Ferenczi 1933, p. 156). According to Ferenczi, a confusion of tongues is created when people of lesser status (children, supervisees, or patients) become "tongue-tied" (p. 159) and cannot speak about their own experience in the presence of the powerful authority (parent, supervisor, or thera-pist) with whom they have had an abusive relationship. The core psy-chodynamic is that the individual's functioning is compromised by the authority's denial of his own exercise of power, control, and status to fulfill narcissistic needs. Since the individual's own reality is dismissed as fantasy or lies, a dissociative process ensues. The victims of such trauma come to doubt their experience, perceptions, and understanding of such abuse of authority. They come to believe the authority's view of events as real and, when in conflict, their own as distorted or wrong.

The methods used to maintain such a state of regressive dependency and traumatic vulnerability are varied. Clearly, outright humiliation in front of one's training group was as effective as it was painful. Such critiques of the trainee could occur over the clothes one wore, incorrect use of grammar, questioning a conclusion of the leader/supervisor, or failing to express proper gratitude for all that was being taught. Confrontations could be stinging and once begun by the leader other group members joined in to provide a Greek chorus. Intense feelings of shame could lead to deep sobbing, and feelings of fear could lead to screaming. As Brothers (2003) has pointed out, such "inflammation of passion" (p. 85) adds to the intense bond between the leader and group followers in regulating uncertainty for both.

Approaching the stimulation of intense affect with a physiological understanding gives further credence to this conclusion. Screaming, pounding a pillow or mattress with a tennis racket until exhausted, sleep deprivation through extended marathon sessions of up to 28 hours, following a pen light beam flashed in front of the eyes while yelling a nonsensical sound, are all methods of "dredging for affect" that I experienced in coercive training groups.

These experiences have the effect of producing an altered state of consciousness with overwhelming, intense emotions while the structures of ordinary thought are diminished. Deikman (1972) writes: "The undoing of automatic perceptual and cognitive structures permits a gain in sensory intensity and richness at the expense of abstract categorization and differentiation" (p. 36). As a result Lindholm (2002) suggests that "although those who have been entranced may feel grandiose expansion they are likely to be hyper suggestible, responding uncritically to instructions and cues of an authority figure." Singer (1990) states that trainees "learn much like hypnotic subjects exhibiting trauma logic how to convince themselves that the group (and I might add especially the leader) is always right even if it contradicts itself" (p. 103). Finally, writing from a psychoanalytic perspective, Hinshelwood (1998) concludes such a "mind-blowing plunge into group emotion" is "both deliciously compelling and personally reducing" (p. 105).

Another more common, yet subtle and powerful, tool to incite shame, humiliation, and traumatic dependency is "gaslighting" (Dorpat 1996, p. 32). This term comes from the film, by the same name, made in 1944 starring Charles Boyer and Ingrid Bergman. In the film Boyer manipulates the glow of the gaslight in an attempt to convince his wife (Bergman) she was going insane. This manipulation is incremental, subtle, and denied, while feigned concern and compassion is expressed. Dorpat, however, uses a more expansive definition of the term: "In my usage, the term *gaslighting* includes a variety of brain-washing techniques. Brainwashers are trying to undermine their victim's belief system and to replace it with another" (p. 33). He concludes: "Studies of individuals and groups subjected to brainwashing show how the victims are first led to doubt or even reject their own judgments at the same time that they are pressured to follow and believe what their victimizer wants them to believe" (p. 35).

A key element here is the orchestrated effort by the leader and group to label a dissident position as a "reality distortion that needed correction." It was preached that only someone who was "fucked up" could make such a dissenting remark. The remark then was evidence of the personal pathology; otherwise, it would never have been said. An example of such an offending remark might be: "You are treating me unfairly." The leader, after acting wounded and eliciting a retraction, would expose this remark as a narcissistic wish to be taken care of in an infantile fashion. No thought was given as to whether the statement was accurate, although the response certainly suggests that possibility.

Theft of Language, in which the Loss of Individual Language Becomes the Language of Regression

Each of the components of indoctrination I have identified so far seeks to curtail independent thought, especially the dissident voice. The very structure of what I am describing as a personal language is undermined, crippled, and ultimately stolen. As I approach the theft of language, I would like to begin with a brief review of language development from a Lacanian standpoint. In the beginning (as it were) there is the mother–child relationship. There is a total identification of one with the other, each experiencing the other as part of him/herself. The mother speaks for the two and thus secures that the child will speak her words and be filled with the mother's tongue. This fusion will be total if nothing is introduced that interrupts what is taking place, taking *hold* between the two.

The child's access into normalcy will be determined by the way he or she will separate from this discourse. The father or symbolic father (any person or function that intercedes to offer space) through triangulation creates an avenue to normalcy ("neurosis" to Lacan because it means living with discontinuity and uncertainty). This separation from mother allows for the development of what I am calling a personal language.

This language when developed, for example, reflects history, familial and cultural influences, education, social status, and orientation to the world. This personal language has preferred word choices, phrasings, intonation, and rhythm, and is rich with idiosyncratic meaning. Such a language is a courageous, if incomplete, act of self-definition. "I am in large part how and what I speak." This language is also how we ask, discuss, describe, demand, exchange, and compromise with others who are separate and distinct from us.

Through indoctrination such language is deconstructed directly via confrontation, ridicule, and dismissal. Since the language is personal, it is viewed as a threat to the search for certainty found in doctrinaire teaching.

Larivière (personal communication, 2003), in a recent discussion of these issues, suggested: "A theft will have been perpetrated. Indoctrination is always totalitarian: it leaves no room for anything *other*. Therefore, no subjectivity, no differentiation is tolerated."

Orange (2003) acknowledges a similar albeit more nuanced process in psychoanalysis: "A special case of closing down inquiry in psychoanalysis can be the self-protection our theoretical language affords us, language that can blame patients, either for their own troubles or for treatment misunderstandings. Language itself, then, becomes yet another intersubjective context for shame and blame" (p. 99).

Personal language is then replaced by the voice of the supervisor or institution. This "new" language of indoctrination is regressive; restriction and simplicity rule over elaboration and complexity. It is a reintroduction of the "mother tongue"—that is, fusion, certainty, and repetition. This language is insistent, unrelenting, and emotionally constrictive to foster the necessary dependency and control what is spoken and how it is spoken. Key phrases and terms provide a cohesive force cementing a unique sense of belonging.

Additionally, certain words and phrases were purged in the BLEA group supervision I experienced. For example, "ambivalent" (e.g., "I am ambivalent about . . .") was eliminated as "too weak," "watered down," or "not straight." Key phrases that contained any qualifiers were put under attack: "I think . . . ," "Perhaps . . . ," "It seems to me . . . ," "I was wondering . . . ," "Could it be . . . ," "Maybe. . . ." There was the strident push for the absolute with no room for either nuance or tact. All supervisees were to speak the same way; all were interchangeable in the pursuit for truth. As Lifton (1961) points out, such attitudes reflect "an underlying assumption that language—like all other human products—can be owned and operated" (p. 430).

Since there was one language and no other, reality was narrowly and rigidly defined. There could be no protest—that aspect of language was taken away, and if it could not be spoken of, it did not exist. This "loading the language" (Lifton 1961) is based on constriction. According to Lifton the individual "is, so to speak, linguistically deprived; and since language is so central to all human experience, his capacities for thinking and feeling are immensely narrowed" (p. 430). A very brief example may be useful here:

P: I would like to say . . .
T: (interrupts) "Would?" You "would" like to or you will say?
P: OK. I think I can say . . .
T: (interrupts again) You "think"? You "think"? Say it or let someone else speak. You are wasting time.

Notice in this brief vignette that the patient was not allowed to complete his thought. He wasn't using the correct language. In this case the patient froze and lapsed into silence. He was then confronted for being self-indulgent (i.e., acting on his feelings of shame) and for pouting. The patient's original concerns were never addressed. Since silence was never tolerated for long, the patient was eventually forced to speak the only language available. There was then apparent agreement between therapist and patient, supervisor and supervisee about what was "real." How could it be otherwise when the therapist (or supervisor) is the "reality" in the room?

CONCLUSION

I have identified and examined five essential characteristics that define the process of indoctrination: (1) charismatic, authoritarian, and dominating leadership; (2) dichotomous and stereotypical thinking; (3) affiliation with an institution or group that fosters multiple conflicting professional relationships; (4) cycling of trauma and retraumatization; and (5) theft of language.

One critical measure of successful indoctrination is the degree to which trainees adopt the expressed language, thoughts, and behaviors of the supervisors/training analysts and make them their own. This is a victory for literalism over figurative language. To eliminate ambiguity, uncertainty, and reify doctrine—figurative language—which provides metaphor, play of meanings, symbolism, and interpretation must be dismantled. Literalism flattens out language and suspends complexity by insisting on unequivocal answers and moral imperatives. The more complete the indoctrination, the more trainees look and sound alike, one voice almost indistinguishable from another. Mimicry reigns. Ferenczi (1933) identified and described this defense as "identification with the aggressor," but for purposes of clarity Anna Freud's (1936) elaboration of the mechanism seems most fitting. She was interested in aggression that most typically takes the form of criticism. For example, out of fear of humiliation trainees learn to enter the minds of supervisors to anticipate and minimize scathing appraisals. To be like the supervisor also provides the narcissistic supplies so necessary yet largely missing for this type of supervisor.

Perhaps most disturbing, the trainee may also appropriate the aggression itself. Anna Freud (1936) suggested such a transformation is "from the person threatened into the person who makes the threat" (p. 113). Laplanche and Pontalis (1973) describe this outcome as "a reversal of roles" and tersely note: "the aggressed turns aggressor" (p. 209).

A cycle of aggression can and often does develop as family members, friends, and particularly spouses become the recipients of unwarranted and intense criticism. Feeling victimized creates a cauldron of unexpressed rage. Since disciples/trainees cannot express these feelings to the leadership for fear of sadistic retribution or abandonment, the rage worms its way into the intimate relationships. To mitigate against feelings of helplessness and to defensively justify their continual involvement, family and friends can be subjected to scathing confrontations when they deviate from the mind set demanded by the training program. Through such a process the circle of indoctrination widens, and sadly casualties continue to mount.

REFERENCES

Balint, M. (1948). On the psychoanalytic training system. *International Journal of Psychoanalysis* 29:163–173.

Bar Levav, I. (1990). Challenging a therapeutic taboo. *Voices: The Art and Science of Psychotherapy* 26(4):44–51.

Brothers, D. (2000). Faith and Passion in Self Psychology, or, Swimming Against the Postmodern Tide of Uncertainty. Paper presented at the meeting of the 23rd International Conference on the Psychology of the Self, Chicago, November.

——— (2003). Clutching at certainty: thoughts on the coercive grip of cult-like groups. *Group Journal of the Eastern Group Psychotherapy Society* 27(2/3):79–88.

Deikman, A. (1972). Deautomatization and the mystic experience. In *Altered States of Consciousness*, ed. C. Tart. New York: Doubleday.

Dorpat, T. (1996). *Gaslighting, The Double Whammy, Interrogation, and Other Methods of Covert Control in Psychotherapy and Analysis.* Northvale, NJ: Jason Aronson.

Falzeder, E. (1994). The threads of psychoanalytic filiations or psychoanalysis taking effect. In *100 Years of Psychoanalysis*, ed. A. Haynal and E. Falzeder, pp. 169–194. [Special Issue of *Cahiers Psychiatriques Genovois*]. London: Karnac.

Ferenczi, S. (1933). Confusion of tongues between adults and the child. In *Final Contributions to the Problems and Methods of Psycho-Analysis*, ed. M. Balint, pp. 156–167. London: Karnac, 1994.

Freud, A. (1936). *The Ego and the Mechanisms of Defense*, revised. New York: International Universities Press.

Ghent, E. (1990). Masochism, submission, surrender: masochism as a perversion of surrender. *Journal of Contemporary Psychoanalysis* 26:108–136.

Harwood, I. (1998). Can group analysis/psychotherapy provide a wide angle lens for self psychology? In *Self Experiences in Group Intersubjective and Self Psychological Pathways to Human Understanding*, ed. I. Harwood and M. Pines, pp. 155–174. London and Philadelphia: Jessica Kingsley.

——— (2003). Distinguishing between the facilitating and the self-serving charismatic group leader. *Group Journal of the Eastern Group Psychotherapy Society* 27(2/3):121–129.

Hinshelwood, R. D. (1998). Paranoia, groups and enquiry. In *Even Paranoids Have Enemies*, ed. J. Berk, S. Pierides, A. Sabbadini and S. Schneider, pp. 100–110. London and New York: Routledge.

Kohut, H. (1976). Creativeness, charisma, group psychology. In *Freud the Fusion of Science and Humanism Psychological Issues*, vol. 9, no. 2/3, monograph 34/35, ed. J. Gedo and G. Pollock, pp. 379–425. New York: International Universities Press.

Langone, M. D., ed. (1993). *Recovery from Cults: Help for Victims of Psychological and Spiritual Abuse*. New York: W. W. Norton.

Laplanche, J., and Pontalis, J. B. (1973). *The Language of Psychoanalysis*. New York: W. W. Norton.

Lifton, R. J. (1961). *Thought Reform and the Psychology of Totalism*. New York: W. W. Norton.

Lindholm, C. (2002). *Charisma*. Retrieved December 18, 2003, from www.BU.com, Boston University. <http://www.bu.edu/uni/faculty/publications/lindholm_charisma/charisma.pdf>

Livingston, M. (1998). Harvest of fire: archaic twinship and fundamental conflict within a community and in group therapy. In *Self Experiences in Group Intersubjective and Self Psychological Pathways to Human Understanding*, ed. I. Harwood and M. Pines, pp. 58–69. London and Philadelphia: Jessica Kingsley.

MacDonald, J. P. (1988). "Reject the wicked man"—coercive persuasion and deviance production: a study of conflict management. *Cultic Studies Journal* 5:59–121.

Orange, D. M. (2003). Why language matters to psychoanalysis. *Psychoanalytic Dialogues* 13(1):77–104.

Pepper, R. S. (2002). Emotional incest in group psychotherapy. *International Journal of Group Psychotherapy* 52(2):285–294.

Phillips, A. (2001). *Promises, Promises*. New York: Basic Books.

Raubolt, R. R. (2003). Attack on the self: charismatic leadership and authoritarian group supervision. *Group Journal of the Eastern Group Psychotherapy Society* 27(2/3):65–77.

——— (2004). Charismatic leadership as a confusion of tongues: trauma and retraumatization. *Journal of Trauma Practice* 3(1):35–49.

Roustang, F. (1982). *Dire Mastery*. Baltimore: Johns Hopkins University Press.

Singer, M. T. (1990). Psychotherapy cults. *Cultic Studies Journal* 7(2):101–125.

Temerlin, M. K., and Temerlin, J. W. (1982). Psychotherapy cults: an iatrogenic perversion. *Psychotherapy: Theory, Research, and Practice* 19:131–141.

Tobias, M., and Lalich, J. (1994). *Captive Hearts, Captive Minds: Freedom and Recovery from Cults and Abusive Relationships*. Alameda, CA: Hunter House.

10

Discussion of the Chapters by Drs. Dorpat, Kavanaugh, Larivière, and Raubolt

Molyn Leszcz

The four chapters in this section of the book, written by four esteemed psychotherapists, psychoanalysts, and group therapists from different orientations, converge in a clear and powerful fashion. Together they demonstrate the scope of professional and pedagogical concern regarding the way in which training and treatment that is intended manifestly to facilitate growth, development, self-awareness, and autonomy may under certain circumstances work against these very same objectives. Covering the territory from the individual and idiosyncratic, to the institutional and systemic, these authors draw our attention to the hazards of training and of treatment that quash growth and development under the weight of hidebound tradition and rigid authority. As an academic psychiatrist committed to the training of residents in the psychotherapies at the University of Toronto for over 20 years, these issues strike in me a powerful note of concern.

The approach that I will take is to discuss each of the chapters individually and offer overview and synthesizing comments that illuminate potential directions that prevent and may remedy these misuses and abuses of treatment and training.

COVERT METHODS OF INTERPERSONAL CONTROL: DR. THEODORE DORPAT

Dorpat's focus on covert methods of interpersonal control posits that the exercise of covert interpersonal control in everyday relationships and in psychoanalytic treatment is widespread. Although there are no empirical data to help us estimate the prevalence and frequency with which this occurs, Dorpat's contentions are well articulated and clearly explained.

This chapter originally appeared in an earlier book by Dorpat entitled, *Gaslighting: The Double Whammy, Interrogation, and Other Methods of Covert Control in Psychotherapy and Psychoanalysis*. It takes its title from the theme in the classic Boyer and Bergman film, in which a husband slowly and methodically seeks to convince his wife that she is losing her mind through a process of his control and distortion of her sense of experience and reality. His ultimate goal: controlling his partner and weakening her trust in her own judgment so as to be able to dominate her and steal her most valued possessions.

Dorpat describes through this chapter a variety of ways in which therapists, both at times by design and inadvertently, may similarly dominate the experience and sensibility of their patients through covert mechanisms of control. Dorpat does an excellent job in presenting the various mechanisms by which this can occur, but he is less comprehensive in explaining the motive behind the exercise of interpersonal control, leading the reader to conclude that interpersonal control is fundamentally driven by the therapist's need for control, power, and influence—the need to distance and diminish a sense of personal vulnerability, through the projection of that vulnerability onto his patient. Without doubt, dynamic issues around power, agency, autonomy, and assertion are prominent in most intensive psychotherapies. In a moment-to-moment fashion therapists will be given an opportunity to be part of an experience that disconfirms patient beliefs about how they are to relate within the world, or alternately, reconfirm these pathological assumptions and entrench maladaptive patterns (Kiesler 1996,

Yalom and Leszcz 2005). In a moment-to-moment fashion, as therapists we are part of our patients' problems or part of their solution. Dorpat illuminates a host of ways in which therapists become part of the problem.

Much of Dorpat's thinking is predicated upon the therapist's use of projective identification, which he understands both as a psychological defense and a form of interpersonal communication. When aspects of the experience of the self are projected into the other, with the unconscious aim of actively containing an unwanted, intolerable aspect of self through this projection, a regressive and ego-weakening process unfolds (Goldstein 1991). Unlike the more common displacement transference in which the object carries projections of other whole objects, in this more damaging form of projective identification what is projected is an experience of a part of the self with attendant weakening of ego boundaries. It appears that Dorpat views the therapist's use of projective identification as intended to achieve and sustain a form of communication to gain control over the victim/patient. This stands in contradistinction to another understood use of projective identification: situations in which the patient projects into the therapist unacceptable aspects of self, hoping against hope that the therapist can contain, metabolize, and detoxify these noxious experiences in ways that enhance therapist empathic understanding, and facilitate offering back to the patient a diluted, more contained, less noxious experience of self that facilitates understanding and growth.

Dorpat lists a number of strategies and interventions that therapists, and for that matter leaders in groups, both therapeutic and institutional, employ covertly, in order to exercise and gain interpersonal control, including gaslighting, questioning, defense interpretation, confrontation, interrupting or overlapping, and abrupt change of topic. Each of these mechanisms aims to destroy or impair an individual's confidence in his own psychic abilities, perception, and judgment, thereby setting the stage for the therapist to seize control over the feelings, thoughts, and behaviors of the impacted individual. Shaming, guilting and humiliation are allied experiences that weaken the victim and enhance the power of the victimizer.

Direct, repetitive, and aggressive questioning is another method, Dorpat notes, that clinicians use to gain control over their patient's mental functions and communications. These forms of questions are not intended to promote self-exploration and free association, but rather are intended to undermine and devitalize the individual's sense of self and capacity to communicate. Questioning is employed not to open up but to shut down: not to gain new information but to discredit the information that the individual has already accrued.

Zealous, aggressive interpretation of patient defenses similarly may be used by therapists to undermine, weaken, and control. This is a particularly important point. As therapists we are responsible not only for our intent, with regard to our intervention, but also very much for our impact. A common therapeutic error that produces negative effects in treatment is the therapist's redoubling of interventions that have already proved unhelpful to the patient, confusing therapist error with patient resistance. Therapists may try to find a content solution to a process problem without taking a step back to reflect on why an intervention that seemed sensible and productive had an inhibiting or destructive effect. The literature on negative outcomes in psychotherapy underscores the pathogenic impact of therapeutic interventions that shame, blame, and criticize and in which the patient feels little choice but to submit to the therapist's will (Aviv and Springmann 1990). Dorpat's elaboration is particularly relevant to all practitioners. It illuminates the hazards of failing to attend to countertransference and of ignoring our impact on our patients, obscured by theoretical conviction—a theme we will return to later in this chapter.

Excessive and critical confrontation, interrupting the patient's narrative, or providing diffuse interventions that move the patient in more than one direction at one time all have the impact of undermining the patient. I would add to this, the therapist who needs to impress his patient with his interpretive prowess or extraordinary sophistication of thinking, is similarly likely to silence, inhibit, or devalue his patient in the interest of bolstering his own self-esteem.

Dorpat moves beyond the confines of the psychotherapeutic and psychoanalytic into the disciplines of linguistics, political science, and feminist studies to highlight the "widespread pattern of relationships in Western societies in which certain individuals and groups exert control and dominance over other individuals," and that result in psychologically and interpersonally destructive behavior. It is evident in the exploitation of the poor by the rich, the weak by the strong, and the female by the male. Dorpat also looks to linguistics, citing the work of

Elgin, who has studied the linguistics of verbal abuse and underscores the subtle, implicit nature of control and domination in language that often, in the absence of thoughtful deconstruction, obscures the impact and power wielded in the communication.

Because we live, work, and practice in a society in which power and mastery are highly valued, therapists must be particularly alert to these dynamic issues within their clinical work, to protect their patients from this form of exploitation. It is but one manifestation of a boundary violation in which the needs of the therapist take precedence over the needs of the patient. The therapy becomes more about the gratification and stabilization of the therapist than the growth of the client.

Reflective capacity is critical to ensure that individuals, patients, therapists, and members of organizations and institutions are able to look at their experience objectively and not blind themselves to an experience that is oppressive or exploitative. The power of denial is great, and within a group, individuals may make a tacit or unconscious choice about what part of their common experience will be denied or reframed so as to permit the perpetuation of status quo. Elsewhere (Leszcz 2004) I comment that not infrequently, individuals recognize that members of their professional community may be engaged in malfeasance or boundary violations, but having denied the early presence of this initially, it becomes progressively harder for them to protest the malfeasance later. Shame and guilt over naive participation and earlier misguided trust generate further collusion. This may in part account for the often recognized phenomenon of colleagues continuing to refer patients to individuals for whom there has been clear and widespread evidence of exploitative behavior with patients. Our allegiances to models, colleagues, and teachers generate enormous and destructive blind spots. As Dorpat notes, denial is a form of unconscious rejection of personal responsibility for action by self or within our community.

Psychotherapists cannot help but exercise power and influence over their patients (Mitchell 1993). Our challenge is to use this power and influence constructively and open-mindedly, without a narrow and blind faith allegiance to our models or without personal self-reflection about our own needs, desires, and countertransferential responses. We must be willing to pierce our denial and tolerate painful and sometimes shameful self-awareness if we are to be consistently effective therapists. Our unwillingness to recognize and accept responsibility for our therapeutic errors generates a form of hubris that interferes with the repair of these mistakes early in the course of our work, setting the stage for much larger and more difficult to repair mistakes later.

ON CUTTING THE GRASS, PSYCHOANALYTIC EDUCATION, AND THE INTERWEAVE OF IDEOLOGY, POWER, AND KNOWLEDGE: AN HISTORICAL AND PHILOSOPHICAL PERSPECTIVE: DR. PATRICK P. KAVANAUGH

Whereas Dorpat's focus is on the clinical interaction between patient and therapist, within the context of the larger, societal exercise of interpersonal control and interpersonal domination, Kavanaugh takes a wholly different slant, focusing on the organization and institution of psychoanalytic training. An analogy he draws between the homogenizing, identity-diffusing, model of contemporary psychoanalytic training and his reminiscence of an early scene from his training in a state hospital is eerie and unsettling. Kavanaugh articulates a parallel between the numbing nature of psychoanalytic training and the crews of men he saw working outside this institution, mindlessly cutting grass, without motivation, without strategy, and without design. Members of the Lobo Brigade—individuals who had been lobotomized— go through the same motions endlessly and repetitively without manifest concern and certainly without manifest self-awareness. It is startling to think that contemporary psychoanalytic training is as routinized, devitalized and lacking in creativity as the work of these institutionalized men. Yet, Kavanaugh proffers a caution to us that there was a time when lobotomies were standard and, in fact, cutting-edge treatment. It behooves us, therefore, to be humble about the practices to which we adhere and place value on presently.

Kavanaugh believes that in many respects "our psychoanalytic institutions, theoretical beliefs, and empirical researches have remained insulated and isolated, behind their own conceptually constructed iron-spiked fence forged from the nineteenth-century positivist philosophic premise, a positivist-medical ideology that houses people in the alphabetized structures of diagnostic and statistical manuals, and an empirical discourse that speaks scientifically produced bodies of knowledge about human beings at the .05 level of truth." It is the interweaving, according to Kavanaugh, of ideology, power, and knowledge that perpetuate the status quo, generating an authoritarian and unsubstantiated certainty that creates psychoanalysts he describes as authoritarian, arrogant, and aloof. Here again we see the echo of irony; a process that is intended to elevate and liberate, reduces and diminishes. Kavanaugh challenges the rigid and codified forms of training that contribute to these undesired outcomes. He argues that contemporary psychoanalytic training in the twenty-first century has advanced little in the last century and is still governed by the same philosophy of science embodied by the Berlin Psychoanalytic Institute founded in 1920.

In Kavanaugh's view, a hierarchically organized structure—candidate, analyst, and training analyst—creates a situation in which to advance in the organization one must identify with and model oneself after one's teachers, supervisors, and training analysts. This cannot but help to reduce freedom of thought and space for thinking. The sanctions leveled against those who do not comply are grave with regard to the loss of prestige, affiliation, and income. He states throughout his chapter, "standards standardize, regulations regulate, and institutions institutionalize."

Kavanaugh raises challenging and provocative questions. Certainly he would not favor such a free form of analytic training that would preclude the articulation or development of standards of practice and professionalism. It seems, therefore, that the key question is how do we establish and maintain standards without undue rigidity that reduces freedom of thinking and reflective capacity. Moderation and common sense appear to be invaluable in striking a balance between the establishment and adherence to standards, and the kind of individual autonomy that the field and its practitioners require.

We also need clarity, transparency, and sufficient humility to recognize the limits in our certainty. Kavanaugh argues that the profession of psychoanalysis would be well served by growth beyond the culture of positivism that guided Freud's original work and in which there was little tolerance for challenges to established reason, logic, and rationality: an era in which there was a "right" way and "wrong" way to think, with little appreciation for the vast space between these polarities.

In reading Kavanaugh's thesis, Thomas Kuhn's (1962) work on scientific revolution comes to mind. According to Kuhn, science is only truly scientific if it can be challenged and disproved. If we foreclose the possibility of such challenge and embrace absolute certainty instead, then we have moved away from science into something less substantial and worthwhile.

Within the clinical context, an important safeguard that protects the working and thinking space of the analyst appears to be liberation from certainty, and liberation from a linear causality that believes only in a one-person psychology in which the past shapes the present. In contrast, by emphasizing the intersubjective reality that is created in a here-and-now fashion between patient and analyst, we will be better able to provide effective, thoughtful, and mindful treatment. We must similarly meld a Cartesian split that blinds us to sources of knowledge and information that seem outside of our scope of conceptualization. Adherence to singularity is an escape from confronting complexity.

Certainty also appears to be the enemy of authenticity and creativity, and invites the passive assumption of knowledge by the candidate, imparted through the actions of the teacher. "Sacred" truths are passed down—anointed even—from generation to generation in this fashion, in a way that Kavanaugh recognizes can reify this knowledge. The anointed recipient of this "sacred" truth cannot help but become arrogant, authoritarian, and aloof. Arrogance, one must add, is not the domain only of the analyst. It comes in large part in any profession in which one carries the power of healing others and is certainly no less a concern for surgeons and physicians than for therapists (Ingelfinger 1980). Perhaps we need that certainty and the power that comes with it to take on the difficult work of caring for the ill. But there is a great hazard that this power will be misused. Kavanaugh cautions further, for example, "knowledge intersects with power and the analyst claims the moral justification, obligation, and power to evaluate the other; to signify his or her meaning, purpose, motive, and intent; and to then directly or indirectly influence if not abridge an individual's political, social, and personal freedoms and responsibilities." Psychoanalytic work can ironically and sadly lose its human and unique capacity for connectedness if the interweave of ideology, power, and knowledge breeds an attitude that encourages practitioners to make rapid sense with surety of everything around them without limits regarding the scope or even access to source data.

One of Kavanaugh's chief concerns is that this interweave freezes analysis in time, resting it on the conceptual foundations of 100 years ago. Kavanaugh notes that we must be particularly cautious about training analysts. He cites Hans Sach, the first training analyst, who is purported to have said regarding the goals for this form of analysis, "one is to transmit the understanding of the unconscious which had been so laboriously accumulated by Freud and his co-workers, and the other is to enforce absolute obedience to the theoretical position of the school." This is scarcely the kind of open-minded education that we wish our trainees to have. Kavanaugh argues that we must be able to examine these issues in our training institutes without fear of hostile reproach or being labeled contemptuously as individuals still struggling with negative transferences to authority figures.

My own vantage point has been one in which I have seen over time many individuals who I felt were intuitively empathic, responsive, and humane therapists become less warm, less responsive, and in many ways less therapeutic as a result of the pursuit of analytic training. In a way that echoes the work of Henry and colleagues (1993) regarding the impact on therapists being trained in manual-based psychotherapy, we must be alert to the costs of training that demands adherence at the sacrifice of warmth, fluidity, flexibility, and actual competence.

How can the situation be remedied? Kavanaugh advocates transparent and pluralistic training. Discovery and creativity should supplant anointment. In addition to pluralism with regard to analytic models, there must be pluralism with regard to educational philosophies, making training more individual and student-centered. The focus should be on the growth and development of the individual student rather than primarily the perpetuation of the institution. It may be hard to imagine an environment in which the kind of relinquishing of control that Kavanaugh advocates could be employed such that "the underlying view of a candidate as self-directed, self-motivated, and self-selecting into a largely self-designed program for the study of psychoanalysis" would become common. But at the same time a move away from a faculty-centered approach to analytic training to a student-centered approach would be a step in the right direction. I would add that a greater emphasis on accountability in training and education would be an important safeguard. Accountability in this situation would be reflected in evaluating the effectiveness of trainees in treating a range of patients, comprehensively and effectively, reducing the number of premature terminations and failed treatments, and creating a feedback loop for

analysts to identify early when treatment in their own hands is progressing and when it is not (Brown et al. 2001).

INSTITUTIONAL CLONING: MIMETISM
IN PSYCHOANALYTIC TRAINING:
DR. MICHAEL LARIVIÈRE

In many ways Larivière's chapter speaks to the same concerns
noted by Kavanaugh. Larivière laments the way in which psychoanalytic training generates a kind of conceptual and practical homogene-
ity that borders, in his view, on cloning. Clearly Larivière is stretching
a point to make a point—it is a leap from identification to mimetism,
or cloning, to the Lobo Brigade noted by Kavanaugh. I also note that
the language and writing style in this chapter is unique and differentiated itself from the others in this section, in a here-and-now articulation of the values and ethos that Larivière espouses.

Larivière begins by commenting that a component of one's identity is always mimetic insofar as we copy, borrow, internalize, and imitate our teachers, mentors, and objects of our admiration. He notes that
this is a particular concern in psychoanalytic training because of the
way in which this process can exaggerate rigid and oppressive orthodoxy
in thinking and practice, not unlike Kavanaugh's three psychoanalytic
A's—arrogant, authoritarian, and aloof. The reward for allegiance
within analytic institutions and the sanctions brought to bear upon
those who challenge leadership and authority are legion. Leo Bellak
(1980) noted the same phenomenon 25 years ago in a paper in which
he advocated that group therapy be provided for analysands as a component of all training analyses to mitigate the pressures of imitative and
stringent identification of the training analyst by the analysand. He
argued that a psychotherapy group is the ideal vehicle to challenge the
pressure toward homogenization. Readers will immediately note the
irony in this statement after reading Raubolt's chapter, but I believe
Bellak's position warrants attention and consideration as a way to foster greater authenticity, creativity, individuality, and self-awareness in
psychotherapy training.

Sandor Ferenczi (Rachman 1996, Rutan 2003) is one of many individuals who tried to think outside of the box and challenge the domi-

nant leadership of his time, only to be met with rejection and even vilification. Only much later was he recognized as making an important and innovative contribution to the practice of psychotherapy, psychoanalysis, and group therapy through his advocacy of disciplined therapist transparency.

In his description of the contributions of Jacques Lacan, Larivière details Lacan's establishment of the École freudienne de Paris, as a model psychoanalytic training institution. Lacan aspired to tackle directly a source of great personal consternation—the tendency of analysands to identify compliantly with their training analysts in a self-perpetuating and constricting fashion. Lacan encountered great resistance in his attempts to challenge the historical authority of the analyst. It is, in Larivière's words, "asking them to question a transferential relation to power and knowledge (as well as the uses thereof)." What incentive would there be for challenging a system that assured followers of continued power and authority? Larivière questions Lacan's thinking, although not his courage, in creating an analytic training institution, hoping that it would somehow be able to operate in a way distinct from the classical and traditional analytic training institutions. How could Lacan have hoped to create a training experience that would not reward submission to authority and the assumption of the anointment of power through identification? Larivière answers this question by suggesting that he believes Lacan hoped his training institution would be able to do what Freud had originally intended for psychoanalysis, which was to identify and accept its limitations and come to grips with uncertainty rather than assume a doctrinaire position of certainty. Perhaps, Larivière notes, Lacan created and dismantled psychoanalytic institutions as an enactment of his recognition of the incompatibility between these two conceptual frames: that of psychoanalysis itself and that of the institutionalization of psychoanalysis.

Again, the theme echoes—a practice that is intended to liberate and humanize has the power to suppress and control. Lacan recognized another paradox: it is difficult to demand open-mindedness without being at some level prescriptive. An unavoidable tension inevitably arose around Lacan insofar as the more Lacan tried to demonstrate an authentic, original form of practice as a psychoanalyst, the more his disciples sought to emulate him and model themselves after him. We are left acknowledging that although Lacan was unique in his challenging of traditional models of psychoanalysis and training, he was unfortunately not unique in developing followers and disciples. Even in challenging "the Führer," according to Larivière, a charged word if ever there was one, Lacan could not but help to draw recruits ready to imitate him. How distressing it must have been for Lacan to realize at some level that as much as he critiqued Freud and tried to distinguish himself from Freud, he was not successful. By trying to escape Freud's authority, Lacan re-created it in another guise and another language.

Lacan argued that the analyst should not defer to any authority outside himself, but there is a powerful if at times subtle vulnerability the analyst experiences in doing the work of analysis. Perhaps it is the fragility, the vulnerability, and the regressive pulls we experience in doing this work that cause us to seek to fortify ourselves through identification with our teachers and predecessors. Perhaps this identification is, as Larivière notes, a way for the trainee to "claim his voice, a voice that will not be confused with those of the other people in the room." It is unfortunate, according to Larivière, that Lacan's disciples, like all disciples, were capable more of remembering than of thinking for themselves. It is this lament that echoes throughout Larivière's chapter.

COERCED DISCIPLESHIP: INDOCTRINATION MASQUERADING AS TRAINING IN PSYCHOTHERAPY: DR. RICHARD RAUBOLT

Raubolt's chapter describes in a much more personal and intimate fashion the impact of abusive and exploitative group therapy training. His description of what he has seen firsthand regarding authoritarian, narcissistic, and self-serving leadership, and the process of leaders controlling, demeaning, and devaluing trainees/patients is unsettling. It is in large measure unsettling not because it is rare and extraordinary, but rather because the phenomenon that Raubolt describes has also been reported as prevalent by many others. It is also not an anachronistic issue, even if it seems that by dint of the need for time to heal pain and to create reflective capacity and emotional distance, descriptions of therapist/trainer mistreatment take many years before they can be articulated publicly (Moses 2003, Rachman 2003).

What makes Raubolt's contribution all the more powerful is that this kind of coercion and abuse in group therapy training can be sustained by virtue of the group trainer hovering close to the edge of respectability. The melding of training and treatment blurs boundaries and intensifies trainee/patient vulnerability and dependence. This only increases the difficulty that an isolated individual may have in challenging the leader's and the group's pressure to submit to the will of the group leader.

Drawing from the work of Sandor Ferenczi, Raubolt describes the powerful way in which the individual's sense of personal language is stolen, restricting opportunities for dialogue only to the specific paradigm established by the self-serving leader. The self-serving leader is interested not in others' growth and development but in sustaining his grandiosity and power. Ferenczi's eloquent articulation of the "confusion of tongues," in which prototypically the adult in control or authority dominates the experience of the vulnerable child to the point of depriving the child of his own personal language, may also emerge at the level of training in certain exploitative environments. It is no small irony that Ferenczi was severely sanctioned by Freud for creating his own language of psychotherapy in the form of an approach that engaged patients in a more human and transparent fashion.

Raubolt's chapter is also important because it underscores the way in which group pressure can be brought to bear by a malevolent group leader to facilitate indoctrination of the individual. Raubolt describes "the process by which a proscribed and organized belief system is systematically imposed on others irrespective of their consent." When this belief system is viewed as anointed and speaking a consummate truth, it becomes even more impossible to resist, as a kind of groupthink (Janis 1982) dominates the environment. Whether it emerges from identification with the aggressor, fear of being the object of attack, or shame about ongoing collusion with destructive behavior, group participants may find it difficult to extricate themselves from the group pressure. These toxic environments deprive members of the capacity for critical analysis; reflective thinking is lost and what emerges is a "deterioration of mental efficiency, reality testing, and moral judgment that results from group pressure" (Janis 1982, p. 9). In some instances, particularly in environments where narcissistically vulnerable individuals join with charismatic leaders, the collusion emerges in response to the Faustian bargain that participants make with the leader, to protect their vulner-able sense of self and the leader's grandiosity. An environment in which critical analysis is attacked as pathological or is interpreted as transfer-ence and resistance, will inevitably lead to silencing, oppression, con-striction, and failure in therapy. As Raubolt notes, what makes this even more damaging is the likelihood that the malfeasance perpetrated be-tween trainer and student in one generation, has a great likelihood of being perpetuated from generation to generation. The cycle of trauma perpetuates itself: the devaluation of the importance of boundaries and mutual respect grows from generation to generation.

Raubolt employs a debundling strategy to examine how this kind of destructive indoctrination can take place. He highlights a number of key elements: charismatic, authoritarian, and dominating leadership; dichotomous and stereotypical thinking; affiliation with an institution or group that fosters multiple, conflicting professional relationships; cycling of trauma and retraumatization; and the theft of language.

Charismatic leadership by itself is not the problem (Horowitz 2000); rather, it is when the charisma of the leader is employed not to pro-tect, benefit, and facilitate development in the group, but rather to control and elevate oneself through the devaluation of others. The leader's intent is an important moderator of this, but it is not without precedent that a good intent may still have a destructive impact. Moses (2003) describes an experience in which she was made to feel at fault, blamed, and undermined because she resisted participation in a group that was led by a group leader who, although highly regarded and re-spected historically, was now clearly in the process of a dementing ill-ness. Raising the idea that the "Emperor was no longer wearing clothes" invited critical attack. Even without malevolent intent, malevolent impact may arise when the trainee's/patient's capacity to question is crushed. Raubolt notes that it requires in this instance two parties—the leader and the trainees—to collude in a mutual regulation of uncer-tainty. If collusion is in fact a force, then what is likely as well is that shame and guilt will consolidate the trainee's submission to this destruc-tive process: "in for a dime, in for a dollar."

Moving beyond the personalities, Raubolt notes an important force in this process of indoctrination is the use of dichotomous and stereo-typical thinking that refutes critical analysis and creates an environ-ment in which things are seen in two dimensions: black or white, with us or against us. Ambiguity or unclarity must be eliminated in this environment so that there is no challenge to the fixed truth. Debate is viewed not as constructive but as rebellion that must be silenced. Raubolt refers to a list of expressions that all serve to quash dialogue and eliminate challenge. It is striking how each of the statements in this litany reflects a therapist-centered form of group therapy in which peers are discounted and the world is viewed in dichotomous fashion, populated by winners and losers, those in power and those who must submit. This is doubtless a reflection of the kind of emotional abuse that can be embedded in language, as Dorpat identifies elsewhere. It is indeed evocative to read about Raubolt's visceral response to revisiting his experience—a powerful reminder of its traumatic potential.

The violation of boundaries and the lack of a secure environment that maintains safety and respect is another important device in indoctrination. The ever-changing boundaries of what is therapy and what is supervision or training, of what is valued and what is unvalued, of who is in the inner circle and who is marginalized—all add to confuse and destabilize individuals. These forces pull members toward the leader as a source of potential security and imbue the group members with fear and panic of being expelled or moved to a position of lower priority and primacy. The commingling of social and professional relationships adds further pressure to this as the stakes become even higher and the pressure grows to belong, to comply, and to fit.

The blurring of supervision with therapy is particularly troubling. Trainees who are treated as patients lose credibility in their protestations. They will inevitably feel undermined, as all protests are dismissed and all challenges are viewed as resistance, transference, or psychopathology. This kind of environment attacks the individual at his most fundamental core. The pressure to buy into the belief system of the environment is powerful, particularly when that group environment fosters dependence, exclusivity, and intensity, the hallmarks of relationships in which projective identification thrives.

An additional important dynamic that Raubolt notes is that of the impact on the individual of the traumatization that occurs in this process of indoctrination. He cites, for example, the use of the term *busting* as a statement of the kind of power with which force was used by trainers in this environment to, in essence, blow open the psyche of trainees. It also speaks to the way in which a supervisor could be encouraged to attack, undermine, and overwhelm trainees through the use of shame, contempt, and marginalization.

What is less clear is what motivates the trainer to behave in such destructive fashion. How do we understand this kind of sadistic response? Perhaps it has to do with the vulnerability that some who seek therapy and who seek training in therapy carry into their therapeutic and treatment experience. Individuals who have suffered trauma are more vulnerable to be exploited by subsequent traumatizing forces. Perhaps the traumatizing trainer is also someone who has been traumatized and is also identified with the aggressor. This kind of therapist seeks to master the experience of having been previously assaulted, controlled, ridiculed, and savaged by perpetrating the same on others in his care. I recognize that this is an alternate view to the wounded healer premise that Raubolt puts forward. The premise of the wounded healer may be an apt explanation for the victims, but I believe we also need to understand further the perpetrator. The wounded healer, accustomed to mistreatment, misattunement, and self-sacrifice, becomes a suitable partner for the abusive, exploitative trainer. A "confusion of tongues" ensues and another cycle is launched. Raubolt provides a graphic description of the way in which ego boundaries were dismantled in the training group in which he participated, how passions were inflamed and boundaries weakened, the way one imagines an interrogation process would occur in a prisoner-of-war camp. Clearly, one need not go to the Gulag to encounter brainwashing and spirit crushing. A confusion of tongues ensures that the dissident voice will be silenced and any personal language is stolen away from the victim.

The graphic illustrations of this loss of personal language are hard to miss. Raubolt alerts us, however, to more subtle manifestations of this process in which patients may feel compelled to close off aspects of self to the therapeutic process because the experience does not fit the model or language of their treater. Indeed, our theoretical models may be powerful sources of our countertransference (Purcell 2004).

CONCLUSION

At first reading, these four chapters have the potential to invite a feeling of despair about the state of our work. I prefer, however, to read them as cautionary notes—real and substantial. They are also experiences that must be contextualized. In the same way that psychotherapy for all our patients has been enhanced by our understanding of treatment of patients with the most severe character pathology, the descriptions of these four articulate authors can help us to ensure that all our training and treatment meet our objectives—promoting growth, learning, and autonomy, cognizant of the risk that we may be inadvertently contributing to the opposite experience.

What are some of the principles we might be able to extract as teachers, supervisors, and therapists that will broaden our reach effectiveness? As much as the transmission of skills, training in psychotherapy involves the transmission of values, ethics, and attitudes. Elsewhere (Leszcz 2004) I offer a number of general safeguards that are useful in the prevention of the kinds of difficulties that have been articulated by Dorpat, Kavanaugh, Larivière, and Raubolt.

These considerations include the importance of therapists being well grounded in their personal lives. Gratification from work should not be the only source of esteem. An allied consideration is the importance of avoiding professional isolation. Isolation inhibits the capacity for reflection and diminishes the space for thinking in one's professional life. Exposing one's work and ideas to collegial examination and utilizing peer and collegial supervision promotes opportunities for continuing professional development. Furthermore, this provides an opportunity to reflect upon and examine countertransferential difficulties that may emerge within the clinical work or training environment or that may be generated from within the therapist/trainer's personal life. Who knows better than us that what is not understood is likely to be enacted?

The principles of congruence and isomorphy are also informative. In the systems in which we work and train, dynamic issues reverberate up and down the system, and processes that occur at one level of the system will gain expression at every level of the system. If there is an issue with the misuse of power at one level, it will gain expression at every other level.

We should aim for congruence. By this I mean that in the values we transmit, we should demonstrate that we train our students and treat our patients in a way that reflects our core values and our commitment to foster growth and development. Values such as empathy, decency, authenticity, mutuality, collaboration, and respect must not only be spoken about, they must be demonstrated, moment in and moment out, in the course of all interaction.

As a field we must accept the need to be accountable. Opening the doors of our institutions and training programs is one way to invite this accountability by encouraging the people who work in these fields to articulate and describe the work that they do, the rationale for why they do it, and its effectiveness. Psychotherapy, group therapy, and psychoanalysis are all powerful forms of psychological intervention. Every intervention that can be of benefit has the potential to be harmful as well if misapplied. Mechanisms must be in place that hold supervisors and trainers accountable and that actually monitor their development and effectiveness and promote genuine and authentic feedback without the hazard of retaliation.

Supervision by definition is only effective when it tracks trainees' concerns and creates a space for thinking, a space for reflection, and a space for the exploration of countertransference. Blurring the boundaries between therapy and supervision is fraught with difficulties. Environments in which trainees feel shamed, humiliated, or exploited are the antithesis of what we seek. These are the emotions and experiences that quash autonomy.

Mark Twain once stated that if all one has in his toolbag is a hammer, then everything looks like a nail. We must think broadly and not become infatuated with or overinvested in our models and methods. It is essential to remember that we use models—they are our tools. We control them, and not the other way around. This kind of attitude will also invite the kind of humility that helps us to strike the necessary balance of confidence and caution, and of reflection and action that creates the best opportunity for learning, growth, and development (Murphy et al. 1996).

REFERENCES

Aviv, A., and Springmann, R. (1990). Negative countertransference and negative therapeutic reactions: prognostic indicators in the analysis of severe psychopathology. *Contemporary Psychoanalysis* 26:693–715.

Bellak, L. (1980). On some limitations of dyadic psychotherapy and the role of the group modalities. *International Journal of Group Psychotherapy* 30:7–21.

Brown, G., Burlingame, G., Lambert, M., Jones, E., and Vaccaro, J. (2001). Pushing the quality envelope: a new outcomes management system. *Psychiatric Services* 52:825–934.

Goldstein, W. N. (1991). Clarification of projective identification. *American Journal of Psychiatry* 148:153–161.

Henry, W. P., Strupp, H. H., Butler, S. F., Schacht, T. E., and Binder, J. L. (1993). Effects of training in time-limited dynamic psychotherapy: changes in therapist behavior. *Journal of Consulting and Clinical Psychology* 61:434–440.

Horowitz, L. (2000). Narcissistic leadership in psychotherapy groups. *International Journal of Group Psychotherapy* 50:219–235.

Ingelfinger, F. J. (1980). Arrogance. *New England Journal of Medicine* 301(26): 1507–1511.

Janis, I. (1982). *Groupthink: Psychological Studies of Policy Decisions and Fiascoes*, 2nd ed., p. 9. Boston: Houghton Mifflin.

Kiesler, D. (1996). *Contemporary Interpersonal Theory and Research*. New York: John Wiley.

Kuhn, T. (1962). *The Structure of Scientific Revolutions*. Chicago: University of Chicago Press.

Leszcz, M. (2004). Reflections on the abuse of power, control and status in group therapy and group therapy training. *International Journal of Group Psychotherapy* 54:389–400.

Mitchell, S. A. (1993). *Hope and Dread in Psychoanalysis*. New York: Basic Books.

Moses, L. (2003). Perspectives on the use and abuse of power in group therapy. Paper presented at the annual meeting of the American Group Psychotherapy Association, New Orleans, LA. February.

Murphy, L., Leszcz, M., Collings, A. K., and Salvendy, J. (1996). Some observations on the subjective experience of neophyte group therapy trainees. *International Journal of Group Psychotherapy* 46:543–552.

Purcell, S. D. (2004). The analyst's theory: a third source of countertransference. *International Journal of Psychoanalysis* 85:635–652.

Rachman, A. (1996). *Sandor Ferenczi, the Psychotherapist of Tenderness and Passion*. New York: Jason Aronson.

——— (2003). Issues of power, control, and status in group interaction: from Ferenczi to Foucault. *Group* 27:89–105.

Rutan, J. (2003). Sandor Ferenczi's contributions to psychodynamic group therapy. *International Journal of Group Psychotherapy* 53:375–384.

Yalom, I. D., and Leszcz, M. (2005). *The Theory and Practice of Group Psychotherapy*, 5th ed. New York: Basic Books.

III

SUPERVISORY
ALTERNATIVES

11

Primum Non Nocere:
A Supervisor's Odyssey

Paula B. Fuqua

Psychotherapy supervision is often described as if it were a standard arrangement with a supervisor and a supervisee engaged in a stereotypical encounter based on teaching and learning. I, myself, have written in this vein (Fuqua 1994). Until the recent past, most authors on the topic have attempted to put forth principles to guide the thinking and interaction of the supervisor (Dewald 1987, Ekstein and Wallerstein 1958, Fleming and Benedek 1966). The apparent assumption is that most of this not very extensive literature is meant for those providing supervision rather than those receiving it. If knowledge is power —and if there is any real knowledge involved—the emphasis on the supervisor's teaching activity already slants the situation toward the supervisor.

A moment's reflection reveals how much variation and inconsistency lie behind the "standard" situation. The supervisee may be a neophyte or an experienced therapist, a trainee in a training program or someone seeking private consultation. Payment may or may not be involved. Either party may or may not have experienced his/her own treatment. All these factors make a difference. Even such basics as the gender of the therapist and supervisor, their race and socioeconomic status, and marital and parental experience fold into the mix, as does the sexual orientation of both members of the pair. (I am leaving out entirely supervision that occurs in a group setting because it is beyond the scope of this chapter.)

The physical setting in which the two meet also affects the total experience. The consultation may be in the supervisee's office or the supervisor's, in a clinic setting or privately—or even in the women's board restaurant of a hospital, a place one of my supervisors liked to meet during my residency.

Presumably, supervisees come to learn, but they may have other multiple and complex motives, such as professional advancement, self-esteem regulation, a covert wish for therapy, a need for referrals, the justification of their work in light of other criticism, or an antidote to loneliness. Some therapists also come in response to a mandate to get help after an actual or threatened boundary violation.

On the side of the supervisor there are also multiple possible motivators. Self-esteem, professional advancement, contractual obligation, money, loneliness, the chance to promote a favored theory, and a chance to exercise power are all common. The supervisee's idealization can be a heady motivator for the supervisor too (Berman 2000).

In the past I viewed supervision as a learning experience and understood it from a classically Kohutian perspective. Supervision was geared toward the growth of the supervisee. It involved a psychological disruption and rearrangement as new mental structures were formed. I saw the function of the supervisor as a regulator of this disruption—a self-object and more (see also Gardner 1995, Muslin and Val 1989, Wolf 1989, 1995). Self psychology and psychoanalysis have developed significantly since 1994. Theories involving mutuality, relational concepts, and intersubjectivity have become prominent. It has become glaringly obvious to me how much of the supervisor's subjectivity I had left out in my previous writing. Other writers have also noted this. Berman (2000), for example, describes the expansion in our understanding of supervision through intersubjectivity theory and urges that the subjectivity of the supervisor as well as that of the supervisee become a part of the supervisory discourse. Buirski and Hagland (2001),

Lecomte and Richard (1999), and Slavin (1997) have also elaborated on the extension of self psychology via intersubjectivity and applied that to the understanding of supervision.

Like any relationship, supervision is a cocreated situation and exists in a social matrix as well. Insofar as the supervisor has in mind the idea that she and the supervisee are equally important in their contributions, though not symmetrical in other ways, the supervisor will wear her authority "lightly," to paraphrase Donna Orange (1995). A shift in theoretical perspective toward the relational direction provides a bit of advantage in preventing the exploitation and abuse of supervisees because it empowers the supervisee to a greater degree. As is the case with every other theory, however, intersubjectivity cannot totally compensate for the tendencies of an individual toward good or harm. Still, relational theory helps.

One trainee's experience with two supervisors illustrates the point. Jason was a very bright and intellectual social worker in a psychotherapy training program. He had a sensitive streak that made him both empathic and defensive. His first consultant was George Brown, a respected clinician and a well-known researcher in developmental processes. The perspicacious reader will notice that hereafter I refer to both Jason and George by their first names, rather than follow the usual practice of calling the supervisor Dr. Brown. This phrasing is meant to emphasize the mutuality in the relationship. In the consultation Jason presented Carl, a patient who was hard to involve in therapy. The work with Carl stimulated Jason to try to engage George in wide-ranging discussions of many theoretical positions. George was committed to propagating his work and felt Jason was challenging its value. Jason tried to bring up their problems in the supervision, but George didn't seem to want to talk about it. Both men became more and more uncomfortable.

Finally, Jason bridled, and he and George clashed. George reported to the training director that Jason was arrogant and resistant to learning. Jason felt the same way about his supervisor. Jason was familiar with intersubjectivity theory and felt entitled to a more collaborative, less critical experience. He needed and expected his supervisor to find him where he was and work from there. I think he needed a chance to understand his first supervisor's position too, but that process could not be articulated without the supervisor's concurrent understanding of the intersubjectively cocreated context of the situation, and his willingness to talk about it on an ongoing basis. With a theoretical approach emphasizing mutuality and working with a second supervisor, Jason was able to avoid submitting to ideas counter to his own before he had an opportunity to think them through. He needed to be able to decide whether or not George's ideas fit for him as a therapist. All too often what happens in situations in which supervisor and supervisee clash is that the supervisee "goes inside himself," becomes devious, and conducts treatment without sharing the relevant details with his consultant (Hantoot 2000). In essence, he lies, and the supervisor concurrently experiences the supervision as flat and rote.

The theoretical shift toward intersubjectivity helps the supervisee, but it also exposes a gap in the literature regarding the subjective experience of the supervisor. What was the first supervisor thinking? How did he feel about losing a supervisee? What about the second supervisor too? Was there a competitive triumph? How did he or she manage to connect with Jason and promote or contain his/her own convictions?

In an effort to fill in the gap in our understanding of the supervisor's contribution, I will describe my own experience in a dilemma full of emotional and ethical challenges. To protect the identity and privacy of the supervisees I have amalgamated aspects of several supervisions, emphasizing what I felt and thought similarly in each case. Two other supervisors have generously shared their experience and contributed to this condensed description as well. Since my focus is more on the inner life of the supervisor, I can be simply straightforward about that aspect. I trust the reader will find my report true to life, despite the disguises of the supervisees and their patients. I believe that if those in supervision see more of the humanness of the supervisor, they will feel more equal. I also hope my report will help supervisors deal more complexly with their experience in supervision, feel less pressure to be all-knowing, and become more comfortable with their dilemmas.

The supervisee I will call Pat, an androgynous name that reflects experience with both male and female consultees. Here we will assume that Pat is a woman. I met her in a clinic where I was consulting to the staff and supervising trainees. We discussed various cases once a week for about a year. Over that time, I developed quite a bit of respect for her therapeutic skill. Some years later, Pat sought me out privately for further supervision when she shifted to an exclusively private practice.

By then she had many years of experience and was in her own analysis. When she came to me, I was complimented that she felt good about our previous work. She was also in supervision with another consultant of a different theoretical bent. She wanted to think broadly and that was fine with me.

Pat was a lively woman who had periods of self-doubt about her abilities. Like Jason, she had had a bad experience with a former consultant who seemed to be a know-it-all. She often left his office feeling angry and insecure.

What was I bringing to the supervision? I was proud of my good reputation as a supervisor. When I wrote about supervision in the past as a learning situation, a big part of my motivation was to exorcise my own bad experience in psychoanalytic supervision. The truth is, despite my reputation as a good supervisor, I never felt I had had a good experience as a supervisee. Most of what I learned about treatment had come from my two analyses and extensive reading. I joked that perhaps I was not teachable. I never felt trusting enough to open up fully to my supervisors. Maybe, I have often mused, the reason was that every instance of supervision was part of a training program and I was always being evaluated. In the 1970s and even the 1980s, personal revelations such as dreams about patients were considered signs of pathology rather than useful pieces of information as they are today. Enactments, too, were thought of as "acting out," and anathema instead of analytic material. Many of us who trained in that era became self-protective and guarded about what we might reveal. I do not feel I hid any big ethical lapses, but I did attend the wedding of a patient in the late stages of an analysis without mentioning it to my analytic supervisor. I believed that what I was doing was therapeutic and that he would not see it that way and would hinder my progression in training. I also believed that it would be damaging to the analysand if I did not participate. She was someone who needed a "witness" in her life that her parents could not provide. I was enacting that provision (Bacal 1985, Shane et al. 1997), and talking about it with her, and not talking about it with my supervisor.

Because of all my own past experience, I bent over backward to get some idea of what Pat wanted to learn—where her active curiosity was most alive and what she wanted from me. Using this approach, I have found supervisees often are very open and self-confiding, whether they are consulting with me as part of a training program or independently. I believe this is partly due to my using a theory emphasizing mutuality and partly due to my personal qualities. A point that relational theories logically lead to is that one's personal qualities are a definitive part of any interchange. In the interchange of two subjectivities, the specificity of the subjects matters and must be recognized.

What I further knew about myself was that I took great pleasure in the admiration and respect I received as a supervisor. I felt important, wanted, and appreciated when things went well. I also liked supervision because I could be more open and at ease than I was in my clinical work. I often felt a conflict between wanting to talk about myself or discuss movies and books with my bright, interesting supervisees and my belief that the supervision was about the development of the supervisee. An intersubjective focus offered me a framework to understand how those pressures interacted. I hope that supervisees will read this and have some perspective on the bilaterality of both the needs and the power in the situation. An understanding that the supervisor has longings and vulnerabilities can enhance the power on the side of the consultee. Ultimately we cannot hope to help our patients achieve a nuanced acceptance of their own lives without our accepting our own, whether we are student, teacher, or seeker of therapeutic help. Of course, if a supervisee is extremely compliant and becomes primarily a self-regulator of the supervisor, such "understanding" can also become a form of domination by the supervisor. A successful supervision, it seems to me, enables both parties to understand this and keep all the understanding "at bay," while exploring the process of doing treatment.

During Pat's consultation I developed great respect for the emotional intensity she brought to her work. She also had a large fund of theoretical knowledge and was widely read in psychoanalysis. We talked about several of her clients, focusing on one for a few weeks and then another. Finally we began to talk only about Libby, who was a special challenge to Pat. She described Libby as a divorced woman who was confused about the future direction of her business career. Libby came from a working-class family. Her emotionally invisible mother kowtowed to an alcoholic, physically abusive father. Libby gradually revealed that she was depressed as a result of her abuse. Sometimes she became panicky and suicidal. She called Pat frequently outside therapy hours for support. As time passed, I could see Pat feeling more and more responsible for maintaining Libby.

Pat was also somewhat confused about how to understand Libby. Libby was very athletic, a big soccer star in high school and college. She felt neither much attachment to her former husband nor much regret about their divorce. Pat told me she thought Libby was a lesbian deep down, but unaware of it. I myself was not sure whether that was true or not.

Pat also told me that her marriage was not going all that well. Her husband was emotionally flat and unresponsive to Pat's feelings. Libby seemed to be providing a sense of intimacy and intensity that Pat needed. I became more and more worried about Pat's intense involvement with Libby. Were Pat's longer and longer phone conversations with Libby in Libby's best interest? They seemed to be helping Libby survive and I was reluctant to interfere. Libby's urges to commit suicide really worried me. I was not one to take a doctrinaire approach, I thought, and I needed to figure out what functions were being served in Pat and Libby's interaction. I wondered what Pat's dynamics were and wanted to be able to show how Pat could use her feelings to help Libby in therapy.

Meanwhile, Pat had another supervisor who knew what was happening with Pat and Libby and was openly disapproving. I did not think I had to emphasize limit setting because Pat was not without a reminder of the slippery slope of her behavior. I felt some relief not to be the only concerned party. I could focus on understanding, which has always been my theoretical bent.

Pat was very open with me about all her interactions with Libby. She was sitting next to Libby and holding Libby's hand from time to time when Libby seemed most upset and needy. Pat felt closer to Libby than she did to her husband. I knew an enactment was happening. If we could understand it, Pat could establish better boundaries. Pat revealed her past sexual abuse by an aunt and elaborated further on her unhappiness in her current marriage. A good friend of Pat's had died recently and Pat observed that you have to go for what you want in life, because life is short. I could see Pat's longing for an intense, intimate relationship being mobilized and gratified by Libby's persistent push for greater contact. I felt a profound sympathy for Pat's yearnings.

At this point I was conflicted about what I should be doing, but not nearly so greatly as I would become. I wondered whether I needed to protect Libby. Could I do a better job of that in some other way than by continuing to try to understand what was going on in Pat's countertransference? Intimations of the other supervisor disapprovingly questioning what was happening with Pat and me made me more nervous. I thought if I insisted Pat break off the treatment with Libby that Libby might kill herself. Even now, though, I doubt that Pat would have done so, had I recommended it. The whole process would have gone underground, not to be shared at all. I was working in the dark as far as really knowing what would happen in the future if I took this or that course of action, but doing my best. I chose to stick to the analytic method of trying to understand everything.

I tried to help Pat explore her feelings about Libby by describing my own intense attraction to a former female patient, Alana. Alana was also a victim of inappropriate parental behavior. She had taken naked showers with her father in her prepubertal years and he had inserted his finger in her anus. Alana was significantly depressed. She would lie on her side on the analytic couch, turn toward me, and describe how she wanted to touch my breasts in an erotic way. I endured this, felt an intense attraction and desire myself, but ultimately weathered my own longings. I understood Alana's behavior as her way of intensifying our relationship to counteract her depression.

With Pat I hoped to create an empathic bond by showing that I had had similar feelings to hers. First, I thought that might normalize intense countertransference feelings as a part of therapy. Racker (1968) described a necessary countertransference neurosis. We needed to see Pat's feelings as a usable and useful part of treatment. If Pat felt a bond with me that might also divert some of her mirroring selfobject needs into our relationship and remove the pressure to cross any more boundaries inappropriately with Libby. Another motive in my sharing my own experience was to create a holding environment by example, so that Pat would be able to "hold" her own feelings while developing a greater understanding.

In my many moments of desperation I asked myself, where was Pat's analyst? Why weren't Pat's needs expressed and managed with her analyst rather than with Libby? I was annoyed. Pat said her analyst was insisting she break off her treatment with Libby and he was threatening to report her. Pat felt guilty and anxious about the threat. She and her therapist had no therapeutic alliance. The therapist and I seemed to have changed roles. Now I was really getting nervous. Could Pat lose her livelihood? Might I be sued, lose my license, be censured ethically?

What was I doing in the middle of this? It was like the war in Iraq. I should have seen trouble way back, but it would be irresponsible to pull out now. Pat needed me.

It will be no surprise that the analyst and I sought a joint consultation with Pat's approval. We met with two consultants. They affirmed my persistent efforts to understand within a system of multiple players. I felt greatly relieved, although I retained a certain concern because none of the problems were solved yet.

I tell this tale in order to fill in the side of a supervisor's experience in a setting of great responsibility and intense vulnerability for all parties concerned. I am attempting to expand one side of the dialogue that is supervision. The story is incomplete without the report from the side of the supervisee, but that is for another day. The patient, too, deserves a say, so we really need a model with multiple perspectives as well as an appreciation for the multiply created system to which all have contributed (McKinney 2000). Besides patient, analyst, and supervisor, we might also want to include in the total system all their therapists, other supervisors, the training institution, if one is involved, and even other significant persons in each of the primary contributors' lives. My report is tantamount to carving out a portion of a moving river for examination. Everything is constantly changing and what we try to describe slips through our hands as we try to convey it. Yet, in the process, we get some idea of what it was like to swim in this particular river.

What happened with Pat and Libby? Pat divorced her husband and began a more helpful analysis and finally, in an appropriate way, did break off the treatment with Libby. I was relieved, but only partially satisfied with the conclusion. I would have wanted Pat to be able to use what she felt within the treatment to help Libby. On the other hand, I felt a great deal of compassion for Pat and was glad that her needs were being better met overall with a new analyst. What about Libby? Things ended amicably and I hear from other sources that Libby seems to be thriving. But we do not really know. I feel the weight of responsibility and at the same time recognize my lack of real control. I most certainly identified more with Pat than Libby. In the end, the supervisor's authority and expertise were a double-edged sword. They have the potential to foster growth or create pain, harm, and havoc, and we don't always know which will result. Retracing my own steps along this portion of the supervisory path reminds me to be humble.

REFERENCES

Bacal, H. (1985). Optimal responsiveness and the therapeutic process. In *Progress in Self Psychology*, vol. 1, ed. A. Goldberg, pp. 202–227. New York: Guilford Press.

Berman, E. (2000). Psychoanalytic supervision. *International Journal of Psychoanalysis* 81:273–290.

Buirski, P., and Haglund, P. (2001). *The Intersubjective Approach to Psychotherapy*. Northvale, NJ: Jason Aronson.

Dewald, P. (1987). *Learning Process in Psychoanalytic Supervision: Complexities and Challenges*. New York: International Universities Press.

Ekstein, R., and Wallerstein, R. (1958). *The Teaching and Learning of Psychotherapy*. New York: Basic Books.

Fleming, J., and Benedek, T. (1966). *Psychoanalytic Supervision*. New York: International Universities Press.

Fuqua, P. (1994). Teaching, learning and supervision. In *A Decade of Progress: Progress in Self Psychology*, vol. 10, ed. A. Goldberg, pp. 79–97. Hillsdale, NJ: Analytic Press.

Gardner, J. (1995). Supervision of trainees: tending the professional self. *Clinical Social Work Journal* 23:271–286.

Hantoot, M. (2000). Lying in psychotherapy supervision. *Academic Psychiatry* 24:179–187.

Lecomte, C., and Richard, R. (1999). The supervision process: a self-supervision developmental model for psychotherapists. Paper presented at the meeting of the 22nd annual conference on the Psychology of the Self, Toronto, October.

McKinney, M. (2000). Relational perspectives and the supervisory triad. *Psychoanalytic Psychology* 17:565–584.

Muslin, H., and Val, E. (1989). Supervision: a teaching learning paradigm. In *Learning and Education: Psychoanalytic Perspectives*, ed. K. Field, B. Cohler, and G. Wool, pp. 159–179. Madison, CT: International Universities Press.

Orange, D. (1995). *Emotional Understanding: Studies in Psychoanalytic Epistemology*. New York: Guilford Press.

Racker, H. (1968). *Transference and Countertransference*. New York: International Universities Press.

Shane, M., Shane, E., and Gales, M. (1997). *Intimate Attachments: Toward a New Self Psychology.* New York: Guilford Press.

Slavin, H. H. (1997). Influence and vulnerability in psychoanalytic supervision and treatment. *Psychoanalytic Psychology* 15:230–244.

Wolf, E. (1989). A psychoanalytic self psychologist looks at learning. In *Learning and Education: Psychoanalytic Perspectives*, ed. K. Field, B. Cohler, and G. Wool, pp. 377–394. Madison, CT: International Universities Press.

——— (1995). How to supervise without doing harm: comments on psychoanalytic supervision. *Psychoanalytic Inquiry* 15:252–267.

12

Clinical Supervision: A Process of Self-Reflexivity in the Development of Therapeutic Competence

Conrad Lecomte

Numerous issues have been raised regarding supervision and training of psychotherapists. Many of these concerns pertain to the emotional toll it takes on therapists and the challenge they face dealing with patients reporting problems that are ambiguous, contextually unique, and continually shifting, and the challenge they face dealing with emotions, ranging from anxiety and depression to anger and hostility (Begley et al. 1994). Consequently, several questions have been raised: How does a therapist create an appropriate emotional distance from the patient? How does a therapist avoid becoming too emotionally distant, or the opposite, becoming too involved? When all attempts have been made to deal with complex situations, what is a therapist left to do? When faced with doubt and uncertainty, how is it possible for a therapist to avoid feelings of discouragement or disillusionment? Finally, how is it possible to maintain and develop an active engagement in the development of therapeutic competence, and at the same time offer quality services?

When faced with these questions, therapists have their own way of seeking answers, based on personal history, work environment, past experiences, personality, as well as personal values and beliefs. Many consult colleagues for answers or support, which frequently result in concrete advice on how to intervene or how to avoid such difficult situations altogether. In either of those cases, therapists can easily conclude that they are incompetent, merely based on the fact that their colleagues seem not have experienced as difficult a situation as their own. Others try to find answers in books or articles relating to their clinical practice. Unfortunately, despite the importance of these resources, many therapists find it difficult to apply what they've read in practice. Too frequently, recommendations from colleagues or professional and scientific documents may implicitly undermine a therapist's sense of competence. In addition, published case studies often report positive outcomes, even with difficult clients. This can serve to further challenge feelings of competency because if the therapist were more competent, he too would achieve positive results. Consequently, such experiences can engender feelings of shame and humiliation, which in turn may lead therapists to conceal their problems. Talbot (1995) notes that embarrassment and shame can accompany disclosures in response to questions pertaining to personal or professional issues or personal weaknesses. It is not an uncommon experience for a supervisee to decide not to reveal or discuss problems following an embarrassing or shameful experience, opting instead to divulge cases that demonstrate initiative, autonomy, and competence! Unfortunately, such a situation can have detrimental effects on the development of therapeutic competence by leaving supervisees to assume they can rely only on themselves or to feel like an imposter, thereby leading to feelings of isolation. Some other therapists seeking a deeper longing for a near-miraculous transformed sense of competence or a search of an idealized state may become enslaved to the sadistic omnipotent control of an idealized supervisor. In a desperate search for competence, supervisees are vulnerable to being controlled by surrendering exclusively to a supervisor's perspective.

It remains true that most of university clinical training and supervision programs tend to advocate approaches centered on the acquisition and mastery of techniques and specific strategies (Bernard and Goodyear 1998). This model is based on the principle that therapeutic competence and effectiveness come from mastering the application of these techniques and strategies. The trainer-supervisor is defined as the expert, using modeling, feedback, coaching, and practice to facilitate the development of competency in the pursued objectives. These technical procedures and specifications are often offered in treatment manuals. Such "manual-guided" psychotherapy training has led to a clinical practice based on empirically supported psychological treatments.

Other training and supervision approaches recommend, first and foremost, knowledge of the patient's characteristics (Frawley-O'Dea and Sarnat 2001). A therapist who is capable of diagnosing as well as clearly describing and explaining the functioning and dynamics of a patient is considered competent. Training and supervision, therefore, focus on the examination and analysis of the patient's characteristics. The trainer-supervisor viewed as an objective expert proposes, teaches, and recommends the course of action.

Training programs that are therapist-centered promote the exploration and clarification of the therapist's subjective experiences (e.g., subjective reactions, resistances, perceptions, etc.). However, supervision processes that concentrate on the trainee run the risk of being confused with psychotherapy processes that can be felt as intrusive by the therapist-supervisee (Lecomte 2001).

Finally, at the core of other training and supervision approaches is the professed parallel between the therapist–patient relationship and that of the therapist–supervisor (Frawley-O'Dea and Sarnat 2001). It is thought that analyzing and clarifying the similarities between the therapist–patient and therapist–supervisor relationships affords the opportunity to understand and repair any difficulties experienced by the supervisees, thereby enhancing their professional competence.

The comparison of these different approaches allows for a reflection of the pertinent factors in training and supervision. First, by focusing on one perspective, each of these approaches favors a particular way of "knowing." Supervision that focuses on techniques and strategies favors the development of professional competence based on "know-how." Supervision centered on the subjective experience of the therapist primarily aims for clarifying the experiential dimension of "being," while supervision that focuses on patients seeks to promote "theoretical knowledge."

Each of these approaches offers both advantages and limitations. A patient-centered supervision and training model can help the therapist develop clear reassuring and well-defined intervention procedures. Thus, the therapist learns to work in a structured manner while avoiding making personal involvement a part of the process. However, a patient-centered approach offers little flexibility when it comes to the vicissitudes of human relations. In effect, when the therapy does not proceed as anticipated or when there are ruptures in the therapist–patient relationship, it is the patient who tends to bear the responsibility. Similarly, when problems arise in the supervisee–supervisor relationship the cause is often attributed to the subjective reactions of the therapist. In consequence, when the patient is the primary focus of the supervision process, the needs of the supervisee become secondary, if not ignored. Moreover, believing that teaching specific techniques is essential to improving a patient's well-being can prove to be ineffective and problematic. How can supervisee-therapists learn and apply complex theoretical and technical recommendations for the well-being of the patient while they are withholding personal concerns, doubts, and often negative reactions to the supervisor? Although patient-centered supervision and its interventions undoubtedly are useful for comprehending and managing some interpersonal obstacles to learning, it should not be expected to offer guidelines to teach complex therapeutic skills. Technical or theoretical adherence has no positive correlation with therapeutic competence or positive treatment outcome (Binder 1993). Furthermore, a major pedagogic problem is posed by the gap between theoretical understanding of the patient and of the technical procedures and the experience of actually doing the therapy (Corradi et al. 1980).

The training and supervision approach centered on the experiences of the supervisee-therapist has the advantage of dealing with the internal subjective experience of the supervisee. This approach seeks to understand and clarify the role of the therapist's personality on the psychotherapy process. The therapist-centered model attributes difficulties encountered in the psychotherapy to the therapist's personality. In this supervision process, less attention is accorded to the influence and contribution of the supervisor or the patient. As a result, the supervision can be experienced as an intrusive, if not a humiliating, process. Many argue that supervision should avoid discussion of the supervisee's personality issues (Arlow 1963). Some have even asserted that the supervisor should not even comment on what he observes as countertransference difficulties. As contemporary intersubjective models of supervision developed, some ventured to suggest that an impenetrable boundary between professional and personal issues in supervision is neither desirable nor achievable (Fossaghe 1997a). Even though this dichotomy no longer seems to be a meaningful distinction, we need to establish a distinctive ongoing difference between therapy and supervision.

Supervision that emphasizes the learning and mastery of techniques, on the other hand, offers advantages. Learning principles can be applied within a clearly defined and systematic framework. The therapist-supervisee is invited to participate in the mastery of these techniques in an active and collaborative manner. However, therapists dealing with personal difficulties experienced with a patient, or even questioning their professional identity, may not be at ease with this type of learning process. Consequently, when grappling with a strained therapeutic relationship, therapists may hesitate to discuss, if not disclose, these difficulties in the supervision, or may attribute the problem to their incompetence. The supervisees' professional existence could be at jeopardy if they revealed personal or negative reactions. Despite the potential importance of the topics of supervisee disclosure and nondisclosure for the efficacy of supervision, Ladany et al. (1996) report that 60 percent of the supervisees don't disclose relevant personal issues, inadequacy of performance, and negative reactions to their supervisor, thus inhibiting their learning process.

Most supervisors recognize the importance of each of these variables, be it patient characteristics, the personality and subjective experience of the therapist, techniques and the therapeutic alliance, or the supervisor–supervisee relationship. As has been described, each of these models has a tendency to favor one category of variables over another. We need a model of supervision as a fully integrative learning process encompassing relational patterns alive in both supervision and therapy as well as professional and personal issues. But is it possible to generate a model that integrates these different perspectives, and if so, to ensure that the needs of both the patient and the therapist-supervisee are met? And finally, how will such a model utilize techniques and strategies within a relevant framework, while at the same time recognizing the contribution of the therapeutic relationship? Although the experiences of the therapist-supervisee touch on the questions of knowledge, know-how, and being, training and supervision models tend to emphasize only one or the other of these modalities. For that reason, an integrative supervision model is needed to take into account the entirety of the experiences and needs of the therapist-supervisee. Such a model involves teaching and treating that both permits and directs supervisors to focus on the vicissitudes of the supervisee's self-esteem and self-cohesion potentiated by the supervisory process.

CRITERIA OF AN INTEGRATIVE TRAINING AND SUPERVISION MODEL

The first and ultimate aim of clinical training and supervision is the development of therapeutic competence, as demonstrated in the therapist's skill to facilitate positive change in the patient. Psychotherapy research findings have contributed greatly to clarifying the factors that lead to positive therapeutic outcomes.

In their exhaustive review of research results spanning the last 40 years, Norcross (2001), Sexton and Whiston (1994), and Lambert and Barley (2001) conclude that the most effective therapists are those who create a helpful therapeutic relationship with the patient. However, this finding is more complex than it initially seems. Luborsky (1994) suggested that positive outcomes result when there is an optimal meeting of techniques and therapist–patient characteristics in the therapeutic relationship. It is not a matter of isolating one variable over the other, but rather of emphasizing the importance of the therapeutic relationship as a mechanism of change in therapy. It is in this frame that Kahn (1997) affirms that the quality of the therapeutic relationship constitutes the most discriminant and determining element of successful therapy.

The establishment of a helpful therapeutic relationship is strongly related to the personal characteristics of the therapist. Lambert (1989) reports that after patient variables, the influence of the therapist's personality constitutes the second most important source of influence. Despite these convincing findings, however, research continues to focus to a large extent on theoretical approaches and techniques, ignoring to what extent therapists vary in their effectiveness. Even though common sense dictates that therapists vary greatly in their professional competence and effectiveness, clinical research projects continue to disregard the significance of therapist variables. Using research designs regarding therapists homogeneously, little attention is given to the wide variability that exists in the skills and personal qualities of the therapists.

In the twenty-first century, researchers aspire to empirically validated interventions that can be uniformly applied to a diverse range of patients, thereby diminishing or ignoring the influence of the therapist. Meanwhile, as Mahoney (1995) and Lambert (1989) point out, clinical practice and research repeatedly demonstrate that therapist characteristics are a determining factor in therapeutic outcomes. Based on meta-analytic findings, these researchers report that therapist characteristics are eight times more important than specific therapeutic techniques. Because interactional processes are more challenging to measure, reciprocal effects are not studied. Instead unidirectional hypotheses continue to dominate research on treatment outcome.

Supervision and training models reflect this controversy to a large extent. Even if the influence of therapist characteristics and the quality of the therapeutic relationship are known, the more widespread practice is to put the emphasis on the mastery of techniques, therapeutic approaches, and theoretical understanding of patient psychic functioning. For whatever reasons, the field continues to put emphasis on subject matters that are more objective and less risky than studying the personal aspects of effective therapists (Garfield 1997). Therapist, patient, and supervisor variables are often considered in isolation. Yet, it seems more and more evident that without examining the contribution of therapist characteristics, the progress of clinical interventions is compromised. An initial implication brought forth by this contribution is that an integrative supervision and training approach cannot ignore therapist characteristics. The more complex question, however, is how to take into account therapist variables in a training and supervision process. A salient study by Skovholt and Ronnestad (2001) conducted on therapists with a mean age of 74 offers important points to reflect on. To the question: "What aspect of your training and supervision experience do you wish you could have improved?" the majority of therapists responded that the development of their therapeutic competence was intimately related to the integration of personal and professional characteristics. Their main conclusion focused on the integration of personal and professional experiences as a crucial base for the authentic development of therapeutic competence.

The compilation of works from the past 40 years underscores that the most effective therapists are those who know how to establish a therapeutic relationship (Sexton and Whiston 1994). Thus, the comparison of "more effective" and "less effective" therapists demonstrates that effective therapists are the ones who regulate the therapeutic alliance by being more empathic, less defensive, and willing to recognize their mistakes (Najavits and Strupp 1994). Beyond knowing the importance of the therapeutic relationship, few training and supervision approaches are willing to deal with improving the complex process of regulating the therapeutic relationship. Yet, numerous authors have concluded that negative outcomes in psychotherapy are most frequently related to difficulties regulating the therapeutic alliance (Binder and Strupp 1997). Regardless of the theoretical approach, numerous studies have demonstrated that therapists have difficulty responding optimally to negative patient reactions (e.g., anger, criticism, demands, mistrust, etc.). Therapists have enormous difficulties detecting reciprocal hostile interaction patterns that inevitably arise to disrupt therapeutic alliances. Most therapists have negative reactions often as a result of perceived therapeutic failures. The skills required to manage intersubjective impasses constitute perhaps the most important facet of therapeutic competence. In retrospective studies (Rennie 1992, Rhodes et al. 1994), patients report that often their negative feelings in therapy are not explored, and further, they concealed these reactions for fear of instigating negative reactions from the therapist. Those patients who chose to share their negative experiences in the therapy felt they were not heard. These results may partially explain why 46 percent of patients drop out of therapy (Wierzbicki and Pekarit 1993).

These findings demonstrate both the importance and complexity of regulating the therapeutic relationship. Too frequently, the therapeutic relationship is considered in a partial or static manner. Establishing and maintaining a therapeutic alliance does not necessarily amount to an idealized or inflexible position as therapeutic neutrality. Such an equation risks limiting the reasons for relationship impasses strictly to technical difficulties or unidirectional factors. What corresponds better to the reality of this process is an understanding that a therapeutic relationship is a nonlinear, dynamic process in which two people are attempting to reach an emotional agreement to work toward carrying out therapeutic tasks and objectives. The effort, from both the therapist and the patient, to work cohesively will pass through moments of uncertainty, fluctuations, doubts, and deceptions, if not ruptures. Therapeutic progress largely depends on the capacity of the therapist to regulate these difficult moments with the patient. The optimal regulation of these difficult relationship experiences often represents critical turning points in the evolution of the intervention process. It should be no surprise that the majority of therapists fail these relationship tests (Binder and Strupp 1997) if they have not benefited from clinical training and supervision experiences that prepared them for such tribulations. The skills required to manage these interpersonal processes seem to constitute the most important factor of therapeutic competence. These skills involve much more than adherence to theoretical perspectives or prescribed techniques. Strict technical or theoretical adherence tends to produce poor therapeutic process and outcomes (Castonguay et al. 1996).

The elaboration of an integrative model of training and supervision involves exploring criteria that brings to the forefront the centrality of the contribution of the therapist and the therapeutic relationship. This conclusion suggests that in order to use therapy techniques in a relevant and competent manner, while taking into account patient variables, therapists must learn how to regulate their proper experiences within the therapeutic relationship. This means that the impact of techniques or interventions is closely related to the therapist's personality and the quality of the therapeutic relationship. Therapists agree: when one is able to be comfortable with oneself and the patient, it is then possible to offer optimal interventions. But like we all know, putting this program into practice is a complex feat.

Above and beyond theoretical and technical support, psychotherapists need a reflective space in supervision to consider their own regulation and interactive regulation. It is only when therapists achieve optimal self and interactive regulation that they can begin to use therapeutic techniques effectively. In this sense, clinical practice necessitates a space for reflection in clinical supervision, irrespective of the professional experience of the therapist. Many therapists, after 10 or 15 years of professional experience, do not dare to ask for supervision. It is assumed that after 10 years we should be competent for life. On the contrary, the development of professional competence depends on the capacity of the therapist to recognize the ongoing complexity of psychotherapy processes and consequently, to find room for self-reflection in supervision throughout one's career. To help therapists in their efforts at interactive and self regulation and in the competent use of techniques, it is important to offer a supervision and training approach that permits harmonious and pertinent integration.

SUPERVISION: A PLACE OF INTEGRATION

For the majority of therapists, supervision is a determining experience in the development of their identity and professional competence (Borders and Fong 1994, Rodenhauser 1997). Supervision offers support, feedback, a model, and stimulation in the overall view of developing professional competence and assuring a quality service (Savard 1997). Supervision is the most frequently used means of training in the development of professional competence (Lambert and Ogles 1997). The complex role of the supervisor is more clearly understood when Michels (1994) writes that the supervisor must take into consideration (1) the patient, including the problem, dynamics, life situations, and treatment goals; (2) the supervisee, along with his developmental level, intellectual comprehensions, countertransference, and career goals; (3) psychotherapy and supervision processes; and (4) the institutional and professional context in which the supervision takes place. Considering the complexity and importance of supervision, it is paradoxical that only 10 to 15 percent of supervisors have received training in supervision.

The question, therefore, is how to favor an integrative supervision approach. Instead of considering the experience of the therapist in a piecemeal fashion, the supervisor should aim to establish coherent links among techniques, patient variables, characteristics of the therapist, and the therapeutic relationship. Too often, training and supervision are considered from a Cartesian reasoning perspective based on the notions that professional development is logical and categorical, even though human experience is chaotic, nonlinear, and charged with affect. Behind the mask of professionalism, some training and supervision programs offer a procrustean bed, disregarding individual differences or special circumstances. These supervisors impose their agenda rather than taking into account the supervisees concerns and needs. Instead of promoting an integrative and reflective approach, these supervisors tend to one-size-fits-all theory and supervision. The experience of the therapist is in fact based, more or less, on discordant back-and-forth movements among knowledge, know-how, and being.

The dimensions of knowledge, know-how, and being interact in a manner to facilitate a creative and dynamic change in the therapeutic relationship with the patient. Theoretical knowledge determines the know-how dimension, which influences the being dimension. The know-how dimension, for its part, is a materialization of theoretical knowledge and a translation of being. Finally, the being dimension permits a transformation of theoretical knowledge and know-how; it is essentially a place of meaning and transformation.

Therefore, supervision becomes a place for the exploration and comprehension of the tensions between these dimensions of knowledge so that eventually they are integrated in a dynamic fashion. Integration models accord a dominant place to the being dimension. "Being" here refers to self-regulation processes (e.g., regulation of self-esteem and anxiety) and to relational knowledge, namely interactive regulation that manifests concretely from this knowledge (Beebe and Lachmann 2002). This proposition reflects the centrality of therapist variables and the therapeutic relationship (Sexton and Whiston 1994). The integration of techniques and theoretical knowledge operates by means of the interaction between the therapist's characteristics and the therapeutic relationship (Luborsky 1994).

In exploring the inevitable tension among theoretical knowledge (e.g., "Am I sure I understand the client?"), know-how or theoretical technique (e.g., "I tried the recommended technique but it did not work"), and being (e.g., "I'm fed up, I'm discouraged, I can't get out of this situation"), the supervisor creates a reflective space for the therapist to make sense of these questions, establish coherent links, and facilitate an integration of these aspects. In creating a reflective space for experience and practice, the therapist can progressively develop an awareness of his/her self regulation, interactive regulation, and their impact on the intervention process. In facilitating self-reflection, the supervisor emphasizes the integration of the therapist's diverse facets of experience and permits him/her to substantially

improve his/her therapeutic competence throughout his/her professional life.

When we think of supervision and training, we often forget to
consider what is fundamentally at stake in the process of learning. Many
training and supervision programs define the different logical and linear steps to go through to attain professional competence. These linear steps, for the most part, progress from the most simple to the most
complex (Thelen and Smith 1994). However, missing from these steps
are the factors that can destabilize the learning process.

For most therapists, the decision to engage in supervision and
training is a complex one. It involves choosing to show your vulnerabilities to someone else and risk being evaluated, if not judged. It also
entails being subjected to questions, expressing one's point of view and
doubts, as well as being exposed to others' points of view. One can question how such a process can become a learning environment that contributes to the development of therapeutic competence.

Crucial to the supervision process is the supervisor's ability to
understand and to validate therapists' tensions among their motivation
to change, their need to improve intervention processes, and simultaneously their need to maintain their self-esteem and self-cohesion so
that the supervisee can handle both de-structuring and reorganizing
learning experiences. These tensions can take many forms, depending
on the unique characteristics and experience of the therapist. The learning process will also take on a different importance depending on the
nature of these tensions. Piaget (1971) described this process using
the concepts of assimilation and accommodation. Thelen and Smith
(1994), using a framework based on a dynamic systems theory approach,
explained these experiences as ones of dynamic self organization and
chaos. Assimilation is the process by which the individual integrates
new information and existing psychic structures. Tensions between new
and old perspectives are optimally integrated when therapists discover
new perspectives that are compatible with their own organization. It
is without doubt that most therapists would like supervision to be an
experience of assimilation—not having their intervention style or way
of being fundamentally questioned. Supervisees seek, spontaneously,
novel information that they can easily incorporate to improve their
therapeutic effectiveness and competence. Although these assimilative
modifications are demanding, the supervisee's internal cohesion and

self-esteem are not threatened in this framework. It involves a learning experience that allows for the articulation and consolidation of the professional and personal experiences of the therapist.

When therapists are faced with new data concerning themselves, their theoretical understanding of the patient, the adequacy of their interventions or of the quality of the therapeutic relationship that they cannot integrate with existing psychic structures, then they must engage in the process of accommodation. Accommodation involves transforming old structures in order to respond to and integrate new information. Such a process requires the de-structuralization of past knowledge, which often results in destabilizing and confusing experiences. Without optimal support from the supervisor, these experiences can become intolerable and result in disabling and shameful experiences that prevent the emergence of a new and better-adapted, functioning psychic structure. The emergence of this new structure passes through an awkward learning process before becoming a more flexible way of functioning, whereby the processes of assimilation and accommodation act in tandem.

Even if the supervisee wishes to maintain existing structures, the difficulties experienced in clinical practice will point toward something missing and something that must be provided for change to occur. If the supervisor is able to listen and help supervisees make sense of their states of disruption, it is possible that a process of exploring and understanding the tensions between assimilation and accommodation can be initiated. On the other hand, if the supervisor is not open to such an experience, the supervision will be limited to unsatisfactory efforts at assimilation. How many therapists have reported supervision experiences that did not permit learning how to establish such a process of self-awareness? Many supervision models seem to indicate that the learning process is limited to the assimilation of new information within already-existing structures or submitting to the supervisor's perspective. Unchecked display of erudition, cleverness, or superiority by the supervisor may result in defensive operations and concealment. Defending a rigid boundary between personal and professional issues may infantilize supervisees instead of joining with them in a reflective exploration of their experiences. Throughout one's career, there are continual challenges relating to assimilating and making accommodation in existing cognitive, affective, and behavioral structures. Accommodation experiences implying profound structural changes require sufficient time and mean-ingful supervisory conditions to process disruptive experiences such as anxiety, mourning, shame, hurt, and anger. Unfortunately, many thera-pists have insufficient time for professional reflection.

Many authors describe the development of the professional self as passing from the stage of theoretical knowledge of the patient and mastery of techniques to complex awareness of the centrality of the therapeutic relationship and of having to use oneself in an authentic fashion while using theories lightly. This analysis suggests that the de-velopment of therapeutic competence goes backward and forward be-tween assimilation processes that seek to maintain existing structures and accommodation processes that demand destabilizing modifications. As mentioned by Skovholt and Ronnestad (1992), therapists that have not yet negotiated the complex and uncertain process of psychotherapy risk having a practice that is either unsatisfactory and disengaged, or exhausting and depressing, or more so, having the illusion of a pseudo-developed therapeutic competence. If therapists are not able to reflect on their experiences, they may select out, reduce, change, or distort their conception of the demands on the self. Overwhelmed, too anx-ious, or because the professional self is threatened, therapists may enter a pseudo-development. Depending exclusively on the work of others, supervisees avoid facing the anxiety of choosing their own identity and unconsciously repeat rigid ways of thinking, feeling, and behaving with their patients.

SUPERVISION: A SPACE
OF INTERSUBJECTIVE REFLEXIVITY

Research on infant development (Beebe and Lachmann 2002), and numerous clinical observations, have highlighted that personal experience emerges from, and is constructed and organized within, the context of relationships with others. From birth, we are inscribed in a relational, familial, and sociocultural matrix in which we continually develop. Such a perspective allows for the conceptualization of the therapeutic processes as an intersubjective experience, created by the interaction of two subjective worlds, that of the patient and that of the therapist, organized in different ways. Between these two subjectivities, there is an engagement of a therapeutic dialogue and therapeutic processes in an attempt to understand and transform the patient's suffering. The therapeutic relationship is a dyadic and dynamic system with both participants influencing how the therapeutic process unfolds. Both the patient and the therapist participate in the distortions, enactments, and ruptures that occur in the therapeutic alliance. Clinical supervision also unfolds in an intersubjective field. A dynamic regulatory system evolves in which supervisees' signals of moment-to-moment changes in their state are heard and responded to by the supervisor in supervision. This time it involves the interaction of three subjectivities: the supervisor, the therapist, and the patient. The intersubjective interaction between the supervisor and patient is virtual, but nevertheless significant.

In this perspective, it is not possible to understand or explain problems or difficulties, both in therapeutic and supervision situations, without considering the interactions of all the participants involved in the intersubjective field. As Winnicott (1965) put it so well, it is not possible to talk about a child's problems without considering the mother. It comprises a system in which the participants are indissociable. Understanding that difficulties experienced with a patient are situated within a dynamic intersubjective system means moving from a categorical or one-dimensional explanation to a world in which experiences are co-constructed and multidimensional (Stolorow et al. 2002). Instead of looking for answers in the patient or the therapist, we recognize the active contribution of each one, situated within a process of mutual influence. This is one of the most fundamental dimensions of clinical supervision. The supervisor has to define and organize the supervision process within this intersubjective perspective.

As much as this position can be reassuring because it contextualizes and puts into perspective difficulties encountered in the therapeutic and supervisory situation, it can also be unsettling when responses are not always clear-cut. Further, when considering intervention and supervision processes within the intersubjective perspective, it is recognized that there is no longer a distinct and objective position. The subjectivity of the therapist becomes indistinguishable from that of the patient so that they are both part of the problem and the solution.

Therefore, as much as subjectivity can be a resource for the therapist, it can also become an obstacle to therapeutic progress. The same goes for the supervisee–supervisor interactions.

Clinical supervision attempts to create an intersubjective space for reflection that permits therapists to explore, understand, and modify their self regulation and interactive regulation so that they can offer optimal interventions. The creation of a reflective space compels the supervisor and therapist to go beyond searching for a linear or unidirectional cause and effect to a third position in which they both reflect on the issues. An intersubjective space opens the therapists to new perspectives that enable them to envision and reflect on their interactions and interventions with the patient.

HOW TO CREATE REFLECTIVE SPACE IN SUPERVISION

Supervision implies that therapists disclose their doubts and questions concerning their competence and effectiveness. Many supervisees have described this experience as demanding, tiresome, and even shameful. Most supervisees (97.2 percent) do withhold information from their supervisors. The content of the nondisclosures most often involved negative reactions to the supervisor, personal issues, and clinical mistakes (Ladany et al. 1996). Therefore, how can conditions be established to create a reflective space that allows the supervisee to feel supported, understood, and validated? How can the supervisor facilitate a close encounter with the supervisee's professional and personal inner world?

Aware of the intersubjective nature of supervision and therapy on the one hand, and the emotional implications of professional disclosure on the other, the supervisor must provide an environment in which the therapist-supervisee's experience can be shared and an emotional dialogue can be established. This position fosters an empathic-introspective, affect-attuned approach to listening to and exploring the therapist's experience. Listening with empathy and introspection represents the efforts of the supervisor to feel and understand the experience of the supervisee so that in turn, the supervisee can feel emotionally connected to his/her experience (Lecomte and Richard 2003). By means of empathic understanding, the supervisor contributes to creating a secure environment that permits the supervisee to risk self-disclosing. The introspective component corresponds to the way in which supervisors attempt to reconnect with their own internal emotional experiences. This self-awareness is important not only to better understand the supervisees and their influence on the supervisor, but also to guide the supervisees in their self and intersubjective regulation. For example, when faced with a supervisee who fails to prepare for a supervision session, supervisors may be tempted to attribute their irritation and impatience to the supervisee's behavior. But if the supervision is grounded in an affect-attuned, empathic-intersubjective approach, supervisors will more likely seek to explore and understand how this experience affects their interaction, in particular in their attempts at emotional dialogue. All the while looking to understand their own contribution, supervisors maintain a fallible and vulnerable perspective. The result is an expanded process of shared consciousness that favors the emergence of new relational experiences. Instead of defining oneself as a neutral expert or detached observer, supervisors recognize the mutuality of relational processes, not so much to relinquish their responsibilities, roles, or functions, as to protect and to facilitate the reflective intersubjective space.

The supervisor attempts to listen and understand empathically the therapist-supervisee's experience, which rests on the capacity to enlarge one's own perspective in order to accommodate that of the supervisee's. Empathic listening presumes the ability to maintain a certain psychic distance permitting the supervisor to listen to oneself and the therapist. This psychic distance, based on the emotional availability of the supervisor, permits the establishment of an optimal working alliance.

However, even if the supervisor aims to sustain an empathic, respectful, and interested attitude, fluctuations and ruptures in the supervisory alliance inevitably arise. The attempt at an emotional dialogue between two subjectivities, organized in different ways, does not pass without moments of more or less pronounced emotional disjunction. It is illusory to think that both the supervisor and therapist can be empathic without fault. Being aware of moments of disjunction in which the working alliance is more or less compromised is crucial to the evolution of the supervision. Without such a dialogue, meaningful and authentic learning in supervision becomes difficult, if not impossible. Instead of facilitating a shared dialogue of professional and personal difficulties, supervision is then restricted to technical and peripheral issues. To help supervisors in their own self and interactive regulation with the therapist-supervisee, several indicators situated on a continuum are proposed (Lecomte and Richard 1999). These indicators seek to waken the awareness of the supervisor and invite a reflective undertaking with oneself and the therapist-supervisee.

A triadic intersubjective view of the supervisory interchanges is developed using the concepts of intersubjective conjunctions and disjunctions (Stolorow and Atwood 1992). Through this triadic intersubjective model, fluctuating understanding and responsiveness functions of the supervisor can be described.

Optimally, supervisors' empathic, affect-attuned listening is based on resonant-attuned receptiveness that enables them to sense what the patient may feel and to understand the latter's differing or similar perspective. This understanding can be defined as a widening of one's perspective to accommodate that of another. Stolorow and Atwood (1992) described inevitable instances of intersubjective disjunctions and conjunctions as either facilitating or obstructing the understanding and responsiveness functions of the therapist. According to them, the facilitation depends on the ability of therapists to become reflexively aware of their own organizing principles, thereby regaining their subjective centeredness. The obstruction refers to a variety of therapeutic impasses in which the therapist misunderstands the patient. Applying these principles to the supervisory process can illuminate the complicated relatedness of supervision and supervisee, and clarify how each contributes to the regulation of the other's behavior. In the disjunctive phenomena, supervisors either assimilate the differently organized supervisee's perspective to their theory, altering its meaning, or they get stuck.

It can happen that supervisors, feeling impatient or irritated, want the supervisee to see things according to their perspective. To different degrees, this position can become a type of imposition, resulting in a relationship characterized by opposition and tension. Thus, faced with an emotionally unavailable supervisor, therapist-supervisees may feel invalidated and thus no longer engage in the process of exploring and understanding their experience with their patient. This position can be described as dissonant. In the conjunctive phenomena, supervisors merge their similarly perceived, organized perspective to their supervisee or they surrender their perspective to their supervisee. Supervisors feel under pressure, as well as responsible and inadequate in their efforts to respond to all of the needs of the therapist-supervisee. Supervisors completely adjust to the world of the supervisee, thereby losing their own perspective and psychic distance. Paradoxically, in wanting to do everything to maintain the relationship, the meaningful work of exploration and understanding is compromised.

In the practice of supervision, these three positions are spread out along a continuum of disjunction, junction, and conjunction. Given the intersubjective field in which supervision takes place, the supervisor will experience one or more of these positions despite empathic attempts to talk with the supervisee. At certain moments or with certain therapists, the supervisor may take on a more dissonant interventionist style, while at other times the supervisor may let himself be overcome and defined by the difficult experience of the therapist. When supervisors come to recognize, explore, and understand these fluctuating experiences, they can hope to resolve the relational impasse with the therapist. These fluctuating positions can become significant markers of one's self and interactive regulation. These instances of disjunction and conjunction are the results of the unconscious mutual influencing processes between the two subjectivities. Therefore, when supervisors are able to recognize, explore, and understand these fluctuating positions in themselves, it permits not only a resolution of the impasses but it is a most valuable source of information on the supervisee's unconscious organizing activity. Being able to contain and to understand these reactions enables supervisors not only to regain their subjective centeredness but also to respond optimally to the supervisee. Understanding and responsiveness constitute critical supervisory and therapeutic abilities that the supervisor aims to develop in the therapist-supervisee through an educative-therapeutic-experiential process. Supervisor competence can then be defined as the self-awareness and regulation of one's own ongoing organizing activity in interacting with similarly and differently organized perspectives.

It is within this intersubjective field of mutual influence and reciprocity that these fluctuating positions have their contextual significance. Thus, the dissonant and consonant experiences of the supervisor are best understood in the interaction with the therapist. Even though these experiences are co-constructed by their interacting worlds of experience, supervisors have the responsibility to acknowledge their participation and to pay attention to their own psychic functioning. The reflective work of the supervisor takes into account these two levels. Communication flows in both directions: both supervisor and supervisee affect and are affected by the other. It is in this climate that a reflective intersubjective space can be constructed between the supervisor and therapist.

THERAPEUTIC COMPETENCE: FROM EXTERNAL SUPERVISION TO INTERNAL SUPERVISION

The most challenging and disruptive discovery for the therapist is without doubt that of the complexity of change. The demands of the patient are ambiguous. The intervention process is essentially uncertain. In the quest for professional competence and identity, many therapists seek some form of professional security and certainty by learning techniques and theories and by imitating experts, before gradually discovering the importance of the therapeutic relationship and the influence of their own characteristics (Halgin and Murphy 1995). This recognition of the eminently subjective and intersubjective character of the therapeutic situation implies a constant revision of one's perspective based on the unique nature of the interaction.

Psychotherapists quickly discover that they have personal and professional limits, that techniques are insufficient and theories are poor teachers. Therapeutic competence can then be defined as the recognition that optimal responsiveness facilitating positive change in therapy comes about through the influence of therapists in touch with their internal experiences and sensitive to the intersubjective context and attentive to the patient's experience. The competent therapist is one who has optimally integrated a combination of theoretical knowledge, know-how with regard to technique, and strategy in the interaction with a specific patient. Even though the main task of supervision is on promoting professional competency and agency while learning the application of theory and technique, the self and the use of the self of the supervisee has to be addressed and sustained in order to achieve these objectives.

The main objectives of clinical supervision are then to facilitate the establishment of professional competence and the development of self-reflectivity, while at the same time supporting the therapists' attempt to integrate their own theory of change, theoretical orientation, experiences of self and interactive regulation, and to help bring to light the therapists' clinical choices in the therapeutic relationship. In doing so, the therapist-supervisee gradually moves from an external supervision to an internal supervision.

I will now examine briefly how the supervisor can accompany and help the supervisee move from an external supervision to an internal supervision. By attempting to listen empathically and understand the supervisee's experience, the supervisor can negotiate a working alliance in supervision and promote and facilitate the development of the supervisee's ability to regulate affects and self-esteem. In the framework of this relationship, the supervisor is sensitive to grasp and to make sense of the therapist's oscillatory movements of assimilation that are accommodations that manifest by means of open and closed behaviors and attitudes. It is not until the supervisee can feel and maintain a sufficient level of self-esteem and agency that he can come to experience and integrate disruptive learning experiences. It would be difficult, for instance, to help the supervisee to overcome feelings of shame and incompetence without the concrete empathic support of the supervisor. Basically, it is when therapist-supervisees can feel that the supervisor is in emotional harmony with them and is sensitive to their affective experiences, particularly shame, underlying oscillations, and tensions between experiences of openness or expansion and closure or contraction, that the learning process and development of professional competence can take place. A lack of recognition of the supervisee's self and of the complicated relatedness of supervisor and supervisee will of necessity distort the supervision process. The supervision then shifts from the goal of learning and development to one of survival for the supervisee, as well as frustration for the supervisor.

Creating a learning environment that challenges existing ways of being and doing is far from a small task (Bernard and Goodyear 1998). When such a setting is present the description of the objectives, tasks, and procedures of clinical supervision takes on another meaning. The process of defining with the supervisee the objectives and expectations of supervision, and specifying the roles, duties, and modes of functioning within a dynamic, intersubjective learning process, facilitates the process of meaningful integration. After defining the framework for supervision (objectives, expectations, procedures, roles, and duties), reflective work can begin on the interaction of the three fundamental parameters of supervision.

Therapeutic practice is basically characterized by the interaction among the intentions-goals, the behavioral interventions, and the subjective experience of the therapist (Lecomte 1997, Schön 1987). The objectives pursued by the therapist, based on personal views of suffering and healing and espoused theory, influence the aims of supervision. Personal beliefs and hypotheses also shape the intended aims of supervision. In the reflective work of supervision, therapists may discover a discrepancy between their espoused theory and their personal views or their practical theory. This discovery may help to clarify important aspects of the intervention process. Schön (1987) emphasized the importance of understanding the theoretical basis for professional actions. Professionals' descriptions of the theoretical basis for their therapeutic behaviors often bear little relationship to their actual behavior in therapy. If their espoused theory and their practical theory do not match, supervisors should help supervisees to bring the two theories into line. Without the development of a congruent theory of practice, supervisees may follow on what others think instead of developing their own reflective skills. Therapeutic interventions are defined as observable professional behaviors and their impact on the patients. In describing their professional behaviors and their impact (for example, interpretation, cognitive restructuring, relationship ruptures), therapists are speaking from an objective self-awareness perspective. On the other hand, the subjective experience is comprised of an "I" experience in the form of a subjective self-awareness; this subjective experience encourages therapists to explore and understand the influence of their subjective experiences and personal characteristics on their behavioral interventions and intentions (Aron 2000). The tensions and interactions among the aims, the interventions, and the subjective experience of the therapist-supervisee constitute the fundamental parameters of the process of clinical supervision.

The following observations can be made from an analysis of this model: (1) A difference between the aims and the interventions and their impact on the patients will have an influence on the therapist's perceived level of competence and effectiveness. Therapists risk perceiving themselves as incompetent or ineffective if these aims are not applied successfully. The degree of perceived discrepancy will take on a different meaning for each therapist. (2) A discrepancy between the aims and the subjective experience will manifest the degree of satisfaction experienced by the supervisee. It is usually the first issue discussed by the therapist. (3) A discrepancy between the felt subjective experience and the objective experience of professional behaviors indicates the degree of difficulty a therapist has in trying to reach an integrated experience of "who I am" and "what I do." This tension between the objective experience and the subjective experience may also reflect the difficulties of integration between professional and personal aspects. It is in the continued effort to integrate these two poles that the therapist comes to use one's self in a satisfactory and optimal way. If the discrepancy is too great, the therapist risks having professional experiences that are exhausting or unsatisfactory, or based on a sense of pseudo-competence. This process is both an intellectual and emotional process. It involves the mediation of the self-as-subject with the self-as-object, the "I" and the "me."

Throughout their professional life, therapists attempt to make sense of this inevitable tension between observed and experiencing functions, to illuminate and improve their continuous professional reflection. The exploration and understanding of the tension between subjective self-awareness and objective self-awareness is a key dimension to professional development (Aron 2000). This long-term internally directed process, so central in the development of the therapist, involves continually reflecting upon and processing one's experiences (Karasu 2001).

The supervision and training process rests to a large degree on the exploration, understanding, and modification of the discrepancies and tensions between these three parameters. Considering the complexity and demands of working with individuals suffering from emotional dysregulation and deficits in mentalistic functions in situations in which biological psychiatric positions and biopsychosocial interventions confront each other, a reflective space where one can share questions and difficulties becomes almost an essential service to ensure the quality of professional services (Gabbard 1992).

Throughout the supervision process and more so at the beginning of each supervision session, the supervisor makes sure to appreciate and especially validate the difficult felt experiences of the tensions. This

244 / *Power Games*

empathic validation is essential to help therapist-supervisees fully recognize the discordant experiences between what they want to do, what
they are doing, and their internal subjective experience. The exploration of these tensions, centered on the objectives and needs of the
supervisee, often initially turn to a search for external causes and solutions. Considering patient characteristics, particularly the severity of
symptoms, as a primary explanation tends to lead therapists to technical or theoretical solutions. Frequently, therapists try to reduce the
discrepancy between the aims of therapy and the adequacy of their interventions and their impact. Therapists frequently ask: "What can I
do to realize my objectives and have a positive impact?" The exploration of the therapist's subjective experiences or more personal aspects
are either ignored or minimized. However, a reflective and empathic
exploration gradually makes the therapist-supervisee aware that these
factors are not the only cause of the tensions among the three poles.
Of course, patient characteristics and techniques are important and
useful to comprehend and manage some emotional and interpersonal
obstacles, but more and more, therapists come to recognize repetitive
patterns in their practice and ways they regulate these tensions. They
may discover that despite attempts to use different techniques or to
conceptualize the patient's problem in a different way, the desired results still do not come about; or worse, therapists relive relationship
impasses without an apparent way out. This is often a painful and disruptive experience. It is when therapists have at their disposal a supervisor who is capable of offering a supportive and validating reflective
space that they can engage in the exploration and comprehension of
their repetitive patterns. Thus, this work enables them to consider the
influence of their own characteristics on the relational and intervention processes.

    To avoid mistaking the reflective work of supervision with that
of psychotherapy, the supervisor assists therapists in pursuing their
learning objectives while establishing fluid and dynamic connections
between personal and professional aspects (Lecomte 1997). This process of clarification and comprehension serves to help the therapist find
explanations for such questions as: "How is it that I find myself in repetitive and difficult therapy situations, despite my efforts to understand
and my attempts at different types of interventions?" In helping therapists gain self-awareness and understanding of their contribution, thera-

pists discover that the techniques and the quality of the therapeutic relationship make sense and have value when they use their authentic self, including their resources and limitations. To help strengthen this self-reflexivity, the therapist is invited to reflect with the supervisor, to consider as well as to choose to put into practice new modalities of self and interactive regulation. It is here that the relevant use of techniques takes on its importance. Inevitable disruptive and restructuring experiences are to be expected of any meaningful learning experiences. The supervisor has to go beyond the therapist role to provide concrete support to facilitate optimal structural disruption and increase self-cohesion and self-esteem by helping the supervisee incorporate required changes into a new structure. The supervisor, being sensitive to the fundamental tension between the need for openness, differentiation, and competence, and the need for self-cohesion, self-esteem, and self organization, attempts to offer optimal support to the therapist's efforts at learning. For many therapists, putting into practice new methods of self and interactive regulation comes from learning new strategies in the supervision process through the use of relevant exercises, self-observation scales, audio and video recordings, note taking, etc. By offering optimal and concrete support in the therapist's exploration, comprehension, and application of new perspectives, the supervisor helps the therapist move from an external supervision to an internal supervision. More and more, the therapist manifests a reflective self-awareness stance in the presence of the supervisor. A supervisor should be delighted to notice when supervisee-therapists become more and more capable of a sustained exploration of the dynamic tension between their subjective self-awareness and objective self-awareness, while being attentive to their therapeutic aims and interventions.

A CLINICAL SUPERVISION VIGNETTE

Situation

A psychotherapist-psychologist with more than 10 years experience in the field of psychiatry asked to meet with me, although with much hesitation. She was already in a supervision group at her work setting. Even though she benefited from the diagnostic and theoretical knowledge she gained from these meetings, she had the impression that this was not an environment in which she could share her doubts and anxieties. Her work continued to be exhausting and difficult, in particular with a patient who not only suffered from depression, but also manifested behaviors of a borderline personality. She began to dread more and more the sessions with this patient. Although her colleagues attempted to reassure her and highlight that with such a patient one should expect emotional and chaotic behaviors, she remained perplexed and confused. What was really going on? Was she contributing to this difficult situation? In the group supervision, she was told no. Despite all of this, she still questioned herself. Within such a context, she had doubts that supervision could help her. Up to this point, her experience with supervision mostly focused on diagnosis, theoretical considerations, and treatment modalities to use with this patient. In this group supervision, there was an implicit boundary between personal and professional issues. Drawn to the most commonly known treatment approaches, she felt she had tried everything she could with this patient. Thus, she was inspired by the works of Linehan, Kernberg, and Masterson to attempt to better treat this situation.

Despite the therapist's best efforts, the patient criticized her insensitivity, lack of understanding, and the fact she had done nothing to help her. The patient continued to be aggressive and defeatist, regularly threatening to leave therapy.

Regulation and the Intersubjective Field

Skeptically the therapist came to individual supervision with me, expecting to be disappointed and abandoned. Believing she needed to describe her patient in detail, she proposed a meticulous and thorough analysis of the therapeutic process. The thickness of the patient's dossier attested to the multiple efforts she undertook with this patient.

After listening to her case presentation, I asked her to specify the objectives she hoped for in the supervision and invited her to share with me her subjective experience with this patient. A bit surprised and interested, she put the heavy dossier on her knees and began to explain the various failures and unsatisfying experiences she's had with this patient. To reassure me, and no doubt to reassure herself at the same time, she concluded by saying: "Like everyone has told me, such situations are normal in the field of psychiatry; it comes with the territory."

Faced with my genuine interest in understanding her subjective experience, she explained that she would like to know how to have a positive impact on such a patient and feel better about herself. She believed that if she were to become more competent and able to have a greater impact, perhaps then she could stop constantly doubting and questioning herself. Yet, she said, "I've undertaken numerous training programs to become more competent in order to work particularly with borderline personality disorders." In describing to me her experience with her patient, she shared her feelings of powerlessness and shame. She had the impression that despite all of her efforts, there were no results, and she frequently felt isolated and discouraged. She came to question her work in this psychiatric unit. At the end of the meeting, she felt better about trying to address her issue, but also felt anxious about our work. She asked me: "When are we going to start supervision?" For her, supervision meant discussing patient's issues only. In exploring her expectations and objectives, we agreed on two objectives for supervision: (1) how to intervene with more competence and impact, and (2) attempt to understand why she is so affected in her professional work with this patient.

From the start of this first meeting, a regulation process between our two subjectivities began to take place. She seemed to expect me to play the role of expert, that after listening to her, I would give her effective solutions. When, instead of playing this expected role, I invited her to talk about her experience, she spoke of her difficulty in self regulation and in appeasing herself. When she communicated her experience of feeling isolated as well as her serious pursuit for competence, I felt myself oscillating between a position of consonance (wanting to protect her) and dissonance (wanting to explain like an expert what I thought was going on for her with this patient). In concentrating on and being open to her experience, I felt a fragile reflective process was gradually created between us. The formulation of the expectations and objectives seems to give direction and sense our work.

Tension Among Goal, Professional Behaviors, and Subjective Experience

Subsequent supervision meetings demonstrated that she had gathered strong theoretical and practical knowledge regarding issues related to her patient. Her colleagues even consulted her for information and references on personality disorders. The question she came to ask herself was: "How is it that, despite my knowledge and professional experience, I have not yet come to feel competent and effective?"

She began to describe the phenomenology of her experiences. Even though she knew to expect fluctuations and ruptures in the relationship with a patient with a borderline personality that would have demanding implications, these situations still made her feel inadequate. Gradually, she began to observe that this subjective experience made her feel tense. She just wanted to retreat and avoid her patient. When the patient questioned her in a personal way, she became impersonal and distant. She even imagined becoming angry and telling the patient what she really thought of her. She also knew she could never dare to make such a gesture. This exploration allowed us to recognize how difficult it was for her to sustain a satisfying integration of her professional behaviors and her subjective reactions.

The recognition of these modalities of regulation was enlightening, but remained painful and overwhelming. Experiencing uncertainty and ambiguity still seemed almost intolerable. We were still struggling to create a significant reflective space among her subjective experience, her professional behaviors and their impact, and my subjective experience, my goals, and my interventions. Recalling specific therapeutic interviews with her patient, she was overwhelmed by feelings of powerlessness and sadness combined with an unbearable experience of shame. For her, it was not acceptable to find herself in such a position after 10 years of professional experience.

Parallelism and the Unique Experience of Supervision

The more she recognized and felt her relational impasse, the more she would ask me what to do. The experience of feeling powerless combined with the experience of shame pushed her to want to find effective and immediate solutions so that she would no longer feel this way. She wondered if I, as her supervisor, could really help her. She said to me: "Maybe she is an impossible case to help." Considering that she felt she had made no progress and even had the impression that the patient was worse than before, she questioned the pertinence of pursuing supervision with me.

It was tempting to explain our relational experience by referring only to a parallel experience that exists with her patient. Considering that she was looking for answers for her painful relational experiences with her patient, we can expect to find a certain correspondence in what will be set up and played out in our supervision relationship. But this should not prevent us from paying attention to what is specifically taking place, or is otherwise being constructed between her and myself. In fact, communicating with intensity how intolerable and shameful she found her situation, I felt more and more stuck and restricted in my intervention process. Despite my effort to validate, recognize, and explore her experience, it seemed my words were not enough. How could we come to create a reflective space between us? In looking at my own subjective experience, I became aware of the shame I felt in not being able to do more or make the situation better for her. I attempted to reassure her by highlighting her resources and her determination; then, with the help of interpretations, I tried to help shed light on her experience. But that was not enough. It was not until recognizing my own experience of powerlessness and shame that I began to understand more about our mutual experience in the supervisory interaction. In contact with my own internal experience and sensitive to the intersubjective context, I felt more available to her both verbally and nonverbally. I discussed with her the idea that it was in wanting too quickly to interpret her experience and reassure her that I prevented myself from being supportive of her experience of powerlessness and shame, and in doing so, she found herself once again feeling abandoned and not heard. She welcomed this exchange with a profound feeling of sadness and relief. She finally felt heard. Thus began the formation of a reflective intersubjective space based on emotional attunement.

The Inevitable Interpenetration of Professional and Personal Issues

Attempting to bridge her professional difficulties and her subjective experience frequently led to revisions of her personal narratives about the self and relationship to the world. Too often, some supervisors attempt to erect an arbitrary wall between these two facets of the same dynamic organization. The more complex question consisted of determining how to explore those inevitable personal aspects to improve therapeutic competence and effectiveness. Within an empathic, affect-attuned, intersubjective regulation process, she began to feel more secure in letting herself come into contact with this new relational experience. At the same time, this experience of finally being heard brought up painful childhood memories of feeling, despite her best efforts, that she could never meet her parents expectations and needs. Even though those infantile ideals had been explored in personal therapy, she was surprised and distressed to see how much they were still influencing her clinical work. She felt that she had been cheated by former supervisors' maintaining a strict boundary between personal and professional issues. Revisiting this childhood history and revising the painful emotional conclusions of powerlessness and shame offered her a new perspective and profound understanding of the relational impasse she had with her patient. This new understanding allowed her, on the one hand, to establish an important reflective space between her subjective experience and professional behaviors, and on the other hand, to envision new methods of self and interactive regulation.

CONCLUSION

In the recent evolution of psychotherapy and research, a "false" debate has arisen between empirically supported treatments and techniques versus the therapeutic relationship and therapist characteristics. In a society centered on quick and observable results, it seems that, more and more, the empirical movement dominates. In responding to only observable empirical criteria, however, we end up ignoring the wide variability of patients and therapists. The myth of homogeneous patients and therapists, however, has been denounced time and time again (Kiesler 1966). No two therapists practice in the same manner. Therapists are not interchangeable and psychotherapy is not a homogeneous treatment. Manuals in the conduct of therapy do not eliminate the complex elements of the therapeutic encounter. Moreover, in such a perspective, the therapist is not only ignored, but left to fend for himself.

Research on the effectiveness of psychotherapies from the past 40 years supports, unequivocally, the importance of the quality of the therapeutic relationship and the influence of the personal and professional qualities of the therapists. Therapy is first of all a relational endeavor. The most effective therapists are those who (1) are capable of conceptualizing the dynamics and needs of the patients by listening to and understanding their unique experiential subjective world; (2) are capable of flexible cognitive and emotional self regulation and inter-active regulation in order to offer new specific, unique, and necessary relational experiences; (3) are open to their own affective experiences and to those of their patients in a continual process of self-reflexivity; and (4) use their techniques in congruence with their ways of being in their therapeutic relationship with their patients.

To help the therapist feel and be competent and effective, clini-cal supervision needs to become a space for reflection and integration of theoretical knowledge, techniques or know-how, and experiential being. The more the therapist develops a coherent integration of his espoused theoretical model and intervention methods, his personal theory of suffering and healing, his personality, values, beliefs, and life experiences, the more deeply he will be committed to and the more competent he will be in his work. The development of professional competence and effectiveness relies on this process of self-reflexivity.

REFERENCES

Arlow, J. (1963). The supervisory situation. *Journal of the American Psycho-analytic Association* 11:576–594.

Aron, L. (2000). Self-reflexivity and the therapeutic action of psychoanaly-sis. *Psychoanalytic Psychology* 17(4):667–689.

Beebe, B., and Lachmann, F. M. (2002). *Infant Research and Adult Treatment: Co-Constructing Interaction.* Hillsdale, NJ: Analytic Press.

Begley, S., Rosenberg, D., and Ramo, J. C. (1994). One makes you feel larger, and one makes you feel small. *Newsweek,* February 7, pp. 37–40.

Bernard, J. M., and Goodyear, R. K. (1998). *Fundamentals of Clinical Supervi-sion.* Toronto: Allyn and Bacon.

Binder, J. L. (1993). Is it time to improve psychotherapy training? *Clinical Psychology Review* 13:301–318.

Binder, J. L. and Strupp, H. H. (1997). Negative process: a recurrently dis-covered and underestimated facet of therapist process and outcome in the individual psychotherapy of adults. *Clinical Psychology: Science and Practice* 4:121–129.

Borders, L. D., and Fong, M. L. (1994). Cognitions of supervisors-in-training:

an exploratory study. *Counselor Education and Supervision* 33:279–293.

Castonguay, L. G., Goldfried, M. R., Wiser, S., Raue, P. J., and Hayes, A. H. (1996). Predicting the effect of cognitive therapy for depression: a study of unique and common factors. *Journal of Consulting and Clinical Psychology* 64:497–504.

Corradi, M., Wasman, M., and Gold, F. S. (1980). Teaching about transference: a videotape introduction. *American Journal of Psychotherapy* 34:564–571.

Frawley-O'Dea, M. G., and Sarnat, J. E. (2001). *The Supervisory Relationship: A Contemporary Psychodynamic Approach.* New York: Guilford Press.

Gabbard, G. C. (1992). Psychodynamic psychiatry in the decade of the brain. *American Journal of Psychiatry* 149:991–998.

Garfield, S. L. (1997). The therapist as a neglected variable in psychotherapy research. *Clinical Psychology: Science and Practice* 4:40–43.

Halgin, R. P., and Murphy, R. A. (1995). Issues in the training of psychotherapists. In *Comprehensive Textbook of Psychotherapy*, ed. B. Bongar and L. E. Beutler. Toronto: Oxford University Press.

Kahn, M. (1997). *Between Therapist and Client: The New Relationship.* New York: Freeman.

Karasu, B. T. (2001). *Psychotherapist as Healer.* Northvale, NJ: Jason Aronson.

Kiesler, B. T. (1966). Some myths of psychotherapy research and a search for a paradigm. *Psychological Bulletin* 65:110–136.

Kohut, H. (1984). *How Does Analysis Cure?* Chicago: University of Chicago Press.

Ladany, N., Hill, C. E., Corbett, M., and Nutt, A. (1996). Nature, extent, and importance of what trainees do not disclose to their supervisors. *Journal of Counseling Psychology* 43(1):10–24.

Lambert, M. J. (1989). The individual therapist's centralization to psychotherapy process and outcome. *Clinical Psychology Review* 9:469–485.

Lambert, M. J., and Barley, D. E. (2001). Research summary on the therapeutic relationship and psychotherapy outcome. *Psychotherapy* 38:357–361.

Lambert, M. J., and Ogles, B. M. (1997). The effectiveness of psychotherapy supervision. In *Handbook of Psychotherapy Supervision*, ed. C. E. Watkins. New York: Wiley.

Lecomte, C. (1997). La supervision clinique et le développement de la compétence professionnelle en psychothérapie. Paper presented at the first Colloque Elliott Sokloff, Montreal, Quebec.

——— (2001). From external to internal supervision: the development of self-reflexivity. Paper presented at the Psychiatric Department of the Jewish Hospital of Montreal, Québec.

Lecomte, C., and Richard, A. (1999). From external to internal supervision: an integrative developmental model. Paper presented at the annual convention of the Self Psychology Association, Toronto.

—— (2003). De la subjectivité à l'intersubjectivité: pour une psychothérapie pleinement relationnelle. *Revue de la Psychologie de la Motivation* 35:64–73.

Luborsky, L. (1994). Therapeutic alliances as predictors of psychotherapy outcomes: factors explaining the predictive success. In *The Working Alliance: Theory and Practice*, ed. A. Horvath and L. Greenberg, pp. 38–50. New York: Wiley.

Mahoney, M. J. (1995). The modern psychotherapist and the future of psychotherapy. In *Comprehensive Textbook of Psychotherapy*, ed. B. Binger and L. E. Beutler. New York: Oxford University Press.

Michels, R. (1994). Foreword. In *Clinical Perspectives on Psychotherapy Supervision*, ed. S. Greben & R. Ruskin, pp. xi–xii. Washington, DC: American Psychiatric Press.

Najavits, L. M., and Strupp, H. H. (1994). Differences in the effectiveness of psychodynamic therapists: a process-outcome study. *Psychotherapy* 31: 114–123.

Norcross, J. C. (2001). Empirically supported therapy relationships: summary of the dimension 29 task force (special issue). *Psychotherapy* 38(4).

Piaget, J. (1971). *Biology and Knowledge: On Survey on the Relation Between Organic Regulation and Cognitive Processes*. Chicago: University of Chicago Press.

Rennie, D. L. (1992). Qualitative analysis of the client's experience of psychotherapy: the unfolding of reflexivity. In *Psychotherapy Process Research: Paradigmatic and Narrative Approaches*, ed. S. G. Toukmanian and D. L. Rennie, pp. 211–233. Thousand Oaks, CA: Sage.

Rhodes, R. H., Hill, C. E., Thompson, B. J., and Elliott, R. (1994). Client retrospective recall of resolved and unresolved misunderstanding events. *Journal of Counseling Psychology* 41:473–483.

Rodenhauser, P. (1997). Psychotherapy supervision: prerequisites and problems in the process. In *Handbook of Psychotherapy Supervision*, ed. C. E. Watkins. New York: Wiley.

Safran, J. D., and Muran, J. C. (1995). Resolving therapeutic alliance ruptures: diversity and integration. *Psychotherapy in Practice* 1:81–92.

Savard, R. (1997). *Effets d'une Formation Continue en Counseling sur les Variables Personnelles Relatives à la Création d'une Alliance de Travail Optimale*. Thèse présentée à la faculté des sciences de l'éducation de l'Université de Montréal, Montreal, Canada.

Schön, D. A. (1987). *Educating the Reflexive Practitioner*. San Francisco: Jossey-Bass.

Sexton, T., and Whiston, S. (1994). The status of the counseling relationship: an empirical review: theoretical implication and research directions. *Counseling Psychologist* 22:6–78.

Shapiro, D. A., and Firth, J. A. (1987). Prescriptive vs exploratory psychotherapy: outcomes of Sherfield Psychotherapy Project. *British Journal of Psychiatry* 151:790–799.

Skovholt, T. M., and Ronnestad, M. H. (1992). *Evolving Professional Self: Stages and Themes in Therapist and Counselor Development*. New York: Wiley.

——— (2001). What can senior therapists teach others about learning arenas for professional development? *Professional Psychology: Theory, Practice and Research* 32(2):207–216.

Stolorow, R. D., and Atwood, G. E. (1992). *Contexts of Being: The Intersubjective Foundations of Psychological Life*. New York: Academic Press.

Stolorow, R. D., Atwood, G. E., and Orange, D. M. (2002). *Worlds of Experience: Interweaving Philosophical and Clinical Dimensions in Psychoanalysis*. New York: Basic Books.

Talbot, N. L. (1995). Unearthing shame in the supervisory experience. *American Journal of Psychotherapy* 49(3):338–349.

Thelen, E., and Smith, L. B. (1994). *A Dynamic Systems Approach to the Development of Cognition and Action*. Cambridge, MA: MIT Press.

Wierzbicki, M., and Pekarik, G. (1993). A meta-analysis of psychotherapy drop-out. *Professional Psychology: Research and Practice* 24:247–258.

Winnicott, D. (1965). *Maturational Processes and the Facilitating Environment*. New York: International Universities Press.

13

Authority Relations in Psychodynamic Supervision: A Contemporary View

Joan E. Sarnat

How does a relational psychodynamic supervisor view her authority and its origins? What are the implications of this view for how supervision is conducted? What differentiates authority within a relational model of supervision from other supervisory models?

On one point all supervisory models agree: the supervisor's authority derives, in part, from the supervisor's community. If a supervisor works in a private practice setting, the colleagues who refer to her[1] as well as her licensing board bestow the status of "supervisor." If she works for an agency, the training site or program that recruits her to supervise bestows that role. Along with the role comes conferred power and authority.

---

1. For clarity the supervisor and patient will be referred to with feminine pronouns throughout this chapter, and the supervisee will be referred to with masculine pronouns.

Beyond that core source of authorization, different supervisory models view the supervisor's authority and its origins quite differently. In nonrelational models of psychodynamic supervision, the supervisor's authority is assumed to derive primarily from her knowledge of theory and technique, and from her status as an objective expert. Martin S. Bergmann provides a recent example of a nonrelational supervisor's stance toward his authority in his contribution to the Symposium on Psychoanalytic Training and Education, published in *Psychoanalytic Dialogues* (2003). Despite the knowledge of contemporary clinical theory that he displays, he employs a decidedly nonrelational, patient-centered, didactic approach (Frawley-O'Dea and Sarnat 2000) to supervision. He relies on his ability to teach theory and technique for his sense of legitimacy. For example, when asked by the editors of *Psychoanalytic Dialogues* to describe how he would supervise, based on actual case reports submitted by two therapists, he launches into a 16-point description of his therapeutic philosophy. The detail with which this philosophy is articulated shows Bergmann's investment in his particular conceptualization of the psychoanalytic process.

Describing Bergmann's supervisory approach Margaret Black (2003) comments: "He seeks, when possible, to build on the candidate's thinking, inviting her to speculate and discuss ideas that may be newly formulated. But he also supplies his own crystal clear vision of analytic functioning *and expects it to take precedence*" (pp. 368–369, emphasis added). It is from this "crystal clear vision" that Bergmann draws his sense of his authority as a supervisor. There is little room here for negotiation of meaning between supervisor and supervisee, or for discussion of disagreements based on the supervisee's theoretical views, preferences, or differing assessments of his patient's psychology and therapeutic needs, however respectful the supervisor might be of the supervisee. The supervisor's vision of the patient, technique, and how the supervision should be conducted takes precedence.

In contrast, the relational supervisor depends less for her authority on her personal construction of theory and technique. She regards herself as an involved participant in the supervisory relationship, who holds a particular point of view, but not necessarily the "truest" point of view. Knowledge and authority are assumed to be distributed between the members of the supervisory couple, although the existence of a knowledge and experience gradient between supervisor and supervisee is not denied. In such a process-oriented, supervisory-matrix–centered model of psychodynamic supervision (Frawley-O'Dea and Sarnat 2000), knowledge is understood to be perspectival. It is from the quality of relationship that she establishes with her supervisee that the relational supervisor considers herself to be authorized—and necessarily reauthorized as the process unfolds—to exercise influence.

This relational revisioning of the supervisory relationship, which has been articulated in the recent psychoanalytic literature on supervision (Berman 2000, Caligor et al. 1984, Frawley-O'Dea and Sarnat 2000, Leary 1997, Pegeron 1996, Rock 1997, Teitelbaum 1990) has been inspired by contemporary clinical models. Following contemporary relational theory (Aron 1996, Hoffman 1998, Mitchell 1997, Pizer 1998), these supervisors think of themselves as co-creaters of what transpires between themselves and their supervisees, appreciate the irreducibility of the supervisor's subjectivity, see knowledge as perspectival, and understand the important role that negotiation plays in supervisory relationships. A contemporary model of supervision is well suited to teach a contemporary form of psychotherapy because it provides a supervisory medium that is consistent with the supervisory message.

A supervisor working from a relational model helps the supervisee to utilize theory to develop his own way of working with a particular patient as much as she teaches her own construction of theory. A relational supervisor prioritizes the creation of a supervisory environment in which much can be thought, felt, and known about both the clinical and supervisory relationships, even if some of that thinking goes contrary to her own assumptions. Her openness to reflecting upon her own mind as it impacts the supervision, and her interest in her supervisee's experience of the supervisory relationship, contribute to creating an atmosphere of mutual vulnerability. Frawley-O'Dea and I (2000) put it this way: "Since the transformative power of the supervisory relationship is understood to reside in this mutual vulnerability and openness to interpersonal influence, the supervisor chooses to encourage the empowerment of his supervisee rather than depending on his power as a supervisor to impress, intimidate, coerce, or instruct" (p. 80).

Inclusion of the supervisor's own psychology in the supervisory discourse also makes it safer for the supervisee to bring to his supervisor, without undo feelings of shame or failure, the kinds of problems that trouble him most (Sarnat 1992).

While the supervisor brings significant power to the relationship—deriving from her status, experience, knowledge, and role as evaluator—the supervisee brings into the supervisory relationship firsthand knowledge of his patient and their relationship, which gives him a source of authority that the supervisor lacks. Supervisor and supervisee must therefore mutually negotiate the meaning of what goes on in the supervised treatment and in the supervision itself. The supervisor invites evaluation from the supervisee, as well as evaluating the supervisee, throughout the process.

We can look again to the *Psychoanalytic Dialogue*'s symposium (2003) to illustrate authority relations in a relational model. In contrast to Bergmann's statement, as Mary Gail Frawley-O'Dea (2003) writes about how she would work with the two therapists' material, she finds it impossible to specify what she would try to teach them. She states:

> Because I am not in relationship with these clinicians, I cannot easily approach their work from a relational supervisory perspective. When addressing [this] case material, therefore, I focus mostly on what appears to me to be missing from their discussions [such as description of the therapist's countertransference experience] and on the kinds of material I would hope to *elaborate with* [the two therapists] in our work together. [p. 356, emphasis added]

Here, in the place of Bergmann's description of his therapeutic philosophy, Frawley-O'Dea alludes to a process of getting to know her supervisees and their patients in their individuality. Bergmann's didactic approach is replaced by an emphasis on "elaborating with"—a process of co-construction that is assumed to lead in unknowable-in-advance directions. Rather than presenting her philosophy in authoritative fashion, this supervisor positions herself to receive and respond to an emerging process. Here surprise and discovery are as much a part of the supervisor's experience as they are a part of the supervisee's experience. Both participants are learners as well as teachers.

One advantage of this approach is that it invites the supervisee into a more engaged learning process. Traditional role expectations, with their roots in the family, are violated here, with the hope of stimulating development. As Cooper and Gustafson (1985) state in their discussion of dependency dynamics in supervision groups, "In order to be loyal to traditional authority and give them [e.g., supervisors] the power and deference one assumes unconsciously they deserve and need, one willingly sacrifices . . . the capacity to think clearly, critically, and independently" (p. 8). In a relational model of supervision, a nondeferential teaching and learning relationship is the goal, even if that entails moments of tension and conflict between supervisee and supervisor.

A supervisor thus demonstrates by example as well as by instruction her openness to her supervisee's relinquishing of unconscious debilitating loyalties. By welcoming negative as well as positive feedback from her supervisee, and by reflecting upon her own negative as well as positive impact on the supervised treatment, the supervisor implicitly grants her supervisee permission to think independently and critically about the supervisory process as well as the clinical process.

None of this means that a supervisor, functioning within a relational model of supervision, allows herself to be treated disrespectfully. It means instead that genuine respect is granted not only to the supervisor but also to the supervisee and to the process that evolves between them as well. Nor does this approach overlook a supervisor's responsibility to teach her supervisee. Didactic teaching instead becomes one of many ways that a supervisor may help her supervisee to grow and develop. Offering theoretical guidance or even concrete advice to a supervisee who is floundering, especially an anxious beginner, is one of the crucial ways that the relational supervisor may offer containment to help the supervisee manage disruptive levels of anxiety. But as she teaches, the relational supervisor thinks about the meaning of this transaction within the supervisory relationship, and is aware that received knowledge has its limitations. She remains open to the possibility that didactic teaching may outlive its usefulness at any moment, as she watches for new developments within the supervisory relationship.

Authority in a relationally based supervisory relationship can be summed up as *mutuality in the context of asymmetry* (Aron 1996). Some of the necessary asymmetries of the relationship include the supervisor's responsibility for managing the boundaries of the situation, for representing standards for competent and ethical practice, and for structuring evaluation. Asymmetries in experience and competence also (one hopes) differentiate the supervisor from the supervisee. Yet despite these essential asymmetries, the processes of generating material and negotiating meanings in a relationally oriented supervision are deeply mutual ones, with both participants aware of themselves as people with conflicts, defenses, and unconscious responses. Within such a model, the supervisor is less likely to abuse the power that she wields, although she is more likely to openly acknowledge the power that she actually does possess.

I would like to further illustrate how a relational view of power and authority shapes the supervisory process by addressing four specific topics: (1) the supervisor's role in challenging a clinician's enthrallment with an "authoritative" clinical theory, (2) the supervisor's attitude toward her own psychology as it enters the supervisory relationship, (3) how the supervisor balances respect for the supervisee's consciously made choices with respect for the supervisee's unconscious needs, and (4) the supervisor's availability to negotiate aspects of her style that the supervisee finds problematic.

THE SUPERVISOR'S ROLE IN CHALLENGING A CLINICIAN'S ENTHRALLMENT WITH AN "AUTHORITATIVE" CLINICAL THEORY

Purcell (2004) brings to our attention the problems inherent in a therapist's assumption that any theory provides an "authoritative" view of the patient and the analytic process, and the potential role that the supervisor can play in challenging his relationship to too-well-loved theory. Purcell asserts that any clinical theory is only one lens among many, and notes that many clinicians lose track of this reality after a period of immersion in a particular theory, thus persisting in a particular approach even if it is not working with a given patient. He examines the impact of the analyst's unreflecting relationship to his preferred theory on his countertransference, a crucial source of information for the analyst:

> The analyst has conscious and unconscious transferences . . . determined by his internal object relationship to theory. . . . To the extent that an analyst's countertransference is a product of theory and simultaneously

a fundamental modality in the apprehension of the patient's transference, it becomes apparent how crucial and also potentially problematic our theories are in the construction of the phenomena of every analysis. [p. 647–648]

Purcell points to supervision and consultation as a source of perspective for the therapist who gives too much authority to his preferred theory. He suggests that if therapists are exposed to supervisors of different persuasions, these supervisors' different approaches can "offset the detrimental effects of loved theory " (p. 649). Thus Purcell views the supervisor as having an opportunity to correct for some of the limiting assumptions in a therapist's clinical thinking.

Important as these ideas about the role of the supervisor are, in my view they do not go far enough. Just because a supervisor speaks for an alternative theory doesn't mean that the supervisee will necessarily be helped by that supervisor to think more openly and flexibly about the patient and the work, will be able to implement the suggested technical shift successfully, or will be helped to modify the authoritarian or idealized nature of his relationship to theory. Indeed, a supervisor who believes that she is working from a "better" theory than the supervisee may actually activate an authoritarian relationship with the supervisee within the supervision, thus reinforcing those very qualities in the supervisee's internal object world. Engaging in a supervisory process that demonstrates a different approach to authority relations is also necessary in order to overcome the stultifying effects of loyalty, be it to people or to theory. An example illustrates this distinction:

A licensed clinician, Adam, working from a self-psychological perspective, came for consultation, concerned that his patient was not progressing. His consultant, Maggie, bringing a conflict model of narcissistic defense to bear, pointed out that the patient was subtly denigrating Adam and the therapy, a fact that Adam seemed not to notice or at least to give much importance. Maggie wondered why Adam was not aware of feelings of anger in his countertransference since the patient was subtly but continually attacking his efforts to help. Adam explained that he viewed the patient's behavior as a symptom of her fragmented self. Viewing her pathology with this theoretical lens, he felt quite accepting of the patient's attitude, and was trying to be a "good selfobject" to the patient until she developed a more cohesive self. He realized, however, when Maggie brought the issue to his attention, that this development did not seem to be occurring and that he had been blinding himself to an important aspect of the transference/countertransference.

Maggie advised Adam to use a different (Kleinian) theoretical lens and different clinical technique in order to bring the patient's subtle narcissistic resistances into clearer focus and engage his patient in a more active way. Adam felt some doubt about the timeliness and appropriateness of the shift, but also knew that the treatment was stuck, and felt that he should give Maggie's advice a try. With some suppressed misgivings, Adam began to shift his stance toward the patient, confronting his patient's devaluing of the therapy and the therapist along the lines his supervisor suggested.

Things did not go well. Adam was somewhat brusque in the way that he implemented this new approach, which he had not fully made his own. And because of his unaddressed conflict about the change, he was also insufficiently emotionally available to work with his patient's emerging anxiety and anger. In response to this treatment, the patient became progressively more defensive and oppositional. Unaware of the full extent of Adam's difficulties, which Adam was not internally free to observe or describe in supervision, Maggie accepted the patient's increasing defensive hostility as the expectable result of Adam's new interpretive stance and the disruption of the patient's narcissistic defenses. She considered the patient's anxiety a sign of progress, although of course difficult for both of them, and encouraged Adam to hold to steady. Adam did not feel free to express his doubts to Maggie, and so soldiered on. After several weeks of struggle between Adam and his patient, the patient abruptly left treatment.

In this example, Maggie helps Adam by pointing out the limitations of the theory he is using, and how that theory might be obscuring an "appropriately" negative countertransference that might have motivated Adam to confront his narcissistically stuck and subtly destructive patient. Maggie is able to make use of her own countertransference response to the patient to offer technical advice that might lead the clinical dyad in a fruitful direction. However, because she does not attend to the process that is unfolding between Adam and herself as she makes this intervention with him, Maggie is also failing Adam. Adam complies with the advice offered, and because he is not invited to do otherwise, keeps his doubts and negative feelings out of the supervisory relationship. Adam then unconsciously exports what is unresolved in the supervisory relationship into the clinical relationship, unconsciously identifying with— and maybe even caricaturing—Maggie, who challenged his approach without also attending to the impact of her intervention upon him. As a result, the tone of Adam's confrontation with his patient is harsher than it might otherwise have been, and he doesn't help his patient with her feelings about the unfolding process between them.

If Maggie had explored with Adam his reactions to the recom- mended change in technique, Adam would have had the opportunity to experience firsthand in supervision the kind of relationship that he needed to learn how to provide to his patient. As things actually un- folded in the supervision, he was insufficiently prepared to help his patient work through her responses to his sudden change in technique. Adam got the didactic instruction that he needed, but not the accom- panying relationship experience that would have helped him to effec- tively implement it. And so, in a sense Adam exchanged a compliant attitude toward one theoretical approach for a compliant attitude to- ward a new approach, without being helped to address the underlying relational themes (compliance with an idealized other, resentment of the disruption of an idealized bond) that contributed to his difficulties.

THE SUPERVISOR'S ATTITUDE TOWARD HER OWN PSYCHOLOGY AS IT ENTERS THE SUPERVISORY RELATIONSHIP

A serious and self-reflective beginning trainee, Karen, arrived at supervi- sion with a blouse that gaped open a bit across her bust. During the super- visory hour, her supervisor, Doris, silently debated how to address the issue with her. She felt that she needed to say something, because presenting oneself appropriately when working with patients was a nonnegotiable value of hers, but she wanted to bring up the matter in a way that would facili- tate rather than shut down discussion. She feared that she would make her supervisee feel criticized, and would arouse feelings of shame no matter how she raised the topic. As the hour proceeded, Doris came increasingly to feel her own discomfort with raising this issue. She realized that she was having an unusually strong reaction, and as she associated further in her own mind, she became aware of her own harsh conscience regarding issues of sexual seductiveness and exhibitionism. This was territory that she had previously become familiar with in her own analysis.

Doris finally brought up the matter, in what she hoped was a light way, at the end of the hour. First she asked Karen if she were going to see patients today. When Karen said that she was, Doris commented that she might want to find a pin for her blouse, since being careful not to "dress exhibitionistically" was an important part of the therapist's role. (Here Doris substituted "exhibitionistically" for "seductively" out of her own discomfort with the implications of the term *seductive*.)

Karen seemed quite embarrassed, and surprised that her blouse was gaping. She said that she would be sure to fix her blouse before seeing her patient. Doris was relieved by her student's receptiveness, but still felt significant tension between them as Karen left the session. Doris was concerned about the impact she might have made with her comment.

Doris sought consultation from a colleague, after which she decided that she would return to the issue with Karen at the start of the following hour. She began by inquiring about Karen's experience of the interchange. Karen said that although she had felt embarrassed to have her lapse brought to her attention, she also was glad that the supervisor had spoken: she had rushed out of the house that morning without paying close attention to her appearance and wasn't aware of the problem. Then Doris disclosed that she had felt uncomfortable about making the comment, realizing that it might have caused the supervisee embarrassment. She mentioned her own conflictual feelings around seductiveness, and how those feelings had complicated her intervening. Doris also said that although at the time she thought that she had waited until the end of the supervisory hour to save Karen embarrassment, she had realized afterward that waiting had also been a defensive maneuver on her own part. The tension in the room lessened after this discussion, and Karen presented her work in an apparently comfortable way during the rest of the supervisory hour.

In this vignette, Doris exercises her rightful authority by speaking up for a standard of appropriate therapist behavior. A comment such as this one, made in a relationship with a power and status differential, can cause embarrassment and shame under the best of circumstances, and it is not surprising that Doris felt a bit uncomfortable about making it. For Doris, however, this was an especially loaded intervention, because an unintegrated judgmental aspect of herself had been activated. In speaking up, Doris felt a bit like a disapproving parent, making it more likely, she realized, she could misuse her authority by making Karen feel like a "bad" child.

As a result of some informal peer consultation, which she sought out after the hour, Doris decided to share something of her own conflict with Karen. The effect of this disclosure was to create an interpersonal context in which both supervisee and supervisor were understood to have conflicts, and to be far from perfect, with the supervisor taking partial responsibility for evoking the shameful feelings that her supervisee experienced. Leaving the situation as "improper supervisee/ proper supervisor" or "conflicted supervisee/conflict-free supervisor" would have been less than honest. It would also have been destructive to the supervisory relationship if Doris had not acknowledged the impact of her "harsh parent/bad child" internal object relation on the supervisory relationship. In making her disclosure, Doris also demonstrated for Karen how one can work with one's own conflicts while in the role of "helper." Of course, the question of when one actually discloses a countertransference reaction when working in a clinical context as opposed to a supervisory context was a separate issue that would also need to be addressed when it became relevant to Karen.

The issue of supervisor disclosure, like therapist disclosure, is a complex one. Each supervisor must find the style that works best for her, and that fits in best with the clinical theory she is trying to teach. Although every supervisory relationship is different, I am in general more likely to disclose my reactions to supervisees than to patients. In part this is because the helping relationship that exists between supervisor and supervisee coexisits with a collegial relationship, between a senior colleague and a junior colleague, while this is not necessarily the case in a clinical relationship. In this collegial relationship, I am conscious of wanting to demonstrate a self-analytic process, by speaking about the workings of my own mind as it shows up in our relationship. A relational model of supervision views such disclosure as part of an effort to make the supervisory relationship process consistent as well as content consistent, by showing the supervisee what to do as well as telling the supervisee what to do.

At the same time, I try to consider when disclosure will likely muddy the waters of the supervision by unnecessarily burdening the supervisee or detracting from other needed experiences. I try to be mindful of disclosing my internal conflicts to a supervisee if he is, for example, an anxious beginner who needs the chance to idealize me in order to manage her anxiety.

HOW THE SUPERVISOR BALANCES RESPECT FOR THE SUPERVISEE'S CONSCIOUSLY MADE CHOICES WITH RESPECT FOR THE SUPERVISEE'S UNCONSCIOUS NEEDS

A consultee, Coreen, saw her consultant, Jana, on an intermittent basis. Coming in to see Jana after an interval of several weeks, Coreen announced that she wanted to change consultants, and in fact had already met with someone new. Coreen gave a number of reasons why such a switch made sense to her at this time, including her desire to work with a consultant who was a member of an organization where Coreen was herself beginning to supervise. Coreen thought that the fact that she and the new consultant belonged to the same organization might be helpful to her as she began to supervise there.

Coreen emphasized that she was not dissatisfied with Jana's consultation. She had considered whether she might be avoiding something by leaving, since once before she had interrupted their consultation relationship precipitously. But after considerable reflection, she had concluded that her reasons were sound.

Jana was taken aback by this sudden announcement. Although she felt confused about what was going on, Jana felt that she needed to respect Coreen's decision. She told Coreen that she didn't understand the timing of this decision, but that Coreen seemed clear that it was right for her, and so she accepted it. Coreen seemed relieved by this response.

Having acknowledged Coreen's right to choose, Jana was tempted to back off from the question altogether. She felt narcissistically wounded, and she didn't want to appear overly concerned about Coreen's departure. Yet letting the matter go felt to her like an abandonment of Coreen, and so she gently continued to inquire, not in an effort to get Coreen to change her mind, but in order that both of them should better understand. And now Coreen, feeling that she was no longer at risk of being talked out of her decision, seemed more willing to explore her reasons.

Jana asked Coreen what she remembered about their last meeting. Coreen said that she had found it helpful and unproblematic. Jana said that she remembered having the feeling of offering something useful to Coreen. But as Coreen continued to speak about the session, it became evident that more had been going on than either Jana or Coreen had at first been able to be aware of. Coreen recalled that she had discussed a case that she had recently presented in her consultation group, which was led by an analyst. (Jana was also an analyst.) Coreen had mentioned to Jana in the previous hour that she had felt inadequate because her presentation to the group had revealed her countertransference issues with the client. Jana realized that she had not appreciated at the time the degree of anxiety and shame this presentation had caused Coreen. As Coreen spoke more about the presentation, powerful feelings welled up in her, taking both herself and Jana by surprise. In tears, Coreen spoke about the gulf that she thought separated her skills as a therapist from the skills of both the group consultant and Jana. As she listened, Jana felt moved, and regretted her earlier insensitivity to this underlying concern of her supervisee. As Coreen continued to talk, Coreen realized that she had been overwhelmed by a fear that she could never learn to work in the way that her group consultant and Jana did, and that she would therefore be better off learning from someone like the new consultant, who was not an analyst, and whose background and training were more similar to her own.

Now both Coreen and Jana understood Coreen's desire to switch consultants as her unconscious effort to cope with these painful feelings, which had been neither thinkable nor speakable in the previous consultation hour. Jana noted that Coreen did not seem to anticipate receiving help with these feelings in consultation, and so contacting them and bringing them into the relationship had not been possible for her.

Coreen chose at this point to take more time to think about her decision, a choice that Jana could wholeheartedly support. Coreen also began to consider that she might be able to work through her feelings in consultation, rather than needing to flee them.

In this vignette, Jana did not try to use her authority to undermine Coreen's choice. But on the other hand, Jana remained open to the possibility that other aspects of Coreen, aspects that were for some reason currently inaccessible, needed to be heard from as well. Jana sustained an analytic attitude, although she felt under some external as well as internal pressure. After doing some silent work on her own narcissistic vulnerability,[2] she was able to express acceptance of Coreen's conscious motivation, and to simultaneously invite exploration of Coreen's unconscious motivation. She neither opposed nor prematurely condoned action; she neither fled this upsetting material nor pushed

---

2. A parallel process seems to be involved here. Perhaps Coreen projected her anxiety about being inadequate onto her supervisor, who then had to work it through in the supervisory countertransference before she could be of help.

her supervisee into exploring it as a means of managing her own anxiety. Her stance created space where something new could emerge. In the end their shared understanding of a previously warded-off aspect of their interaction helped to prevent a potential rupture in the consultative relationship.

THE SUPERVISOR'S WILLINGNESS TO ADAPT TO HER SUPERVISEE'S NARCISISSTIC VULNERABILITY

Two brief vignettes illustrate different supervisor stances toward a supervisee who finds her style of intervention problematic because of injury to his narcissism:

Early in the supervision of my second control case, during my own psychoanalytic training, my supervisor pointed out something that I had missed in the presented hour, and told me how she would have handled it differently. I felt devastated by her critique, but in that hour could say nothing. In the next hour, having recovered a bit, I told her about my reaction. She showed surprise and immediate concern that her intervention had affected me in that way. She said that she had mistakenly thought that I was more secure in my abilities than was the case, and that this effort to teach me something did not mean that she felt I was doing a bad job.

This intervention allowed us to repair our relationship, and I felt able to proceed. My supervisor was careful to take heed of my vulnerability in offering feedback to me from then on, although she did not hold back her point of view. Sometimes, however, she reassured me that my difficulties were occurring in the context of good work, and were the kinds of issues that all psychoanalysts face, especially early in their training.

Many years, and many hours of training later, the same supervisor made another blunt statement about what she felt I was missing in a session. I recalled the earlier experience with her, and realized how different this comment felt to me from the previous one. Now I was able to hold on to a more complex and secure experience of myself, my supervisor, and also my own analyst, as mostly skillful but also each bringing our human limitations to our work.

By contrast, a colleague described to me a very different way of relating to her supervisees. She told me that although her supervisees often feel wounded by her commentaries on their work, she does not see this as her problem. She feels that it is every analytic psychotherapist's responsibility to confront directly the limits of his own understanding. She said that in her frequent consultations on her own analytic work, she is continually faced with how much she misses with her patients, and that supervisees who expect to be spared that disturbing experience are asking her for something that a supervisor cannot provide. She accepts it philosophically when supervisees react to her bluntness by electing not to work with her, viewing it as a commentary on their limitations, rather than a problem that needs to be worked with in the supervisory relationship.

These two supervisors had very different degrees of flexibility in responding to the narcissistic vulnerability that is part of the experience of most supervisees. My supervisor took some responsibility for the distress she caused me, even though she was very much aware that my own issues were involved. She adapted her style in order to establish a working relationship that I could tolerate. She did not hold back her critique of my work, but instead supplemented it with commentary that protected me from narcissistic injury until I developed a more benign attitude toward my limitations.

The second supervisor, unwilling to negotiate how supervision would be conducted, felt less obligation to adapt to her supervisees' distress. As a result of her unwillingness to negotiate the terms of the supervision, and her insistence on the correctness of her own stance, some supervisees left that supervisor.

Negotiation has become a nodal concept in relational thinking. As Frawley-O'Dea and I put it (2000): "The concept of negotiation implies that both members of the supervisory dyad have some, although not necessarily equal, authority in deciding what is true and what is best. . . . But for every supervisor there are limits to what can—or should —be open to negotiation" (pp. 76–77).

A relational view of the supervisor's authority, emphasizing the importance of a negotiation process between supervisor and supervisee, makes it likely that supervisory stalemates and ruptures will occur only when a disagreement about core values—things like the basic need for confidentiality in the clinical situation, for example (Greenberg 1995) —are at stake. In all other cases the relational supervisor assumes that she and her supervisee will work together, with a sense of mutual empowerment, to find their way through the difficulty.

Because theories of supervision have lagged behind clinical theories, only recently has a more mutual view of the supervisory relationship, where authority is distributed between the supervisory couple and negotiation between the parties is assumed to occur, begun to be elaborated in the literature. In the absence of such a well-elaborated theory of supervision, and the guidance it provides, it is human nature that supervisors should simply do to their supervisees as was done to them by their supervisors. The contemporary model of supervision elaborated here offers a new framework for authority relations within the supervisory relationship, and offers an opportunity to those engaged in psychotherapy training to reflect anew on their pedagogical approach.

REFERENCES

Aron, L. (1996). *A Meeting of Minds*. Hillsdale, NJ: Analytic Press.

Berman, E. (2000). Psychoanalytic supervision: the intersubjective development. *International Journal of Psycho-Analysis* 81:273–290.

Bergmann, M. (2003). A contribution to the supervisory panel. Symposium on Psychoanalytic Training and Education, *Psychoanalytic Dialogues* 13: 327–340.

Black, M. (2003). Afterward. Symposium on Psychoanalytic Training and Education, *Psychoanalytic Dialogues* 13:367–376.

Caligor, L. Bromberg, P., and Meltzer, J., eds. (1984). *Clinical Perspectives on the Supervision of Psychoanalysis and Psychotherapy*. New York: Plenum Press.

Cooper, L., and Gustafson, J. (1985). Supervision in a group: an application of group theory. *Clinical Supervisor* 3:7–25.

Frawley-O'Dea, M. G. (2003). Supervision is a relationship too: a contemporary approach to psychoanalytic supervision. Symposium on Psychoanalytic Training and Education. *Psychoanalytic Dialogues* 13:355–366.

Frawley-O'Dea, M.G., and Sarnat, J. (2000). *The Supervisory Relationship: A Contemporary Psychodynamic Approach*. New York: Guilford Press.

Greenberg, J. (1995). Psychoanalytic technique and the interactive matrix. *Psychoanalytic Quarterly* 64:1–22.

Hoffman, I. (1998). *Ritual and Spontaneity in the Psychoanalytic Process*. Hillsdale, NJ: Analytic Press.

Leary, K. (1997). Supervision and contemporary clinical practice: deconstructing and re-negotiating clinical authority in the psychological training clinic. Paper presented at the 17th annual spring meeting of the

Division of Psychoanalysis (39) of the American Psychological Association, Denver, CO.

Mitchell, S. (1997). *Influence and Autonomy in the Psychoanalytic Process.* Hillsdale, NJ: Analytic Press.

Pegeron, J. P. (1996). Supervision as an analytic experience. *Psychoanalytic Quarterly* 65:693–710.

Pizer, S. (1998). *Building Bridges: The Negotiation of Paradox in Psychoanalysis.* Hillsdale, NJ: Analytic Press.

Purcell, S. (2004). The analyst's theory: a third source of countertransference. *International Journal of Psycho-Analysis,* 85:635–652.

Rock, M., ed. (1997). *Psychodynamic Supervision.* Northvale, NJ: Jason Aronson.

Sarnat, J. (1992). Supervision in relationship: resolving the teach-treat controversy in psychoanalytic supervision. *Psychoanalytic Psychology* 9:387–403.

Teitelbaum, S. (1990). Supertransference: the role of the supervisor's blind spots. *Psychoanalytic Psychology* 7:243–258.

14

Effective and Efficient Supervision: Doing It in Group

Arthur A. Gray

In our field we have become increasingly aware of the supervisory process, although for me this awareness began in 1976 early in my analytic training. I began group supervision with a supervisor whom I admired as sensitive, caring, and dedicated to his work. However, I struggled through his group supervisions.

I remember one specific supervisory session where only the presenter spoke and the rest of us looked on in silence. The supervisor analyzed the case presented and then spoke of Fenichel's (1945) prescriptions. I learned how Fenichel documented the theory of psychoanalysis from Freud's original conceptions up to 1945. Something seemed to be missing from those analytic formulations and in the supervisory process yet I was too much of a neophyte to be able to articulate what was missing.

As I came to appreciate the complexity of psychoanalytic work, I also came to appreciate the evolution in psychoanalytic thinking (Bergmann and Hartman 1976). As I immersed myself in the explosion

274 / Power Games

of diverse, contemporary psychoanalytic knowledge, I found myself questioning the supervisory process.

In his review of Wallerstein's (1981) *Becoming a Psychoanalyst: A Study of Psychoanalytic Supervision*, Lachmann (1982) clarified how hazily defined the supervisor's role is in the life of a candidate:

> Every aspect of the life of the candidate, as the prospective analyst is called, is open to analysis, and, of course, the psychoanalytic literature provides the focus for the teacher. The boundaries for the supervisors are far less clear. They are narrower than those for the training analyst and broader than those for the teacher. Yet, although the value of supervision is explicitly acknowledged in psychoanalytic education, its contribution to the "becoming" of a psychoanalyst is still in dire need of study. [p. 801]

In the past 10 years while studying the supervisory process, my interest in group therapy led me to develop a model for supervising in a group modality. I have been haunted by that early group supervisory process where I learned of Fenichel. Though I was then excited about the potential for group supervision as a modality that could be efficient, a question remained. Could it be effective? I did not find my early group supervision effective. Yes, I learned of Fenichel, but that was all. So, what was still missing?

Group supervision is efficient because several people can be exposed to supervision at the same time. However, such a group process has potential pitfalls. It can either be too constricted or too chaotic. When it is constricted the group leader directs the supervision, talking to that one person who is presenting. The others in the group simply watch and listen as if the supervisor is lecturing. Occasionally, one of the other supervisees will ask a pertinent question. Usually this pertains to the supervisor's "lecture." This process is often not only constricted, but can be boring to those not presenting. Such a process usually takes place when the supervisor is not experienced in group work but is asked to lead a supervisory group.

Supervisors with group experience usually have a different problem. The supervision can become chaotic and arbitrary. As a supervisee presents a case and the other participants in the group supervision get a sense of the case, they begin to suggest alternate ways of thinking about it. Many times these alternate suggestions lead to other reactions and discussions as different supervisees react to different aspects of the presentation and the preceding comments. This is the beginning of the chaos. If someone makes a comment or suggestion that is in keeping with the group supervisor's preferences, then the supervisor will tend to take the group in that particular direction. This is often considered a focus. However, the original presenter's question or focus usually gets lost in this haphazard process. What dominates is the supervisor's preference. When a case is presented for supervision, the presenter is often uncertain of the most pertinent question to be raised. A chaotic group process does not help in defining the issue. The supervision becomes a platform for the supervisor's preferences rather than the supervisee's needs.

Supervision is usually just between supervisor and supervisee. If that process is hazily defined, then imagine the fuzziness added by attempting to provide supervision in a group context. The process of supervision must be brought into sharper focus so that the process of supervising in a group context can be defined.

Parameters of the supervisory process can be brought into sharper focus by asking and answering the following challenging question. Is our supervision, as a part of the training process, considered some kind of therapy, didactic training, or some combination of the two? Several authors such as Ekstein and Wallerstein (1972), DeBelle (1981), and Issacharoff (1984) have discussed this. Doehrman (1976), in addressing this complex question, suggested that while supervision and psychotherapy might have some qualities in common, a crucial difference exists. She believes that the goal of supervision is to allow the candidate to become a competent clinician. In contrast, the goal in psychotherapy is personality and behavioral changes.

The concern for the supervisee's competence raises still another key question. Does the supervisor treat the patient through the supervisee, or does she guide the supervisee as the latter treats the patient? Clearly, the focus should be on the supervisee's treating the patient (Ekstein and Wallerstein 1972, Fosshage 1997).

Two major convictions guide my thinking in this chapter. The first is that the goal of supervision is to promote the competence of the candidate in functioning as a mental health professional. The second is that the candidate's work is treating his patients, and supervision facilitates how he develops in his work. The supervisor nurtures the candidate.

The candidate treats the patient. This Cyrano de Bergerac approach directs the attention on the supervisee's way of working. This approach privileges the supervisor's authority while at the same time respecting the candidate's own authority, learning needs, and emerging professional identity. That is, the two assertions promote not only attention to the student's developing competence, but also attention to how he authoritatively communicates his unique style of clinical work. The application of these two assertions is contained in a model called "A Format for Group Supervision" (FGS).

A FORMAT FOR GROUP SUPERVISION

The FGS provides a six-step model that organizes the group supervisory process:

1. The presentation of the situation
2. The presenter's approach to the situation
3. The problem to be addressed in supervision
4. Can the presenter's approach address the problem?
5. Alternative approaches to the problem
6. Conclusion—what have we learned?

These six steps can be used in a group context not only to supervise candidates, but also to train supervisors in the use of this model. As a matter of fact, the model was developed to train directors in a social service agency with many satellite clinics. Since these directors were already supervisors, they were being supervised on supervising their supervisors in a group context.

The remainder of this chapter elaborates on these six steps. The model allows for the expertise of the supervisor. But it allows also the presenting candidate to define with the supervisor the candidate's unique needs in any given supervisory meeting. The focus remains on the candidate's needs. Together the supervisor and the candidate define what those needs are. The authority of the supervisor is relied on to foster the collaboration between teacher and student. That authority is used to define the unique learning of the candidate. In other words, the six steps in this model facilitate a co-created (Beebe and Lachmann 2002, Stern 2004), collaborative supervisory process.

For each of the six steps in this model, I begin with a brief description. Then I elaborate on that description and its application. Finally, I discuss the theoretical foundation and some practical issues that can arise in that particular step. As I describe the model and present a vignette about a therapy group, the group in the vignette is referred to as the *treatment group*. As shorthand, our supervision group will be referred to as the *group*. I attempt only to identify the group as a context consisting of at least three people (Gray 2001). I attempt to avoid anthropomorphizing any group; that is, I avoid implying that it is an entity with a life of its own. The leader and the other members in the group create together the experience, and are responsible for it. The group leader guides this process.

SETTING THE STAGE

Before applying the model to a supervisory group, that group must be prepared. It is recommended that the supervisor inform the group that she plans to approach the supervision in a different manner. It takes a minimum of 45 minutes to complete the supervising of one person when using FGS. In fact, in the FGS each member in the group receives supervision simultaneously with the presenter. In other words, the allotted time includes much discussion from all participants in the process—not only the presenter. More than 45 minutes can always be taken for a single presentation. The time factor depends on the makeup of the supervisory group and the experience of the person leading it. Furthermore, there is another practice that takes additional time in a supervisory session. Consider an example where a candidate named Rashad presents in the first week of the supervision. Then, for the first 5 to 10 minutes of the next supervisory meeting, Rashad is asked to give feedback to the group on how the previous week's supervision influenced his work with the patient. Following this feedback session, Shoshana begins her presentation. Therefore, each week a different person in the group will make the main presentation.

THE SIX STEPS OF THE MODEL

1. The Presentation of the Situation

To begin with, the first step in the six-step process is different from what one usually expects. The person presenting is asked to present a situation to the group. For candidates this is usually an event having to do with treating a therapy case. However, the candidate need not restrict his presentation in this way. He might want to present some other problem that might have arisen in his training. He could even choose, for example, to question whether he is going to stay in the training program. Or, he might present that he has difficulty knowing what to present to the group. In other words:

> The presentation of the situation is a brief and specific definition of the who, what, when, where of some event relevant to training.

Elaboration

The situation refers to the manifest narrative that the presenter provides at the beginning of the group supervision. Should the material not appear clear to the supervisor or the other members of the group, then the supervisor actively helps to clarify, and make more coherent the details of the situation. The group does not listen for problems or unconscious content (Lichtenberg et al. 1996). The focus is on the narrative of the situation being presented. The members of the group are encouraged to participate in this effort to clarify this narrative. This participation between the presenter and the group is continued until the presenter states convincingly that the group has heard what is presented. Through this process the presenter tells what important concern he or she wishes for us to consider in the supervision. When this process has been completed then the supervision moves on to step 2, below.

For the sake of this discussion I will assume that the presenting candidate is bringing in a case vignette. This first step of the model emphasizes the need to listen to what the presenter would like us to attend to in his vignette. The vignette is the situation.

Viewing the vignette as a situation is an extremely important matter. I wish to emphasize that a situation that is presented is not inherently a problem. Still there is the tendency for the supervisor and supervisees to listen for a problem in the case. For example, the supervisor and the group of supervisees might interrupt the presentation to show how he missed a certain level of disturbance in the patient. Or, they might even begin by reassuring the presenter: "You shouldn't be so hard on yourself. After all, this is a difficult patient." Such interventions are discouraged in this model.

The members are asked to focus on the who, what, when, and where of the vignette presented. Working with a patient is not inherently a problem. Similarly, patients are not inherently difficult. It is this specific presenter who finds the work with this particular patient challenging. This first step gives the authority to the presenter. The presenter has the opportunity to state how he is uniquely challenged by his patient.

So, in this first step the group members clarify the situation by repeating what the presenter has said. In so doing, they focus on what the presenter wants to question or emphasize in his work with his particular patient. In some presentations, the candidate might think highly of his work, and want to address a complexity that emerges out of how effectively he has been treating the patient. In such a presentation the group members accept the description of the patient. They do not challenge the candidate's sense of the patient. His description identifies the question that he wishes the group to address. However, the candidate does not always understand the question or the focus he is addressing. The group can help identify the focus from the who, what, when, and where of what is presented. A key factor in identifying the candidate's question is to listen carefully to his opening remarks. In these remarks he communicates his primary concern, even though it may be vague.

For example, after Shoshana had given a 10-minute feedback about how the previous week's supervision had influenced her work, Mark was scheduled to present. This was to have been Mark's first time presenting. As Shoshana gave her feedback, he seemed to have questions that would have taken her feedback in a totally new direction. If followed, his line of questioning would have extended the feedback session far beyond the 5- to 10-minute limit.

I said to Mark that we needed to leave time for his presentation. He said, "Okay." However, under his breath he said, "I really don't want to present."

Mark's presentation gave extensive detail about each member in his therapy group. The other members in the supervisory group were baffled. When Mark finally began talking about the process in the therapy group, the presentation remained vague and unfocused. Remembering that he had said, "I really don't want to present" informed me that he might have been feeling embarrassed about being unclear about what to focus on in his vignette. He prided himself on "being there" for his patients. However, "being there" was a haphazard process of vague responses to whatever a patient brought up at the beginning of his group.

From the who-what-when-where, I suggested a focus on whether or not to comply with one of the therapy group members' request to change the day the group met. Being there for his patient, Mark changed the day. In our supervision group, other members concurred that they too thought this might have been his question. Mark, however, rejected our suggestion, and perked up for the first time in the supervision. "Ah hah, that's it," he said. "I want to know how to deal with their disappointment. The person who requested the change had not shown up. They were disappointed about this absence. They have all suffered several major disappointments and abandonments in their lives."

The example of Mark demonstrates that the process involved in the first step is to listen empathically (Ornstein 1985) to the presenter. That is, the group members listen to the presenter from the presenter's perspective. We rely on the knowledge we all share about how we communicate even when we do not verbalize explicitly what we are sharing and how we are presenting ourselves. The FGS model provides ample time to understand the case material from a clinical perspective. However, the case material is not the focus in this first step. In this first step the focus is on defining what the presenting candidate wants us to address. Mark's who-what-when-where description became understood as his need to define more specifically his general sense of "being there" for his patients. His "being there" needed to be more specific. He wanted to address an issue he saw as relevant to the therapy group on that day. I and the other members of our group initially attempted to help Mark focus on the issue of agreeing to change the day his therapy group was to meet. However, that was not the focus he had in mind. For Mark to grow in his work, he needed the group to begin with his focus. He had the authority to define the avenue to his growth as an analyst.

When the presenter's question is understood, he usually will respond with, "Ah hah, yes. That is what I am asking," as Mark had done. When the presenter expresses spontaneously and convincingly a sense of having been heard, the group moves on to the next step which is the presenter's approach to the situation.

Another additional note is that Mark's extremely detailed presentation of the situation meant that step 1 took up the complete supervisory time for him. This is acceptable in the model. Usually the description of the situation and understanding the presenter's focus takes about 5 to 15 minutes. All six steps need not be completed, if this is not possible. Completing any number of steps from one to six is valuable to the supervisory process. Mark could handle only step 1.

2. The Presenter's Approach to the Situation

When the group is ready to move on to step 2, then the presenter and participants define and agree on the presenter's approach.

Elaboration

The focus in this step is on how the presenter approached the situation he or she described. That is, the presenter and each member of the group clarify and understand how the presenter approached intervening in the situation that was presented. At this juncture members of the group are asked *not* to present differing points of view on how to approach the material. The presenter and the other supervisees must agree on the presenter's approach. The supervisor actively facilitates this process. The approach could be the presenter's theoretical orientation or simply how he or she intervened in the situation presented. Not until the presenter and the other supervisees agree on the presenter's approach can the discussion move on to step 3, below.

Discussion

It is important that the supervisee's approach be defined and appreciated before going further in the model. This step in the model ensures further that the presenter is understood from his perspective.

The authority remains in the hands of the presenter. The supervisor's expertise and authority facilitates the learning process.

Understanding the presenter from the presenter's perspective also includes understanding how he approaches his work within the therapeutic setting involved. To understand the supervisee empathically (Ornstein 1985) requires understanding his theoretical perspective, as well as what he does in his work. As Lachmann (2001) states, "the devil is in the details."

Another way to understand this step in the model is that at this point the group seeks an example of what the presenter actually does in his work. In this step other supervisees in the group focus on understanding the presenter's way of working. At this point supervisees tend to want to make suggestions to the presenter. As stated, this is actively discouraged. The presenter feels appreciated and understood when the focus is on understanding what he did in working with the vignette without attempts to correct him. There will be plenty of time to address other perspectives on the presenter's work. However, this is not that time. Instead, the members in the group reflect back to the presenting candidate their understanding of how he approached working in the situation presented. The supervisor promotes this process of clarifying and understanding the presenter's way of approaching the work. The supervisor makes sure that each of the members of the group has the opportunity to verbalize her understanding or questioning of the presenter's approach. Making sure that each member participates (Gray 2001) by asking questions provides for each of the questioning members a form of supervision.

After the presenter feels that his approach is heard, understood, accepted, and respected (Coopersmith 1967, Lichtenberg et al. 1996), then the group is ready to move on to the third step of the supervision —defining the problem faced in the supervision. This step is the most difficult and elusive aspect of the supervision as the group decides how to best address the question the presenter is bringing to the group supervision. It is the most essential step in contributing to the effectiveness of the supervision.

3. The Problem to be Addressed in Supervision

Here the question is asked: Does the presentation of the situation and the approach to it illustrate a *learning problem* (pertaining to learning how to handle the case), a *problem about learning* (from presenter to supervisor), or a *problem with administration* (either in the supervisory setting or the setting of the vignette or both) (Ekstein and Wallerstein 1972, Fleming and Benedek 1966, Jacob et al. 1995)?

Elaboration

These three types of problems distinguish supervision from psychotherapy. Psychotherapy addresses emotional issues through exploring transferences emerging in the therapy sessions. Supervision addresses how the presenter learns to handle various work challenges (DeBelle 1991, Doehrman 1976, Ekstein and Wallerstein 1972, Issacharoff 1984) through exploring problems that emerge in the supervisory session. How the candidate's personal, emotional issues influence the learning is not the explicit matter of supervision.

In step 3 the supervisor, the presenter, and the rest of the group consider the situation presented in step 1. And they consider the approach to the situation presented in step 2. From these data they formulate and agree on the type of problem the supervision is facing with the presenter. Step 3 is the first time a problem is addressed in FGS. There are three possible problems: (1) A learning problem is one arising from the candidate's not knowing how to handle a specific treatment issue. The treatment issue could arise in individual therapy, group therapy, or milieu therapy. But in this chapter I focus on candidates being trained in individual or group therapy. (2) A problem about learning is one arising between the supervisor and the presenter, highlighting some difficulty the presenter has about learning from the supervisor. And (3) a problem with administration arises out of the presenter's struggle with the administrative structure of the present supervisory setting or with the setting where the vignette took place, or both.

In step 3 an interesting occurrence can take place. Together, the presenter and the others in the group might agree that a question initially identified by the presenter is not the most relevant focus. A very different one might be identified and agreed on by the presenter, supervisor, and the other supervisees in the group. When this kind of redefining occurs it is usually accompanied by a delightful sense of discovery and often surprise. Below I discuss an example of this kind of redefining.

Discussion

By step 3 in the supervision the presenter's question for supervision is known. The presenter's approach to his work is also known and appreciated. But the supervisor and other candidates in the supervision group still could intervene by responding to any number of points in the presentation. Within group supervision any of the participants might determine what that particular point of intervening is. However, to avoid this remaining haphazard possibility this third step ensures that the presenter's need determines the point of intervening. Instead of having an indeterminate number of points of intervention, this step narrows the points to only three possibilities: (1) a learning problem, (2) a problem about learning, or (3) a problem with administration. Each of these possibilities makes specific the problem that confronts the supervision. Knowing the specific problem helps the group address more effectively the presenter's needs.

The important question implied in the problem that the supervision group faces with the presenter is that of the difference between supervision and psychotherapy. As the group specifies the problem it faces with the presenter, his emotional issues that might challenge how he does his work often become clear. As noted, emotional issues are *not* the explicit domain of the supervisory process (Doehrman 1976, Gray 1995). The supervision focuses on helping the presenter to do his work more effectively. In this process, he will often experience the emotional issue that might stand in the way of getting that work done. As the supervisor stays with the clinical context, the presenter can continue over time to experience the emotional challenges without feeling criticized. Defining within the clinical context the kind of problem facing the supervision group vis-à-vis the presenter often helps him appreciate personal, emotional challenges affecting his clinical work. In this event the presenter may ask for a therapy recommendation. The presenter may also be in therapy or a training analysis in which he can address his emotional needs emerging implicitly in the supervisory group. When following this FGS model, usually it is not necessary for the supervisor to suggest that the presenter needs to be in his own therapy, or, "Take this problem up with your analyst."

When the supervisor is attempting to define the nature of the problem that the presenter brings to the group, the complex task of identifying that problem can be aided by what Ekstein and Wallerstein (1972) call the clinical rhombus. The clinical rhombus is a diamond-shaped figure that summarizes the supervisor's role in any training institution. Through the clinical rhombus Ekstein and Wallerstein clarify that the supervisor professionally positions herself equidistant from the presenter, the patient, and the administrative setting. That is, the supervisor has equal responsibility to the other three aspects of any training institution—the candidate, the patient, and the administration.

The administration is both the setting in which the supervisor supervises and the setting in which the presenter sees his patients. For both supervisor and candidate the setting includes the ethical and professional responsibilities of our work as mental health professionals. It is the responsibility of the supervisor to attend not only to how the candidate upholds that professional responsibility but also to how the administration upholds its professional responsibility to the candidate and to the profession as a whole.

However, while Ekstein and Wallerstein clarify that the supervisor has equal responsibility to candidate, patient, and administration, I augment their thoughtful prescription. I believe that the supervisor's primary commitment is to the learning needs of the presenter. The supervisor does not treat the patient through the presenter. The supervisor is responsible for the presenter mastering the skills required to do his work effectively and ethically in his setting (DeBelle 1991, Doehrman 1976, Gallagher 1994, Gray 1995, Issacharoff 1984, Rock 1997). However, at the same time the supervisor is committed to the administrative setting and the patient being treated.

The stated interrelationship among supervisor, candidate, patient, and administration can help to make it clear that as a presenter gives case material, that material itself might not be the actual focus of the problem facing the supervisory group. The problem could be about the difficulty the presenter is having with the supervisor, the supervisory group, or someone in the supervisory group. Or it could be about the presenter's difficulty with administration.

Earlier I stated that while FGS can be used to conduct effective and efficient supervision in a group context, it can also be used to train supervisors on how to supervise in a group. When FGS is used for supervising candidates, then this third step is not stated explicitly. It is implicitly culled from the discussion of the case material. That is, the supervisor formulates it from the presentation and discussion of the situation and the approach to it. Her formulation is then further implicitly explored with the supervision group in order to confirm it. When the model is used to train participants in how to supervise using a group context, then the decisions made in this step are explored explicitly, and discussed among leader, presenter, and all other members present in the supervision group. This exploration done implicitly or explicitly with all members in the group ensures that the supervisor is not autocratically determining the problem in the supervision.

In a group for training supervisors, the presenter's problem is first identified and openly discussed. When everyone is satisfied with the formulation of the problem, then the group is ready for step 4: can the presenter's approach address the problem?

In the case of supervising candidates, the supervisor subtly relies on her reactions and the reactions of the supervision group to formulate whether a learning problem, a problem about learning, or a problem with administration is being addressed. When she is adequately convinced that the problem is accurately defined, she then slides into step 4. This decision determines how she handles the remaining steps of the supervision.

A Clarifying Case

Dr. Shiner (Gray 1995), who was in individual supervision with me, provides an example of how defining the specific problem effectively addressed her supervisory needs. While this was an individual supervision, I relied on the FGS model to guide me in addressing her supervisory needs. Throughout her 2-year supervision, she provided an example of each of the three problems that can emerge in the supervision.

In Dr. Shiner's first session, after she described her background and her practice, she told me she wanted to learn more about working psychoanalytically in contrast to the effective though primarily intuitive way she had been working. In her second session she referred to having terminated a group and wanted to discuss the new group she was establishing. We discussed the constellation of the new group, and she agreed to bring in process recordings starting with the next supervisory session.

Though she looked forward to our supervisory sessions, she had to cancel our next scheduled appointment—the third session. The fourth appointment was disrupted by some personal matters. She requested that we hold our supervisory session by phone. I agreed to do this. The fifth session was disrupted by a snowstorm requiring that she leave town early to return to her children in New Jersey.

At this point I thought it essential to address her difficulty coming to her supervisory sessions. I did this over the phone. I interpreted to her that she might have some apprehension about revealing the limitations in her psychoanalytic sophistication. I explained to her that, to this point her work had been highly successful, but she had been working primarily intuitively, and the success gained was through her ability to convey to her patients her great degree of enthusiasm and caring. It was now time for her to master the more complex process of working through in therapy. To do this, it was necessary for her to make time to come to supervisory sessions.

This intervention was addressing her problem about learning from me. I implicitly, but carefully, assumed that she was avoiding the supervision. At the same time I accepted wholeheartedly that she did want to attend the supervisory sessions, as she had expressed. In my intervention I was testing my hypothesis.

When she came for her fifth session, she angrily told me of her fear of my trying to bring her into the psychoanalytic fold. She thought my implicit efforts would rob her of her creativity. This issue had come up during her very first meeting with me. There she had stated that she wanted to learn more about psychoanalysis but respected her effective, intuitive way of working. I addressed her angry concerns reassuringly. She never again missed a supervisory session for almost two years despite a very busy schedule.

During her first year in supervision with me, she was required to write a paper for graduation from her group therapy program. She decided to reevaluate the group she had terminated and discover how her limited psychoanalytic experience created problems that led to her ultimately disbanding the therapy group. Her difficulty working with her patients in that group represented her learning problems. This issue had been raised already in her second meeting with me. By further exploring these questions she wrote an outstanding paper on the limitations of charismatic leadership in the working through phase of group therapy. Ultimately she was invited to teach in the institution from which she at one time had felt alienated.

Her alienation from the psychoanalytic orientation of that institution also represented her problem with the administration. It was clear that her doubts about the psychoanalytic emphasis of this institution did spill into how she treated her patients. Her emphasis on unorthodox, creative interventions caused much difficulty for many of her patients. The result was that they left treatment. For other patients her charismatic style was inspiring and emotionally helpful. Early in the supervision when I had demonstrated how working psychoanalytically would not destroy her creativity, I was also addressing the ways in which her struggle with the administration interfered with her treating some of her patients. She ultimately discovered the extent to which that struggle with the administration created an atmosphere within her therapy sessions that at times had more to do with her battle with administration than with the patient's needs. For example, she often emphasized her more charismatic tendencies in coping with a challenging patient concern, rather than exploring in supervision an approach with more tested psychoanalytic principles. Of course at the same time the FGS model allowed us to question "tested psychoanalytic principles" comparing them thoughtfully with her charismatic ones. This approach emphasizes the supervisory effort as a collaborative one.

Once a presenter's problem to be addressed in supervision is clarified, step 4 can be addressed.

4. Can the Presenter's Approach Address the Problem?

At this point in the supervision, given the candidate's approach, which has been defined in step 2, how can the group help him to address the problem identified in step 3?

Elaboration

The focus here remains on the presenter's perspective. Throughout the model, the authority of the presenter is maintained. So, given the question raised by the situation the candidate presents in step 1, and informed by his approach to that situation clarified in step 2, step 3 identifies the problem to be addressed in the supervision. Then, in this fourth step the supervisor asks, "Can we stay within the approach of the presenter and solve effectively the problem confronting the supervision?" If so, how? That is, can the supervisor and members of the group make suggestions on how the presenter could have achieved his stated approach even better, and so address the question he was raising? However, the group attempts are guided by how the problem confronting the supervisory group has been defined. That is, is the supervision trying to refine his approach so that he can deal with the learning problem, the problem about learning, or the problem with administration? The group stays with how the presenter defines his needs in the supervisory setting. His authority is as paramount as that of the supervisor or anyone else in the process. All members of the supervision group including the presenter explore thoroughly this effort to refine the presenter's approach. When the question is answered to the satisfaction of the presenter and all involved, the group moves on to step 5—alternative approaches.

Discussion

The supervision continues to focus on the presenter's unique approach to his work. It stays with his approach to see if it can enhance it in order to effectively address the problem identified in step 3. Respecting the way the presenter works is the key to effective supervision. The group members do not impose other theoretical orientations. For example, if the presenter is using an object-relational approach and the supervisor works from a self-psychological perspective, the supervisor continues to accept and respect the presenter's approach (Coopersmith 1967). The model provides ample opportunity for the supervisor and others to present alternative approaches, which brings the group to step 5.

Two outcomes are possible in step 4. One is that the presenter's approach, when aided by suggestions from the group, does work better and does address the problem confronting the supervision. Another outcome is that the presenter will comfortably admit that his approach does not effectively address the problem. In either case, all the group members including the supervisor and presenter explore these two possibilities thoroughly. When everyone is satisfied with the conclusion, the group moves on to the next step.

The example of Dr. Shiner relying on her charismatic, intuitive style demonstrates what takes place in step 4. In supervising her, I explored thoroughly her use of her charismatic, intuitive style. We appreciated how it did work with some of the people in her group. We discussed ways she was able to use her style more effectively. She appreciated this understanding and comfortably raised questions about why her style failed with other members of her group. Seeing the limitations of her approach, she readily inquired about and explored with me alternate approaches.

However, consider a situation where the presenting candidate introduces a learning problem that refers to questions about how to treat his patient. What if it is discovered in step 3 that, to the presenter's surprise, he is having a problem with administration? If so, the group explores in step 4 how the problem with administration might influence the way he treats his patient. Together they might figure out how his approach could be used more effectively once he clarifies his struggle with the administration. They could also discuss how, in future supervisory presentations, he might further address this struggle with administration.

For example, Dr. Shiner's insistence on using her charismatic approach to help her patients was based partly on her battle with the administration of her group therapy training department. As she understood how some patients did benefit from her charisma, while others were overwhelmed by it, she accepted the limitations of her approach. As stated above, she came to appreciate how a blanket charismatic approach overwhelmed those patients who needed a more analytically oriented exploratory process. She even came to understand how her charismatic approach could be used in ways more in keeping with an analytic stance. These understandings led to a tempering of her struggle with the administration.

Dr. Shiner, in understanding and tempering her struggle with administration, began to recognize the differing needs of her patients. She then began to explore with me more details about alternative approaches to her work.

5. Alternative Approaches

At this point the supervisor and the group members can offer and explore alternate approaches that address both the question initiated in step 1 and the problem confronting the supervisory group in step 3. Here, references from clinically relevant literature can be introduced, explored, and elaborated.

Elaboration

Finally, this is where each of the group members is free to make alternative suggestions. If the problem in step 3 cannot be solved sufficiently using the presenter's approach, what other approaches may be considered? If the presenter's approach was used effectively to address the problem presented, then this step is not necessary unless requested by the presenter, or by any one of the supervisees in the group. If the focus of the supervision is on teaching a new theoretical approach, then step 5 would compare the presenter's approach with the alternative model being taught.

The problem being addressed in supervision (a learning problem, a problem about learning, or a problem with administration) represents the supervisee's specific learning needs. Reference material from clinically relevant literature should be geared to these specific needs. These references clarify the alternative approach. They also provide a backdrop for comparative readings to understand how the presenter's approach is similar to and different from the ones being discussed in this section on alternative approaches.

It is essential to reserve alternative approaches to this stage in the supervisory session. The tendency to offer alternate perspectives from the very beginning of the presentation can create chaos in the group and excessive frustration for the presenter. When alternative approaches are reserved for this stage, the presenter can be more open to them. In turn, each group member can feel freer in expressing his or her perspective. By this time the presenter's question has focused the supervision. In the context of this focus, alternate suggestions contribute more specifically to the learning needs of the presenter and of each group member.

When the discussion of alternative approaches seems to have satisfied the needs of the presenter and those of the other members of the supervision group, they move on to step 6.

Discussion

When all members have a sense that alternate approaches have been sufficiently explored, the supervision moves on to the sixth step. Time constraints also weigh in on this decision.

The next goal is to end the supervisory session by returning the focus to the original presenter. This goal is achieved in step 6.

6. Conclusion: What Have We Learned?

At this point the group compares the original approach with the alternate approach or approaches.

Elaboration

The focus here is on comparing the implied effectiveness of the approaches discussed. The presenter's approach, spelled out in step 2, is compared with suggestions made in step 4, if there are any. The presenter's approach from step 2 is compared also with the alternative approach or approaches offered in step 5. Everyone participates. Finally, the presenter is asked to comment on the experience of presenting to the group. His responses are discussed by all.

Consider a supervisory group that meets weekly. As stated earlier, the candidate presenting in a given week will take 5 to 10 minutes of the next supervisory session to report on the impact of the previous week's supervision. During those 5 to 10 minutes, the supervisor might hear and clarify for the presenter other issues. The supervisor can then recommend that the candidate brings these other issues up in his next full presentation.

Discussion

The limits to this conclusion are usually time related. It is important to end the supervisory session addressing the presenter. The presenter has the opportunity to tell of his experience in the group supervision. This step ensures that neither the supervisor nor the group had overlooked anything that might have been important to the presenter. In my experience, when FGS has been followed effectively, the presenter usually leaves with a sense of satisfaction, having been heard in a highly respectful, critically thoughtful, and nonjudgmental atmosphere.

CONCLUSION

When FGS is carefully followed, this six-step model can provide for the supervisor a platform on which to use her expertise in a group context to supervise candidates. On this platform she can co-create (Beebe and Lachmann 2002, Stern 2004) with a presenting candidate a group supervisory experience that is both effective and efficient.

In this co-creation the supervisor and supervisee team up. The supervisor uses her experience and knowledge to carefully understand the situation the supervisee chooses to present. From the presented situation, supervisor and supervisee agree on a question, focus, or issue to which the supervisee wants to attend. The situation implies the question, focus, or issue. Together, along with the rest of the group, they agree on what it is. However, the presenter has the final word.

In addressing the candidate's agreed upon focus, the supervisor does not impose her approach—theoretical or practical—on the supervisee. She focuses on elaborating clearly the candidate's approach. Through the presenter's approach, the supervisor begins to co-create with the candidate a viable means of collaborating on how the student can grow from this presentation. This collaboration is fostered by the supervisor's understanding learning problems, problems about learning, and problems with administration. These three problems that confront the supervisory dyad and group provide a key to how the candidate organizes his learning experience within the psychoanalytic training context. In any given supervisory session, the presenting candidate will confront the supervision with one of these three problems. Each of the three problems represents the transference-like experience of the candidate in the supervisory sessions. In a session the supervisor organizes her interventions in ways that are in keeping with the one problem that is most salient.

Finally, respecting the approaches of presenter and all group participants, the supervisor creates an atmosphere of learning in a dynamic group process. In this process differing perspectives are explored. Through this exploration emerging clinicians grow to appreciate and strive to master the unfolding complexity of psychoanalysis and psychotherapy. A Format for Group Supervision presents a collaborative process between supervisor and candidate that can be explored in an interactive group process that is highly stimulating for the presenter and all participants.

REFERENCES

Beebe, B., and Lachmann, F. M. (2002). *Infant Research and Adult Treatment: Co-constructing Interactions*. Hillsdale, NJ: Analytic Press.

Bergmann, M. S., and Hartman, F. R. (1976). *The Evolution of Psychoanalytic Technique*. New York: Basic Books.

Coopersmith, S. (1967). *The Antecedents of Self-Esteem*. San Francisco: W. H. Freeman.

DeBelle, D. E. (1991). Supervisory styles and position. In *Becoming a Psychoanalyst*, ed. R. S. Wallerstein. New York: International University Press.

Doehrman, M. J. (1976). Parallel process in supervision and psychotherapy. *Bulletin of the Menninger Clinic* 40(1):9–104.

Ekstein, R., and Wallerstein, R. S. (1972). *The Teaching and Learning of Psychotherapy*. New York: International University Press.

Fenichel, O. (1945). *The Psychoanalytic Theory of Neurosis*. New York: W. W. Norton.

Fleming, J., and Benedek, T. (1966). *Psychoanalytic Supervision*. New York: Grune and Stratton.

Fosshage, J. L. (1997). Toward a model of psychoanalytic supervision from a self-psychological/intersubjective perspective. In *Psychodynamic Supervision: Perspectives of the Supervisor and the Supervisee*, ed. M. H. Rock. Northvale, NJ: Jason Aronson.

Gallagher, R. E. (1994). Stages of group psychotherapy supervision: a model for supervising beginning trainees of dynamic group therapy. *International Journal of Group Psychotherapy* 44(2):169–183.

Gray, A. A. (1995). Learning problems and problems about learning in supervision: implications for distinguishing supervision from psychoanalysis. Paper on supervision receiving the Emanuel K. Schwartz Memorial Award at Postgraduate Center for Mental Health, New York, May.

——— (2001). Difficult terminations in group therapy: a self psychological perspective. *Group* 25(1/2):27–39.

Issacharoff, A. (1984). Countertransference in supervision: therapeutic consequences for the supervisee. In *Clinical Perspectives on the Supervision of Psychoanalysis and Psychotherapy*, ed. L. Caligor, P. M. Bromberg, and J. D. Meltzer, pp. 89–105. New York: Plenum Press.

Jacob, D., David, P., and Meyer, D. J. (1995). *The Supervisory Encounter*. New Haven, CT: Yale University Press.

Lachmann, F. M. (1982). Mission impossible: to supervise psychoanalysis. Book review of Wallerstein, R. S., ed. *Becoming a Psychoanalyst: A Study of Psychoanalytic Supervision*. New York: International Universities Press, 1981. *Contemporary Psychology* 27(10):801–802.

——— (2001). The devil is in the details. *Psychoanalytic Dialogues* 13(3):341–353.

Lichtenberg, J., Lachmann, F., and Fosshage, J. (1996). *The Clinical Exchange*. Hillsdale, NJ: Analytic Press.

Ornstein, P. H. (1985). Clinical understanding and explaining: the empathic vantage point. In *Progress in Self Psychology*, vol. 1, ed. A. Goldberg, pp. 43–61. Hillsdale, NJ: Analytic Press.

Rock, M. H. (1997). Effective supervision. In *Psychodynamic Supervision: Perspectives of the Supervisor and the Supervisee*, ed. M. H. Rock. Northvale, NJ: Jason Aronson.

Stern, D. (2004). *The Present Moment in Psychotherapy and Everyday Life*. New York: Basic Books.

15

Toward a Quadro-Partite Training Model, or from Identification-Relations (of Power) to Introjection-Relations (of Love): The Case of Identification with the Aggressor[1]

Gershon J. Molad and Judith E. Vida[2]

SOME NOTES AS AN INTRODUCTION

This chapter is drawn from the larger context of our work-in-progress, which we call "The Clinical Relevance of the Autobiographical Dialogue." In the area of its relevance to psychoanalytic training, we suggest that making explicit and visible the autobiographical dialogue between analysts may lead to a crucial developmental change: a movement from the classical tri-partite model (of personal analysis, theoretical and clinical seminars, and analyses conducted under supervision) to

1. An earlier partial version of this chapter was presented in a workshop "*Psychanalyse, Histoire, Rêve et Poésie*" (Psychoanalysis, History, Dream, and Poetry), organized by the European Association for Nicolas Abraham and Maria Torok, Paris, October 9 and 10, 2004.
2. Since we write in the context of an ongoing mutual dialogue, the order of names intermittently alters and is of no significance.

the inclusion in the training model of what we see as the missing fourth part, the autobiographical dialogue between analysts (Molad and Vida 2002 and 2005).

Moving to the immediate topic of this chapter, we examine the case of identification with the aggressor as a most central and difficult issue in psychoanalytic training. Looking into the essence of identification with the aggressor, we find a previously unrecognized layer of relatedness, which introduces a two-step idea about the basic nature of identification with the aggressor:

1. The deeper layer of identification with the aggressor is not an identification within or of the *victim as an aggressor*, but an identification with the *aggressor as a victim*.
2. The mechanism of this deeper process is introjection rather than identification, as introjection has been understood by Nicholas Abraham and Maria Torok.[3] In the actual traumatic event that gives rise to what is currently thought of as identification with the aggressor, the power of the "aggressor" can be seen as expressing an inner split that iterates what had happened to the aggressor in an earlier instance. We propose the origin of such aggression as itself the failed outcome of an identificatory holding, containing, and circumscribing of the life experience of the aggressor. It is introjection that begins to bridge the inner split that lies in the heart of aggression.

Notions of identification and introjection have to do with love, but in different forms. When love takes the form of submission, a giving-up of oneself to the other, the power motif is visible. On the other hand, surrender and giving-in (yielding) are more suggestive of something quieter, like devotion. We see identification as a means of maintain-

---

3. In their way of thinking, identification refers to a kind of internalized copying of an other, whereas with introjection what one takes in is the established or constituted desire for the other, especially the thwarted, unmet desire. In the comparison of these notions of identification and introjection, we notice two distinct ways of generating the subject, the "I," that is, myself. Identification offers a simple way of (re)creation, whereas with introjection, I know myself by means of my desire, irrespective of achieving it, and I will know myself differently according to how my desire is met.

ing and consolidating power, a joining of self to other in a holding, containing, and circumscribing process. Identification operates with submission and giving-up as its subtext; this is the role of authority. On the other hand, we see introjection as essentially egalitarian, maintaining the right-to-be of self and other, recognizing and valuing aspects of self in the other; here the subtext is surrendering and letting in, generosity rather than authority.

We see the basic mechanism of identification with the aggressor as an imagined healing or transformation of the other that is generated by a longing to move the nature of relating from submission (to the powerful expression of a single and singular voice) into a context of love (with a dialogical polyphony of multiple voices). In our words, this is a movement from biographical monologue to autobiographical dialogue, where what matters is not who rules with the best/right/perfect story but rather playing together by telling all our stories. This is a kind of regression, though in the service of relatedness, not simply of the ego but for a relational ego.

Our reconceptualization of identification with the aggressor as introjection-relations with the aggressor represents a shift in our current understanding and usage of the concept. The shift is from a focus on survival and self-preservation (the territory of object relations) and the split-off dynamics of the victim, to a focus on (a more subject-relational) developmental and therapeutic circumscription. This is circumscription in the sense of accepting the being and existing of the inner dynamics of the aggressor. The aggressive act is experienced by the other as not only victimizing but also as victimized, that is, originating from victimization. Through a mechanism of something like projective identification, the victimization of and within the aggressor can be discovered, along with that person's yet-unattained developmental yearning.

In the autobiographical dialogue that takes place (mostly covertly) between analysts in training, teaching, and supervision, there is a meeting, simultaneously, by way of collusion and immersion, between the two kinds of dynamic relations with the aggressor: the split-off identificatory dynamic of failed containment, and the introjective dynamic of being and existing, which is a containment that works.

Based on a conceptualization of psychoanalytic training as fundamentally an autobiographical dialogue, our approach emphasizes a mutual investigation of the dynamics of relations with the aggressor that includes its ethics.

A CONVERSATIONAL LETTER

While we were working on this chapter, Judy wrote to Gersh, on August 8, 2004:[4]

Dear Gersh,

Of course I[5] have to write this as a letter. I like the tone of my writing self best when writing to you. The pleasure of writing is laced with a kind of melancholy and longing, sometimes more so, and sometimes less, that infuses the reading with softness, my wanting to reach and be reached.

After we talked yesterday, I became quite agitated. What you were saying about identification with the aggressor was more theoretical than I like, and I started to feel that there wasn't going to be enough time for us to get through this with each other, much less write it into a finished form. I made myself remember that recently I have felt better about this subject than I did at first. I've had a "set piece" of reactions to the notion that is very different from your take, so I was outside and even opposed for a long time. (Isn't this how it always is with us? You're out ahead and I scramble to catch the train, but I have to remember that sometimes it is me.) Still, as we talked I was able to listen, and then it hit me with force, unexpectedly, an awareness of your strange deep optimism. It's the same optimism that you have always used to portray what happens in clinical space, an optimism that surprises me, given your disappointments.

---

4. All correspondence extracts are from Vida and Molad (2004a).

5. In the dialogue of our work there is a continuous fluid movement between the voice that is "we" and the separate voices that are "Gersh" and "Judy." An alternating "I" in the text reflects not only the way of writing but also the "how" of the actual presentation, how it is read in the conference, namely, that Gersh reads one part and Judy, another. In this chapter, "I" refers in turn to Judy and to Gersh, who wrote much of this in the form of letters to one another. Opening up and presenting this complexity, in both the written-read and the presented-listened-to texts, is of some importance, as it tells something and demonstrates the polyphonic nature of dialogue among the many voices within the text and the many voices in the listening audience and within the reader of the text. This becomes, therefore, an in-vivo demonstration of the love-making of dialogue and autobiography.

I, with an open-family-relation with my long-ago analyst, have been much more cynical about what happens in clinical space.

This reminds me of Ferenczi and Freud, and what Ferenczi wrote about optimism in "Stages in the Development of a Sense of Reality" (1913):

> We can only repeat: All children live in the happy delusion of omnipotence, which at some time or other—even if only in the womb—they really partook of. It depends on their "Daimon" [their own genius] and their "Tyche" [the goddess of fortune] whether they preserve the feelings of omnipotence also for later life, and become *Optimists*, or whether they go to augment the number of *Pessimists*, who never get reconciled to the renunciation of their unconscious irrational wishes, who on the slightest provocation feel themselves insulted or slighted, and who regard themselves as step-children of fate—because they cannot remain her *only* or *favourite* children. [p. 232]

I always marvel over this passage, because Ferenczi, whom Freud often criticized as intensely rivalrous from having been one of too many children of a harsh mother, was the therapeutic Optimist, and Freud, self-described as his mother's never-displaced favorite, was the notorious Pessimist.

When I heard that note of unmistakable optimism in your voice yesterday, I almost laughed, from a pleasure I wasn't expecting. All of a sudden I understood something deeper about how you came to your concept of the illusionary door-frame between clinical space and conference space [the door frame that marks our inability to embrace the other analyst's trauma in conference space]. I know that for you there has long been an openness and wholeness of experience that you have access to in clinical space that the rituals of conference space do not recognize, and that, despite your usual stance of quiet diffidence, that failure of recognition makes you irritable and angry. I have to think about how I am different.

Gersh wrote back:

Dear Judy,
    I want to join you here, and play some thoughts along your lines. By way of depicting and exploring our dialogue, you touch here two issues:
    One is the issue of the "alive dialogue," psychoanalysis as a way of life which shows that thinking and theory are so very personal and

emotional. At the center of this is the feeling of joy and love in making the dialogue and being in it.

The other issue is the resistance to and within the dialogue. In a natural way, resistance appears here as "the differences in an autobiographical dialogue," and the ways we as optimists and pessimists carry and handle them.

Saying it like this helps the reader and audience approach a somewhat different idea, as they listen to something that is new in both its content and its form. As in a musical piece or a novel or a good conversation, the themes slowly and partially present themselves, so when it is time for an open full presentation, there is no need to say any more.

This is what I call "a proactive interpretation" in therapy and analysis (and what you have referred to, borrowing a term from football, as a "through ball"). This is different from the classical retroactive interpretation, the interpretation of what was said or done. Here, what is being said and done creates and is the interpretation in an openness and wholeness of experience, so that the usual form of interpretation, the culminating sentence, is just a name, sometimes merely a redundant verbalization, the way a mountain is named by its peak.

And this is how interpellation (the call upon the other's identity) takes the place of interpretation: the conversation in context, the autobiographical dialogue, comprises our understanding as an alive dialogue of differences (Molad 2003, 2004). The external process of this kind of dialogue is what Ferenczi wrote, which can be paraphrased: "My best thoughts are person-relational, closely bound to the imagined mutual-being with another person, the love object," and the internal process is of an introjective nature, a subject we will soon touch.

What is of importance here is the Ferenczian proposition that challenges the classical distinction between process and content: interaction, intersubjective relations and the autobiographical dialogue are the content. Or, to say it more radically, this is the deep meaning of mutual analysis, as content and form mutually analyze each other, and in doing so mutually transform into each other. In the in-between phase that is blurred, the Freudian anxiety about chaotic death (anxiety about the loss of power, the loss of format and order, the loss of meaning and sense, the loss of containing identification) is being met here by the Ferenczian staying and being within the anxiety, being and existing with the pain of lost love, introducing the pleasure of relational play.

Judy's letter continued:

Until you and I began our collaboration some years ago, I never thought about how I was being met, in either clinical or conference space—that is, outside of the usual parameters of "transference" and "counter-transference," those theoretical word-shields designed to ward off the register of feelings in a personal way. What I thought I was supposed to do was to master those feelings so I didn't have them or let them bother me. But when you and I started working together, you presented an altogether different possibility: I listened to your proposal that instead of working always so damned hard to find a way through and around people's objections to or dismissal of my ideas, I could consider the reaction, the difficulty, the resistance, to be a part of the whole picture, and if embraced, something unpredictably new could happen. I watched it happen to you at the Ferenczi conference in Tel Aviv, and then I started to notice it happening to me. In fact, I began to look back on many years of complicated experience, and see that a part of me had been struggling for a very long time, not at all consciously, to do that in partial ways, and to reach just that awareness.

Gersh:

I want to say something here. You speak of embracing the resistance and difficulty, and this is exactly what you're doing to and with our dialogue. I am so tired at the moment that I cannot extend an embracement of the difficult, an overview that simultaneously reveals and makes meaning. But this is what you're doing here. You mentioned melancholy before: the pleasure of maintaining dialogue and writing, which "is laced with a kind of melancholy and longing, sometimes more so, and sometimes less, [and] infuses the reading with softness, wanting to reach and be reached." That melancholy of the ever-longed-for yet unattained is in me, too. In part I envy your "holding it lightly," and at the same time I feel some compassion in its being part of our dialogue, and some real pleasure at how my fears of "not having enough to get through" disappear as we talk.

Judy:

Whether I describe them as crumbs or as pearls, I look back now over very many years and see so clearly these small bits of myself yearning and lurching toward a voice of my own, a voice anchored in my direct experience that I would not have to apologize for or retract or disguise. What I say to people who are curious about this unusual collaboration of ours is that the context of our relations (our work and our dialogue) is actually a basket into which I can gather all these crumbs or pearls and hold them together for the first time. When I describe them as pearls, I say that, despite being of many different sizes, now they can all be strung on a single strand. When I describe them as crumbs, I am using a metaphor for ter-rified efforts to find my way out of the dark woods.

Gersh:

Yes, and the connecting link here is that the yearning toward a voice of one's own is predicated upon being able to embrace the broken voice of the other. It is in this mutual embrace that disturbance creates beautiful pearls strung on form and identity, and the anxiety of crumbs, facing nostalgic pain for the nonexistent whole bread, seeks remedy in Love.

Judy's letter continued:

I mentioned my agitation after we talked. When I complained that our talk was all theoretical, that what we were missing was the juice, you said, well, the juice comes to us, one of us has a dream, or something. I may have taken that partially as an instruction, because I went on to have a dream last night:

DREAM 1 ("OPTIMISM ABOUT MY LIFE")

The French artist Sophie Calle was in it, and I was surprised that she was talking to me as though I had some information for her (it is Stuart[6] who has worked with her over many years on exhibitions, installations, and catalogs). It was friendly. Then I, much younger than I really am, was spending time with a man near my age; we seemed to be getting to know one another in a very nice way and were considering some serious inten-tions; I was even talking to his mother. As arrangements were starting to be made, I said that there was someone else in my life, another man, who I also spent a lot of time with, and this was important to me and would continue, though any sense of "outcome" was unclear and unspecified. This was met with matter-of-fact acceptance, an "of course." Again to my surprise, I spoke without hesitation or shame, without apology or defensiveness. There was a background sense in the dream that this would

---

6. Judy's husband.

be a life of complexity and richness. I'm not sure why I woke up when I did; I was still sleepy, and it was not yet half past five. It was as though I was in a hurry to reach the surface. I noticed a lot of thoughts swirling around, some leading to this presentation for Paris, some leading to ideas for our advanced seminar, and all of them connected. "I've got it!" I crowed to Stuart when he woke up. That's when he told me that he heard me laugh in my sleep in the middle of the night.

Now this is quite rambling, but I promised myself that when I sat down to write, I was going to let myself go, to enjoy the experience of writing freely. I don't want to push too hard to impose a form on this, but even I can see the optimism in my dream about Paris ("Sophie Calle") and the optimism about my life.

What I see is that finding my voice has led me away from stultifying identifications—for example, using my formerly prodigious memory to get through medical school—into a much more introjective stance with all the people in my life, not only clinically and professionally. Think of my new relations with my mother, when, after shouting at her with a voice suppressed for almost six decades, I am now able to think about her experience separately from mine, and she at the age of ninety is beginning to think about me as separate from her. I thought, there's something in here surely of your own story, some aspect of finding your own voice that once found, you have not been willing to suppress (or to suppress completely), and this has something to do with your professional rites of passage. It's relevant too, and connects to our seminar-project.

DREAM 2 ("ISOMORPHISM")

A week later, in a letter on August 15, 2004, Judy wrote of another dream:

I was with a group of people in our profession, mostly women. There was a homeless older man, demented or psychotic, quite paranoid, walking around muttering to himself but every now and then shouting out an accusation at one of us. At first the accusations were random, but they came to be centered on me. It seems that I had interfered with his relationship with his daughter, who was also there, looking bewildered and trying to stay away from him. The quiet murmurings in the group of people was about how to increase the distance between the man and the daughter, and how to protect ourselves, if that was possible. The interior began to look like an old-fashioned emporium, with dark wood fixtures and display cases in a room only dimly lit. The group of mostly women began to form a semicircle around me, awaiting the arrival of the Inquisition, a kind of tribunal. I knew what was going to happen—my ritual sacrifice (the ritual sacrifice of me) and the panic I felt at first gave way to calm acceptance. It was because of the stance I took with the young woman or how I talked about it. The semicircle grew tighter, and I felt the warm concern of these women. In my mind was the thought that now I could understand martyrdom, what drew martyrs to their fate and what made them not avoid taking the position that cost them their lives. The warmth of the women felt like enough. In the last minutes before the arrival of the tribunal, I knew what the means of my death would be: "isomorphism." It's an actual word from the last paragraph of my published "Teratoma" paper (2001), a paragraph that I omitted in my presentation on Saturday because I didn't want to end on a distancing theoretical note. What it meant in the dream was that I was condemned to die in a battle with dogs, who would kill me by ripping off my skin, and initially I would be allowed to try to rip off their skin in turn. It felt fair and balanced, at least starting out as symmetrical. I was worried that it might hurt too much, but then I thought, I will just have to enter into it. I can do that.

A COMMENT

Nicholas Rand (1994) tells us that for Abraham and Torok, "the secret is a trauma, whose very occurrence and devastating emotional consequences are entombed and thereby consigned to internal silence, albeit unwittingly, by the sufferers themselves" (p. 99). This touches a criticism recently made of our work: that we appear to make no distinction between "personal" and "private." "Private" is what consensus decrees should be hidden. For us, the reason to keep something private is out of fear for being or becoming traumatic, either pretraumatic or posttraumatic. But Abraham and Torok's "secret" is intrapsychic. "It designates an internal psychic splitting; as a result two distinct 'people' live side by side, one behaving as if s/he were part of the world, and the other as if s/he had no contact with it whatsoever" (p. 100). Thus identification with the aggressor by way of introjection of the aggressor is actually the healing of the precariously split-off trauma in the aggressor that enacts itself on the victim. Their idea of introjection is at the heart of our work: a "principle of gradual self-transformation in the face of interior and exterior changes in the psychological, emotional, relational, political, professional landscape" (p. 101). And Torok's argument speaks very much to our point: "It is not the children's failure to accept the adult's rejection or prohibition of incest wishes that is most likely to lead to neurosis, but the degree of disarray in the parents' own state of desire" (p. 104).

Ending her letter, Judy wrote:

> Here is something good to end with, a paraphrase from Rilke that Sharon Bassett sent: "Perhaps everything terrible is in its deepest being something helpless that wants help from us."

AFTERTHOUGHTS: A NOTE ABOUT THE EXPERIENCE OF READING-AS-TRANSLATING, WITH SOME IMPLICATIONS FOR "A MUTUAL UNDERSTANDING OF THE OTHER" AS AN INTROJECTORY MODEL OF SUPERVISION AND TRAINING

Reading can be thought of as translation: a movement from one personal language "into" another, but this is of course impossible. During that movement there is both destruction and creation, in the form of a new and intermediate conversation. A truly blurred area is created, where the words of the writer are lost and a new paper is offered by the reader-translator (and vice versa). A read-translated paper is thus in continuous movement between figure and ground, a circumstance both inevitable and fortuitous, and for this chapter, first presented in an earlier form at an Abraham and Torok conference, it is more than fitting:

> Abraham and Torok found that patients suffering from a secret identification with a departed love-object invented particular forms of obfuscation in their speech. The patients obscured beyond recognition the linguistic elements that might reveal their secret's existence and contents to themselves and to the world. . . . What leads people to make themselves unintelligible . . . [by means of] new linguistic mechanisms whose aim seems to be to disarray, even to destroy, the expressive or representational power of language [?] [Rand 1994, p. 105]

So, perhaps the work of reading as translating, the work of the departure and loss of language-love-objects, is the work of introjectively mediating in language the experience of the hidden trauma, a mixed work of mourning and enjoying the concealing and revealing of the traumatic and the posttraumatic. The reader-translator carries openly the burden of this work of mourning and transformation. Listening to the other reader-translator, we observe the mutual tuning of our developing thought streams, as we move between identification and introjection, as we move between power and love relations, and as trauma is taken in and accepted as an immanent part of life.

It seems useful to add that the two of us are aware that our written prose can at times be confusing or confounding to the reader. In some places words are applied like paint, or as chords or complex chromatics in musical notation and ought not to be read in a straight-on linear fashion. These passages work best when approached differently: sideways, or skimming, yet slowly enough to allow visual or emotional associations to cluster. Some readers tell us of "getting it" long after they have stopped reading, despite the inevitable irritation and frustration.

Again and again we see that this kind of painted reading-translation is the work of both dialogue and correspondence. Translation-reading as a dialogical correspondence goes beyond identificatory appropriation (which "kills and consumes" the subject) to introjective relations of a mutually responsive and responsible answering of other and self. This is answering not by telling but by taking in, allowing what is taken in to exist as it is. An introjectory model of supervision is a natural extension of this, a welcoming of what has been and is, not requiring anything to be different. The supervisor-reader-translator creates correspondence, by a kind of com-responding (like the response of soloist and chorus in a Bach cantata to a recitative), by being the sponsor, the accountable person who takes responsibility for the text's life. In doing so the supervisor-reader-translator introjects not only the form and content of the dialogue but, even more significantly, the manner of correspondence of the authors,[7] of the consulting analyst and analysand.

---

7. This is the way the two of us have entered into a correspondence of psycho-analysis with life (Vida and Molad 2004b).

THE ETHICS OF INTROJECTION RELATIONS: TOWARD A QUADRO-PARTITE MODEL OF TRAINING IN PSYCHOANALYSIS

When we understand the importance of the "correspondence" that is at the core of the autobiographical dialogue, we realize that the establishment of autobiographical dialogue between analysts may lead to a crucial developmental change in psychoanalytic training. This is a change that may counterbalance the effects of power-based identification relations, which is at heart an identification with the aggressor.

What we suggest is a move from the tri-partite model of personal analysis, theoretical courses and supervision, to a quadro-partite model that includes the autobiographical-dialogue between analysts as an essential component of the training experience. Teaching that has as its aim the explicit development of one's own voice as a recognized part of the formal training has the potential to change the scene of power relations. This involves a use of self and other under a different code of ethics, a code that emphasizes responsibility, generosity, and forgiveness. When the issue is abuse of power, "forgiveness" may present a difficult obstacle. While responsibility and generosity may function as prophylactic measures, only something like forgiveness creates movement beyond the impasse. We offer for consideration our enlarged understanding of the dynamics of identification with the aggressor, as well as our notion of a forgiveness, which serves neither the forgiver nor the forgiven but is directed toward achieving a state of forgiveness. Our sense is that a state of forgiveness may be of some help in relieving the training-related posttraumatic bitterness, pain, and anger that all too often undermine the analyst's capacity for genuine tenderness and compassion. This version of forgiveness involves the recognition that difficulty and conflict are inevitable, to which the autobiographical dialogue can supply a human face.

In recent years we have had opportunities to introduce the autobiographical dialogue to students and candidates as part of their training program.[8] Although candidates who have been dismayed by the

---

8. Since 2001, Judy has introduced the autobiographical dialogue in a required seminar that began as an integration of theory for fourth-year candidates at the Institute of Contemporary Psychoanalysis in Los Angeles, and is now titled "Finding One's (Own) Way as a Psychoanalyst (FOOWAP)"; Gersh has taught versions of the autobiographical

absence of the personal have tended to respond enthusiastically, our previous accounts of these experiences (Molad and Vida 2002, 2004, and 2005, Vida 2004) describe how unsettling it can be for other candidates to engage with the personal and autobiographical after years of indoctrination in their exclusion. Not long ago, a recently graduated analyst who had been one of the enthusiastic participants suggested presenting the notion of the autobiographical dialogue at the outset of training, as well as at the conclusion. From having been there all along, appearances of the autobiographical could be collected and considered more integratively at the conclusion of formal seminars. Judy's first response to this was "Oh, no; that's too hard; the institute would never go for it; and I'm not sure I have the energy for persuasion, much less to do it." Only later could the importance of the suggestion be seen, taken in, and worked with.

Thus what we have found over the years is that in suggesting that the idea of the autobiographical dialogue moves us toward a quadro-partite model of training, we have to deal not only with the resistance-difficulties of the students, but also with the resistance and counterresistance of our teaching colleagues, including ourselves. Little did either of us suspect that the demonstration of that resistance would be such an organic part of this chapter itself—but, of course, it always is.

Our parting gesture is to offer a footnote from another paper that has as its subject the typically complicated response that meets our work:

> Our use of the word "resistance" from the beginning has drawn a lot of heat from readers as well as audiences. To American ears and eyes, it comes across as a vestige of Freudian authoritarianism. On the one hand, it would have been better to use a neutral word like "objection," which is what, in fact, we mean, although "resistance" in its non-Freudian sense does convey a vital pushing-back, which "objection" does not. We have immense respect for "resistance" in its larger applications. (As Alice Walker [1993] said so notably, it is the secret of joy.) And then the rea-

---

dialogue in his postgraduate seminars about Sándor Ferenczi in the Post-Graduate Psychotherapy Program at Tel Aviv University. Together we offer seminars in the autobiographical dialogue, at both basic and advanced levels, and presented so far in Pécs, Hungary (2002), and Los Angeles (2002, 2003, 2005). The Los Angeles seminars have been and are free-standing, unaffiliated with any formal program of training.

son for not simply using a different word here is to allow for the visibility of our contribution to the difficulties we encounter in our everyday use of analytic terms. But on the other hand, we may assume that what we encountered at that moment was "resistance" and "counter-resistance": as we were experiencing "the resolution of transference-based love-differences among colleagues," the colleagues being us. [Molad and Vida 2004 and in press]

It is here, in the resolution of these transference-based love differences among colleagues, that "forgiveness" meets "resistance" in the working through of power in analytic training, which is the main issue of this book. This is a good moment to look at what Freud wrote about the "practical task of psychoanalysis": "The overcoming of resistance is the part of our work that requires the most and the greatest trouble" (1940, p. 179). But if we apply what we've been saying about the autobiographical dialogue in training, and try to figure whose "work" and whose "resistance" it is, we may reach some understanding that in finding one's own way as a psychoanalyst, it is the student-candidate's "work" to resolve his teacher-analyst's "resistance" and to transform institutional training's "greatest trouble" into personal and professional hope.

REFERENCES

Ferenczi, S. (1913). Stages in the development of a sense of reality. In *First Contributions to Psycho-Analysis*, trans. E. Jones, pp. 213–239. London: Maresfield Reprints, 1980.

Freud, S. (1940). An outline of psychoanalysis. *Standard Edition* 23:141–208.

Molad, G. (2003). From interpretation to interpellation: introductory remarks on the nature of transformational dialogue between analysts in conference space, and some notes on resistance. Paper presented to "The Transformational Conversation," fourteenth annual interdisciplinary conference, International Federation for Psychoanalytic Education, Pasadena, CA, November.

——— (2004). How the soul gets accustomed to the mutual "need for the other:" thoughts on the practice and ethics of the dialogue between analysts. Paper presented to "Sacrifice," the fourth annual conference of the Tel Aviv University Psychotherapy Program and School of History, Tel Aviv, December.

Molad, G., and Vida, J. (2002 and 2005). The autobiographical dialogue in the dialogue between analysts: introductory notes on the use of relational and intersubjective perspectives in conference space. Earlier versions were presented to Tel Aviv University Postgraduate Psychotherapy Departmental Seminar on Supervision, April 15, and to "Clinical Sándor Ferenczi," International Conference organized by Università Degli Studi Di Torino, July 21. A chapter for *Relational and Intersubjective Perspectives in Psychoanalysis*, J. Mills, ed. Lanham, MD: Jason Aronson.

Molad, G., and Vida, J., with Barish, S., Bassett, S., and DuBois, P. (2004 and in press). A responsible controversy about failures of love: some comments on the ethics of presenting and listening in conference space. Based on a panel presentation at the International Federation for Psychoanalytic Education, 15th annual interdisciplinary conference, Chicago, November. In *Psychoanalytic Inquiry*, issue "Analytic Love," D. Shaw, ed.

Rand, N. (1994). New perspectives in metapsychology: cryptic mourning and secret love. In *The Shell and the Kernel*, ed. N. Abraham and M. Torok, ed., trans. N. Rand, pp. 99–106. Chicago: University of Chicago Press.

Vida, J. (2001). Ferenczi's "Teratoma": a result, not a process. *International Forum of Psychoanalysis* 10:235–241.

——— (2004). "Cure" is a strange notion. Paper presented to "Exploring Transference and Cure in Contemporary Psychoanalysis," Institute of Contemporary Psychoanalysis, Los Angeles, June.

Vida, J., and Molad, G. (2004a). Correspondence. Unpublished.

——— (2004b). The Ferenczian dialogue: psychoanalysis as a way of life. *Free Association* 11:338–352.

Walker, A. (1993). *Possessing the Secret of Joy*. New York: Pocket.

16

Individual and Group Supervision, Consultation, and Autobiographical Dialogues Between Analysts and Colleagues

Irene Harwood

I feel privileged and honored to discuss the contributions of such distinguished colleagues as Drs. Sarnat, Fuqua, Lecomte, Gray, Molad, and Vida. I am in awe, not only of their contributions to this book, but also of their entire body of work in our interesting and complex field. In starting to discuss their contributions, I feel very similar to what I have felt before in front of a colleague or supervisee. For the most part I feel in parallel process with both the supervisors and supervisees of these chapters. However, I have been given the privileged task to discuss, and my perspective will be guided by my professional and personal history. Even if I am in twinship with the authors and have a similar subjective take about the content of the chapters, I hope I can focus a light on a different part of the stage in these interesting intersubjective dialogues.

Even though Heinz Kohut's self-psychological theory spelled out an empathic stance and implied sensitivity toward the other, it did not specifically focus on the subjectivity of each person and what it contributed to the relationship, regardless whether it was clinical, su-pervisory, or collegial. The authors whose work I am discussing are very familiar with intersubjectivity and relational theory. They understand that each participant contributes to the dynamics of the relationship, and how each contribution influences the texture of the intersubjective matrix. However, there is no way to compare these chapters, since each puts the spotlight on a different aspect of our intersubjective dialogue with our mental health colleagues.

Though there is a distinct difference between supervision and con-sultation, some authors often use the term *supervision* when they mean *consultation*. I will use "consultee" and "consultant" when it is a con-tracted process between colleagues. I will use "supervisee" and "super-visor" when there is a legal or professional responsibility. I will address each author's contribution separately, and provide an overview of the intersubjective process that occurs between clinicians at all stages of personal and professional development.

Supervision is different from consultation in that the supervisor, unlike the consultant, carries a legal and professional responsibility for the patient, since the supervisee practices under the license of the su-pervisor. When the work of a licensed therapist is overseen by a more experienced colleague in an advanced training institution, this is also called supervision. But in this case, while the supervisor does not bear legal responsibility, the supervisor carries a professional responsibility to help advance the already-licensed therapist to another level of pro-fessional expertise. Along with meeting other requirements, if this process is considered successful, it will lead to a more advanced and pres-tigious title or degree.

I believe there are also many conscious and unconscious factors that often subtly influence both supervision and consultation. An im-portant factor to consider, for example, is how the existence or lack of a financial arrangement affects the process. Where the professional supervision is taking place (whether it is in an institution such as a clinic, graduate school, or the supervisor or consultant's private of-fice) also affects the tone of the process. How the dialogue takes place, whether face to face, over the phone, or by e-mail (which slows down both the reflective and reactive process), introduces a totally different quality and dimension. The process is also affected by whether the consultant considers the consultee to be a junior colleague or one of equal experience. The intersubjective dialogue takes on a totally different coloration when it takes place between trusting colleagues, possibly friends, or even best friends.

In an unacknowledged way, these chapters seem to concern themselves primarily with the classical versus relational theoretical and philosophical orientations that influence the intersubjective dialogue of the supervisor or consultant. At the same time the authors are quite open in acknowledging how their stance has been greatly influenced by their own early experiences in the role of supervisee. But what I hoped would have been addressed more and with personal discussion in these interesting chapters is how, regardless of the role that each person occupies, the intersubjective dialogue is greatly influenced by the intersection of each person's individual history, emotional development, defensive structure, and particularly previous narcissistic injuries.

For example, in a supervision I conducted with a graduate student, one of the dominant themes that influenced and instructed the relationship was that the supervisee did not want another woman supervisor (Harwood 1982). As a beginning supervisor what helped me work with him was that for some reason his response did not seem to threaten me. I tried to analyze this more closely—I did not grow up with a brother, and I wondered, if I grew up with one who was rejecting, whether I could have been as empathic and nondefensive with a male supervisee. Self-reflecting on how I grew up with older half-sisters, I was fairly sure the process would have been much harder for me, if a woman supervisee presented me with the same issue. My ability to respond nondefensively would have been greatly stretched. The supervisee's reactions to my potential defensiveness and protectiveness would also have been different. Looking back, I think I could also respond more sensitively to the early fears and longings of a male supervisee because, at that time, I was also the new mother of a baby boy.

Given a different history and a different time in my life, the success of the supervisory process would probably have been different and may have entailed more ruptures, but possibly more repairs as well. Where we came from, what affects us today, and how far we have come in working through our own past issues will affect at any time what we will offer as supervisors or consultants.

JOAN SARNAT

How does one discuss a paper of an author one does not know professionally or personally? Is it similar to supervising or consulting with a
colleague one does not know? Am I in the same parallel process with
my author/colleague Dr. Sarnat that she is in with the colleagues that
come to her for supervision and consultation? It appears that as a discussant I am placed in an unofficial role as a professional consultant
whom she did not choose. Thus, I will discuss my "discussant/consult-
ant" process.

I have the same anxiety in starting to write a discussion about her
paper that I have in starting to supervise or consult with a colleague. The
questions that arise are: Will I be helpful? Do I have something to add,
or will I just fill the time or pages in this book? If I have something to
add, will it be perceived as a criticism of what my colleague has said
already, or will it be seen as just another addition to an intersubjective
dialogue where each subjectivity is valid and appreciated?

Reading this excellent chapter I find myself in the same circumstance as with a very bright, capable colleague or student: narcissistically wanting to have something of value to add, but finding one can
only stand back with a glimmer in one's eye applauding and smiling in
a pleased validating manner. And since we both seem to have a similar take on things, we appear to be in a celebratory twinship.

I do not have the benefit of first meeting Dr. Sarnat and establishing an intersubjective right brain to right brain communication (Schore
2003) where we could first just appreciate and accept each other as
human beings, trying to give each other respectful space and attention,
as I hope I do with my new patients, as well as my supervisees and
consultees. I try hard to be sensitively and gently facilitating for each
to start leading the way. At the beginning, I try to read the affective
stance of each patient, supervisee, or consultee. I remind myself that
there might be a need for control over one's emotional visibility or
transparency to another human being. I try to keep in mind that each
individual may want an optimum distance or closeness. But I realize that
I cannot read what kind of "experience distant or near" discussion/re-
sponse would be optimal for Sarnat.

I also try to remember that everyone covets respect of selfhood and
of each private piece or jewel they dare bare and disclose. Each person

is in a different place on personal and professional developmental continuums. Because of the lack of information about our supervisees' and consultees' history and dynamics, at the beginning it is harder to ascertain where each stands on the continuums and which specific functions each might require. It is harder to know at what point I might cause a narcissistic injury or trigger, by my manner or words, previous impingements and traumatizations. One needs to be vigilant for ruptures that will need repair.

I also try to remember (metaphorically and developmentally speaking) not to treat a 4-year-old as an infant, since that would be condescending and annoying. But I recognize that I as a human being also have not only my adult self, but a feisty 4-year-old and a vulnerable baby within me as well. Thus, as a supervisor/consultant I think it is important to heed Sarnat's (and her acknowledgment of Frawley-O'Dea's) values—to first encourage empowerment of each supervisee/consultee, as well as create an atmosphere of mutual vulnerability where it is safe for both to learn and explore.

I agree with Sarnat about the importance of welcoming negative feedback from the supervisee. I would also suggest that at the very beginning of the relationship we specifically let the supervisee know that we invite such feedback. Then when it is courageously brought up, we indeed should welcome it and accept it by recognizing the courage it took to bring it up. Though difficult, it is also important to consider and reflect nondefensively on the supervisee's subjective perception of us as supervisors.

Sarnat wisely counsels supervisors to present the self-disclosures of one's own mistakes only when such disclosures will not weaken the idealization of the supervisory relationship. Idealization, she believes, is of particular importance at the very beginning of the learning process. I believe that she would not disagree with the notion that not every supervisee requires idealization, but instead may require a twinship experience in which the supervisor is also fallible. Sharing my mistakes many years ago with my male supervisee allowed him to trust me and not experience me as an "all-knowing" authoritarian woman who was looking down on his struggles. In addition, as Sarnat agrees, at the beginning of the supervisory/therapeutic journey, validation of the novice's strengths is also important in order to develop a successful working alliance with the supervisee's patients as well.

Thus, with our supervisees/consultees, as with our patients, we need to understand which functions are required at that specific time of the evolution and development for that specific psychotherapist or psychoanalyst. Sarnat, in her "relational revisioning" of the supervisory relationship, considers herself as a co-creator of what transpires in the supervisory hour. It is from the "quality of the relationship" that is established that she feels authorized, rather than from the already established authority. She states that the supervisor "remains open to the possibility that didactic teaching may outlive its usefulness . . . as she watches for new developments within the supervisory relationship."

Sarnat is in agreement with Winnicott (1965), who entreated us to provide specific functions until they are all used up. Otherwise, they begin to become not only irrelevant, but burdensome. Thus, supervisors need to provide specific functions to specific supervisees when they are specifically needed and geared to the specific stage of the development of that specific individual, therapist, or burgeoning psychoanalyst.

Like Winnicott, Sarnat warns against supervisory compliance, which often leads to identification with the aggressor—in this case the supervisor as well as a false therapeutic self. Sarnat also offers examples of how to struggle with one's own conflict and share it with the supervisee. She teaches self-reflection and self-analysis by modeling. She does not invoke: "Do as I tell you, but don't do what I do." She offers us a lovely example of how a supervisor who had enough developmental flexibility of her own was able to repair a rupture (Beebe 2003) and to attune her interventions to the vulnerability of a beginning supervisee.

Later, having acquired greater professional cohesion and expertise, that same supervisee could self-reflect on her limitations without the shame that beginning therapists feel about their therapeutic errors. In the last example offered, she not only describes a supervisor who is rigid in a professional theoretical approach of tough love, but a supervisor who herself has not, developmentally or therapeutically, received enough empathy for her own vulnerabilities, and thus does not have the capacity for empathy for others.

Sarnat gives us a rich taste of different intersubjective configurations that can happen between junior/senior, and later between more equal-experience colleagues. These configurations implicitly also demonstrate not only the theoretical stance of the particular supervisor, but how far each has traveled on the empathic developmental continuum.

PAULA FUQUA

From the beginning Dr. Fuqua's chapter draws us into the complexities of supervision. She makes the important legal distinction between the supervising and consulting responsibilities and roles. She asks us to consider who is in front of us. Is it a neophyte or a more experienced therapist? Is it a colleague who comes to us primarily to be a sounding board, or one who requires whatever additional insight we might have? In her own way, she reminds us to filter our supervisory process through the notion of specificity (Bacal 2004). She eloquently states: "In the interchange of two subjectivities, the specificity of the subjects matters and must be recognized."

In her clinical supervisory example she courageously talks about her own human needs, concerns, and fears as a supervisor. She challenges us to look at a complex crisscrossing of intersubjectivities in a training institution's group matrix. In this setting, she points out how each individual person has needs, longings, and fears that can be in conflict with what is in the interest of the patient, the supervisee, the training analyst, and the supervisor.

In her example, the supervisor insisted on adhering to the analytic method in order to maintain an understanding, noncritical stance, while also trying to appreciate the different subjectivities of all the players and the multiplicity of dynamics involved. Utilizing the subjectivities of different theoretical models, different supervisors, clinicians, and theoreticians could argue that the supervisor should have intervened earlier and taken measures to redirect the treatment. On the other hand, one can agree with the stance of this supervisor and state that the consequences could have been much worse, if the supervisee lost trust in the supervisor. As a consequence of the latter, the worst possibility could have been a suicide. Thus, here again we can encounter different subjectivities from one theoretical pole to another, and most likely many more in between. I can agree with Fuqua that subjectively each supervisor does the best that s/he can, given the personal needs, motivations, and theoretical orientations that legitimize them.

Fuqua's chapter makes it clear that although she uses the same sensitivity with a supervisee that she would use with a patient, she does not have the benefit of the same data. In supervision, though one starts accumulating knowledge about the historical emotional development and dynamics of the patient, one only infers from the interventions and affects presented in the supervision what the historical dynamics of the supervisee are that might get in the way of the patient's treatment. Fuqua tells us that she hoped the training analyst would do more. In her chapter she reminds us how much more difficult the role of supervisor is in needing to be more careful not to cross the personal boundaries and psychological issues of the supervisee, while also keeping in mind the best interest of the patient. Thus, Fuqua reminds us, compared to the role of the therapist, how much more difficult and circumscribed the role of supervisor really is.

Fuqua walked a very fine sensitive line with Pat. It was not clear whether Pat was her supervisee or consultee. It was also not clear whether there was a professional responsibility that Fuqua had for Pat, since usually two supervisors do not supervise the same patient in a training institute or in a graduate school. It also was not evident whether Pat's analyst was a training analyst. I do remember that Fuqua said that the example was an amalgamation of supervisees/consultees. Thus, it is difficult to comment on the specifics, except to repeat again that I think our own dynamics are influenced if we have a legal or professional responsibility as a supervisor. For myself, I find that the role of consultant allows me greater flexibility, as well as comfort.

I am trying to reflect on my own learning dynamics through my different graduate schools and analytic training. I know that at the beginning I would have very much appreciated Fuqua's gentleness and object-presenting explorations. As I matured as a therapist and felt more competent and also less vulnerable, I would have appreciated more directness. At this point, as one colleague to another, I think I would be ready for her to not mince any words with me, but gently of course!

ARTHUR GRAY

From his expertise as a group therapist and supervisor, Dr. Gray makes a unique and welcomed contribution to this group of chapters by adding group supervision to the discussion mix. He discusses how, from his own training experiences, he has become quite sensitive to both the emotional and learning needs of the supervisee. He developed and follows his own six-step model: "A Format for Group Supervision"

(FGS). In his unique contribution he obviously invites others to learn from it and to use it. He suggests that before implementing the FGS model, the supervisor set the stage for it.

Therefore, I will follow his suggestion, and set the stage for my discussion by stating that I will follow his delineated six steps in discussing his paper: (1) presentation of the situation, (2) presenter's approach to the situation, (3) problem to be addressed in supervision, (4) can the presenter's approach address the problem? (5) addressing alternative approaches, and (6) conclusion.

Presentation

Gray's chapter presents (the who) his own beginning process in a group supervisory situation (the when). Though he points out that he liked his first supervisor as a person, his present aim is to contribute more, and facilitate a different, more satisfying and participatory group supervisory process (the what). He holds that his Format for Group Supervision (FGS) model is applicable to both individual and group supervision in a training institution and in private practice (the where). The FGS model that Gray presents is a creative suggestion for repairing existing problems in supervision, particularly in group supervision.

Approach

In his model, Gray attends to the subjective needs of each supervisee. Indeed, Gray is careful in the first steps of the process to attend to the possible (or probable) vulnerability of the presenting supervisee in the group process. His care is not unfounded, since individuals are usually more vulnerable to criticism or shame in group. At the same time supervisees may feel more recognized and celebrated, when validated by a group.

I did not have the benefit of a direct interchange with Gray while writing this discussion; thus I can only assume or hope that we agree on the understanding of his approach. I applaud his setting the stage for facilitating a supervisory group process where each member can participate by asking clarifying questions of the presenter and thus "participating." At the same time Gray asks for all the "supervisees to agree on the presenter's approach." I wonder if "attempting to understand from the presenter's perspective" is always possible for each member, or even necessary, in order for the process to move forward. Sometimes others "just don't get it" or prefer to honor their own subjectivity and not to contribute at that specific juncture. I hope my own written verbalization, in trying to clarify the individual and group dynamics in step two, poses a "question" about Gray's approach, and is experienced by him as a clarifying question, rather than questioning his approach.

Gray's multifaceted approach is not only psychoanalytical, but also self-psychological/intersubjective, and inclusive of Beatrice Beebe's (2003) infant research. He pays attention to the entire intersubjective field between dyads and the whole group, minimizing the possibility for narcissistic injuries and facilitating a learning atmosphere. In Gray's facilitating environment, creativity is both created and co-created among all the participants in the group, or in other instances between the individual supervisee and supervisor.

The Problem

The problem that Gray addresses appears to be how to develop a more positive facilitating atmosphere in the supervisory learning process where a supervisee's strengths and abilities are recognized and validated and where creativity and good work is celebrated. Gray suggests distinguishing three different problems: a learning problem (pertaining to learning how to handle a case that is being presented, that is in supervisory learning), a problem about learning (which he is offering to the entire mental health learning community), or a problem with administration (a problem in the supervisory setting or the training setting).

But I am confused about what Gray says in the third step of his FGS model when he writes, "emotional issues are not the explicit domain of the supervisory process. . . . As the supervisor stays with the clinical context, the presenter can continue over time to experience the emotional challenges without feeling criticized" and what he interprets to his individual supervisee, Dr. Shiner, about "her difficulty coming to her supervisory session."

Is he suggesting that depending on the situation his model can be modified as long as one is attuned to the specific unconscious or conscious needs of an individual supervisee? I would not have an argument with that adjustment.

Does Approach Address the Problem?

The short answer is yes. Gray's FGS model indeed does address the prevention of many of the problems and narcissistic injuries created in supervision, especially in group supervision. But whatever model or intuitive process we adhere to in supervision or consultation, I believe that Gray would agree that no one theoretical model can provide a complete blueprint for perfect understanding where no one's feelings get hurt. The best we can do is pay attention to reactions and enactments and investigate the subjective meanings of each impingement or injury. We can hope that by investigating the subjective meaning of each "rupture," "repair" (Beebe 2003) can occur and the process can be enriched, deepened, and moved forward and not left to fester.

Alternative Approaches

I am not ready to present any alternative approaches or models to Gray's. I am actually very simpatico with his attunement and approach in working with therapists individually and in group supervision. I also appreciate how he invites other supervisees to reflect and participate in the process, while the focus is on someone else.

But as long as his model allows for someone else's subjective contributions, I will try to "object-present" (Winnicott 1965) other thoughts for consideration or clarification.

1. If Gray at times deviates from his proposed format, what are the reasons behind those deviations?
2. Is there any significant difference in his approach with an individual supervisee/consultee and why?
3. Does he adjust his format to the experience level of the individual supervisee/consultee? Thus, is there any difference in his approach or interventions with an unlicensed therapist for whose work he may have a legal responsibility vs. a licensed therapist who comes for consultation?
4. Does he adjust his approach to the personal psychological/ developmental qualities of the person in a one-to-one supervisory process?
5. Would he vary his approach with an experienced therapist/

colleague vs. an experienced therapist/colleague/and good friend?

6. Would his FGS differ in a private practice group supervision/consultation vs. a graduate institution setting where he bears a professional responsibility to the institution?
7. Does Dr. Gray change his approach if different supervisees/consultees are at different levels of personal, professional, or experiential development?
8. Last but not least, I wonder whether and how Gray utilizes relational theory? Does he wonder about how his own personal history, affects, and reactions interact with each supervisee and group and whether he shares any of these reflections with his supervisees and consultees?

Conclusion

I feel enriched by studying and considering Gray's six steps, particularly for group supervision. The six-step format for group supervision seems to take great care in providing safety for the presenter, as well as ensuring active inclusion and participation for the other members. Gray could provide us with yet another useful model if he could specifically delineate a format for individual supervision and consultation.

CONRAD LECOMTE

Dr. Lecomte offers both supervisees and supervisors an integrated model of supervision. He delineates the several models of supervision, and in his chapter he exemplifies the different approaches. By offering an integrated model, he indeed provides us with new knowledge and know-how. Two of the supervisory approaches he explains are focused on the experience of the patient and on technique of skills training. He also focuses us on a way of being in supervision where the focus is on the experience of the therapist, and the experience of the supervisor, not only in parallel process to the patient, but also to the supervisee.

He suggests that all of these approaches should be integrated as part of the background with a primary focus on the quality of intersubjective relationship between patient and therapist, and therapist and supervisor. The principal prerequisite is to provide a holding, containing safe environment in which the supervisees' strengths are first validated, which then allows the supervisee to self-reflect about the experience one has with the patient and what feelings and associations it produces from one's own therapeutic work in progress.

As a seasoned therapist and supervisor, Lecomte knows that ruptures are inevitable. His proposed approach sets the stage for an atmosphere of a greater probability for repair of these ruptures, after a trusting environment has been established. He leaves us with a wise caveat and a warning against idealization not only of techniques and theories but also of supervisors.

His supervisory approach is similar to Winnicott's transitional space in which the supervisee is invited to enter into a safe space, experience self-regulation and cohesion, and then play with ideas and feelings in a self-reflective way in the presence of a supervisor who provides a holding experience. Once the self-reflecting functions are well established, the supervisee can be on the way to self-supervision.

Lecomte gives us an excellent integrated model of self-reflexivity where the focus can shift flexibly on the subjectivities and relationships between the patient and therapist, and supervisor and supervisee. This new capacity to be alone with one's own self-reflection and self-supervision does not preclude sharing one's ideas in a reciprocal manner with other trusted colleagues, since as we know even Freud, Winnicott, Kohut, and others also needed selfobject functions from their colleagues, as well as a mirror held up to their unconscious.

GERSHON J. MOLAD AND JUDITH E. VIDA

In reading and rereading this interesting chapter I tried first to understand the gestalt of this most unusual communication. I found myself drifting from my cognitive left brain into my more intuitive right brain. I left my cognitive self and came more experience-near to my own emotional self. I believe this process could be closest to what Ogden (1994) describes as the analytic third, where one listens to one's own associations. I will now share my first impressions of reading this paper, because after each rereading I gained a different level of richness.

Judy Vida and Gershon Molad elevate the supervisory/consulta-
tion training collegial discussion to a totally different level. They have
introduced the autobiographical dialogue as a fourth dimension to the
tripartite model of psychoanalytic training that Vida also brought to
the Institute of Contemporary Psychoanalysis in Los Angeles.

I wondered how the autobiographical dialogue could be introduced
and, if necessary, adjusted in a supervisory setting for beginning therapists who are not even required to have any therapy of their own. My
left brain responds with caution, my right brain believes it could be liberating for gifted future clinicians to find their own true therapeutic self.
And what about the less gifted, I ask? My left brain answers, they will
always have the "how-to" manuals.

In their chapter they do not really offer a definition of the autobiographical dialogue, and thus leave it up to the readers to approximate
through their own subjective understanding of what the autobiographical dialogue may be to each, by leaving the reader no alternative but
to enter into one's own reverie about the meaning of the unique and
special collegial/friendship/love-working relationship Vida has with
Molad.

They write: "We see introjection as essentially egalitarian [opposed
to identification], maintaining the right-to-be of self and other, recognizing and valuing aspects of self in the other" and further "to move the
nature of relating from submission to the powerful expression of a single
and singular voice into a context of love (with a dialogical polyphony of
multiple voices). The emphasis is on 'playing together by telling our stories.'" They continue: "This is a kind of regression, though in the service
of relatedness, not simply of 'the ego' but for a relational ego."

For this invitation "to join a mutual play space" to become an actual reality, colleagues and co-players have to be at somewhat similar
developmental stages of self-confidence and vulnerability (Livingston
2001). Not only should there be a mutual readiness to dance while accepting each other's awkwardness and occasional clumsiness in step-
ping on each other's toes, there has to be enough balance on the side
of trust, the existence of capacity for concern, and the ability to repair
the ruptures without breaking anyone's toes.

I turned to their course syllabus to see if I could further my understanding of their autobiographical dialogue. Excerpts from the syllabus
read as follows:

"Our concept of 'the autobiographical dialogue' is based on the premise that whatever we say, do, and write as theory or practice is understood and interpreted mainly in the context of our personal story." They further believe that "psychoanalysis has had a conflictual relationship with the autobiographical . . . beginning with Freud's self-censorship in *The Interpretation of Dreams*, and including the eventual refusal to share with Jung and Ferenczi his complete associations to the dreams they had agreed to analyze mutually."

In their seminars they encourage analysts to reach beyond the tradition of self-censorship and self-protectiveness. They look at the development of "the voice of the analyst from historical, personal, and experiential perspectives." They emphasize the holding of trauma within the autobiographical dialogue and the failure of love.

It appears to me that Vida and Molad's autobiographical dialogue is written primarily in mind for individuals who are in psychoanalytic training. Most individuals at this level of training can be at a place of readiness for this kind of dialogue, given previous professional experience, training, personal analysis, and life experience.

At this point of reflecting on this chapter, I still did not feel I had a clear enough understanding of how the "autobiographical dialogue" works in their psychoanalytic seminar. The editor of this book directed me to another of their papers.

In the paper titled "'Cure' Is a Strange Notion" (2004), Vida states that indeed she has introduced this candid and playful dialogue into psychoanalytic training and that there have been mixed results. It appears that these results were not just because of Judy's less than perfect teaching self, awkwardness, and continuous self-reflections on what ruptures she caused and how she can repair them, but on what Judy would perceive to be each trainee's holding onto their idealized protected false self based on analytic identification.

Thus, the openness that Judy asks from each psychoanalytic trainee in the autobiographical account of the development of each particular candidate's psychoanalytic voice (Vida 2004) she inevitably and openly struggles with herself. In parallel process, she recognizes after a difficult class that "too much archaic fear had been activated in me to risk being quite so vulnerable." She does go back to her class, and discusses vulnerably and courageously her self-reflective self-analysis. Only by modeling the vulnerability one invites others to embrace, and by surviving it and growing from it, will other courageous souls venture forth.

I have other fleeting thoughts about the origins of the "autobiographical dialogue" as I read Judy's observation of Freud's life view of pessimism and Ferenczi's contrasting optimism: "Ferenczi, whom Freud often criticized as intensely rivalrous from having been one of too many children of a harsh mother, was the therapeutic optimist, and Freud, self-described as his mother's never-displaced favorite, was the notorious pessimist."

It seems that Vida and Molad both fall (by different degrees) into the optimistic camp of human relatedness. They are trying to move the optimism of being held and safely known through understanding in the clinical space into the collegial supervisory, consultation, and conference exploratory space. It is in the safety of the clinical space that the patient in each of us moves forward in our self-understanding and in our travels in the journey of life. It is from the protective mother's arms that a baby feels safe enough to positively venture into the world. It is from the safety that these authors have discovered, not only in their own families' arms, but in the evocative dialogues with each other, that they invite other colleagues to participate similarly.

I applaud their invitation to stretch the emotional, nondefensive, self-reflective creative dialogue of their colleagues. I observe how in their letters to each other they demonstrate a collegial openness and reciprocity in their intersubjective dialogue. They are not afraid to be vulnerable while lovingly sharing and defining oneself with one's differences. Their capacity to learn from each other, self-reflect, and self-transform suggests to me the existence of a psychological secure-enough structure from which they venture in their intersubjective explorations.

At the same time, my mind wanders between two different scenes of two 4-year-olds, one of whom has been greatly impinged by her mother and is trying to still get some inner control of her world by closing her eyes whenever anyone addresses her or invites her playfully to explore. Not being allowed to have much "continuity of being" (Winnicott 1965), this little girl could only hold onto whatever "being" she had. Openness to any other is out of the question. Thus, some of our supervisees or colleagues can only hold on tightly to their own theoretical being. They can only envision exploration into other theoretical ideas after their own sense of being has been allowed some continuity in an environment of safety and has been recognized as valid, just because it is theirs! These are not likely on their own to sign up for Molad/Vida's autobiographical (supervision) seminars, but will possibly watch from the sidelines as a conference audience until it becomes safe-enough.

But unlike the previous 4-year-old, the second 4-year-old observed I consider ready to sign up for the Vida/Molad autobiographical dialogue. Like many other times, this 4-year-old brought his colorful drawing to his mother. She sensitively pointed out many positive aspects about his picture. Having yet another positive experience of validation, he was ready to move on. For him the function of continuous validation was all used up by now! He exclaimed: "You always tell me what is good about my picture; you need to tell me what I can do to make it better."

Vida and Molad state in their syllabus: "We will work to create an atmosphere safe-enough for such a dialogue to emerge." As good group therapists, they know that the group conductors set both the atmosphere and the values of the group. I applaud them for their efforts to bring the loving nondefensive, self-reflecting, and self-transforming communication with each other into the greater psychoanalytic world of training and collegial interchange.

As I understand it, the autobiographical dialogue is informed by the context of each personal story. All the traumas, impingements, and validations are engraved into the archaeology of each psyche. We not only have dialogue from our explicit formulations from our left brain, but also react implicitly with our early encoded affects from our right brain. Our ability as psychoanalysts and conference colleagues to venture out to truly hear and digest the offerings of someone else is indeed determined by our personal story. As colleagues, supervisors, and consultants of trainees, we need to remember that those we interact with, like the two 4-year-olds described, may be at different developmental stages of self-reflection, exploration, and communication.

CONCLUSION

Each of these authors has successfully presented a format for talking with supervisees, consultees, colleagues, and friends within an atmosphere or format where there would be minimal narcissistic injuries and maximal possibilities for openness, self-reflection, and learning.

Although I do not know any of them personally, I venture to guess that their approaches include part of their own story. They have embraced the relational theory of intersubjectivity and call for greater self-reflection on the part of the supervisee as well as the supervisor.

For those of us who cling to whatever self-structure we have and dare to venture out to explore with others their psyche as well as our own, there are a few tenets we may want to hold onto:

- There is no such thing as perfection. Therefore, we can only move and struggle in the direction of perfectibility in our communications.
- In listening to someone else's subjective take on our communication, we do filter it through our own self-reflection that is instructed by all of our history.
- What all of us, supervisors and supervisees, explicitly and implicitly remember of our story and how we present it and interact with others is determined by what impingements, functions, and losses are carved into depths of our archaeological unconscious.
- Our unconscious is the bedrock of implicit memories and relational affects, which were opened up affectively. If we had loving interchanges, these memories continue. The longings for these interchanges spring from an old unconscious affective well, and we thus continue longing for that special understanding relatedness of two separated lovers.

REFERENCES

Bacal, H. (2004). Specificity theory: conceptualization of a personal and professional quest for therapeutic possibility. Paper presented as the Kohut Memorial Lecture at the 27th annual international conference of the Psychology of the Self, San Diego. November.

Beebe, B. (2003). Brief mother-infant treatment: psychoanalytically informed videofeedback. *Infant Mental Health Journal* 24(1):24–52.

Harwood, I. (1982). A four-year supervisory relationship and growth. Paper presented at the Dynamics of Supervision—Student and Supervisor Perspectives Symposium at the annual convention of the California State Psychological Association in San Diego. February.

Livingston, M. (2001). *Vulnerable Moments: Deepening the Therapeutic Process.* Northvale, NJ: Jason Aronson.

Ogden, T. (1994). The analytic third—working with intersubjective clinical facts. *International Journal of Psycho-Analysis,* 75:3–20.

Shore, A. (2003). *Affect Regulation and the Repair of the Self.* New York: W. W. Norton.

Vida, J. (2004). "Cure" is a strange notion. Paper presented at the ICP Exploring Transference and Cure in Contemporary Psychoanalysis, Conference, Los Angeles, June.

Winnicott, D. W. (1965). *The Maturational Processes and the Facilitating Environment.* New York: International Universities Press.

17

Concluding Reflections

Richard Raubolt

I was special editor of the September 2003 issue of the journal *Group*, entitled, "Charismatic Group Leadership: Theoretical and Ethical Issues." I realized, from the responses I received, that some of my experiences with and ideas about the dangers of such leadership found a receptive ear with other professionals. Specifically, I participated as a member of an advanced training group that was authoritarian, dogmatic, and cultlike. I found I was not alone in my experience, as many psychotherapists and psychoanalysts reported similarities in their training. From this realization came the idea for this book.

The chapters in this book represent a variety of writing styles and experiences. Some are deeply personal (Raubolt and Brothers, Richard, Fuqua), some are poetic and evocative (R. Raubolt, Vida and Molad), others are a blend of the personal and theoretical (Shaw, Gray, Lecomte, Sarnat), and a few are historical, theoretical, and personal (Larivière, Kavanaugh). The authors have been encouraged to write with their own voice in their own style. Recognizing and respecting the variety of individual expression in writing, as in psychoanalysis and psychotherapy, has been a guiding principle of this book and stands in opposition to doctrinaire training and practice. Discussants have been encouraged to write in a similar fashion.

I have come to an even deeper recognition that training in psychotherapy and psychoanalysis is often marked by authoritarian practices, some subtle and many pronounced. These practices instill fear and foster simplistic obedience to the favored proclivities of the leading proponents or authorities of the training institute. Such practices hinder the development of the field. Both training candidates and their prospective patients are limited from developing creative, authentic, and meaningful experiences when they are forced to rely on authority that lies beyond question. Fiscalini (1985), as quoted by Epstein (1997), has aptly termed this process "analysis by ventriloquism" (p. 290).

As knowledge is foreclosed by such constraints, psychotherapy and psychoanalysis, as both science and art, are dealt crippling blows. One essential reason for such rigidity is that the traditional prevalent training model is neither scientific nor educational but rather religious, where highly organized systems of beliefs are held with ardor, faith, commitment, and devotion. At their core, such institutes demand submission to a higher authority for truth, certainty, and ordained knowledge. Dogma replaces inquiry; belief trumps exploration. Roustang (1976) has applied the term *discipleship* to this practice.

Kirsner (2002) in his exceedingly well-documented research on psychoanalytic training institutes concludes:

> Most psychoanalytic institutes are unfree associations of psychoanalysts where the spirit of free inquiry has been replaced by the inculcation of received truth and the anointment of those who are supposed to possess knowledge. Through their institutions, psychoanalysts become blind to the spirit of skeptical inquiry on which psychoanalysis was based. This method is rarely applied to their institutions, which are mostly unfree oligarchies, and which rewarded conformity and punish difference. [p. 9]

The spirit of free inquiry is replaced with an attitude and structure with cultist features. Many analytic and psychotherapy training programs have developed an esoteric, mysterious, and highly ritualized language understandable only to the initiated, that is, the candidates and faculty members of the particular institute. Language then becomes the vehicle to define and promulgate "truth," the more complex, ambiguous, and jargonized, the greater the claim of knowledge in an attempt to "own" the very realm of the unconscious.

Such attitudes lead to paradoxical and conflicting results—on the one hand, arrogance, righteousness, and a sense of superiority by faculty and by candidates as well. They are the chosen, and, whatever their private doubts or reservations, they work to promote and defend their training program. They can become insulated from new developments in the field and rigidly resist theories, techniques, or practices not developed by one of their own. Leadership in the field can be claimed even when not earned.

On the other hand, a conflicting and disturbing ambiance may develop in a parallel yet disavowed fashion. Beneath the veneer of superiority, anxiety may begin to flourish as the modes of operation (i.e., selection, instruction, and evaluation) rigidify. The institute structure then seems to dictate and constrain the thinking, attitudes, identity, and even well-being of all involved. It is as if the training program is separate from those supposedly directing or benefiting from it. Law has replaced procedures. In presenting an astute analogy Stelzer (1986) has used Roman Polanski's film *The Tenant* to dramatically illustrate this point. In the film a young man who is new to a big city moves into an apartment, only to find he gradually takes on the identity of the previous tenant who had committed suicide. He is unalterably conflicted by his wish to remain himself and yet also belong to a place. Since he is unable to resolve this dilemma he loses his identity and ultimately his life as he commits suicide in the same fashion as the previous tenant. The power of the film is the gradual transformation to become someone else in order to have a place (to belong). The place has rules of its own greater than the individual.

The negative effects of these conflicting experiences are often most apparent in clinical supervision provided to trainees. Rock (1997), in reviewing three different surveys of over three hundred trainees (psychoanalytic candidates in training and graduate students in psychology), found authoritarian and intrusive supervision still in practice and still damaging to trainees. Such supervisors are experienced as harsh, critical, theory bound, and controlling. Supervisees are then left with a severe internal critic inhibiting their clinical work.

As described throughout this book, authority-driven clinical supervision is fraught with misunderstanding, confusion, and injury to the supervisee. If these problems are addressed directly, as in the models presented in the last section of this book on supervisory alternatives, the supervisees/therapists emerge from the experience with greater self-understanding, knowledge, and a voice of their own about what makes most sense in therapy/analysis. If, however, the supervision remains authoritarian, the effects can become so menacing as to be traumatic producing wounded healers. Especially vulnerable are those trainees who have experienced previous trauma(s) in their lives.

Signs that such trauma or retraumatization is occurring in supervision may include:

1. A sudden flatness of affect or alternately a sudden increase in anxiety.
2. Difficulty organizing and presenting pertinent clinical information on a patient.
3. Lateness or a pattern of canceling supervision.
4. An abrupt change in the transference–countertransference paradigm between supervisor and supervisee or supervisee/therapist and patient.
5. Paucity of information provided on patient–therapist interaction.
6. Unquestioning compliance by the supervisee to the supervisor's interpretations or directed interventions.
7. Overly solicitous or alternately aggressive stance taken with the supervision.
8. Development of somatic complaints or sudden appearance of physical symptoms of distress just prior to or during the supervision hours, such as rapid, shallow breathing; pronounced sweating; pale skin color; dilation of pupils, suggestive of acute anxiety or panic.

Wolf (1995), writing from a self-psychological perspective, offers a quite different type of supervision to consider, as is suggested in the title of his paper: "How to Supervise Without Doing Harm." In discussing what psychoanalysts know about facilitating learning, he writes: "One of the most basic aspects of supervision or consultation should be the reduction of the student-analyst's fragmentation anxiety and the first aim the strengthening of the student's self. Teaching has to merge into healing before it will result in learning" (p. 261). The process through which such healing takes place has been identified by Wolf (1988) as the "disruption–restoration sequence" (p. 110). I believe this sequence forms a foundation for supervision that is both effective and emotionally responsive and a relational perspective makes it even more potent. When supervision is proceeding well, the supervisee feels respected, nurtured, listened to, and accepted in a mutually self-sustaining dialogue with the supervisor. Learning is active and alive with possibilities. There will be times, and inevitably so, when the supervisor and supervisee are misaligned. The supervisee comes to feel misunderstood and the supervisor in turn may well feel surprised, defensive, or perhaps hurt. Each experiences disappointments as expectations are unmet. The supervisee can feel that the climate of respect and attentiveness is disrupted by the ill-attuned supervisor, and fragmentation of the supervision and self state may result. The supervisor, in recognizing the fragmentation distress, communicates his acceptance and understanding and invites the supervisee to share in a mutual dialogue that reestablishes the relational connection. Reciprocal responsiveness is again restored. Important learning has thus taken place where disruptions can be responded to, worked with, and integrated, so the learning can continue.

The disruption–restoration sequence is an essential experience in supervision as well as analysis. Since there is no perfect match, differences need to be recognized and addressed as part of the learning. Healing of disruptions serves as a necessary foundation to the success of the enterprise. The major responsibility for restoration falls to supervisors. They can use their authority as teachers to create an ambiance of empathic sensitivity, patience, and determination to encourage supervisees to explore disconnections and lapses in responsiveness. This is in-vivo learning, where trainees experience both emotional and intellectual grounding in theory and benefits from their experience of influencing the supervisor.

Berman (2004), writing from a relational viewpoint, would seem to concur with the goals of the process I have delineated. He writes:

Our clinical effectiveness and our theoretical potency alike are dependent on flexibility, creativity, and a capacity to use ourselves fully to observe emotional reality freshly, in ourselves and in the other, and to become attentive to our own blind spots and the rigidities that stand in our way. Increasing such capacities is a primary goal of psychoanalytic training, and the factors that hinder them must be of great concern to us. [p. 121]

From this perspective, the designation of "standard technique" is an anachronism, especially when set apart from the personality, subjectivity, and experience of the supervisee. Supervision/training, if it's to help inculcate a unique state of mind and particular sensitivities, needs to recognize and respect the mutual, reciprocal, if asymmetrical, influences between supervisor and supervisee. Supervisees then recognize that the influence of the supervisor is not a one-way street and that with dialogue they may effectively and helpfully influence the supervisor. This process leads not only to less fear of losing oneself but to greater confidence and trust as a therapist/analyst, which can lead to finding one's own therapeutic voice and the ability to believe in oneself rather than in time-honored techniques.

This book, I believe, has demonstrated the need for paradigms in professional education that focus on finding "truth" in the supervisee and in the supervisor through the mutually developed relationship between them. Looking at the broader educational design, we would do well to create fresh instructional/interactional processes. Here are my recommendations for such training:

1. Encourage open, meaningful, and in-depth discussion of various distinct theoretical points of view.
2. Actively elicit the development of each candidate's unique voice as a therapist, a voice that recognizes and appreciates the autobiographical influences.
3. Intersubjective and democratic principals should be utilized in focusing on empathic conflict resolution where differences arise. Such a process aims to be growth enhancing for both trainee and supervisor.
4. Trainees would benefit from supervision from several senior consultants of their choosing.
5. While supervision and training retain an asymmetrical element, careful attention, via joint trainee–faculty meetings, should be given when new policies or requirements are considered.

6. Trainees should have a greater say in their own education. They should guide it in the selection of courses and choice of personal therapist/analyst and supervisor.

7. In order to alter the insulated, arcane microcosm of training institutes, a broader base of subject material must be added to the curriculum. Prominent theories of philosophy, literature, literary criticism, film studies, and artistic expression need to be offered to expand the knowledge and sensibilities of candidates. Cultural Studies, long viewed as the bastard stepchild of many universities, should be afforded a special place of recognition. Candidates who are steeped in highly theoretical and esoteric studies may lose touch with and therefore also lose an appreciation for the issues and trends that help shape their personal and professional worlds and particularly those of the people they see in psychotherapy and psychoanalysis.

8. Careful recognition needs to be given to the crucial fact that by virtue of their position, senior mental health professionals have the potential to inflict great hurt and potential damage on supervisees and junior colleagues. Specialized training in understanding the vulnerabilities of the human psyche and a growing sophistication of the dynamics of trauma and abuse can provide vehicles for addressing the expression of unresolved aggression and rage by senior analysts and therapists. [Giselle Galdi, (personal communication, 2004) called my attention to these concerns.] Ad hominem attacks, public and personal criticism, humiliation, belittling, and coarse descriptions of students are unwarranted. Such behavior needs to be challenged, evenhandedly but firmly, by other senior faculty and colleagues.

9. No formal certification of competency should be awarded by any training institute. Instead, a certificate of attendance and letters of recommendation may be offered. This is of course my opinion and is not necessarily supported by a number of authors, even in this book. My reasoning is that no one can certify a therapist as competent, given the nature of the unconscious (see Larivière in this book) and the complex, ever-shifting variety of clinical situations and patients each of us must deal with. Further there is too much room for bias or for what Balint (1948) and Reeder (2004) refer to as the establishment of a superego

complex: practicing by rules that stultify creativity and potentially compassion.

REFERENCES

Balint, M. (1948). On the psychoanalytic training system. *International Journal of Psycho-Analysis* 29:163–173.

Berman, E. (2004). *Impossible Training*. London: Analytic Press.

Epstein, L. (1997). Collusive Selective Inattention to the Negative Impact of the Supervisory Interaction. In *Psychodynamic Supervision Perspectives of the Supervisor and the Supervisee*, M. Rock, ed. London: Jason Aronson.

Kirsner, D. (2002). Unfree associations inside psychoanalytic institutes. *Academy for the Study of the Psychoanalytic Arts*. Retrieved August 1, 2004 from http://www.academyanalyticarts.org/kirsnerintro.html.

Reeder, J. (2004). *Hate and Love In Psychoanalytical Institutions*. New York: Other Press.

Rock, M. (1997). *Psychodynamic Supervision Perspectives of the Supervisor and the Supervisee*. London: Jason Aronson.

Wolf, E. S. (1988). *Treating The Self*. New York: Guilford.

——— (1995). How to supervise without doing harm: comments on psychoanalytic supervision. *Psychoanalytic Inquiry* 15(2):252–267.

Index

Bacal, H. A., 29, 85, 213, 319
Balint, Michael, 26, 67, 174–175, 339
Bar Levav, I., 177
Bar Levav, Reuven, 39, 40, 41, 42–43, 49, 53
Bar Levav Education Association (BLEA), 37–55, 173, 182. See also Coerced discipleship; Michigan Group Psychotherapy Society (MGPS)
Barley, D. E., 226
Bateson, G., 109
Beebe, Beatrice, 50, 51, 231, 234, 277, 293, 318, 322
Begley, S., 221
Behavior modification therapy, covert interpersonal control, 109–111
Bellak, Leo, 196
Benedek, Theresa, 144, 209, 283
Benjamin, J., 68
Benson, S., 108
Bergman, Ingrid, 180
Bergman, Robert, 110n3
Bergmann, Martin S., 256, 258, 273
Berlin Psychoanalytic Institute, 124–126, 128, 143, 147
Berman, E., 71, 80n5, 210, 257, 337–338
Bernard, J. M., 222, 241
Bernfeld, Siegfried, 151
Bevan, W., 141
Binder, J. L., 16, 224, 228, 229
Bion, W. R., 95, 113
Black, M., 256
Boesky, D., 138
Borch-Jacobsen, Mikkel, 164n1
Borders, L. D., 230
Borges, Jorge Luis, 167
Bornstein, M., 137

Boston Psychoanalytic Institute, 2, 3
Boyer, Charles, 180
Brainwashing
    China, 3
    covert interpersonal control, 108
Brenner, Charles, 114
Breuer, Joseph, 17, 124, 130, 163
Brightman, B., 66
Brothers, D., 15, 23, 25, 26, 28, 29, 37, 50, 51, 172, 178, 333
Buirski, P., 210

Caligor, L., 257
Canetti, Elias, 166
Capra, F., 135
Carter, J., 102, 104, 111
Cartesian theory, 13, 133, 134, 135. See also Institutional organization
Cassriel, Dan, 38
Castonguay, L.G., 229
Celan, Paul, 166
Center for Feeling Therapy (CFT, Los Angeles, California), 12–13. See also Coercive training program
    coerced discipleship, 177
    collapse of, 22–23
    described, 16–19
    discussed, 28–32
    media, 12
    psychodynamics at, 23–27
    therapy at, 19–22
Change of topic, covert interpersonal control, 100–101
Charisma
    coerced discipleship, 171–172
    vulnerability, trauma and, psychoanalytic training, 83–89
Chicago, University of, 5–6

350 / Index